EFFECTIVE
FLOWERING SHRUBS

MICHAEL HAWORTH-BOOTH, F.L.S.

EFFECTIVE FLOWERING SHRUBS

With forty-seven plates in
colour photography by the author

COLLINS
ST JAMES'S PLACE, LONDON
1951

PRINTED IN GREAT BRITAIN
BY WILLIAM CLOWES AND SONS, LIMITED, LONDON AND BECCLES

TO MY WIFE
AND CHIEF COLLABORATOR

CONTENTS

COLOUR PLATES

9

FOREWORD

THROUGHOUT this book I am out for flowers—large, bold, beautiful flowers equal to, or surpassing, those borne by herbs, bulbs, annuals, orchids or anything else. I have no use for dowdy shrubs. These wretched things are so commonly put forward that a large section of the gardening public takes it as a matter of course that shrubs are inferior in flower to other kinds of plants.

One even hears the expression 'shrubs or flowers' and, no doubt arising from this mistaken attitude of mind, there is even a tendency to make out that Roses are not flowering shrubs, presumably because no one can deny their superlative flowers.

I hold that the finest, most effective, gardenable flowers are borne by flowering shrubs and, in the following pages, I shall do my best to prove it.

MICHAEL HAWORTH-BOOTH
Farall Nurseries,
near Haslemere,
Surrey

INTRODUCTION

THE phase of gardening which dominated the early part of this century was that of the botanist-gardener who was interested in growing the largest possible number of species. This arose from the amazing wealth of new plant material which poured in at that time from the Orient and many other parts of the world. Later, this flow waned, and, having grown and observed the new plants, we became able to take stock of their value. Selection, breeding and hybridisation then began. The assessment of the relative value of the selected forms and hybrids followed. Now, most gardeners are interested in the study of the cultivation and the arrangement of the finer products of this previous work, so that the best possible use may be made of this splendid plant material so as to form a satisfying garden.

The works of the late Alfred Rehder, the late Adolf Engler and Mr. L. H. Bailey, between them, cover the whole field of the species. The particulars given in such works of a species of flowering shrub of outstanding value can only be very brief, as all the other species of the genus are equally dealt with. The selected garden varieties and the hybrids, which are far the most important plants from the gardener's point of view, can only receive a short mention. In this book the purpose is to record and to give all possible information concerning only the most effective species for garden decoration and their hybrids and garden varieties. Hence its title.

Personal likes and dislikes as regards plants vary widely, so I have laid down a specification of what, in my opinion, constitutes an effective flowering shrub for the garden. Thus the basis of evaluation can be transferred from the realm of personal fancy into that of fact. The facts, only, can decide whether or not the plant measures up to the prescribed standard. A flowering shrub is taken to be effective if it fulfils the following conditions:—

1. It must be a good garden plant, able to grow healthfully and vigorously under conditions of soil and climate possible in a large proportion of British gardens.
2. The flowering must be of such vividness, profusion and good presentation as to colour the bush or pattern the whole with blossom for a reasonably long period.

13

3. The habit of growth must be such as to make the plant a decorative feature of the garden at all times of the year.

A plant fulfilling these conditions in an outstanding manner is described as first class. There are, of course, minor complications. I hold that the flower beauty of the garden should continue in uninterrupted sequence from spring to autumn and there are therefore periods when the selection is more limited than at others. Under such circumstances the best plants available are given the benefit of the doubt.

The order in which the plants are described is as nearly as possible, in the sequence of their flowering. Thus the species are grouped by their fellowship of blooming together rather than because they share certain botanical characteristics.

Accuracy is so essential that I have sought it to the best of my ability. In particular the colours of the flowers are described by the colour names used in the Horticultural Colour Chart whenever possible. These hues are distinguished by capitals and, when available, the number of the tint, or shade, of the hue, according to the Chart, is also given in brackets. By reason of the clarity and accuracy that it brings to colour evaluation I consider the Chart to be one of the most valuable achievements in horticulture today. The vagueness and chaos previously reigning in these matters made many colour descriptions quite useless.

In addition to the absolute accuracy obtainable, the Chart has clarified colour problems for many gardeners in another way. It has enabled them to visualise the colours as a circle in which every hue has its ordained place.

Starting at a point on the circumference with pure yellow this hue passes through orange and becomes more and more suffused with red until pure red is reached. Red in turn becomes progressively more and more tinted with blue until, passing through purple and violet, we arrive at pure blue. Blue, in turn, is gradually tinged with yellow until, passing through green we finally return to the pure yellow from which we started. After using the Chart for some time a sort of "absolute pitch" is attained which enables the gardener to state the exact colour of any flower that he sees.

The plant names used in this work are those adjudged to be correct by the late Alfred Rehder according to the second edition (1947) of his great work "Manual of Cultivated Trees and Shrubs". In cases where another name is commonly used in catalogues, etc. I have placed this in brackets alongside. By rights,† the specific names of hybrid races should carry the multiplication sign—e.g. *Ceanothus* × *Delilianus* 'Gloire de Versailles.' I have, however, omitted this sign in the interests of readability and, instead, have stated that the plant is a hybrid.

Distinctions bestowed by the Royal Horticultural Society are significant as they give useful information on the quality of the plant and the date that it came to the notice of gardeners. Of the first importance among these, to the ordinary gardener, is the Award of Garden Merit, written A.G.M. This signifies a plant of outstanding excellence for general garden use, having been tried out at the Society's gardens. There is also the First-Class Certificate issued after trial at the Society's gardens. This is written F.C.C.* and shows that the variety is an improvement on its predecessors and the standard varieties. It does not indicate suitability for all garden conditions but that it is one of the best under suitable conditions. Next comes the Award of Merit after Trial, written *A.M. This is a slightly less high distinction similarly granted. In addition there is the First-Class Certificate, written F.C.C., given to a plant or piece of one exhibited at one of the Society's shows to the appropriate Committee. This indicates a fine decorative plant eminent among its fellows, but does not necessarily indicate that it is a good garden plant everywhere. The Award of Merit, written A.M., is a similar but slightly lesser distinction.‡

As far as possible botanical terms are either eliminated, or explained on the spot if they are so useful that their employment is thought desirable. Examples of really helpful words that save much explanation are those describing the way the flowers are assembled on the plant. For instance:—

CORYMB—A short and broad domed cluster whose outer flowers open first and which has the flower stalklets springing from various points on the main stalk. Common example, *Hydrangea macrophylla*.

CYME —A broad, domed or flat-topped flower cluster whose central flowers open first. Common example, *Viburnum Carlesii*.

† *R.H.S. Journal*, Vol. LXX, pt. 6, p. 180 (1945).
‡ For an interesting account revealing the highly competitive nature of Rhododendron Trials, see "The Trials of Hardy Rhododendron and Azalea Hybrids", by N. K. Gould, *The Rhododendron Year-Book*, 1946, R.H.S.

RACEME—An unbranched, elongated assembly of stalked flowers, whose terminal members open last. Common example, *Wisteria floribunda*.

PANICLE—A branching raceme in which the terminal flowers open last so that the growing point may extend while the basal flowers are opening. Common example, Lilac.

The shapes of leaves are fairly straightforward. Oblong just means oblong with the corners rounded off. Elliptic means of the evenly-curved shape of an ellipse. Ovate means shaped like the outline of an egg with the leafstalk at the big end. Obovate is the same but the stalk comes at the small end. Lanceolate is shaped like the head of a lance with the leafstalk at the blunt end. Oblanceolate is the same but the stalk is at the narrow end. Orbicular means circular in outline.

The terms for leaf-tips are a little more complicated. Acute means tapering evenly to a point, the sides of the leaf being convex or nearly straight. Acuminate is the term used when the point is so drawn-out and pronounced that the tapered sides are concave in outline so that the point looks longer.

There are innumerable other terms, but their use is so rarely required in this book that there is no need for me to use them, but a few are so convenient and exact that they are worth explaining.

A clone means one of a group of individuals resulting from vegetative (as from cuttings, layers, buds or grafts) and not seed propagation, from one individual plant and therefore identical to it.

A "miff" is a plant that, although appearing healthful, suddenly dies for no evident reason. A "mimp" is one that neither flourishes nor dies outright. Reginald Farrer invented these words some years ago and they are so useful that gardeners have used them ever since.

The "type" form of a plant is the original type first discovered and named. Usually it is the original wild species, but in some cases, where the plant comes from far countries whose inhabitants have been gardeners since time immemorial, the "type" is a garden form.

As far as possible the names of the colours standardised in the Horticultural Colour Chart are used in my descriptions of flowers and these are signalised by capital letters. A second volume has now been added to the Colour Chart which shows abnormally deep shades and also hues to which black has been added. In my view this makes matters too complicated for the average gardener and my hope that the Colour Chart would come into common use has received a setback.

Actually I have found no flower which cannot be quite sufficiently accurately charted by the use of Vol. I, except certain very dark Roses whose petals are suffused with black. Such flowers and also those of slightly greyed hues would seem to me to be amply described by the addition of the words "deep" or "very deep" to the hue, and those of the second type by the addition of the words "dull" or "very dull".

The illustrations are from my own colour photographs, mostly taken of actual growing shrubs. Such photographs are a more difficult matter than studio pictures as the photographer must cope with wind and cloud and rain. I think, however, that they give a more truthful picture of a plant's natural habit and the presentation of its flowers than can be got from pieces arranged in the studio. The colourings will be found to be correct on reference to the Horticultural Colour Chart.

In the preparation of this work I am much indebted to the officers of the Royal Horticultural Society for their kindly assistance at all times, both at Vincent Square and at Wisley; and in particular to Mr. Patrick M. Synge, editor of the *R.H.S. Journal*, and to Mr. W. T. Stearn, librarian of the Lindley Library; also to the late Alfred Rehder for his invaluable "Manual of Cultivated Trees and Shrubs" and for his personal kindness in sending me an advance copy of parts of his new work, "The Bibliography of Cultivated Trees and Shrubs".

Acknowledgment is made in the text to the numerous works referred to, as cited.

CHAPTER I

GARDENING
WITH FLOWERING SHRUBS

LAYOUT

WITH flowering shrubs a naturalistic layout is best. Rectangular beds and straight lines do not take advantage of the natural, year-round symmetry and beauty of the plantings possible with shrubs. Island-like curving shapes are much more pleasing.

Laborious tasks such as weeding are eliminated to a great extent by mulching, which is also essential to the health and growth of the shrubs.

Hoeing is avoided, as it destroys the feeding roots of many kinds and also the self-sown seedlings which are an added pleasure and often of considerable value.

A favourite general principle in design today is to provide a lawned glade stretching away as far as possible in a curving line with informal beds of shrubs at the sides. There are often two irregular lines of these: those nearer to the viewpoint having, mostly, lower-growing subjects and those at the back the taller species. Small flowering trees are set as specimens in the turf, so that they afford some shade to the occupants of the beds. Such a scene, in the natural style, is more pleasing to our eyes, surfeited by the straight lines and artificial enclosures of the ever-increasing towns, than more formal arrangements.

There are one or two new types of planting arrangement which I have found singularly satisfactory from both the cultural and the æsthetic points of view. They are mentioned in the chapters on species and varieties but perhaps require a little further explanation.

The first is the carpet, in which an area is planted with low-growing, creeping shrubs such as Evergreen Azaleas, Lithospermum, alpine Rhododendrons, alpine Phloxes, dwarf Genistas, Thymes, dwarf Brooms, Helianthemums, Heaths and *Cotoneaster Dammeri*. The secret is to associate all these kinds closely, so that the carpet is flowery all summer long, and to limit the planting to evergreens for the most part so that the carpet remains furnished attractively all winter. Here and there a taller, mounded tuffet may emerge with bold effect. In Nature, Heaths and alpine Rhododendrons provide hundreds of miles of such floral carpets.

The second is also an arrangement that is common in Nature. The flowers are in three storeys; tree-flowers above under-shrub flowers, and lowlier flowers beneath these. In the garden, this may work out as Cherries above Rhododendrons and Camellias above Lilies, Primulas and Meconopsis, or as such tall, tree-like Genistas as *G. cinerea* and *G. virgata* above Hydrangeas above tiny bulbous plants and Primulas. On the chalk one might have *Rosa Moyesii* above Viburnums above *Genista dalmatica* and Periwinkles. There are innumerable delightful combinations possible. Light shade is helpful to the majority of shrubs in the south of Britain and the frost protection afforded by the canopy, and the leaf mulch that it helps to provide, are often decisive advantages that make all the difference between healthful growth and failure. Another important gain is that the three tiers of flower help us to concentrate floral beauty in a small space, for in this way we may have nearly three times as many flowers per yard of ground.

The third treatment affects the town gardener. In these times of increasing congestion of buildings, the only garden that some of us command is a small, deeply shaded courtyard perhaps only a few yards across. Formerly such places were given up as hopeless for fine plants. There could be no greater mistake. If one can afford to remove the foul soil to a depth of two feet and replace it by fresh, rich, black, sandy stuff, many lovely species will find just the conditions that they like best. Camellias and woodland Hydrangeas, set off by Primulas, Hepaticas, Cyclamens, velvety Mosses and graceful Ferns can make the place delightful.

In a cold district, if it can be afforded, there is much to be said for enclosing the area in glass to keep out the worst of the frosts. Furthermore, electric lighting may be installed so as to give sufficient light to grow many more kinds of plants. The General Electric Company have done much useful research in this field. In this way a house may be transferred from shabby, cold and bleak surroundings into the atmosphere of a tropic isle. An old army hut, thus encircled, is actually one of the most charming dwellings that I know, embowered in Vines, Fuchsias, Hydrangeas and Plumbago.

The salient point in the new style of layout for the flowering shrub garden is that every foot of cultivated ground is decorated and made beautiful—winter and summer. Beauty is more concentrated as the available space is smaller. I have a demonstation garden available to prove that this is practicable and that such an arrangement makes for both ease of maintenance and the better growth of the plant material.

FLOWER COLOUR ARRANGEMENTS

There are various schools of thought in these matters. Some gardeners are interested only in the botanical side of gardening and even use the adjective "mere" in connection with flower colour. Others admit an interest in colour, but are sometimes so encumbered with plants that they find indispensable in spite of their flowers being of a purplish-pink colour, that they must label as "difficult to place" any having flowers of pure and vivid colourings. Another large section of gardeners, among whose ranks may be numbered many of the most experienced and highly skilled, find a fascination in exploiting the rich, pure and beautiful flower colours now available to us. They hold that the only colour which is difficult to place in the garden is a muddy, pale, purplish pink. As this hue is the least effective in the garden landscape the simple course of doing without it provides an easy remedy.

In the body of the work, flowers of pure and vivid colourings are specially recommended. Readers will have their own views on their favourite colour harmonies.

The colour that prevents our enjoying the full value of vivid and pure colours is purplish pink. Unfortunately almost a majority of flowers in northern Europe affect this colour. If the gardener is sufficiently determined he can, however, cut it out altogether and I have no doubt that this is really the right course. Pure reds, yellows, oranges, blues, violets and purples can then be enjoyed without fear of clashes and the effect is far finer in every way.

Only bees like the Magenta colours—reddish purples or purplish pinks ranging from Solferino Purple and, going bluer all the time, through Magenta itself, Fuchsine Pink, Fuchsia Purple, Rhodamine Purple, Peony Purple and Mallow Purple to Cyclamen Purple. Next, and still going bluer all the time, we reach Orchid Purple—the colour of *Hydrangea villosa*, and the Scots Heath *Erica cinerea*, and this is just bearable, as is Petunia Purple—the colour of a bad *Rhododendron ponticum*. Then we reach Mauve and Imperial Purple which are followed by the Violets and all these are enjoyable. Anything less red than violet is blue and almost everybody loves a blue flower.

For the benefit of those without the Horticultural Colour Chart it may be worth while to describe the pink and red colours in their sequence. If we go redder from Solferino Purple all the way, we first find Rose Bengal, a slightly purplish pink, like that of the common Rhododendron 'Cynthia'; then Phlox Pink which is a rather better pink than cake-icing, and is the colour of Azalea 'Hinomayo'; then Tyrian Rose, the charming colour of the pink part of Dicentra or

"Bleeding Heart"; Rose Madder, which I would call rose pink; Neyron Rose, a warmer, better pink, and then Crimson—the colour of *Malus purpurea* and the best red Hydrangeas. Carmine comes next—the colour of *Tropæolum speciosum*; Turkey Red is, near enough, just a deeper shade of the same hue. Then comes that lovely hue Carmine Rose, the colour of Rose 'Picture'. Now we reach Geranium Lake; we are, of course, going more orange all the time, and this is the colour of the best red Camellias and "Japònica" (in particular *Chænomeles superba Simonii*). Scarlet is now reached and Signal Red is, near enough, a deeper shade of it. Getting still more orange, Vermilion follows, and this is the colour of the finest deciduous Azaleas. Azalea Pink is a slightly warmer and paler hue and is commoner for these Azaleas. Mandarin Red is an exquisite colour only attained by the Pomegranate flower, a few choice Azaleas and *Chænomeles* 'Knap Hill Scarlet'. Shrimp Red is really a soft orange only attained, so far as I know, by one or two Rhododendrons such as 'Fabia' in some forms. Thus we arrive at Poppy Red which speaks for itself and Capsicum Red which is attained by the Embothriums and *Leonotis Leonurus*. Fire Red is nearly orange and some forms of *Azalea Kæmpferi* can equal its paler tints. In a few more gradations of hues seldom found in the flowers of shrubs we come to Orange which is favoured by the Azaleas 'Flamingo' and 'Emil Liebig'.

To be brief with the Yellows, we may start at the green end of the arc with Sulphur Yellow where we shall find *Rhododendron Keiskei*. Getting warmer in tone the next is Primrose Yellow which explains itself and then Dresden Yellow which gives us several Rhododendron species and some of the Potentillas. A little warmer is Canary Yellow with *Mahonia japonica*, *Senecio laxifolius*, Mimosa and Laburnum. Then comes Empire Yellow, the soft hue of *Cytisus præcox*, and Aureolin the colour of Spanish Broom, Forsythias and the tall Genistas. Lemon Yellow is now reached with *Rosa Ecæ* and *Hypericum calcynum*, and Straw Yellow—the colour of the common Yellow Azalea. Buttercup Yellow colours *Hypericum patulum Forrestii*, Gorse and *Kerria japonica*. The warmer Indian Yellow and Chinese Yellow are exemplified by a few choice Azalea varieties. Saffron Yellow and Maize Yellow begin to approach a soft orange and Rhododendron 'Goldsworth Orange' shows the latter hue. Cadmium Orange is now reached and Azalea 'Anthony Koster' and the buds of *Berberis stenophylla coccinea* give us this colouring. True Apricot follows but no shrub flower quite equals it and Tangerine Orange has only *Buddleia globosa* to offer us. Orpiment Orange is the colour of *Berberis Darwinii* and it is just one hue redder than the peel of the average orange.

SOILS

With flowering shrubs, garden soils may first be divided into two different types which each support quite a different flora. These are limy (or alkaline) soils and acid soils.

Naturally limy soils, or those that have been made limy by applications of artificial lime, although favourable for herbs and vegetables, will only grow a limited selection of flowering shrubs. Those that will tolerate such soils are always so described in the body of the work and I have been careful to include a large selection of these.

Acid soils are, fortunately, found in Nature over the greater part of the British Isles, particularly in well wooded areas. All kinds of flowering shrubs will grow well in acid soils mulched with fallen leaves and bracken. So-called lime-loving plants will grow to perfection even in very acid soils if given a light dressing of bonemeal occasionally.

In gardens, such soils have often been made alkaline by applications of artificial lime. This is very disadvantageous for flowering shrubs. Iron starvation, and other shortages caused, prevent the growth of Rhododendrons, Azaleas, Camellias, Pieris, most Heaths, Eucryphias, Embothriums and many other genera. Apples and Roses can be grown, but often less well than in neutral or acid soils. The acidity of soil is measured by a scale called the pH scale. Between pH 5 and pH 6 the acidity is ideal; pH 7 is neutral and any pH figure over this must be classed as limy.

Both types of soil may be again divided into sandy soils and clay soils. Sandy soils are warm and pleasant to work and to live upon. If kept mulched, all flowering shrubs *including Roses*, grow well on sandy soils which are also acid. Clay soils need much humus added, such as peat, leafmould or bracken, to keep them open, fertile and easily worked. Care must also be taken to provide drainage. If a bed is deeply dug in clay soil the undug soil surrounding it and below it forms a utensil from which water cannot escape. Shrub roots thus waterlogged soon die and this is a very common cause of the failure of Roses. Drainage must be provided and this can be a troublesome business on bowl-shaped or, even, level sites. Where drainage is available, acid clay soils grow most flowering shrubs quite well but, being colder, some kinds fail.

Mellowness is an important requirement of soil fertility. It means that the soil is so homogeneous—or completely mixed and blended—that there are no lumps of different character and colouring. Often a layer of dark topsoil overlies a pale, sterile subsoil. The layers must not be jumbled into a mixture of lumps of the two kinds. They must be kept separate with care, even though, as in bastard trenching, both layers may be loosened up and some humus may be incorporated with the lower layer. If, in this process, some admixture takes place it is necessary to fork the bed over, perhaps several times, until mellowness is achieved.

Sour soils are those which are so tightly packed or waterlogged that the soil atmosphere is driven out. The soil life, composed of teeming organisms essential to fertility, therefore cannot exist. Without them and without air, the roots of the shrubs or other plants cannot grow. The remedy is to break up such soil thoroughly and to mix—in humus —not lime—if flowering shrubs are to be grown.

If soil for flowering shrubs has to be purchased at any time, it is wise to specify dark, acid, sandy soil. Otherwise a heavy, limy soil, admirable for cabbages but most unfavourable for flowering shrubs, will be delivered.

CULTIVATION

Farmyard manure is not necessary, or even desirable for flowering shrubs. Enrichment of the soil is best achieved by annually mulching the surface with a layer of fallen leaves or bracken fronds. Owing to the fear that these may blow about the garden, and ignorance of the correct method of applying the mulch so that this does not occur, the mistake is often made of allowing the leaves to rot elsewhere first. In consequence their feeding value is largely lost. The composted, spent material is admirable as a rooting medium for seedings, etc. but, like used tea-leaves, lacks strength.

Fallen leaves may either be collected or secured by arrangement with Local Authorities whose lorries collect enormous quantities from roadsides in wooded districts. To mulch a bed, take a full, tight double handful of the fallen leaves, which must be wet, and plant them firmly, just as they are, on the surface of the ground at one end of the bed. Do not spread them out or loosen them at all; keep them tightly pressed together. Place the next and subsequent, tight, double handfuls closely up against the first and so carpet the bed evenly until the far end is reached. Then take a light garden fork and pat down any loose places until all is firm and even. Lastly, if the site is very much exposed to wind, a scattering of ordinary yellow building-sand may be put on over all. No gale will disturb a mulch thus applied although blackbirds may painstakingly pull it out, in places, occasionally in the most annoying manner.

So long as no soil is put over the leaves few weeds appear through such a covering and if any do succeed they are so loosely anchored that a mere tweak dislodges them.

Cultivation of the ground after planting, by hoeing, etc. is not desirable and is rendered unnecessary by the mulch. Helianthemums and Halimiums are the only shrubs that I know that do not react spectacularly to the mulching system. Such small subjects may be given chopped bracken instead of leaves, however, with good results.

Bracken, cut in June before its rich contents descend to the rhizomes (fleshy roots) below for storage, is a remarkably powerful stimulant to rooting and contains many valuable plant foods in readily available form, particularly potash which many shrubs cannot assimilate in its crude state from the soil (see Mr. Colin Brooke, *R.H.S. Journal*, LXXVI, pt. 1, p. 26, (1951). It is, however, much less discouraging to weeds than leaves are and therefore less labour-saving. If it is available, the best way to use it is to lay the fronds on the bed before applying the fallen leaves. All advantages are then secured. On the other hand when a bed is already planted with small subjects it will be found best to cut up the bracken first, either with a spade or a chaff-cutter.

The only cultivation required under the mulch system is a light and very shallow forking of the surface of those parts of the bed that are not occupied by surface roots when the soil has become rather bare just before the next mulching. This is best done by using a ladies'-size fork with one hand, with a jab-twist motion. The mulch should be renewed as often as is necessary to keep a layer of leaves from four to six inches deep over the surface at all times—particularly under Rhododendrons, Azaleas, Eucryphias and Camellias. But the mulch should be kept just clear of the stems, as if it gets piled up around them they may become soft and unhealthy.

The feeding properties of the mulch are not the only benefits. Moisture is retained so that the soil of beds thus covered after the autumn rains will remain moist all through even the driest summer. Furthermore, frost is prevented from damaging the roots and the young, emerging shoots of the shrubs, and planting can often be carried out in winter in unfrosted ground by merely moving the mulch to one side.

GARDEN CLIMATE

This subject is so important and so widely misunderstood that I offer no apology for devoting considerable space to it.

The climates reigning in the British Isles are extraordinarily varied. In America the climatic zones have been plotted very exactly and it will astonish many to find that a given zone will often cover, as a slender band, a range of longitude from 60 degrees to 33 degrees north†. Such zones have not yet been exactly plotted for Britain, so far as I know, but I think the zone extending from Kent through Sussex including south Surrey and all the southern and western coastal counties right up to the north of Scotland would be found to form the most favourable. Next would probably come a zone including those parts of the eastern counties that are close to the seaboard and also the more elevated parts of many southern but not coastal counties. Finally, the coldest zone would include the midlands and extend northward covering the remaining areas.

These zones would, however, only provide a rough guide because so many other factors operate. Katabatics, tree canopy, soil consistency and aspect can all exert a potent influence on garden climate.

The most powerful factor is air drainage or katabatics. The word comes from the Greek, meaning "to afford a means of descent". Cold air is heavy, and, provided that there is an uninterrupted downward path available, flows, like oil, slowly away downhill. Thus an elevated site with such facilities will remain unaffected by early autumn or late spring frosts. In the depths of winter the cold air is so widespread that the elevated site is submerged and quite as cold as anywhere else. At last, as the days lengthen and the quantity of cold air grows steadily less, the time comes when the high site re-emerges above the frost-line. For some while later, recurring frosts may still fill the undrained depressions below. Once spring is well begun, however, there is seldom sufficient volume of cold air to affect the high, air-drained site again.

Thus a site with good katabatic facilities has a remarkably favourable garden climate. The gardener cannot create such a climate in a low site, but many elevated gardens whose cold-air drainage is blocked can have their climate almost miraculously improved by removing the blockage. This is the only purpose for which I would even recommend the employment of a bulldozer if this were economically practicable. As I have said, the degree of cold reached in the depths of winter is no less on the katabatically favourable site. Thus shrubs which die, no matter how well ripened and prepared, when a certain degree of cold is reached are little assisted. On the other hand, the great majority of the more valuable sorts are those whose chief setbacks are due merely to untimely frosts, and these are able to grow with full vigour when given good air drainage. So decisive are these effects that gardens may be found in all parts of these islands whose climate is as favourable as those of places in the far southwest.

Another powerful factor is the existence of a tree-branch canopy.

† Dr. Rehder's " Manual of Cultivated Trees and Shrubs".

Land protected by such a canopy does not readily freeze. Thus woodland, where the canopy is complete, does not provide cold to flow down into a hollow below it. This explains the good climate often enjoyed by woodland dells and even, though to a lesser degree, bare hollows below densely wooded heights. The gardener whose garden climate cannot be assisted by katabatics can yet take advantage of the facilities of the canopy system. To do this, admittedly, he may have to wait thirty years to grow the friendly oaks or other deep-rooting, benign trees required, or he may be able to remove his plantings into the shelter of an available wood.

Those who should know better have said that it is impossible to change a climate. That it is possible to do so for the better is well known to many and that it is only too easy to do so for the worse and turn fertile forest area into an almost rainless desert subject only to freak storms, by the wholesale destruction of every tree in sight, should have become quite plain to an even larger number of persons.

Soil and aspect also play a part in garden climate, although this is a less decisive one. A dark-coloured, sandy soil is warmer than a pale, clayey soil and a south-facing slope is obviously warmer than one that faces north or in any other direction owing to the more direct angle of incidence of the sun's rays.

The most favourable garden climates in Britain, then, are those in the mildest zone having good katabatics, a tree canopy and a dark sandy soil. Gardens favoured by even only one of these factors will still have great advantages over others that have none.

INSTALLATION OR PLANTING

No factor in the life of an individual shrub is more important than the care and skill with which it is first planted out. If this is not well done its vigour and well-being are permanently affected. There is a time in the life of the young plant when a burst of energy is available and the best results are achieved when this is expended to produce new growth in the permanent position. This is the reason why the purchase of small, young plants is advisable in the case of the many species that are not what we call "good movers". With good movers, such as Rhododendrons, the plant is so little affected by transplanting that youth is less important.

Briefly, good planting that ensures a favourable start includes the following requirements:—healthy plant material having latent vigour; carefully prepared soil conditions to suit the subject; exact placing of the plant as regards depth in the soil; well-arranged spreading of the root system so that anchorage will be secure and the main roots so spaced as to enable their rootlets and fibres to exploit a large area of soil; and, lastly, such firmness of the surrounding soil that close contact with the roots is ensured whilst such extreme density as to promote sourness is avoided.

Let us now set out in detail the requirements summarised above. The importance of good plant material has already been partly explained. Sometimes one has to deal with gnarled old plants that have been cut back and moved too often. Their energy is low; they have lost heart, so to speak. Provided that the plant is of a species that can safely be pruned, a drastic cutting-back the moment growth starts will often induce new shoots from the base that will soon form a vigorous new bush. Species that do not submit well to pruning may be planted partly on their sides and have the old growths carefully pegged down. This usually has the same result and, as a plant always tends to keep an exactly proper balance between the size of its roots and its stems, is often, in any case, more advantageous. (See p. 31.)

The type of soil required for the various species is described along with them in the seasonal notes on the different kinds. As one cannot easily change an alkaline soil into an acid one the gardener having such a soil must limit himself to the species described as supporting this kind of soil. An acid soil of good quality will grow both lime-tolerating and acid soil plants equally well. Indeed, I have yet to find a case of lime starvation with any shrub or tree of any kind growing on mulched ground. There are, however, species which insist particularly on free and rapid drainage, such as a chalk soil often affords, and these, although they will usually grow to perfection in well-drained sandy, acid soils, may fail in acid clays where waterlogging sometimes occurs.

Some few acid soils on steep slopes are deficient in certain essential chemicals and mineral elements. In such cases the remedy is not to lime, as this merely causes further shortages by sealing up available iron, aluminium and other minerals. In practice, the mulch supplies all that is required, except in very extreme cases when a complete fertiliser may be given as well.

The exact stationing of the plant in the soil as regards depth is very important. If too shallow, the roots, unless heavily mulched, are exposed to air and frost. If too deep, the surface roots cannot get the air they require and consequently do not function properly; worse still, the basal buds cannot burst out into new shoots to renew the branch system, as many kinds require to do. Mark the point carefully, then, where stem becomes root, and station this exactly at soil-level. Note that Rhododendron and Azalea roots are thus shown to require a position on the surface and accordingly cover them only with mulching material—not heavy, suffocating soil.

The roots must, further, be carefully spread out, individually, if they are bare, so that they radiate outwards and downwards from the centre. Friable soil is made firm about them as planting proceeds. At all times gentleness should be practised. The plant is out of its element, like a fish out of water or a drowning man, until it is re-established and able to resume its vital processes. Finally, one should make sure that the plant is really firm in the ground by gentle squeezing of the soil with the foot all round, and then apply a protective mulch at once in the manner already described.

STAKING

If the bush has a large top and the site is exposed to the wind, or if the subject is a young standard tree, staking will be necessary to prevent wind-rocking. A strong stake of suitable size is given a sharp, tapered point, and, a hole for it having been gently made with a pointed crow-bar, it may be inserted in the hole and hammered in until tight. Then a tie is made by threading a two-foot length of iron wire through a one-foot length of old rubber hose, or proportionately larger or smaller as required. The tie is taken round the stem, then the ends are crossed over and brought together again on the outer side of the stake. Here they are gently twisted, care being taken not to make such an abrupt twist as to kink the wire. Such a tie will hold a tree firmly and without chafing so long as the stake lasts. It must be inspected every year, however, because it will not yield to growth beyond a certain point. To adjust, untwist the wire, slack off as required, and then retwist.

TRANSPLANTING

For transplanting a tree or shrub from one part of the garden to an-other, late autumn or early spring are the best times to choose if the subject is large or known to be of a kind likely to suffer by moving. A trench should be taken out in a circle just beyond the spread of the roots. Soil may be gently teased from these and the trench will then have to be cleared of soil again. Deciduous sorts that move well—such as Cherries or Maples—may have all the soil gradually removed. Specimens as large as a strong man may just carry, with bare roots, seldom suffer even a check if care and gentleness have been used. Evergreens, essentially, and Hydrangeas advantageously, and all fibrous-rooted subjects small enough to handle in this way, should have a ball of soil left enclosing the main root system. Large evergreens such as Rhododendrons and Camellias will require burlap to wrap up the large root-ball that it is essential to preserve, also cords to hold the burlap in position and ropes looped and thrust under the ball to provide a sufficient grip to haul them out of the ground. In such cases the stem must never be pulled at and gentleness, as always, is essential. Very large plants on sloping sites may be slid out on planks into their new positions remarkably easily. So long as the initial work is not scamped, and provided that the roots are intact within their surrounding ball of soil, there is no limit to the size of the plants that may be moved with safety. It is purely a mechanical problem. Gardeners in both Japan and America move even larger specimens than we do in Britain.

As for smaller specimens, we commonly move Azaleas and Hydrangeas of considerable size when in full bloom in the nurseries but, such is the care taken in securing the root system entire within the surrounding ball of soil, that the plants do not flag for an instant. In all such cases immediate replanting is, of course, essential.

PLANTING DISTANCES

When planting a bed, it is helpful to use two kinds of shrubs—permanent plants and temporary plants. This enables the planter to plan his ultimate effect without disadvantageous deference to immediate results and yet secure a good showing to decorate the waiting period. The permanent plants are first put in at such distances apart as will suit their ultimate development. Then the temporary plants are put in, closely filling the spaces between them. These temporary plants may be of sorts that are of little value and whose destruction later will not be regretted; they may be short-lived plants that will probably eliminate themselves automatically; or again they may be valuable plants of species that can be moved easily at any time. Common Broom seedlings and Heathers are examples of the first sort; annuals, Tree Lupins, Cistus and Ceanothus are examples of the second, and evergreen Azaleas of the third. It is essential, however, that they should be shrubs —not herbaceous plants. This is because not only do herbaceous plants spread so as to swamp the permanent shrubs but, in removing the herbs later, dangerous ground-disturbance is unavoidable in order to eliminate their persisting roots. With most shrubs, one good chop just below ground level puts paid to them and their roots may safely be left to rot and enrich the soil. This latter function is performed by leguminous plants with unusual efficiency.

PLANT LABELS

All the pure species should, perhaps, be labelled, and if they are rare it is even very desirable. But if the labels are lost there is no insurmountable difficulty in replacing them. With superior forms and garden varieties, it is quite a different matter. For every hundred persons who can determine the identity of a pure species there may be only one who can name a garden variety. Thus a permanent label is specially necessary. Metal labels inscribed with acid, or impressed, are very durable and probably unsurpassed for this purpose. A tongue of the metal or a piece of lead wire is generally used to attach them securely to the central stem.

Owing to the fact that the labels are attached to the growing plants no fears need be entertained that they will show up too prominently in the garden scene. Indeed, the difficulty is, often, how to find them among the masses of foliage.

PRUNING AND PEGGING-DOWN

Pruning is important in the shaping of young trees. Branches competing with the leader have to be shortened back to a branchlet, or a U-shaped double leader will cause danger. Later in life the tree is liable to split at the base of the U with disastrous results.

In general I would deprecate any but obviously necessary pruning, when an old or straggling branch cries out for removal. Apart from the exceptions, pruning should not, in my opinion, be looked upon as a *necessary routine* in growing flowering shrubs. If they are properly grown and arranged they do not need it. On the other hand with species that do not resent hard pruning a starved, gnarled specimen making poor growth may be first carefully fed and then, when growth starts, cut down with the object of growing a new bush up from the roots. If the plant is grafted or budded, care must of course be taken to make certain that the cutting process is done well above the initiation of the scion (or portion of the superior form).

In almost all cases with shrubs, though not of course, trees, the virtues of pegging down should be carefully considered. In my view this is often much more effective than pruning. A plant always tends to keep an exact balance between its root system and its top. If we remove a portion of the top there is a corresponding slowing down of root growth. But if we bend down a branch and fix it to the ground with a peg or a large stone there is no such severe check. The sap is slightly obstructed by the bend and new shoots not only appear from that point but also, almost magically, from the base. Many other great advantages are gained by pegging down young shrubs when first planting them. They are held firm against wind damage without troublesome stakes, layers are facilitated, the form and habit of the bush is made perfect at once, being fixed so that every branch is decoratively disposed, and the vulnerable stem is protected from frost and sun.

Among the subjects benefiting most spectacularly from this treatment are Rhododendrons, Azaleas, both evergreen and summer-clad, *Senecio laxifolius*, Rose species, large specimen Hydrangeas, Cistus, etc. Convenient pegs perfectly shaped for the purpose are provided by inverting Bamboo stems. *Sinarundinaria nitida* supplies these for the evergreen Azaleas and Cistus, *Pseudosasa japonica* for medium-sized shrubs and *S. fastuosa* for the larger sorts. When the projecting tops of the pegs are cut off above the hooks with the secateurs the bush appears to be naturally of perfect habit and form. By the time the pegs rot, the branches have become fixed in the proper positions and the phenomenal growth induced from the centre makes of the whole a verdant mound of healthful foliage.

CHAPTER II

PROPAGATION

CUTTINGS

ONE of the simplest methods of propagation for the amateur is by means of cuttings of half-ripe shoots of the year, from two to six inches long taken with a "heel" of old wood and placed in the sand box or under a bell-glass. When the branchlet is broken off the branch, the "heel" naturally comes away with it in most cases. It is a good plan to trim the base smooth with a sharp knife or razor blade so that any ragged point is removed and to *cut* off the lower leaves. If these are pulled off it may damage the stem. The cutting is then ready for insertion.

The sand-box is just a strong box about 14 to 18 inches deep, for choice, and about 18 inches wide by two feet long. Drainage holes are bored in the bottom and covered with a layer of crocks on which is next placed a layer of sifted leafmould or chopped bracken about an inch deep, then a layer of a mixture of equal parts of peat and sharp river sand about six inches deep and over all a layer of about half an inch of finer sand. This is a favourite specification; actually, results quite as good may often be had by merely putting six inches or so of "rabbit sand", from outside any new rabbit hole in a sandy spot, into the box. More important is the sheet of glass that is required to cover the box. As often as not, half a dozen odd pieces are used like a jigsaw puzzle held down with stones and bits of wood. When any local builder's yard would supply a pane cut to exactly the right size to make a snug fit for about eighteen pence I think it is worth while to save time and bother by getting a piece of glass cut for each box. Several of these boxes are needed so that there is always room to put in any cuttings that one may receive, at once.

The best method of insertion requires a smooth stick a little thicker than the cutting and about a foot long, and this is best kept handy by the box. The cutting is measured against the stick and the hand is slid down to register the top of the lower two-thirds of the cutting that will be buried. Without moving the hand from the stick this is plunged into the sand, at a slight angle, and the cutting when inserted in the hole

3   33

will be at the right depth. The sand is then firmed round the cutting by a deep prod and twist with the stick, taking the most particular care that the base of the sprig is tightly surrounded on all sides and at the bottom, and the glass is then replaced.

The sand in the box is kept moist and the box stands in the sun where it keeps warm while the deep sides prevent the sun from wilting the leaves of the cuttings. In hot weather a piece of mutton-cloth to provide extra shade is held over the glass by a few drawing pins; better still, a frame of hessian or burlap, supported on sticks, may be suspended two or three feet *above* the glass.

The sand-frame is really only a larger and more carefully arranged and convenient model of this simple appliance. It is more suitable when large quantities of one kind, such as Hydrangeas or Evergreen Azaleas are required. In sharply drained ground the soil inside the frame is best excavated about eight inches deep and replaced with peat and sand mixture up to ground level again. To save labour, we use portable frames and lift them off, leaving the cuttings growing on, *in situ*, feeding them with liquid fertiliser as necessary. The frames are then reset as before in new positions for the next season's cuttings.

Glass bell-cloches are probably the most useful and effective of all propagating mediums for the amateur, (if unobtainable large glass jampots provide a useful makeshift) and sandy beds can be made up in both sunny and shady situations for them. Camellias, for example, strike best in shade, and softer cuttings of many kinds root more quickly when more warm and moist. The cloche cuttings usually keep sufficiently moist without artificial watering owing to the natural moisture of the soil, but mutton-cloth skirts, easily contrived by merely tying one end of this tubular-woven material round the knob of the cloche, are needed on hot days. Too much shading retards rooting, so it is advisable to shade no more than is absolutely necessary to prevent wilting, and in my experience results are notably better when the shading material is suspended high above the cloches.

For certain species that root easily from hard-wood cuttings a north wall-foot is one of the most valuable and labour-saving of all propagating mediums for the amateur. By merely digging out the soil and replacing it with sharp river sand and sifted leafmould we have an excellent propagating bed. Roses, *Kerria japonica*, Cistus, Fuchsias, Hydrangeas, Ceanothus, *Genista hispanica*, *G. tinctoria* and other species are easily rooted from autumn cuttings of firm wood in such a situation and, at a pinch, can be left to grow-on until the following autumn when they may be lifted and set out at once in their permanent situations. In these days, gardens both large and small have to help to pay their way, or at the least save some money having to be spent on replacements and additions, and a few rows of well-grown cuttings of some choice speciality of the garden will go far to achieve this.

SEEDS

The results of seed sowing are slower than those from cuttings in many instances and only in the case of isolated pure species or controlled pollination are the seedlings certain to be of value. But the possible reward of really interesting and even of highly exciting results makes it very well worth while.

This opens up the whole vast problem of plant breeding which is too complex a subject to deal with here. But briefly, it may be said that the objective is, first of all, to prevent the parent flower being pollinated by its own pollen or by chance, and, secondly, to effect pollination with the desired male parent. To give an example, we wished to produce a Hydrangea, of the informal Lacecap type of *H. macrophylla*, having a *red* flower. 'Whitewave' with its hardy vigorous growth was selected as the female parent and 'Arthur Billard', an intensely rich-coloured Hortensia, as the male parent. The 'Whitewave' flower-head was covered with a muslin bag to prevent insect visitation. When ready the fertile flowers were all carefully dusted with 'Arthur Billard' pollen.

Then ensued the long waiting to grow and ripen the seed which is ready only in December. The ripe seed was carefully sown in well-crocked pans of sterilised sifted loam, sand and leafmould in the greenhouse, and covered with a pane of glass. The seedlings, when large enough, were carefully pricked out and grown-on in boxes, then in small pots and finally planted out in rows in a frame. In the case of the Hydrangea mentioned we do not yet know the results. Possibly all will be inferior to the parents; on the other hand one or two may be just what we wanted. Many crosses of other species, such as among the Lilacs, Abelias, Roses and Azaleas also offer interesting possibilities at the present time and the humblest amateur may well make history in the development of his favourite plant.

Where there are special requirements, further details of seed propagation are given in the body of the work under species headings.

GRAFTING AND BUDDING

Grafting and budding are more complicated, but some species such as Cherries, Crabs, Rowans and Hawthorns are fairly easily budded by the amateur and the following account of propagating Cherries can, with minor modifications, serve as a model for many kinds.

As a preliminary it is advisable to line-out young seedlings of the
Gean (*Prunus avium*) or whatever stock is to be used, in early autumn
when they are from about six to eight inches high. They will add a
foot or more to their height during the following summer and be ready
for budding in mid to late July.

The "wood" used for budding is taken from shoots of the current
year, the good buds being located about the middle of the firm "wood".
When cutting out the bud, the tip of the shoot is held towards the
operator and the cut commenced on the further side of the bud which
is removed by a clean slicing motion with a razor blade or sharp knife.
The leaf is then cut off, leaving just under half an inch of its stalk in
position. Next, the sliver of wood is removed from inside by a gentle
pull. Sometimes a tiny piece remains in the centre. This fragment, which
is said to perform the function of feeding the leaf, may also be taken
away, great care being taken not to damage the delicate centre of the
actual bud which will be seen as a tiny indentation surrounded by a
little ridge. If moisture is seen to be glistening on the exposed surface
of the inner bark the bud should be discarded as being too sappy,
probably from wood too near the tip. If, on the other hand, when
removing the sliver of wood the heart of the bud comes away as well,
leaving a pin-head hole, it means that the wood is too hard, having
probably been taken from a portion of the shoot too near the main
stem.

A cross cut, at an angle of about forty-five degrees is now made with
the knife in the stem of the stock, care being taken not to let the cut
go deeper than the actual bark. Then, similarly, a downward vertical
cut is made in the bark from the centre of the first cut forming a letter
T with the top bar askew. With an ivory blade the bark is next gently
lifted on either side of the vertical cut and the bud, on its strip of bark,
lightly pushed down as far as it will go inside the slit. This strip of bark
will now project above the cross cut, and should be cut off so that it
fits snugly in below it. Now, a suitable length of raffia is taken and,
starting at the bottom, just below the cut, carefully wound round stock
and bud in such a manner as to draw the edges of the vertical cut
together round the bud and its strip of bark, both below and above,
care being taken not to cover the actual bud. Finally the raffia is tied
in a reef knot at the top.

It is well to bear in mind that the success of the operation depends on
the nascent life in the bud being preserved in spite of its undergoing a
major operation without medical amenities. Consequently speed and
cleanliness are essential and the exposed surfaces should never be
touched with the hands. As it happens, the leaf-stalk forms a useful
handle for the bud and this should be used exclusively. When bud-wood

has to be sent long distances, the leaves should be snipped off and the cut ends of the shoots should be sealed with wax, and drying out further prevented by the use of damp packing material.

The knife must be specially ground and sharpened to a razor-like keenness; furthermore it must be absolutely clean and free from any decayed vegetable matter, however microscopic, for this might contain fungus spores.

The bud will remain dormant until spring and no further action need be taken until October, when it will be necessary to cut back the stock to about six inches above the bud.

In January, it will be advisable to cut off some grafting wood from those varieties which it is desired to propagate, so as to be in a position to graft any stock whose buds, as evidenced by their not having cast their leaf stalks, have died. These shoots should be of the last year's growth. They should be heeled in, that is to say, have the lower third portion buried in the ground, preferably under a north wall or in a shady spot free from drip. The reason for this procedure is that, in grafting, it is necessary to have the sap in the stock in a more forward state than that of the scion and by this method the ratio should be about right for this operation to be performed in March.

Having all materials in readiness for grafting, the first operation, that of beheading the stock about three inches from ground-level, can be performed. The cut is made horizontally, leaving a clean level surface. Next the scion is selected from the firm middle wood of the shoot. The large end of this is sliced off on one side, leaving the bark undamaged on the other. Assuming that the stock is about twice the thickness of a pencil in diameter, the cut thus made for this purpose would be about two inches or so in length. This length is then measured against the stump of the stock and a similar, opposite, portion of the stock cut away in such a manner that, when the two exposed surfaces are placed together, stock and scion appear as one shoot with the junction almost invisible. Upon the exactitude of this junction, through-out its length, much of the success of the operation depends. Having satisfied himself that this is as perfect as possible the operator then makes the last cut. This is an upward incision, at an angle of forty-five degrees, made in the scion at the point where the bark begins, on the shaved-off side. The cut should penetrate to slightly less than one-third the diameter of the scion. An opposite incision, that is to say one in a downward direction, is then made in the top of the stock in such a position that the little tongue of wood formed in the scion will fit into it, thus assisting in holding the graft firm. Stock and scion having been fitted together in this manner they can now be tied in position with raffia.

The method of tying the graft is slightly different to that employed in budding. The tie is started at the bottom and wound up in a rapid open spiral to the top, then the raffia is wound closely and firmly round, down to the bottom again, where it is made fast by a tuck similar to that used in splicing.

It now only remains to apply the grafting wax in such a manner as to exclude the air completely from the join, and the exposed surface of the top of the stock and of the scion where the tip of the graft was cut off. In order to be able to remove the wax easily and safely later on, in late spring, it is best to keep the non-grafted side clean and free from wax. Then it will only be necessary to cut the raffia to clear the stem by a gentle pull when it becomes evident, by the growth of the shoot, that the necessary callus has been formed.

When spring is well advanced there are few greater pleasures in gardening than watching the first growth of the buds and grafts. These must, however, be carefully tied and staked, or some incompetent bird, misjudging the strength of the union, will break off the precious shoot by alighting heavily upon it. The bud-shoots will require to be tied to the snag left on the budded stocks with successive raffia ties. They usually end up with about three ties, roughly four or five inches apart.

The grafted plants will require to have a stake for each scion firmly stuck in so that they can be secured similarly. The rate of growth, whether from tiny bud or insignificant twig is such as to appear at first sight quite unbelievable, provided caterpillars are kept away, and gives ample reward for all the trouble taken.

Finally, in late autumn when the little trees are in a dormant state, the "snagging" is done. This merely consists in cutting off the last snag of the stock to which the budded plants have been tied. A close upward slanting cut is made and the wound at once painted over with gas-tar. The young plants are now known as "maidens" and can be planted out in their permanent positions if desired, though they may well be allowed another season's growth in the Nursery.

In the foregoing description I have avoided technical terms and complications as far as possible in the hope of encouraging amateurs to try a few buds or grafts for their own amusement. In case it all sounds too serious and complicated may I say that I have, at times, committed most of the worst faults and used the wrong systems altogether and still had highly interesting and sometimes even surprisingly successful results? The fact is that Cherries, Rowans and Crabs lend themselves particularly to this method of propagation.

LAYERING

To layer a shrub, select a low branch which will conveniently touch the ground at a point about a foot from its tip. Scoop out a hole about six inches across and nine inches deep. Very gently and tenderly bend the branch into the hole so that it assumes a U shape with six inches of the tip emerging. Then fill the hole with sand and black mould mixture and make firm. For slender branches the hole may be narrower, as the bend needs to be as abrupt as is possible without breakage. The sap-flow of the branch is interrupted by the sharp bend and thus in the course of the following season roots are put out to keep the tip alive. In the following autumn, having made certain that the tip is now well rooted, the branch may be cut off where it emerges from the ground on the parent plant's side.

Sometimes the layer requires another growing season to make sufficient roots and in all cases of doubt it is wise to leave the layer in position after cutting the main branch. After the further season's growth *in situ* it should be well able to support the move.

The gardener should always *try* to propagate choice shrubs even if he can only apply the most rough and ready methods. Gardening history is full·of amazing happy surprises in successful results. To give a few instances, a rare and precious Magnolia, destroyed by a storm, was preserved for posterity by one of the torn branches being firmly stuck into the ground although the species is usually hopeless as regards propagation from cuttings; one of the finest of the new Camellias was obtained merely by pressing the seed into the ground near the parent plant; a bundle of prunings of a fabulously costly Tree Peony was stuck into a heap of leafmould and all rooted admirably although cuttings are too chancy to be worth while commercially—in spite of long lists of unfilled orders.

CHAPTER III

EARLY SPRING AND APRIL

EARLY SPRING AND APRIL

IN this time of early spring an ample selection of beautiful shrubs comes into flower, but restraint in their planting must be advised in gardens whose bad air-drainage, arising from low-lying or "cul-de-sac" positions, makes frequent spring frosts likely. A later and therefore more reliable effect is to be preferred in such places.

The choice available includes both shrubs of the highest quality and, unfortunately, cost, such as the Magnolias of the *stellata* and *denudata* sections, Camellias, Tree Pæonies, etc., and also a great number of the more inexpensive kinds.

Except for Camellias, Evergreen Azaleas, dwarf Rhododendrons and flowering trees, it is wise to keep the early flowerers to the less prominent positions, as most of them have a comparatively short season of bloom compared with those that flower later. On the other hand, the flowering evergreens mentioned as exceptions have such all-time value in the garden landscape that they may advantageously form the furniture of even the most prominent beds.

One of the earliest effective pictures of the season is made by the blooming of the flowering trees of Plum, Magnolia, Cherry, Peach and Almond. Many small shrubs flower at the same time, but the background scene of naked trees and sere old grass frequently spoils their effect. The blossoming trees have often blue sky and white cloud or, best of all perhaps, dark Pines to frame them.

The problem is to find room for these very early flowerers where they will not obtrude too much in the summer scene when out of flower. The flowering Cherries are perhaps the most effective and therefore the most to be recommended to serve also the useful role of giving light shade to some of the beds. They are more beautiful in form than the others merely as trees when out of flower and give us a second effect in autumn, when their leaves turn to fine shades of red and yellow.

Gardens with limy soils have a wide choice of fine shrubs flowering this month; notable among these are the "Japonicas" (Chænomeles), Moutans (Tree Pæonies), Berberis, Spiræas, Forsythias, Crabs and Cherries, Lilacs and Viburnums. With these the gardener can contrive vivid and beautiful flower effects without recourse to those purplish-pink hues which prohibit the enjoyment of all pure and clean colours.

43

Among the **Plums** the best known are the varieties of *Prunus cerasifera*, the Cherry Plum or Mirabelle. *P. c. atropurpurea* (A.G.M. 1928), often known as *P. Pissardii*, is the commonest. Named by the German gardener Hermann Jaeger in 1881, it was said to have been first sent to France by M. Pissard, gardener to the Shah of Persia, in 1880. It forms a rounded, dense tree about 20 feet high. The delightful white, or less bold pinkish-white, blossoms appear in March or early April as the red young leaves start to open. Unfortunately, the flowering is often sparse owing to the evil work of bullfinches or to an insufficiently open position, and the leaves turn later to a dark, heavy colour. The sudden blob of sullen maroon in the garden landscape is anything but attractive in summer.

An interesting new form with pink flowers—*P. c.* var. *Lindsayæ*, was brought from Persia by Miss Lindsay and received an A.M. at the R.H.S. Show in February 1948. Also shown was the variety *P. c. Purpusii* with dark red, yellow and pinkish-coloured leaves.

A fine variety of *P. c. atropurpurea* is that clonally propagated as *Woodii*. The flowers are bolder, more shapely and long-lasting and of a blush-pink colour.

Particularly decorative is *P. cerasifera nigra*. In this variety the bolder flowers are very profuse and of a vivid pink and the leaves of a darker and richer tint.

The "type", *P. cerasifera*, is a native of the Caucasus and West Asia and has normal green leaves and white blossom of a slightly greenish cast and is quite attractive. It is sometimes used as a hedge, but close clipping, of course, prevents its flowering properly and, if not clipped, it is certain to get bare at the base in time.

Prunus blireiana (A.G.M. 1928) is a hybrid between *P. c. atropurpurea* and the Japanese Apricot, *P. Mume*. It has a purplish-red foliage similar to the first-mentioned parent but the flowers are large, semi-double and clear pink in colour and make it a very showy little tree in blossom. *Prunus blireiana Moseri* is rather similar but decidedly less effective.

It is a pity that *P. Mume* is not generally satisfactory in Britain. It is one of the most dearly-loved trees in Japan where its white or pink blossom often bursts from the bare boughs while snow is still on the ground. Over here, it usually flowers rather sparingly except after unusually hot summers. Possibly an aged plant in poor soil might flower more effectively. It was reported to be free-flowering at Mr. J. C. Williams' famous garden at Caerhays in the West Country, and well-flowered branches were exhibited by Messrs. Hillier in 1948, so it should be worth trying in the South.

Before we leave the Plums, mention must be made of the double-flowered form of our native Sloe, *P. spinosa* var. *plena* (A.M. 1950).

This is a most attractive, dense little bush that does well in even the most exposed positions. According to J. W. Bean ("Trees and Shrubs Hardy in the British Isles", Vol. II, p. 253) it seems first to have appeared spontaneously at Tarascon. It is specially worth noting for gardens whose limy soil precludes the growing of many choicer early flowering shrubs.

Another ultra-hardy shrub that is capable of giving a good account of itself anywhere may be mentioned here.

Mahonia Aquifolium (A.G.M. 1930) is one of the old standbys that one cannot leave out. Though it lacks the bold, arresting architecture of the winter-flowering *M. japonica* and *M. nepaulensis*, it is such a useful, ultra-hardy, evergreen ground-coverer, so free with its fragrant Canary Yellow racemes in April or earlier, and so accommodating, whether the soil be limy or acid, that it finds a place in almost every garden.

It is particularly valuable on an alkaline (or limy) soil, where fewer flowering evergreens are available to furnish the ground with an ever-green covert from which the stronger-growing deciduous shrubs may emerge. A little extra feeding may be necessary in such cases, but the difference in the winter attractiveness of the garden scene is so great that it is worth quite a lot of trouble. In fact I would go so far as to say that on such soils the larger number of deciduous shrubs that have to be grown make it necessary to carpet the ground with such evergreen carpeters as *M. Aquifolium*, Periwinkles, etc. if the winter appearance of the garden is not to be highly bleak and depressing. In autumn many of the Mahonia's leaves turn red or purple and thus add to the season-able décor of the garden.

M. Aquifolium can be increased by dividing up and replanting old plants and by seed which often gives hybrids where other species are also grown. Sometimes a fungus (*Puccinia mirabilissima*)† attacks the plant with a rust disease which has a disastrous effect.

There are a number of varieties:—

M. A. magnifica, a tall form up to eight feet high and very decorative indeed.

M. A. Moseri, a low growing bushy form with particularly richly coloured autumn foliage. Regrettably difficult to propagate, it is one of the rarer and more beautiful evergreen shrubs.

M. A. undulata, a tall form with crenulated foliage, very free-flowering.

† The late Mr. L. de Rothschild, R.H.S. Conference, " Ornamental Flowering Trees and Shrubs", 1938.

Two allied species, *M. nervosa* and *M. repens* are rather rare, they are foot-high miniatures of *M. Aquifolium* in appearance and so restrained that they are even suitable for small rock gardens.

M. japonica, cultivated in Japan, is a striking evergreen of perhaps eight or ten feet, with foot-long spiny, pinnate evergreen leaves and drooping racemes of fragrant yellow flowers in February. It is reasonably hardy. It is a shrub of all-the-year-round decorative value as a foliage shrub of the highest order. Shrubs of this class are seldom given full value in modern plantings, boldly displayed as specimens near important paved areas where they give character and atmosphere to the composition.

M. Bealei, a related species from China with upright, shorter, less fragrant panicles, is often considered to be hardier, if slightly less decorative in flower and less freely branching.

M. B. var. *hyemalis* is by some considered a superior form of the last-named, by others a form of *M. japonica*. When seedlings are grown from either type they appear with all sorts of inflorescences.† The important point is that, whether they are forms or species, certain superior individuals of fine flower and habit are clonally propagated by specialist nurserymen and, quite rightly, they charge more for these more troublesome items than for mere seedling forms.

M. lomariifolia, with much divided, long, evergreen leaves and bright yellow, erect flower spikes in October and November, is another very handsome Mahonia. There appear to be both tender and reasonably hardy forms of this species and, in any event a fairly open position seems to be necessary with good air-drainage so that early frosts may be avoided.

These Mahonias are not particular as to soil, moderately limy ones being quite acceptable. Some shelter from the worst of the winter winds is desirable to give a chance for the untimely flowers to expand. Propagation is not easy for the amateur without heated propagating frames, but if seed is ripened it should be sown with care in small pots as these plants suffer severely in moving.

The **Periwinkles**, without being vividly effective at a distance are useful, hardy, easy-going, low, evergreens with delightful, if often rather sparse and shy flowers that are prepared to make the most of any rough bank that we care to give them. On the other hand, if good forms are given a sunny position in well worked soil they bloom much more freely and soon provide a pleasing carpet seldom without flowers all summer long. In these days a labour-saving carpeter of this kind is

† Mr. R. D. Trotter, R.H.S. Shrub Conference, 1938.

invaluable. They are humble cousins of the Oleander being members of
the tropical Dogbane family, but our Periwinkles have no ill effect
on dogs. They will grow well on limy soils where they may take the
place of the Heaths and Evergreen Azaleas.

Vinca major, the Greater Periwinkle, is a trailing, foot-high evergreen
from south Europe with blue flowers about an inch and a half across
from late April or early May onwards. Once planted in good soil it
can look after itself and will be found very useful for rough banks
where, with an annual trim-over in early spring, it will furnish the
ground attractively for many years.

Vinca minor, the Lesser Periwinkle, is more responsive to good
cultivation and an even better plant for carpeting purposes and a very
charming little thing indeed, worthy of more careful attention by
planters. It often starts flowering as early as March and continues
more sparsely all summer. There are varieties with white, pale blue,
deep blue, violet and purple flowers and these make a delightful effect
mingled together. Owing to the fact that almost any piece will root,
with care, and that it spreads freely, rooting as it goes, it is advantageous
to buy a few plants of the best and most vivid colour forms obtainable.
Even the Lesser Periwinkle is, of course, too invasive for rock gardens
where alpines are cultivated but is quite satisfactory as a six-inch
evergreen carpeter among the stronger shrubs. It grows quite well even
in chalky and shady places and I have seen it, beautiful, about the boles
of great oaks in the woodland, but its flowering is less whole-hearted
there than in sunnier places.

Some named varieties are:—

V. minor "Bowles var." in colour Hyacinth Blue (H.C.C. 40/1).
Flowers one and a half inches across.

V. m. atropurpurea, purple flowers.

V. m. azurea, sky-blue flowers.

V. m. alba, white flowers.

There are also several varieties with doubled flowers or variegated
foliage.

Not particular as to whether the soil is limy or acid, the Periwinkles
flower more freely if it is fairly rich, and, indeed, an occasional top-
dressing is desirable for the more valuable Lesser Periwinkle.

Propagation is easily done at any time by detaching rooted pieces.

Vividly effective in flower, the **Forsythias** are an easygoing family
very commonly planted.

Forsythia Giraldiana, from China, is one of the first to open its
very pale yellow flowers and has a stronger and more shapely

habit of growth than the commoner sorts, attaining about six feet in height.

In March, *F. ovata*, from Korea, often precedes it in opening its pale amber-yellow flowers, produced on a bush of lower stature and more shapely form than any. It was introduced by E. H. Wilson in 1918 and is said to be the hardiest of all the Forsythias.

Another Korean, *F. viridissima*, has a more upright habit and the bright yellow flowers have a greenish cast. The variety *koreana* is said to be superior, another—var. *bronxensis*—is a dwarf only a foot high.† Var. *elegantissima* is a good form.

F. suspensa, from China, with its flopping habit, is somewhat untidy, but the variety *Sieboldii* carries the trait so far that it has a certain attractiveness when hanging down over a cliff or draping an arbour. The flowers are Aureolin Yellow (H.C.C. 3/2).

F. s. atrocaulis is a fine and distinct variety with a more upright habit, blackish bark and large, less profuse, Primrose Yellow flowers boldy presented.

The most effective Forsythia is undoubtedly *F. intermedia* var. *spectabilis*, a hybrid which received the Award of Garden Merit in 1923, having large Lemon Yellow flowers. If pruned after flowering to encourage new shoots the latter will often flower all along their length in a most spectacular manner.

All these Forsythias can be struck from cuttings very easily indeed, and grow well in any soil in a sunny position. They are especially valuable for gardens on limy soils.

Many of the Forsythias are highly effective when in flower, with masses of vivid yellow of several hues. So much so that they are amply prominent when in flower even when placed in out-of-the-way positions in the background. These are the places to put them, for delightful as they are when in flower they are very dull and ugly bushes for the rest of the year. Care in arranging a lively and gay colour association is very well rewarded, though seldom seen; the unrelieved yellows are too startling alone. A groundwork of blue Periwinkles or the deep blue herb, *Pulmonaria angustifolia*, and contrasts with the soft orange of *Chænomeles japonica* and the white blossoms of the flowering Plums, the Yulan, the Sloe or the Spring Cherry and the softer yellow of the pollen-bearing, male form of the Pussy Willow (*Salix caprea*) and other early flowerers can afford novel and striking arrangements of great charm.

Another "ironclad" is *Ribes sanguineum*, the **Flowering Currant,** with flowers that appear a somewhat muddy pink that is difficult to

† *The Gardeners' Chronicle*, Vol. CXXV, p. 90 (1949).

Magnolia mollicomata

Rhododendron venustum Jacksonii

Camellia japonica 'Adolphe Audusson'

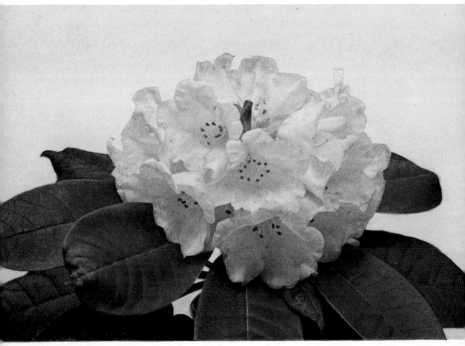

Rhododendron lacteum

place near the purer and more vivid colours advocated, though actually it is Rose Madder (H.C.C. 23/2) with Crimson buds. It was introduced by David Douglas when collecting in western North America for the old Horticultural Society in 1836. The var. *splendens*, having Crimson flowers, is somewhat brighter, if less vigorous, and received the Award of Garden Merit in 1928.

While we are still in the beginning of springtime we may consider one of the earliest flowering sections of the **Magnolia** family. This is that centred about *Magnolia stellata*, all having somewhat strap-shaped petals and sepals (collectively sometimes called tepals) and coming from Japan.

Magnolia Kobus (A.G.M. 1936) is a tree said to be up to seventy feet high in its native forests of Japan and, according to Alfred Rehder,† it is the hardiest of the Asiatic Magnolias. It does not usually flower at all until it is eight to nine feet in height. The northern form, *var. borealis* is, however, a remarkably fast grower and makes a fine shapely tree that is particularly fine when grown as a standard and much superior to the "type" form. The larger trees in this country are seldom more than thirty or forty feet in height and this appears to be the maximum size that it can be expected to attain here. The flowering time, late March or early April, is a dangerous one and the pure white fragrant flowers, about four inches across, with thin narrow tepals, are easily damaged by strong winds and may be destroyed overnight by five or six degrees of frost. Unlike the other Japanese species, *M. Kobus* will grow on limy soils.

M. salicifolia (A.G.M. 1941) is rather similar in flower. There are two forms—the "type", which is the most handsome of the two, and the variety *fasciata* which has a somewhat besom-like habit. The flowers are produced on quite small trees and the willow-like leaves have a lemon-verbena scent when crushed. It is one of the most desirable small trees for the garden and gives a reasonably quick return.

M. stellata (A.G.M. 1923) is the most valuable of the three for really small gardens, perhaps, as it not only flowers freely when very small but remains a low bush for many years in most soils, although it may ultimately reach ten or twelve feet in height. Like the other members of the section, the flowers, with ten or more rather strap-shaped tepals (petals and sepals) are a peculiarly pure white. This Magnolia was brought from Japan in 1862 by Dr. George R. Hall who gave it to Mr. S. B. Parsons of Flushing, Long Island, who distributed it as *M.*

† "Manual of Cultivated Trees and Shrubs", 2nd Edition, Macmillan, N.Y., U.S.A.

4

Halleana, and it reached England in 1877. There is a pretty variety—var. *rosea*—with slightly rosy-flushed flowers, also var. *rubra* with pale Fuchsia Purple flowers.

Considering the often excessive earliness of its flowering—March–April—*M. stellata* makes a very good showing, because if the first batch of flowers is frosted, or pounded to pieces by gales, it often manages a second flowering a little later.

M. Loebneri is a hybrid (*M. stellata* × *Kobus*) having larger leaves and also larger flowers with about twelve tepals. This excellent Magnolia will probably become more common as new methods of propagation are now being perfected. It grows well on chalky soils.

As regards the cultivation of these Magnolias, plenty of leaf-mould in a deep soil and sufficient wind shelter to preserve the delicate flowers from the worst buffetings of March gales are the first essentials. With a very limited space available, one cannot always afford the uncertainty of such early flowers and in such circumstances better value is offered by the summer-flowering section of the Magnolia family, dealt with later. In the wood-garden, on the other hand, these Magnolias and those of the *M. denudata* section are supreme, and let us hope that planters will soon be busy planting them in the regional gardens of the new National Parks which should, I think, make a point of exploiting the excellence of our climate for gardening purposes and thus help to give future tourists something worth coming to England to see.

Seeds, layers and cuttings (see p. 33) offer the best means of propagation.

We now come to that beautiful but much miscultivated plant **Camellia japonica** (A.G.M. 1930). Introduced in 1739 by Lord Petre, the earliest importations soon died as they were kept in a warm greenhouse. Gradually it was learnt that the plant enjoyed less warm conditions and for many years it was a popular cool greenhouse shrub. More recently it has been discovered that it is perfectly hardy out of doors so long as it is grown in a really shady place in a reasonably moist, acid soil rich in humus.

In its natural state, *C. japonica* grows in the Japanese forests under large trees. Among flowering shrubs of unusual beauty grown for their charm as individuals as opposed to those grown for mass effect, this Camellia holds one of the highest places. It is, indeed, also so colourful that it is only its costliness, and the shaded and sheltered position that it requires, that prevent this absolutely first-class flowering shrub being used for mass effects as well.

Though there are several species, the best garden plants are provided by *C. japonica* in its innumerable garden varieties, and certain hybrids. Such is the variation of these, not only in flower, but also in habit of growth, that it is difficult to generalise on their height and appearance. On the average, a height of 10 feet and an even larger spread would appear to be about the maximum size usually attained by old plants growing under good conditions. The habit varies greatly, some varieties being almost procumbent, others sturdy and upright.

The wild species, with small single red flowers as a rule, is not often seen here as the garden varieties are much more decorative. Most of these, though, were produced in the Victorian era for use as cut flowers from the greenhouse. Tastes have changed, and we care little for the over-symmetrical and elaborately doubled flowers often with blotched and spotted colourings merely due to weakness which comprise a large proportion of these. Identification is difficult, for each outstanding variety is merely the figurehead of a collection of half a dozen or more sister seedlings all of which have been named.

In the following list many of the best reds are described as Geranium Lake (H.C.C. 20). For the benefit of those without access to the Colour Chart, this colour may be described as between Scarlet, on the oranger side, and Carmine, on the bluer side. (Crimson is, of course, still bluer than Carmine.)

Among these red varieties *C. j.* 'Adolphe Audusson' is one of the very best of all for outdoor planting, making a strong, shapely tall shrub of free growth with exceptionally large and vivid Geranium Lake semi-double (sometimes too double) flowers unusually boldly displayed in profusion. This fine habit and the glorious flowers make it an outstanding example of a first-class flowering shrub.

C. j. Kelvingtoniana is a free-flowering vigorous and highly effective variety; one of the best for an effect of massed colour. This is a slightly less vivid red than 'Adolphe Audusson', approximating to Carmine. The flowers are double but not excessively so and have the merit of opening out flat.

C. j. 'Tokayana' is one of the most beautiful of the reds as the flowers are perfectly shaped singles and thus achieve a greater perfection of form than is usually obtained with semi-double or double flowers. Three or four inches across and opening out flat to display the central boss of golden stamens, the Geranium Lake flowers are amongst the most exquisite borne by flowering shrubs.

C. j. 'Mars' is a superb Geranium Lake variety with two rows of petals of superior richness. 'Mercury', 'Apollo' and 'Juno' are very similar, and all these are among the finest of early varieties.

C. j. 'Fred Sander' has a double, deep Geranium Lake flower, fringed like a Carnation. It is usually free-flowering and the flowers are well presented. The habit of the bush is dwarf, close and compact. (See illustration p. 64.)

C. j. latifolia. This is an extra hardy variety with cup-shaped, Crimson, semi-double flowers that are sometimes less shapely than one would wish. It is one of the best for planting in cold districts, not opening too early and having a good habit of growth which assists the formation of a shapely bush.

C. j. 'C. M. Hovey' is a large-flowered, double, Turkey Red variety.

C. j. 'Rosette' has dark red flowers with a slightly separate tuft of petaloid stamens in the centre. Similar but slightly less effective are *anemonæflora*, *althæflora*, *Blackburniana*, *Childsii*, 'Professor Sargent' and 'Arejishi'. All these are apt to flower rather dangerously early—in March instead of April.

C. j. Mathotiana rubra is a dark red double of formal shape with evenly graduated petals.

C. j. 'Lady de Saumarez' has semi-double flowers of a paler Geranium Lake (H.C.C. 20/1) which is one of the loveliest colours that a flower can be. There are two rows of petals and a perfect centre and this variety is very free-flowering, with admirable presentation. Rather early.

Now we come to pink varieties. *C. j.* 'Lady Clare' is quite remarkable. The very large, semi-single flowers are $4\frac{1}{2}$ inches across, having about twelve petals, in colour Carmine Rose (H.C.C. 621). Most of the flowers are beautifully formed with a fine central "boss" of Buttercup Yellow stamens, but some have extra, partly-formed petals among the stamens. This outstanding variety, whose flowers are particularly attractive when cut and seen by artificial light, is somewhat low and sprawling in habit. Unless disbudded it may almost flower itself to death after a hot summer.[†] It is singularly attractive when grown so as to overflow an "Ali Baba" jar in a courtyard.

C. j. 'Hinomaru' ('Hatsukiri') is a single Phlox Pink with a fine central boss of golden stamens and a porcelain-like quality of petal.

C. j. 'Gloire de Nantes' is in some ways a more robust and upright-growing, but less beautiful, version of 'Lady Clare'. Thus in unfavourable gardens it may take her place with advantage.

C. j. 'Empress' is a large-flowered, semi-double variety of a good warm pink and not too early-flowering.

[†] Illustrated in colour in "The Flowering Shrub Garden", by Michael Haworth-Booth, 2nd edition, Country Life, 1947.

C. j. 'Minerva' is a clear pink single with a delightful boss of golden stamens filling the centre.

C. j. 'Lady Hume's Blush' has a very double and symmetrical flower but of very shapely rose-like form and a delicate flesh colour; unfortunately it is apt to flower too early for safety outdoors in any but specially favoured gardens.

C. j. Mathotiana rosea is a formal double with evenly graduated petals of a pure Phlox Pink.

The following are variegated and splashed varieties.

C. j. Donckelaarii is a very fine, hardy and free-flowering variety. The marblings of white which occur on the large crimson, narrow-petalled, semi-double flowers are really the result of starvation, but this and the succeeding varieties are unusually prone to this colour variation. Introduced from Japan by von Siebold in 1830, it is one of the finest outdoor varieties provided that it is well and regularly fed.

C. j. Chandleri elegans. This old variety is also unusually hardy and vigorous. The cherry pink, semi-double flowers are often splashed with white and variegated with paler pink. Like 'Rosette' they have a central tuft of petaloid stamens.

C. j. tricolor Sieboldii. The semi-double or single flowers are white, pink or red or variegated with a mixture of these colours. A famous old bush at Grayswood Hill, Haslemere, bears flowers of all colours at the same time.

C. j. 'Marie Louise' has double flowers with a pale blush-pink or white basal colouring regularly striped with red. A very pretty variety in the artificial style. 'White Vansittart' and 'Comtesse Lavinia Maggi' are very similar, but not quite so fine as flowering bushes.

The following have white flowers.

C. j. 'Legeman' has large, fluffy, semi-double yellowish-white flowers with petaloid stamens and petals intermingled in a novel and strangely attractive manner, delightful for ultra-sophisticated flower decorations. Best in a cold house, perhaps, it is very fine out of doors in favourable gardens in a good season.

C. j. Gauntletti has large-cupped, double, white flowers with loosely grouped golden stamens, *alba grandiflora* is similar but less congested and perhaps of still better shape.

C. j. magnoliæflora. This delightful variety is well named, as the flowers have a superficial resemblance to those of *Magnolia stellata*. It is said not to be quite so strong and hardy as some, but, with me, it has suffered no damage from the severe winters of the war years. The flowers are pearly white, sometimes flushed with pink.

C. j. 'White Swan' is a pure white, single-flowered variety with a fine central boss of golden stamens.

C. j. alba simplex is rather similar, but the flowers of these white varieties do not last long, soon turning brown and unsightly. This is regrettable as the flat-opening, waxy, pure white flowers, set off by the vivid yellow, stamens are very beautiful.

C. j. 'Devona' has smaller semi-double, white flowers, slightly more resistant to browning.

The garden value of *C. japonica* and its varieties is very high indeed because not only are its flowers large, beautiful, of delightful colouring and produced over a long period, but it is hardy enough to withstand over thirty degrees of frost and is an evergreen of the highest winter beauty, the shining leaves being of a rich deep green colour that is extremely attractive. It should have its place in even the smallest gardens, for every detached house has a north wall and I know no shrub that will decorate this more superbly, particularly on either side of the entrance porch. Even in the darkest courtyards this Camellia will grow perfectly so long as there is open sky overhead and the soil is made really good, and it is worth the trouble.

I find that after a hot summer these Camellias over-flower even in such completely shaded situations and have to be somewhat disbudded in late winter so as to husband their strength. In disbudding, the aim is to leave well-spaced, single buds of three sizes—large forward buds, medium-sized buds and also the very smallest and most backward. The last are the most important of all perhaps, often enabling the bush to put up a fine show later, if the first batches are spoiled by frost. In good weather this method will ensure a long season of bloom with all the buds producing good flowers for weeks on end, provided that "dead-heading" is regularly attended to and feeding is lavish.

Shade is an essential in the southern and eastern parts of Britain and a north wall has the further advantage of retarding the flowering.

The chief precaution to be taken when planting is that of removing the poor and unhealthy, lime-mortar-ridden soil usually found in such situations and replacing it with a mixture of turf loam, leaf-mould, peat, and a little of the original soil—a very rich acid loam on the heavy side being aimed at. It is also important to make sure that the soil-level is such that the ground keeps sufficiently moist.

A vitally important point in the growing of Camellias is regular routine feeding. They soon exhaust their soil by the enormous crops of heavy, solid flowers that they bear, particularly if these are tidied away after they fall. Not only should the spent flowers be left so that their material may be re-absorbed, but a mulch of fallen leaves should also be applied annually over the roots and, in addition, a light sprinkling of a complete fertiliser should be given. Furthermore, if the growing season is a dry one, weak liquid manure should also be applied at that time.

Camellias are very sensitive to the mineral deficiencies so easily brought about by unwisely "neutralising" the soil with lime. Iron starvation is manifested by sickly yellow blotched leaves and white-splashed flowers. This is curable by spraying the foliage with a solution of $\frac{1}{4}$ oz. of sulphate of iron to two gallons of water and by adding acid material such as natural leaf-mould from woods *and* decaying leaves or bracken. Rotted dung may also be used but so much of its goodness has usually been already leached away that it is not, as is commonly thought, much of a fertiliser. It is, rather, a growing medium (see section on soils and fertilising p. 23).

Buds dropping off or flowers blotched with white are other signs of starvation. The remedy, of course, is to feed the plants, remembering that they can only absorb liquid nourishment. If dry, the richest soil is inadequate.

With these attentions the later-flowering varieties of *Camellia japonica* are good garden plants, particularly suitable for the dark and shady places in courtyards and between buildings. But I will repeat that really good fresh mould must be substituted for the existing rubbish, and annual feeding must be given, or failure is to be expected.

The propagation of Camellias is slow and difficult compared with that of many other shrubs. I have not found it easy to root Camellias from layers, probably because I have used wood that was too old, (one-year-old wood is best), but the careful propagator can produce young plants from leaf cuttings. A slice of twig with a leaf, and the bud in its axil intact, is half buried in one-part peat and three-parts silver sand compost in March in a closed frame with bottom heat.† More rapid in growth, for the single-flowered sorts, are ordinary cuttings of half-ripe wood, taken in July with a "heel" of old wood, treated, according to the directions given, with one of the proprietary growth-promoting compounds, in the sand-frame. This is one of those cases where the treatment makes all the difference between success and failure.‡

"The American Camellia Year-Book" recommends, according to Dr. Maurice Amsler, a well-known authority,§ that Camellia seeds be packed in glass jars in a medium of damp peat moss or sphagnum, and kept in a warm spot such as a greenhouse or kitchen. As soon as seeds

---

† Francis Hanger, *R.H.S. Journal*, Vol. LXXII, Pt 2, 1947.
‡ "Further Experiments with Growth Substances and the Rooting of Cuttings", Dr. M. A. M. Tincker, *R.H.S. Journal*, LXIII, Pt. 5 (May 1938), p. 210 *et seq.*
§ *Gardening Illustrated*, Jan. 1949, p. 12.

are seen to be sprouting, these are taken out and planted in pots of suitable soil and kept, frost-free, under glass to grow on. Good strong Camellia bushes are obtained quite quickly provided that care is taken to keep growth vigorous and unchecked. The flower quality varies, of course, but a surprisingly large percentage of such seedlings will be found to be excellent garden shrubs.

Besides the admirable *C. japonica* there are a number of other species and hybrids whose charms should be exploited by those with favourable gardens.

C. reticulata is a Chinese garden variety of great beauty, with crimped, semi-double, crimson flowers 6 inches across. It is, unlike *C. japonica*, not really hardy enough for any but exceptionally warm gardens, though superb, perhaps unbeatable, as a shrub for a cold house where the worst of the frost can just be kept off. The wild form was only fairly recently found by the famous plant collector, George Forrest. It has single flowers, but half the size; unfortunately it does not appear to be any hardier than the garden variety. In the mild western coastal area of Britain, from Dorset to the north of Scotland, *C. reticulata* often does well on a south wall. The wood is well ripened and flowering is particularly free. In the south and east such a position would probably get too much sun heat.

A number of previously unknown garden varieties of this species from temple gardens in Yunnan are described and illustrated in the R.H.S. Report on the Camellia and Magnolia Conference 1950, p. 13 *et seq*. Some of these may be available in years to come.

A fine seedling of the wild form, *C. r.* var. *superba* was raised by Mr. C. Williams of Caerhays. It has eight to ten wide-spreading, vivid Carmine petals, the flower being four inches across; Illustrated in colour, *R.H.S. Journal*, Vol. LXXIV, Pt. 4, t. 41.

C. saluenensis, found by George Forrest in Yunnan in 1917, has small, but often shapely, pale rose flowers, in the forms generally obtainable in this country. It first flowered at the late Mr. J. C. Williams' famous garden at Caerhays. It is so free-flowering that "eight or nine flowers may be found on a shoot only six to eight inches long",† and the buds may continue to open in mild spells from January to April. It is noticeably hardier than *C. reticulata* and I have had a plant on an exposed slope seldom much damaged by frost for some years, so far as either the flower buds or the foliage is concerned, but the flowers are often spoiled, as they appear in March or early April. Seedling forms vary greatly:

† Lord Aberconway, C.B.E., V.M.H., "Ornamental Flowering Trees and Shrubs", p. 224, R.H.S., 1938.

some have flowers that open out flat, while other, undesirable forms never open their flowers properly. Some present their flowers beautifully in attractively massed sprays, others have them partly concealed. It is therefore important to select when in bloom.

Hybrids have been bred at Caerhays between *C. saluenensis* and the hardy *C. cuspidata* which has small white flowers, and also with *C. japonica*.

The first-mentioned cross produced the beautiful white-flowered semi-single *C.* 'Cornish Snow'. The result of the latter cross, *C. Williamsii* var. 'J. C. Williams' (A.G.M. 1949) is a plant of outstanding beauty, unusual hardiness and great freedom of flower which will surely be one of the elect garden shrubs of the future. 'J. C. Williams' is not only free-flowering to an extraordinary degree, and over a period of several weeks, but has the merit of dropping the beautifully formed pink flowers as soon as they begin to fade. Thus the shrub always looks neat and tidy, and has a hardy nature which enables it to withstand zero temperatures, at any rate against a wall, and which should make it possible to grow it anywhere in England. Cultivation, of course, has got to be good, but such a fine thing is worth every care. It strikes fairly easily from cuttings. Other hybrids by the same raiser are described in *R.H.S. Journal*, LXXIV, Pt. 8, p. 348 (1949).

One of the finest of the Camellia hybrids as regards the individual flower, that I have seen, is *C.* 'Inamorata', a cross between *C. reticulata* (wild form) and *C. saluenensis* bred at Exbury†. It has large, waxy, pink flowers of delightful form, but it apparently produces these only from the ends of the branches. Possibly one of the sister seedlings of this cross may prove to have the free-flowering quality of *C. saluenensis* more strongly developed; such a plant would be a great acquisition.

The very early-flowering habit of these Camellias, (January, February, March or early April), however, leads me to doubt their being likely ever to supplant entirely the later-flowering and hardier varieties of *C. japonica*, which are really good garden plants.

C. Sasanqua is really a winter-flowering species, with single or double pink or crimson, slightly fragrant flowers, that is sometimes seen. I confess I am pained rather than pleased by these unseasonable, miserable efforts and though a good form is effective enough to be well worth while in a "cold house", it has always appeared to me a pathetic sight outdoors as it struggles to open its flowers amid the prevailing icy blasts. Some of the older varieties are apparently much less free-flowering than the more recently imported forms, but 'Hiryu', a fine double crimson, is as free as any.

An interesting allied, Chinese species is *C. oleifera* with pale green

† *R.H.S. Journal*, Vol. LXXIII, p. 283 (1948).

leaves and an upright habit. The shapely, four-inch, single white
flowers, slightly rosy in the bud, have a particularly sweet scent and
last well on the plant or when cut. They open during early winter
making this a very desirable shrub for a glassed-in veranda or a cold
house. In very mild districts it may be grown outdoors. Almost extinct
at one time it is now available at nurseries.

The cultivation requirements of these other Camellias are similar
to those described for *C. japonica*.

Propagation, except in the case of *C. reticulata*, is somewhat easier
as seeds are more freely produced and cuttings strike rather more
readily.

Before Camellias went out of fashion, at the time of the first world
war, a number of hybrids were bred by skilled head gardeners between
C. reticulata and *C. japonica* varieties. Most of these, being conserva-
tory plants, have probably been lost. Now that Camellias are again in
fashion, the cross will probably be repeated, although later flowering
and greater hardiness would, I think be more valuable than a mere
increase in the size of the individual flowers. In colour, shape of flower
and hardiness, *C. japonica* is not approached by any species that I have
seen.

One of the most beautiful in flower of all early spring-flowering
shrubs that will grow in a limy soil is the dwarf **Japanese Quince**,
Chænomeles japonica, (A.G.M. 1943). It is another victim of name-
changing. First Thunberg, the Swedish Botanist, to whom we owe the
discovery of so many lovely Japanese plants, found it in 1784 and named
it *Pyrus japonica*, but the plant was not introduced into Britain until
1869 when it was imported by Messrs. Maule of Bristol and, in 1874,
was distributed as *P. Maulei*, this name being given it by Dr. Masters
of the *Gardeners' Chronicle*. The tall-growing commoner species vul-
garly known as "the Japonica" had meanwhile usurped the name of
P. japonica. More recent work by Alfred Rehder has shown that these
red-flowered shrubs are sufficiently distinct to require a separate genus,
so Lindley's original suggested name is now to be followed and the
common Quince, alone, comes under Cydonia and the subject of this
note becomes *Chænomeles japonica*.[†] Chænomeles means, literally, split
apple. All the same, I would recommend anyone wishing to order this
plant to put *Pyrus* (or *Cydonia*) *Maulei* in brackets after the name
because the trade, as yet, show no signs of accepting the change.
This dwarf Japanese Quince, then, is a low-growing cousin of the
taller and commoner plant. Its hybrids with the latter, *C. speciosa*

† *R.H.S. Journal*, LXVI, Pt. 12 (Dec. 1941), p. 451.

(*C. lagenaria* Rehder), which are known as *C. superba*, include some of the most attractive of all deciduous early-flowering shrubs. These Quinces are not so often seen, used for massed effects, as they deserve to be, though they are definitely in the first class. The habit of growth of the "type" species—*C. japonica*, itself, is bushy and spreading, seldom exceeding four feet high. The flowers, over an inch across, are a soft orange-scarlet (Fire Red, H.C.C. 15/2) and borne on year-old and older shoots, and well displayed in good forms. The fruits are apple-like, yellow flushed with red and, unlike those of the taller species, make good jelly. As this Quince will grow in limy soil it is of the highest value to those whose gardens suffer from this drawback, for it provides a large part of the brilliant colour range of the Azaleas and Camellias.

On such soils the gardener will be well rewarded by trying all the varieties and giving them the careful attention that the gardener on acid soil will give to the great races of garden shrubs mentioned above.

The flowering time is unfortunately rather too early, both from the weather point of view and the æsthetic. The garden is still just too bare of leaves to do justice, as a background, to the effect. This is also particularly likely to be spoiled at this time of year by masses of purplish pink from the blossom of Almonds, Plums and Peaches. Thus, to give the Japanese Quinces full play with their vivid and lovely colourings, only white-flowered blossoming trees should be allowed near them and an occasional Forsythia and blue-violet Periwinkles. Where Camellias can also be grown the soft orange-red of the Chænomeles forms the perfect bridge between Forsythia yellow and Camellia Geranium Lake.

C. j. alpina (*Sargentii*) is a dwarf mountain form with smaller and more cup-shaped flowers less orange in hue. It is useful where a small shrub of alpine character is required but is less showy than others.

C. j. alba has white flowers that often fail to open fully on the more exposed parts of the bush if the weather is unusually cold and windy.

C. j. 'Naranja' has large orange flowers and a very dense, dwarf habit.

C. j. atrosanguinea has dark red flowers with purplish calices.

As regards cultivation *C. japonica* requires an open, sunny position that is yet sheltered from the bite of north-east winds. I find that it grows quite well in peat though less vigorously than in a good turf loam, which appears to be the ideal soil for it. Layers and seeds afford an easy means of increase for the amateur, seeds, in particular, often yielding fine plants which will flower in their second year in many cases.

Quite outstanding as first-class flowering shrubs of medium size are the varieties of the hybrid race **Chænomeles superba** (*C. japonica*

× *speciosa*). In an open position they make shapely bushes four or five feet high.

One of the finest of all the deciduous flowering shrubs that can be grown on a limy soil is, in my opinion, a well-grown bush of *Chænomeles superba* var. 'Knap Hill Scarlet'. A shapely shrub of five feet, or eight feet on a wall, it flowers with amazing freedom, well out to the tips of the branches. These flowers open fully and are 2 inches or more across and exquisitely shaped, with five petals and perfect centres filled with undistorted golden stamens. Opening a paler tint, the flowers mature to the full glory of that most lovely hue, Mandarin Red (H.C.C. 17). I have counted as many as twenty-eight of these on a 6-inch length of stem. They open about ten days later than those of most of the other varieties. Perhaps because it is rather slow-growing at first, this is one of the most undeservedly neglected of the finer varieties of common flowering shrubs. When cut and brought indoors the flowering sprays are indeed superb and last for ten days or more. Should a branch wilt, cutting off 2 inches or so of stem *under the water* with secateurs (care being taken never to allow air to come into contact with the cut end) will almost invariably cause the flowers to freshen up again completely. It is a fine example of a hybrid carrying the best qualities of both parents without their faults.

C. s. Simonii, another fine hybrid, is more frequently seen and received the Award of Garden Merit in 1924. The flowers are of various shapes and sizes—mostly about 1½ inches across, and deep Vermilion (H.C.C. 18/1) in colour. It has been described as "the best coloured of any in the group"† but I still think that 'Knap Hill Scarlet' is an even more lovely colour and shape, and that it makes a finer show of colour at a distance than *Simonii*. None the less, this is a first-class shrub of good habit and high decorative qualities that is all too seldom planted.

C. s. rosea is described as having "scarlet flowers with usually six to eight petals and larger and broader leaves". (A. Rehder).

C. s. 'Incendie' is a new variety from Messrs. Lemoine of Nancy, having Vermilion flowers and deep green leaves tipped with red. It is of rather low and compact habit.

C. s. 'Boule de Feu' and 'Rowallane Seedling' are rather similar, but taller.

C. s. 'Phyllis Moore' has a shapely, double flower 2 inches across, in colour Scarlet of the full hue, and is a superb, but somewhat straggling, variety for those who prefer double flowers. It is admirable for a buttonhole.

† "Some Good Garden Plants", R.H.S. 1946, p. 16, and photograph facing.

C. s. 'Knap Hill Radiance' is a fine new variety with single flowers of Geranium Lake (H.C.C. 20) of similar size on a big strong plant favouring *C. speciosa* in size and habit.

C. s. perfecta flowers very early and has flowers of a creamy tint maturing to a pinkish hue.

C. s. contorta has oddly twisted branches and white flowers that blush later to pink.

A number of new varieties of *C. superba* have been bred in California by Messrs. W. B. Clarke of San José and the following is a selection:—

C. s. 'Coral Sea' has flowers of Chinese Coral (H.C.C. 614/1) to Mandarin Red. They are described as being often $1\frac{3}{4}$ inches across and the plant is of moderate growth with small leathery leaves.

C. s. 'Crimson and Gold' is a small plant with large cupped flowers of a blood red colour with prominent golden stamens, already obtainable in England.

C. s. 'Early Appleblossom' has pink and white flowers that open early.

C. s. 'Early Orange' is a medium-sized bush with very freely borne, cupped, orange flowers. It flowers earliest of all, often being in bloom in November and December in California.

C. s. 'Juliet' is a variety with flowers of a soft salmon colour.

C. s. 'Stanford Red' has large flowers 2 inches in diameter opening flat and in colour Geranium Lake. It is almost thornless. Already obtainable in England.

C. s. 'Pink Lady' has clear pink flowers that open early.

C. s. 'Ruby Glow' has flowers of Currant Red.

C. s. 'Snow' has large white flowers $2\frac{1}{2}$ inches across opening late in the season. It favours *C. speciosa* in habit.

Most of the above varieties will shortly be obtainable in England.

These hybrids vary somewhat in habit, a few being inclined to make larger bushes 6 feet or more across. Pruning, so as to secure ripened wood set with flowering spurs, is desirable, and pegging down the outer branches and removing over-crowded young shoots encourages freedom of flower.

These Quinces can be propagated by spreading out and earthing-up branches and so inducing them to form roots above the main stem, by layering, or by seed.

A new race of hybrid Chænomeles has also been bred of late years by Messrs. W. B. Clarke of San José in California. It started with a seedling form of *C. superba* which was named 'Coral Glow' and this was crossed with *C. cathayensis* (Schneider). This central Chinese species is considered to be a variety of *C. speciosa* by most authorities, but to the gardener it appears to be quite a distinct species, and Rehder stated that it is much less hardy than either of the other species†. In its typical form it is not an attractive plant in this country and has little resemblance to *C. speciosa*. It is a coarse-growing, gaunt, erect, spiky shrub of Crabapple-like appearance, flowering on young laterals, with narrow leaves and unexciting pale flowers blotched with pink. Most of us discarded it years ago. But Messrs. Clarke were clever enough to see the advantages of the characteristic of flowering on young lateral branches as opposed to that of flowering only on old wood as in *C. speciosa*. The cross mentioned was accordingly made and from 1939 onwards the following fine hybrids appeared. They are large thorny shrubs flowering very freely from the laterals and often produce three crops of bloom followed by very large fruits. Messrs. Clarke do not consider them quite so hardy as the *C. superba* hybrids in America, but their hardiness is amply sufficient for the British Isles. For this hybrid race Messrs. Clarke proposed the name ***Chænomeles californica*** Clarke.‡

C. californica 'Enchantress' has large rose-pink flowers, often somewhat unevenly coloured when first opening. It has the stiff branches with thorny lateral twigs and narrow leaves of *C. cathayensis*. It is obtainable in England.

C. c. 'Fire' has large, full flowers of a vivid red and is a very vigorous variety often producing three crops of bloom.

C. c. 'Masterpiece' has freely borne, rosy red flowers that open unusually early.

C. c. 'Mt. Everest' has white flowers tipped with lavender-rose flushing later to pink.

C. c. 'Afterglow' has double flowers of the same colouring.

C. c. 'Pink Beauty' is early, with pink flowers shaded with rose and often gives two further crops of flowers later.

C. c. 'Cardinal' has dark red flowers (H.C.C. Cardinal Red 822/1) and is one of the finest of this group.

C. c. 'Rosemary' is a mid-season flowering variety with pink to red flowers.

C. c. 'Sunset Glow' is similar, but the flowers are a deeper rose, maturing to darker red. This variety often gives a second crop of bloom.

C. c. 'Cynthia' (*C. japonica* × *cathayensis*) has large bicoloured flowers of pale and deep rose shades which mature to a peach pink suffused with buff. It flowers in late spring.

The above varieties will shortly be obtainable in this country.

† "Manual of Cultivated Trees and Shrubs".
‡ "Garden Aristocrats", by W. B. Clarke, II, p. 12 (1944).

Chænomeles speciosa (*C. Lagenaria* Rehder) (A.G.M. 1927) is really the correct name of "*Pyrus japonica*", that well-known old cottage garden favourite, the tall red-flowered Japanese Quince often called merely "the Japonica". It is not, however, a Japanese plant but is thought to be a native of China, being merely cultivated in Japanese gardens.

C. speciosa was introduced as long ago as 1796, in which year it arrived at Kew. Commonly grown against walls it has really no need of such a position and is often even more decorative grown as a lawn specimen. Thus placed, it offers free play for the exercise of cultural skill, for its natural suckering habit can be kept in check with great advantage and the older branches kept spurred-back and the plant thus assisted to assume the full elegance of picturesque growth attainable.

None of the great plant-hunters appear to have recorded seeing the prototype of this shrub growing wild, so far as I can discover, but it is thought to be Chinese, and it has that look. Studying the plants of Japan, China and America, one comes to form a picture of the "Chinese look" in one's mind. The flower may be spectacularly beautiful, as *Magnolia denudata*, *Campsis grandiflora*, or *Rhododendron Simsii* (the greenhouse Azalea) yet there is a hint of coarseness, a faint, earthy, toad-like quality that is absent from the Japanese or American counterparts. Be that as it may and common as the plant is, *C. speciosa* is a very lovely thing, the "type" having flowers of a pale Geranium Lake (H.C.C. 20/1 and 20/2), and many of the varieties are delightful in both form and colour. In the rush for novelties, often much less beautiful, many of these older varieties have been lost. Still available are:—

C. s. umbilicata, rose pink, rather small flowers.

C. s. Mærlœsii, white, with a rosy flush at the heart.

C. s. nivalis, pure white.

C. s. Wilsonii, flowers salmon pink, leaves reddish-furred beneath.

C. s. cardinalis is a glorious scarlet but the flowers are sometimes obscured by the foliage.

C. s. 'Aurora', soft rose suffused with orange and yellow.

C. s. rosea fl. pl. has double salmon pink flowers freely borne on a bushy plant. Also known as 'Falconet Charlot'.

It is in winter effect that both the species of Chænomeles and their hybrids fail so lamentably. All winter long there is nothing to see— just a few dim sticks, drab as the prevailing drabness; whilst the Japanese Azaleas and other flowering evergreens delight the eye with mounds of richly varied greenery. Thus it will only be in a limy soil that precludes these more year-round-effective garden furnishings that the Quinces will be planted "*en masse*". Then we shall find the true dwarf,

C. japonica and *C. superba* varieties the more generally effective for massing as they can be backed by such evergreens as *Choisya ternata, Siphonosmanthus Delavayi, Ceanothus Veitchianus, Escallonia langleyensis*, and others, so as to give solidity and winter effect to the beds. Near the house, the Quinces will take the place of the Camellias so valuable for such positions on acid soils.

Indifferent as to whether the soil is limy or acid, cultivation is simple enough in any fairly open and sunny spot sheltered from the east wind, and increase may be made by detaching rooted suckers, by layers or by seed. The varieties, of course, do not come true by the last-named method but it is easily done, and seedlings are often interesting in their variations. Provided poor sorts are firmly culled no harm is caused.

Grafted plants are not satisfactory as a rule, owing to the natural suckering habit of the species.

When pruning specimens on walls, the young wood of the year may be shortened back to two buds after flowering, and open-ground plants may be similarly treated. Pegging down long young growths is a good plan, carefully cutting out overcrowded shoots, when necessary, at ground-level. If left unpruned, open-ground bushes of *C. speciosa* in crowded beds usually fail to flower freely and wall plants become a jungle of basal suckers.

From the easy-going Quinces, conditioned to garden life by centuries of cultivation, we turn to a wilder genus that still insists upon a naturally acid soil and a mild climate.

The **Tree Heaths** flower in early spring and though only one or two are possibly first class, according to the strict definition given in the Introduction, they are attractive in elevated gardens on lime-free soils where spring frosts slide away below.

Erica arborea, the Tree Heath, is not reliable, being sooner or later killed by a hard frost, but the superior form known as *E. a.* var. *alpina* (A.G.M. 1933) is, on the other hand, almost "reasonably hardy". It comes from the mountains of Spain, and, from the garden point of view, may be considered a distinct species. Unlike the "type", which is always rather dingy, it forms a dense, deep green, plumy bush, usually about 6 feet high. The ashen-white fragrant flowers appear in early April and last for a considerable time. Though the scent is delightful, the fresh deep green of the bush in winter is perhaps its greatest beauty. Although reported to withstand twenty degrees of frost, it is only reliably hardy enough for use as a permanent foundation evergreen in the more favoured gardens. In such places it is superb in the composition of the winter scene, being one of the most vivid of the evergreens.

Chænomeles superba ' Knap Hill Scarlet '

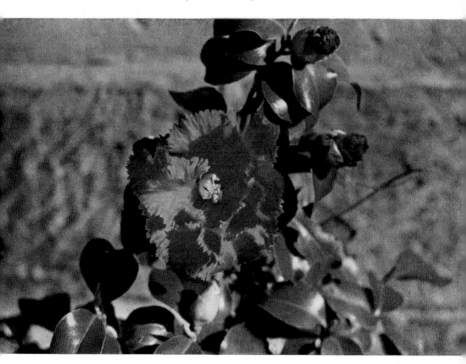

Camellia japonica ' Fred Sander '

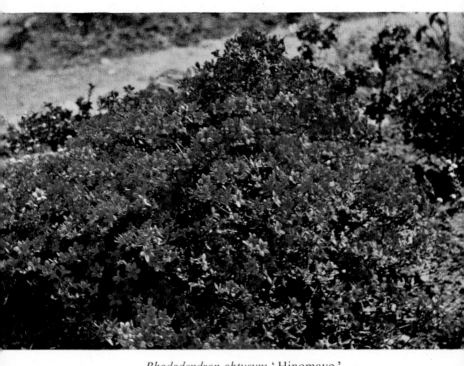

Rhododendron obtusum ' Hinomayo '

Daphne Cneorum

Any straggling branches may be pruned back so as to keep the bush densely furnished to the ground.

E. australis, the Spanish Heath, is still less hardy and is thus only suited to the south and west. It is a somewhat gaunt and gawky grower, but its cylindrical flowers are quite handsome, though the colour is difficult to place, being a bright Rhodamine Purple with black, projecting stamens, and borne in clusters on the tips of the shoots. As it is periodically almost exterminated by hard winters it is not commonly seen in gardens.

A very fine variety with white flowers, found in Southern Spain in 1912 by the late Lt. Robert Williams of Caerhays, perpetuates his name—'Mr. Robert'. It is scarcely hardier than the "type" but is a particularly beautiful April-flowering Heath which received the A.G.M. in 1941.

E. lusitanica, the Portuguese Heath, resembles *E. arborea* but does not grow quite so tall. The foliage is a more vivid green and the white flowers are cylindrical instead of rounded, and faintly fragrant. It is less hardy than *E. arborea* var. *alpina* but particularly at home on dry, sandy or stony soils. The foxtails of white flowers with their pink stamens are very lovely, perhaps the most beautiful of those of the Tree Heaths and its lack of hardiness is therefore particularly regrettable. In the warm sandy gardens of the south and west coasts it is a delightful shrub, and at any rate it is hardier than *E. australis*.

E. Veitchii, Veitch's Heath, is a hybrid between *E. lusitanica* and *E. arborea* var. *alpina*, valuable because while it resembles the former it has the slightly greater hardiness of the latter. The fragrant flowers are intermediate in shape, and, though white, often show a rosy glow from the pink stalks and pistils. It is one of the earliest to flower, often beginning at Christmas time if the weather is mild.

E. mediterranea is a Tree Heath, coming from the Bay of Biscay, hardy enough for planting with confidence in most lime-free gardens. Further, in some varieties, it is one of the more decorative and showy species. Like the others the flowering time is roughly from March to May. The honey-scented flowers appear in upright racemes several inches in length on the previous year's shoots and are, in the type form, Fuchsia Purple (H.C.C. 28/3), deepened by the dark anthers. This is, however, a poor colour for the spring garden. If the soil will grow Heaths it will grow the glorious clean, rich coloured, large-flowered Azaleas and few will wish to have the garden relegated to unnecessary dowdiness by their omission. Fortunately there is an excellent white variety, *E. m.* var. *alba*, and a superlative one, *E. m.* var. 'W. T. Rackliff' which, with their dense evergreen habit and delightfully scented white flowers, form an admirable complement to the vivid

5

Azalea colourings. For those who prefer purplish-pink to white, irrespective of the cleanness of the tint, a grouping of the "type" and the white forms may be arranged apart somewhere. *E. mediterranea* is probably the finest of the spring-flowering Heaths for extensive planting, being a better garden plant than most of the others mentioned.

All the Tree Heaths seem to do best on warm, sandy or stony slopes where cold air and surplus water can drain freely away below.

As for propagation, seeds, cuttings and layers and, with some species, even division after "earthing up", are all possible methods. Seedlings are usually compact and sturdy plants, flowering well in their third year.

Small Heaths transplant quite well, if firmly and somewhat deeply replanted, the opportunity being taken to lay sideways, and then bury up to within a few inches of the tips, any straggling, long branches. These will probably root and so provide more plants.

Except for *E. australis*, most Tree Heaths can be grown from cuttings taken with a "heel" of old wood in July. Unflowered side shoots are the best material. A number of such cuttings may be placed round a pot filled with peat and sand mixture finally covered with silver sand. The pots are soaked from below and then placed in a closed frame in full sun with the glass whitened with "Summer Cloud". Layering may be done by holding branches down into a prepared patch of sandy peat by means of a peg or even a brick or a sandstone rock. Care should be taken to see that the branch is reasonably young and that the "elbow" formed by bending it into the prepared hole is well covered with soil. In this way good plants are soon grown with little trouble.

Where the Heaths will grow another genus of the great family of the Ericacæ may be considered, namely **Pieris**.

Pieris floribunda, from the southern States, is a hardy flowering evergreen of attractive dense habit introduced nearly 150 years ago. The pitcher-shaped white flowers, in erect racemes, open in March or early April and so are very often destroyed by frost. When the weather is favourable it is quite attractive and is perhaps more resistant to exposure than other Pieris.

P. japonica (A.G.M. 1924) is a taller shrub than the preceding, growing up to 10 feet high and is more tree-like in habit; the racemes of similar flowers are drooping instead of erect, opening in March or early April, and more numerous and decorative than those of *P. floribunda*, but still more vulnerable to frost.

P. j. variegata is a variety with leaves neatly margined with white in an attractive manner, otherwise similar.

In gardens where spring frosts are infrequent, *P. taiwanensis* is even more spectacularly beautiful, like a waterfall of porcelain bells, or, rather, urns, but its early flowering habit is a grave disadvantage.

As regards cultivation, the Pieris really need Rhododendron conditions (see page 189) including plenty of moisture at the roots, conserved by a mulch of dead leaves. They may be increased by seeds or by layering.

The first section of the really hardy hybrid **Rhododendrons** opens in April. These are crosses of *Rhododendron caucasicum*, from eastern Europe, and are amongst the toughest and most wind-resisting of Rhododendrons and of dense, low habit. They are, indeed, better when grown "hard", being more compact and comely as evergreens and more decorative when in flower. Two that are commonly available are *R. venustum Jacksonii* "A" † (*R. arboreum* × *Nobleanum*) with flowers of Rose Madder (H.C.C. 23/2) and *R. Caucasicum pictum*, "A", clean pale pink with red spots. There are a number of inferior clones often confused with these. They have flowers of dingy purplish pinks and, in my experience, are particularly addicted to bud-blast. Care should therefore be taken to secure the true varieties. (See illustration facing p. 48.)

These are really hardy and most valuable for cold and exposed spots; *R. caucasicum pictum*, in particular, revels in the full blast of the wind and provides a lovely sight in bloom in places where almost any other variety would be instantly torn to pieces. In the Rhododendron Handbook this Rhododendron is stigmatised by the letter "Y" which means "not up to present day standards in the British Isles". I think this is, perhaps, a case of mistaken identity as, owing to the invaluable sturdiness of the true variety it will, unlike too many choice sorts, flourish and look highly attractive as a flowering shrub in ordinary garden positions. If only more of the starred varieties were up to the standard of this hardy variety *as garden plants for ordinary conditions*, the popularity of the Rhododendron with the general gardening public would receive a tremendous stimulus. R. 'Cunningham's White' is of similar type but is mentioned later as it flowers noticeably later, with the 'Mollis' Azaleas. These three varieties are of admirable size and habit for the small garden and make excellent evergreens for the centres of beds, providing both background and winter form. R. 'Cunningham's Sulphur', listed as Category "B"‡, is slightly less tough and more difficult to grow but has attractive pale creamy yellow flowers that open usually towards the end of April.

† "A" means "hardy anywhere in the British Isles" see p. 84.
‡ "B" means "hardy anywhere in the British Isles, but requires some shade to obtain best results". *Rhododendron Handbook*.

Any lime-free soil, to which some peat or leaf-mould may be added around the root-ball at planting time, seems to suit these Rhododendrons and young stock can easily be raised by layering the outer, lower branches.

The one weakness of the breed is the colour, which is merely pink in the early flowering pair, but this is less objectionable so early in the season, when it may be arranged to harmonise with *R. præcox*, Ribes, Aubrietas, Almonds, Peaches and early Cherries, and makes a fine show of massed flowers beautifully presented on a dense, low rounded bush in full exposure. On the other hand in shady places the growth is rank, untidy and unattractive. Such shade-loving genera as Rhododendron and Hydrangea include exceptional species that require full sun, and it is important to recognize the garden hybrids of these which have inherited this trait. We shall find other examples mentioned later.

At this time of year blossoming trees are specially welcome. The **Almond** (*Prunus Amygdalus*) is an early flowering tree whose positive enjoyment of urban conditions makes it invaluable. Much of this enjoyment is derived from the lack of bullfinches to strip the flower buds and the presence of a sulphurous atmosphere to discourage leaf-curl fungus. Being an Algerian native it asks only for a sunny position and free circulation of air about the branches.

P. A. macrocarpa is a very fine Almond that looks like a distinct species. It forms a shapely tree with large, faintly blushed, white flowers, each over 2 inches across, in clusters of about half a dozen which contrast pleasingly with the dark stems. The nuts of this species are, as the name implies, of unusually large size and, furthermore, are free from the bitter taste, due to the presence of hydrocyanic acid, which makes the nuts of many Almonds unpleasant and even dangerous.

A number of other varieties of the Almond have been described but do not appear to be available in commerce in Britain at the present time. Among these are:—*P. A. albo-plena*, with double white flowers; *P. A. pendula*, a weeping form, and *P. A. fragilis*, a form with a fragile nut containing a sweet kernel. A distinction is also made between the sweet and the bitter Almond. In practice it seems that these forms are so hybridised that it is difficult to find one definitely belonging to either type. Having noted which individuals in a large group of laden trees were attacked by squirrels, we harvest the nuts from these only. It requires a vise to crack them but the nuts are usually of good intermediate quality.

P. Amygdalo-persica, Pollard's Almond (*P. A. Pollardii*), a hybrid with the Peach, from Australia, has larger individual flowers of a rich pink, nearly 2 inches across, and massive dark chocolate-brown wood. It is a tree of outstanding quality, but it is essential to make certain of obtaining the true form which most deservedly received the Award of Garden Merit in 1937. Being more fastidious, however, it can never supplant the common Almond.

P. tangutica (*P. dehiscens*), introduced by E. H. Wilson, is a shrubby species, interesting because it is thought to be the subject of the charming Prunus blossom design of the Chinese Khanghsi vase. It forms a very twiggy bush, of grotesquely angled shoots, up to about 10 feet in height with fragile pale, rosy pink, solitary flowers in March. Unfortunately most of the specimens obtainable from nurseries are grafted on what appears to be Blackthorn and suckers are very troublesome, and I have neither succeeded in layering it or striking it from cuttings. It is worth looking out for by those who like very early flowers and who are not too much troubled by bullfinches.

The dwarf Almond, *P. tenella* (*P. nana*) grows to about 3 feet high and enjoys a hot, dry spot. Some forms have richer pink flowers than others. It has the merit of being fairly easily increased by layering. As grafted plants are not satisfactory, it is best to get such plants on to their own roots in this way as soon as possible.

P. t. 'Fire Hill' form is a very distinct and attractive dwarf Almond brought back from Rumania by Lady Martineau. It forms a shapely dense bush about 3 feet high covered in early spring with carmine-pink buds opening to paler flowers. The leaves are thick and of a dark green, making it a comely bush all summer. Young plants are now available at specialist shrub nurseries.

P. triloba (A.G.M. 1935) is a delightful member of the family, if somewhat artificial-looking in its double form (*P. t. multiplex*). It was found in the gardens of North China by the collector Robert Fortune in 1855. It comes into bloom in early April and in cold districts is best grown on a south wall, although quite hardy. It is usually grafted on the Plum stock which entails endless trouble with suckers, so if a plant can be got on its own roots it is much to be preferred. The pink flowers, of very pretty shape for a double flower, having a typical, musical-comedy flavour, cover the shoots very freely if these are regularly cut back each year after flowering. There is a single-flowered form (*P. t. simplex*) which is said to be less free-flowering and long-lasting. It can be propagated, though not without some difficulty, by cuttings of fairly ripe wood.

Generally speaking the cultivation of the Almonds is a simple matter. Often described as lime-lovers they grow to perfection also on neutral or slightly acid soils if an occasional dressing of bonemeal is given.

Aspect is more important and an open position in full sun is necessary. Weak yellow-leaved shoots indicate infection by "dieback", and these, together with unwanted inward-growing shoots, should be removed at the end of May. Pruning at any other time should be avoided. Most species can be grown from the seeds, or nuts. In sowing, these are half buried on their sides and allowed to get well frosted in winter. If protected from mice, most will germinate the following spring.

Fragrance is a quality that must not be forgotten at this moment of the year and white flowers and a dark evergreen form may complement the slender Almonds by contrast.

Siphonosmanthus Delavayi (*Osmanthus Delavayi*) (A.G.M. 1923), a dense, bushy evergreen, 6 feet or more in height, and perhaps 10 feet wide, has small leaves and tiny, sweet-scented, white, tubular, jasmine-like flowers in clusters in early April. It has the useful quality of being an evergreen that can be grown in limy soil, but in view of the wonderfully wide choice available we must take into consideration the fact that it is a shrub of large size that has only white flowers half an inch across and these insufficiently freely borne to colour the bush solidly. *S. Delavayi*, often known as *Osmanthus Delavayi*, comes from Yunnan, whence the Abbé Delavay sent its seeds to Messrs. Vilmorin of Paris in 1890. It is a "bad mover" and not a fast grower at first. It may be propagated, it is said, by cuttings in late summer in a sand frame with bottom heat, but the amateur is well advised to buy small plants in pots, as it is not easy to strike.

When the spring weather is mild and calm, the most spectacular of the early flowering trees are undoubtedly the large-flowered **Magnolias,** but with some one has to wait a long time before they make sufficient size to flower well. On the other hand, many people enjoy planting and growing young trees, even of species that never flower effectively, and as some of the Magnolias are quick-growing and attractive merely as sapling trees, they should certainly be planted in residential areas in preference to Limes, Elms, Chestnuts, Beeches, etc.

For garden purposes the Magnolias have been conveniently sorted into groups by Lord Aberconway†. Having already described the *M. stellata* section, in this next early-flowering group I will deal with the best of those having affinity to *M. denudata*.

M. denudata, the Yulan, itself is one of the loveliest and best for the small garden. It is hardy and of strong constitution, flowers when very

† "Ornamental Flowering Trees and Shrubs," R.H.S. Conference, 1938, p. 215.

young, even at 3 feet high, and makes a handsome small tree in almost any position in good soil where it is carefully pruned to this end when young, and gets full sun. It has been cultivated by the Chinese since ancient history, and received the A.G.M. in 1936. In a favourable season it is really finer, I think, than any of its numerous garden hybrids, because the great solid flowers appear before the leaves, beautifully presented, and so all are seen with fullest effect. They are a pure creamy white and deliciously fragrant. The nine petals (properly called tepals) are usually in three rows of three alternatively.

Of the hybrids, the most commonly seen is *M. Soulangeana* (*M. liliflora* × *denudata*) (A.G.M. 1932), bred in France by Chevalier Soulange Bodin about the middle of the nineteenth century. It is per-haps a more vigorous grower and an even better garden plant, but the flowers open later, with the leaves, and have a purplish stain at the base, so the effect is less striking. Other hybrids of this type are *M. S. rustica rubra*, *M. S. Brozzonii*, *M. S. spectabilis*, *M. S. Alexandrina*, *M. S. Norbertii* and *M. S. triumphans*. There is really very little difference between them.

M. S. Lennei is another fine variety of similar parentage that is more distinct. Its flowers usually come still later, among the fully expanded leaves, and they are of a rich purplish pink and more globular in shape.

M. liliflora is a rather weakly and unsatisfactory grower in this country, with deep purple flowers. *M. l.* var. *nigra* is a hardier and better form, but it is of little account.

A scarce but valuable Magnolia is *M. Sprengeri* var. *diva*. It is said to be one of the hardiest of the early flowerers and was formerly known as *M. denudata* var. *purpurascens*. The flowers are Mallow Purple (H.C.C. 630/2) and cup-shaped and, if somewhat less spectacular in size than those of *M. Campbellii* and others, are more reliably and freely pro-duced, on a more shapely tree. The seeds were originally sent back to Veitch's Nursery by E. H. Wilson. Another form, 'Wakehurst Seedling', has deeper coloured flowers.

M. Dawsoniana is a fairly bushy tree with about nine, narrower, tepals of a pale purple and has aromatic leaves. It requires some years to reach effective flowering size.

M. Campbellii, from the Himalayas, in time makes quite a large tree but does not flower until it is nearly twenty years old. It is, further-more, such an early flowerer and grower that it gets cut by frost very frequently. None the less, the fact remains that it can provide one of the most superb sights that can be seen. The huge and notably shapely flowers are a soft rose pink, or pure white, in good forms, and when these appear in profusion on a tree of almost forest size the effect is very lovely. In the mountain forests of Bhutan there are rare forms with crimson flowers. Unfortunately it does not flower regularly, even after a hot summer. One of the largest trees in the country, one that I know well, had, I note, not a single flower bud in 1948 although the summer of 1947 was an ideal one.

M. Veitchii is a fine hybrid between *M. denudata* and *M. Campbellii*. There are two forms of this, one having pinkish flowers whose tepals do not expand very widely. In the other, known as 'Isca', the large flowers are white, tinted outside with pale purplish pink. When expanded, they measure about 11 inches across, with eleven tepals. This Magnolia has remarkable speed of growth so that it is very well worth planting as a garden tree on the lawn. The only drawback is that, like so many very fast growers, it requires some shelter from the wind as it is far from gale-proof.

M. mollicomata, a near relative of *M. Campbellii*, from China, was described by Reginald Farrer, with his usual vivid zest, as a tree of supreme loveliness, under the name of *M. rostrata*, though that name actually belongs, it has been found, to a different species. It has the merit of glorious, if somewhat untidy, flowers, some 9 inches across, and makes rapid growth, having flowered from seed at Lord Aberconway's famous gardens at Bodnant, in twelve years. This means that a person buying a strong sapling would not have an unconscionable time to wait. In addition the habit of the tree is more compact than that of *M. Campbellii*. Its pink flowers (actually pale tints of Petunia and Mallow Purple) come a little later than those of the latter, and are more freely and regularly borne, and thus it stands a much better chance of making a good showing. (See illustration p. 48.)

Another early flowering tree Magnolia is *M. Sargentiana*, with large pale purple flowers of informal shape. It requires some years to grow to flowering size and is not very vigorous. It is, however, spindly and tree-like, rather than bushy in habit like the following.

M. S. var. *robusta* is, one of the most spectacular of all Magnolias, though the huge, loose flowers tend to bend over to the horizontal. It also flowers when small, plants only 4 to 6 feet high bearing flower buds.† Needless to say, however, several years' growth is needed to make the lovely display shown in recent illustrations.‡ Seed of this Magnolia has been sown and the seedlings are now becoming available at nurseries.

Few trees are more interesting to grow, for the thoughtful and keen cultivator, or the pruning enthusiast. The wood of the stem often

† Lord Aberconway, *R.H.S. Journal*, Vol. LXX, Pt. 6 (June 1945), p. 159.

‡ Fig. 12, *R.H.S. Journal*, LXVIII, Pt. 2 (Feb. 1943), and frontispiece "Camellias and Magnolias", Report of the Conference 1950.

receives a shock, in moving, from which it seldom really recovers. Consequently growth is slow. But if one can stimulate a young shoot from the base, and then boldly cut away the old stick, this young growth, provided no slugs or pests interfere with it, will shoot up at much greater speed, and make a really healthy stem, free from the die-back that so often cripples maturing specimens. I do not find any bad effects arise from firm pruning of Magnolias, either to get the plant on to fresh young wood at the start, to suppress any rival to the leader or to shorten a too presumptuous side branch.

For years I tried to make a young plant of *M. Campbellii* from an immense low bush, having several stems, but it was not happy and made slow progress. At last I cut away all but one very young shoot and this rushed up in true tree form at a prodigious rate immediately. It may seem fanciful to discuss and recommend such trees as these, when the waiting period is often so long, but they have a niche in the world of the garden from which nothing can displace them. They are the perfect long-term investment. Hundreds of much longer term speculations are made every year by persons planting Elms, Oaks, Limes, Conifers, etc. which take even more time to assume their less spectacular beauties. I would suggest that the great tree Magnolias should be planted instead of these as commemorative trees. They would be really appreciated by posterity and much more likely to be preserved than commonplace sorts. The Soulangeanas are always available in pots and will grow anywhere and for choicer and safer places *M. Veitchii* and others would be suitable.

As regards cultivation, we must remember that these tree Magnolias are forest dwellers, and so give the more delicate kinds the shelter of other trees, if possible, and a rich, woodsy soil. The Chinese species and their hybrids usually tolerate a limy soil, whilst the Japanese do not, but, as the essential is to get your young tree growing quickly, and keep it growing fast, it is worth while preparing a good plot of ground at the start, rich and deep. I have reason to think that we have not really given these trees a chance yet. The early cultivators naturally wished to hustle them into flower as soon as possible so as to know what they were like. If, on the other hand, we plant them with the primary object of growing a strong arboreal framework, allowing plenty of room and letting the flowers come when they may, I think the ultimate effect would be still better. I have no definite proof, but I have reason to believe that more regular feeding is needed. In the forest the leaf-fall feeds the trees annually with Nature's perfect food. In the garden the Magnolias are expected to go on producing barrowloads of flower-petal material with nothing put back to replace what is blown or wheeled away annually. Rather than die the tree husbands its resources. At the best a bad habit of intermittent flowering is initiated. Feed well, then, and regularly; prune to induce a shapely sapling free from the dangers of V-shaped forks of equal-sized branches, and keep the soil over the roots mulched at all times with leaves, like the forest floor.

Knowing that the Chinese have little interest in ornamental gardens compared with the Japanese, I was always puzzled at the explorers' reports of innumerable Magnolias "in cultivation" in China. On going into matters further the mystery was explained. The Magnolias were not grown to be looked at, they were grown to be cut down and destroyed so that an alleged aphrodisiac could be distilled from the sap! The nostrum obtained is said to have no scientific value and the notion is regrettable as it also leads to the destruction of many fine wild specimens.

Seeds often wait a couple of years before germinating and even then growth is often rather slow so perhaps layering is the easiest method of propagation for the amateur. But according to Mr. F. M. Kluis of Boskoop, *M. Soulangeana* can be propagated by means of cuttings, as follows. Small side-branches of half-ripe wood are used, taken in July, the cuttings being 3 to 5 inches long, rather slender for choice, and carefully cut at the node. A "heel" of old wood is not advantageous and sappy shoots or those that are very thick are to be avoided. The cuttings are inserted in 4-inch pots containing a mixture of half sand and half peat-dust and carefully soaked. The pots are then placed in a frame or cool greenhouse. Bottom heat is helpful, but not essential provided that the weather is fairly warm. Great care is taken to remove all fallen leaves and to keep up the moisture content of the atmosphere sufficiently to prevent wilting. Shading is provided against the sun, as the foliage must not be allowed to get dried out. Ninety per cent. have been rooted successfully by this method, under favourable conditions as to material, temperature and humidity. The cuttings were separately potted-on in six weeks from the date of insertion. 1 to 1½ feet of growth was secured in the first growing season, and 2 to 3 feet of growth in the second.

Other Magnolias do not respond well, if at all, to this method. *M. Loebneri* (*M. stellata × Kobus*), *M. glauca* (and, probably, *M. Veitchii*) can with care and suitable material also be rooted in this way, but *M. denudata* is slow and gives a low proportion of successes. *M. Dawsoniana*, *M. mollicomata*, *M. Sargentiana* and *M. S. robusta* are found to be very difficult.

Growth-producing substances, Mr. Kluis reports, did not cause shy-rooting material to form roots: they only induced a greater number of stronger roots.

Later, in the June section, we shall deal with the Magnolias of the summer-flowering types centring on *M. Sieboldii* (*M. parviflora*) and also with that splendid tree *M. obovata*.

In the meantime let us consider that very different race, the **Peaches**; these are sun-lovers relishing an open position and a poor, dry, and even limy, soil rather than the moist rich soil of the mountain forests.

One of the earliest is *Prunus Davidiana* (A.G.M. 1927) David's Peach, named for the good Abbé David who sent its seeds to Paris in 1865 from Pekin. It comes into flower about February when the white or pink blossom often meets a somewhat chill reception. It is therefore hardly worth a place except in large gardens, or in a sunny spot in the woodland among the early Rhododendrons.

Seedlings of the common Peach, *P. Persica*, are very easily grown from stones and are of notably good health and remarkable vigour, compared with grafted plants. If planted out into their permanent places from pots they grow rapidly without check and seem almost immune to the leaf-curl fungus which debilitates grafted plants unless they are regularly sprayed in March with fungicide. Furthermore the fruit from these seedlings is surprisingly often of really excellent quality and their blossom is quite as attractive as that of any of the family. Unlike the Cherries, I find that Peaches often suffer a severe check if moved with bare roots unless every precaution is taken. Even then it is wise to nip off all blossom buds during the first spring in the new position. A further advantage of these seed-grown Peaches is that one may avoid the artificial-looking "standard" shape which one does not always want. The drawback to this shape is that such trees need, for several years at least, a very strong stake and a firm tie owing to their topheavy form. The stake is not an object of beauty; in fact it quite spoils the appearance of the trunk. A young tree put out as a tiny sapling will grow to the wind and assume the perfect form to make the best of its situation, assuming a rightness of look and carefree port that the artificially shaped standard, planted when large, can never do.

A garden variety with double pink flowers is *P. P.* var. 'Clara Meyer' (A.G.M. 1939); it is quite effective in a warm spot. *P. P. alba-plena* is a handsome semi-double, white-flowered variety; 'Windle Weeping' is a double pink weeper from California and 'Helen Borchers' is a semi-double pink of similar origin.

A brilliantly coloured variety is *P. P.* 'Russell's Red'. The flowers are large, and a beautiful rich, crimson red, but it is usually grafted on the Plum and thus a martyr to the leaf-curl fungus unless regularly sprayed, and therefore seldom seen in good health for long. I have, for some time, intended to graft this superior sort on to a strong seedling Peach, to see whether it will do better on this more consanguine host-root than on the usual Plum.† It is one of the most spectacular of all flowering trees and therefore can fully reward the attentions of the determined cultivator. 'Palace Peach' (A.M. 1939), a new variety, is equally rich in colour and it may prove to have a stronger constitution.

There is also a fine, strong healthy Peach with red foliage and pink flowers, *P. P. foliis rubris.* Two new varieties from California are : 'Aurora', semi-double pink, and 'Iceberg', semi-double white.

In cultivation the Peaches require a sunny, open position and well drained soil. Usually considered as requiring extra lime, I find nothing wrong with the vigour of their growth in acid soil if fed bonemeal or with the germination of self-sown seedlings in such soil. Regular spraying with a fungicide such as 'Sulsol' is essential in early spring before the buds open, or the Peach leaf-curl fungus will cripple the trees. "Dieback" should be controlled by cutting out all sickly shoots in late May, annually.

Misunderstanding as to their cultivation have led to their neglect by all but a few thoughtful enthusiasts. Yet of all hardy blossoming trees none can give us the joyous and almost unbelievable cloud of crimson blossom of a good red Peach. Beside it the Magenta tints of the pink Cherries appear poor indeed.

Now we come to some of the most beautiful of all flowering trees as regards form as distinct from colour—the early-flowering section of the **Cherries.**

One of the first to open is *Prunus Conradinæ* discovered in Hupeh, China, by the great plantsman, E. H. Wilson, who sent seeds to the Arnold Arboretum, Boston, Massachusetts, whence they came to Kew. *P. Conradinæ* flowers in January or February, with fragrant white blossoms freely produced on the naked branches. There is a double-flowered form—var. *semi-plena* whose pink flowers, although less shapely, last longer on the tree and make a fuller distant effect. It is too early a flowerer to be generally recommended, but in a sheltered wood-garden its white blossom may fittingly complement the massive red flowers of Rhododendron 'Cornubia' or others of its kindred, amid the fresh green of Bamboos backed by the dark coniferous mass of Pine or Fir.

In the garden we need the more reliable offering of later blossoming and early April or later is quite soon enough.

† Since I wrote the above Mr. Justin Brooks, a commercial Peach grower, has confirmed the essential importance of using Peach root stocks. See *R. H. S. Journal* LXXVI, pt. 1, p. 22 *et seq*, for a most valuable setting-out of all that concerns the grower of Peaches.

Among the early-flowering Cherries that open at this time, a good form of the variable wild Hill Cherry of Japan, formerly known as *P. serrulata* var. *mutabilis*, now *P. s.* var. *spontanea* or 'Shiro-Yamasakura', is one of the most beautiful. This superb hardy flowering tree offers an excellent example of how mere confusion as to name can prevent a good plant becoming known and lead to its almost complete disappearance. In Japan there are avenues and groves of this Cherry, as a tree of full forest size, covered in spring with innumerable small, but beautifully formed, white or pink blossoms opening among the young, unfolding, copper-coloured leaves. By all accounts and photographs, and also many delicate and lovely Japanese paintings meticulously done with great exactitude, these must be some of the most glorious flowering trees to be seen anywhere in the world. E. H. Wilson, described them so glowingly, in particular the immense veterans of the avenue of Koganei, as to excite the interest of all, but unfortunately under the name of *P. sachalinensis*. This latter Cherry has been found to be quite a different species and is also known as *P. Sargentii*. Even now the confusion is not entirely clarified for I note that in the second edition of "Manual of Cultivated Trees and Shrubs", by Alfred Rehder (The Macmillan Company, New York) which I follow in nomenclature, the poor Hill Cherry is relegated to the position of an unspecified form of *P. serrulata*.

Anyhow, as a result of this name boggle, the true Hill Cherry languished for a long time unsung, and even today it is almost unobtainable, most leading Cherry growers having given it up, as no one ever asked for it. However, the few trees existing over here have begun to cast the fame of their beauty abroad and propagation is at last getting ahead. This Cherry has the merit of garden effectiveness to a high degree owing to the great mass of its little flowers and the glorious colour of the young leaves. Forms vary greatly in value and some have more shapely and pure-coloured flowers and brighter young leaves, the latter being a very important part of the effect. The best forms should be selected and *propagated under garden names* so that this lovely tree may decorate the new towns and the avenues of the future Britain now being planned. Small street-sized trees are needed for crowded places but without some trees of full forest size no landscape—urban or rural —can have proper dignity and scale. The Hill Cherry flowers when quite small but some years must pass before it can become large enough to show its true value. It is hardy and of strong constitution and seems to grow well in any reasonably good soil, though in Britain it seems unlikely to make such a tall tree as in Japan.

P. Sargentii, Sargent's Cherry, which was sent to Kew by Professor Sargent of the Arnold Arboretum in 1893, and received the Award of

Garden Merit in 1928, has larger individual flowers of a glowing pink and also a superb autumn leaf colouring. But it is a rather more difficult plant to grow well than most other Cherries. A sapling of 6 feet that I planted in ideal conditions took nearly ten years to reach perfection, but this was well worth waiting for. The tree, nearly 20 feet high, was so densely packed with the large short-stalked bright purplish-pink flowers that it was effective at a great distance and the refinement of form made it delightful on closer examination. A rich, deep, loamy soil and a sunny but wind-sheltered position are needed for this superb Cherry to show its real quality, and it is well fitted to form the high spot of a group of the white and blush-flowered early Cherries also described in this section. Such groups need a preponderance of white to show their full brilliance; too much pink looks merely muddy.

Another species, the Spring Cherry, *P. subhirtella* (A.G.M. 1927) is hardy in all parts of England and has a great number of varieties. The variety most prominent in Japan appears to be a free-growing form, sometimes listed here as var. *ascendens*, which, over there, reaches, according to Major Collingwood Ingram, a height of 90 feet. Evidently this would be a noble Park or commemorative tree that could well be planted in preference to the uninteresting Limes and Elms too often chosen for the purpose. The commonest form over here is one which usually only makes a small rounded tree about the size of a Hawthorn. Provided that the bullfinches are kept away, it makes a fine show of white or pale pink blossom every spring. There are varieties with deeper purplish-pink flowers and also doubles.

A notably fine variety of this Cherry is *P. s.* var. 'Fukubana' with double or semi-double flowers of quite a rich and deep pink, the petals being serrated so as to give the blossoms a charming frilled appearance. At the same time, a good selected form with more abundant, single flowers is really preferable unless one has space to grow several kinds of this delightful tree. 'Beni Higan' is a fine pale pink single and 'Pandora', a cross with 'Yoshino', is very free with larger blush-pink blossom.

The Spring Cherry can be grown from cuttings of the season's growth placed under a bell-glass in midsummer. On their own roots the trees grow better and are more beautiful by reason of having no ugly distortion caused by the graft union. Indeed, for a beautiful and shapely tree, the cutting, and still more the selected seedling, so far surpasses any grafted plant in later life that I, for my part, am prepared to overlook a slight inferiority in shape and colour of flower to attain the handsomer tree. Such seedlings planted out as young "whips" in their permanent places grow to the wind unstaked and assume a beautiful and natural form altogether different from that of the top-heavy transplanted standard secured to its unsightly but necessary stake.

Most frequently planted, perhaps, is the variety *P. s. autumnalis* (A.G.M. 1924) which flowers at intervals during the winter. Often the poor wretch struggles to put forth its tattered semi-double flowers amid the bitter storms of January. It is certainly a wonderful testimonial to the British climate that so many gardeners relish winter-borne flowers. But if one compares the glorious spring picture made by this Cherry among the Daffodils and Primroses of April with the unhappy haze of bedraggled blossom dimly seen against grey skies and naked branches in winter I think most will prefer it, as I do, in its normal form.

The weeping variety, var. *pendula*, can be a very beautiful tree when carefully trained. Failing a seedling tree, I think the best effect is obtained when it is top-grafted on a very tall pole of the Gean (our native wild Cherry) but even then it is necessary to tie up the branches at first so as to get a beautiful gradual curve downwards rather than merely letting the branches hang straight down. There are pink and white forms of the weeping kind, some having starry, thin flowers and others shapely and full ones, and there is also much variation in habit, some having such weak and trailing branches that only a permanent wire umbrella would keep them from hanging straight down in an ugly tangle. Care should therefore be taken to select a good form. It is not a very healthy species in this country, often suffering from "dieback" in parts, or even total sudden death for no cause that I can ascertain.†

The Cutleaf Cherry, *P. incisa* (A.G.M. 1926) is one of the most indispensable delights among the early Cherries for small gardens. It is a good garden plant and will even stand quite severe cutting back, which is often disastrous with the other Cherries. *P. incisa* flowers profusely every spring with solid little white blossoms that look rosy pink at a distance owing to the red calyx (this being the name given to the leafy base surrounding most flowers). Eventually it will make a rounded little tree up to 20 feet, it is said, although usually no more than 12, but it may easily be kept down to a rounded bush 4 or 5 feet high if desired. It flowers freely when only a foot or two in height, and is a treasure of the first order. It is easily grown from seed.

Two outstanding garden-bred Cherries tail along with the early section as to their flowering time and so had best be mentioned at this point.

The first is *P. serrulata* var. 'Yoshino' (*P. Yedoensis*) (A.G.M. 1930). It is thought to be a hybrid between *P. serrulata* and *P. subhirtella*, but

† Instancing this, the remarkable specimen illustrated opposite p. 21 in *The Flowering Shrub Garden* (2nd Edition) by the writer, died outright in the ensuing winter.

in dealing with Japanese garden plants that have been cultivated for hundreds of years there is much uncertainty and it is most convenient to have a handy garden name, whenever the rules allow. 'Yoshino', then, is a fine Cherry with white flowers, often faintly blushed, that cover the naked branches in early spring. It is a good garden plant growing vigorously into a handsome, firm tree in good soil, but it should not be planted where the next to be described is growing nearby for 'Yoshino' looks a poor thing beside 'Tai Haku'.

P. serrulata var. 'Tai Haku' is a very large-flowered variety of absolutely outstanding beauty, pre-eminent among the first six that one would choose for that quality from the many Japanese garden-bred sorts. The shapely single blossoms, each two inches across, are white and appear among the rich bronze-copper colour of the unfolding young leaves. It is a particularly strong and healthful tree, having double the number of chromosomes of *P. serrulata*, and is perfectly happy grafted upon the roots of our native Gean as its unusual vigour matches that of this stock better than most. It flowers a little later than 'Yoshino' and this is the time of year when the first real display of flowers in our gardens had best begin.

Such a spectacularly lovely thing as this Cherry is worthy to take part in an association of harmonious flowerers, one of those delightful colour groupings that distinguish the garden planned with artistry from the mere collection. The building up of these associations is one of the greater joys of the art. An arrangement possible only under the perfect conditions of a good acid sandy loam, where any shrub will flourish, will have alternatives of lesser perfection possible in cold limy clays where the selection is much more limited. At this time, when the big white Cherry blooms, we have a wide choice of complementary plantings.

Among the most beautiful shrubs in bloom at this time are the dwarf mountain Rhododendrons. A charming example that is a really good garden plant is the hybrid 'Blue Tit'. This offspring of *R. impeditum* crossed with *R. Augustinii* was rightly given the four stars of merit, that constitute the highest encomium, by the Rhododendron Association. It forms a shapely mound perhaps a yard across and nearly as high. I started with a little sprig kindly given me by Mr. James Comber, and, a few years later, when I moved the plant, which I had grown under optimum conditions, I was able to divide it into four goodly specimens and also to remove a ring of twelve lusty little seedlings from its perimeter. It is thus a plant that pays its rent very handsomely. The charming evergreen dome covers itself almost completely with flowers of a delightful Aster Violet tint and in the kindly shade of the Cherry, these last long in beauty.

Charming as is an association of two harmonious colours the addition of a third can yield a higher perfection. The colour sought to make up this picture was that of the Primrose, and for years these humble plants have served well enough, but now we find the dwarf Broom, *Cytisus Kewensis*, or the larger *C. præcox*, even lovelier in combination owing to the denser mass of colour they provide.

There are a great number of highly interesting, early flowering wild Cherry species described in detail in "Ornamental Cherries", by Major Collingwood Ingram (*Country Life*, 1948). Most of these are, however, on the whole less effective for the small garden than the varieties described above, but a number of superlative forms, which will, it is hoped, be propagated as clones under garden names, are especially worth noting. Among these are: a seedling form of *Prunus serrulata* var. *pubescens* with "intensely vivid scarlet" autumn tints; a double-flowered sport of the tender *P. campanulata*, interesting for warm gardens; also certain hybrids of this crimson-flowered species and *P. incisa*. A seedling of this cross kindly given me by the author cited above showed amazing vigour in growth but its bright pink blossoms open in March, which is rather too early for safety and the young leaves, unfolding at the same time, fall an easy prey to frost. *Rhododendron præcox*, *Daphne mezereum* and *Pieris japonica* associate pleasantly with it, contrasted with white 'Mirabelle', but one of these mild March spells of calm weather is necessary for the enjoyment of such precocious effects.

Unfortunately *P. cerasoides* var. *rubea* a 100-foot crimson-flowered Himalayan tree is not yet with us, and indeed it never seems to set seed (according to Mr. R. C. Sherriff) in its native habitat.

I have never thought the Bird Cherry, *P. Padus*, really worth growing in the small garden but the variety *Albertii* may be noted as an outstandingly attractive member of an otherwise rather dull family. *P. P. Watereri* (A.G.M. 1930) is also an improvement on the type owing to its longer racemes.

The Chinese Bush Cherry, *P. glandulosa*, is, in most gardens, too much of a martyr to attack by "dieback" to be a good garden plant On the other hand, when on its own roots in an open, sunny spot in a hot, sandy or chalky garden, this little Cherry may grow healthfully enough for its pretty musical comedy appearance to be quite enjoyable. Var. *albi-plena* is a pretty double white variety.

The little Rock Cherry, *P. prostrata*, so widely found wild in the mountains of the world and so seldom seen in the garden, would also be quite delightful if we could only bake and freeze it enough to make it flower really freely. In most gardens it is not very effective.

The Cherries are not so particular as to soil. Sometimes described as
6

lime-lovers, they grow to perfection in acid soils and I know no specimens on chalky lands that approach the size of certain Geans on the greensand.

On the other hand they require an open position, apart from other trees if possible. Spraying to control lichen and black aphis is necessary.

Propagation is described in the special chapter thus headed on page 35. Pruning is restricted to cutting off small branches that are badly placed for the building up of a shapely tree. Rubbing off ill-placed young shoots is even better as fungus attack is the chief enemy of the Cherries. Care should be taken to attend to any wounds caused by broken branches at once, carefully paring away all damaged tissue and painting over the exposed surfaces immediately.

Daphne Mezereum (A.G.M. 1929), a common cottage-garden plant, has great charm. The mauve-pink flowers appear on the naked branches early in the year and smell delicious. It is thought to have been a native but was "collected" to the verge of extinction. Seedlings appear freely from the bright red berries produced among the leaves in summer. There is a rather poor white variety D. M. alba, of more open habit, and also a notably good one, var. grandiflora, which flowers from October onwards with brighter purple and larger flowers. There is said to be a double white-flowered form, var. plena, which I have not seen.

One of the most attractive of early flowerers is D. odora var. elegantissima, a rounded evergreen usually about two or three feet in height with yellow-margined leaves and clusters of pale rosy purple, intensely fragrant flowers during mild spells in late winter or early spring. It is reputed tender but I have found it undamaged in many gardens by the severe winters of the past decade and indeed it has long outlived D. Cneorum and other supposedly more hardy kinds. It has usually the benefit of the foot of a south wall, it is true, but it is at any rate a plant worth chancing owing to the charming nosegays it produces in earliest spring. D. odora itself, (D. odora indica), is a more tender, sprawling, less hardy plant with plain green leaves.

In colder gardens, the hybrids, which go under the names of D. Fioniana and D. Dauphinii, may be grown. According to the late Alfred Rehder these are, botanically, forms of D. hybrida, a cross with D. collina.

D. collina var. neapolitana is a three-foot shrub that is an excellent garden plant for a moist but well-drained, loamy soil either limy or acid, with narrower, more glaucous leaves and smaller, rose pink flowers than the hybrid sold as D. Dauphinii which is very similar to D. odora but considerably hardier and more erect, robust and bushy. These

Daphnes will all grow on limy soils and are not particular as to aspect either. The species may be reproduced slowly but surely from seeds.

Another lime tolerator is **Spiræa arguta** (A.G.M. 1927), the 'Bridal Wreath', a hybrid between *S. Thunbergii* and *S. multiflora* which makes a shapely deciduous bush about 7 feet high and its masses of little white flowers are aglow in April. It is best as a single specimen where its graceful habit is shown to better advantage than when crowded in with other plants, and is generally considered the finest of the spring-flowering Spiræas. It will grow in any fairly good loam, whether limy or not, and is easily propagated from layers.

We have mentioned the excellent little Rhododendron 'Blue Tit' in association with Cherries and now, having done justice to the limy garden, come to consider the great clan of **Dwarf Alpine Rhododendrons** that are among the most fascinating of all garden plants for a lime-free soil.

There are a great number of these delightful little shrubs and it would be a long business to enumerate them all. Grown, as I have seen them all too often, alone without association with other shrubs, their effect is less than that of the common *R. ponticum* which at least boasts a more vivid green leaf. But planted here and there among big boulders in the open, and *complementary plants of other genera*, they are jewels of the highest value. One of the most vital essentials to good planting design is just this embroidery of evergreens of contrasting leaf tones with deciduous shrubs.

Some have condemned the winter value of evergreen Rhododendron foliage as dull, likely to curl up in hard weather and generally un-satisfactory for winter effect. It is too sweeping a statement and with complete confidence I must contradict it. Some species are among the most beautiful of all evergreens, quite apart from the effect of their flowers. If Rhododendrons are isolated in beds by themselves the effect is dreary and dull certainly, and so it would be if Laurels, Hollies, Box or any other evergreens were so tastelessly lumped together. Again, one can hardly expect the best garden landscape to look lovely during a howling east wind with ten degrees or more of frost, but our British winters abound in mild days and on every one of those your hardy Rhododendron foliage sparkles, unfolded, green and lush. Who cares if amid the snow and ice the wise plants huddle down and curl their leaves against the blast? To me it looks a most fitting gesture.

To return to the alpine shrublets, I shall describe only a few of the more outstanding early-flowering members of the various "series" that can be bought from nurseries, leaving out the evergreen Azaleas until later. These Azaleas, I should point out, are the most important section of all for the ordinary garden and are technically known as the "sub-series" *obtusum* of the Azalea "series".

Owing to their great numbers, the system of dividing the Rhododendron species into series of kinship, carried out by the late Sir Isaac Bayley Balfour, has been of the greatest help to all. Thus the innumerable species have been conveniently sorted out into groups showing a family resemblance, and the gardener who knows one member of a series will have some idea of the type of the other members.

Another most helpful short cut is the system of indicating relative hardiness by the letters "A", "B", "C" or "D" which we owe to the Rhododendron Year-Books. "A" means "Hardy anywhere in the British Isles and *can be planted in full exposure* if desired". In practice Rhododendrons so qualified are, of course, by far the most valuable, as they can be grown in the open garden *where they are wanted*, provided that the soil is right. "B" means "Hardy anywhere in the British Isles but requires some shade to obtain the best results". These are therefore less valuable, and, in practice, shelter from wind is also often necessary, but shade can usually be arranged. "C" means "Hardy along the seaboard and in warm gardens inland". Not all of the "C" class necessarily want shade, as for example *R. indicum* ("*Azalea macrantha*"), but the category letter means that the plant may suffer from cold and exposure, and consequently some care must be taken in its placing and it is not to be recommended for unfavourable gardens. "D" means "Hardy in the south and west but requires shelter even in warm gardens inland". This is clearly a danger signal.

So as to maintain as much order as possible, without sacrificing the essential feature of grouping them according to their flowering time in the garden year, I will go steadily through the various series mentioning those in flower during early spring and April. Throughout this book I omit many superb new hybrids, privately bred, because they will not be available in the nursery trade for some years to come.

From one to four stars of merit are awarded to extra fine species by the Rhododendron Group, and this offers a useful guide.

First, in the Boothii series, which is rather a difficult and tender section on the whole, we have the lovely *R. tephropeplum* *** (*R. deleiense*). This was awarded the three stars of merit by the Rhododendron Association but placed in hardiness category "C", which means "hardy along the seaboard and in warm gardens inland", only. Thus if it were not a particularly beautiful species easily grown from seed, delightfully fragrant and flowering at two or three years old, we should not trouble with it. But the best form of this species has these qualifications and in my garden has proved reasonably hardy and a good garden plant, undamaged by all the hard winters of the war when, alongside, Ceanothus, Cistus and Escallonia all perished.

R. *tephropeplum*, in its best form, makes rather an open bush, about 2 feet high when fully exposed, with informal trusses of about six or seven flowers which are of a Rose Bengal (H.C.C. 25/3), not magenta-rose as in poor forms, and wide-open and beautifully full and rounded. The fragrance, which incidentally I have not seen mentioned anywhere, is most enjoyable and scents the air around. In a hundred seedlings there is very little variation, and they are usually in bloom in late April. The form known as R. *deleiense* was found in the Delei valley of Assam "in exposed places on rocky ridges" by Captain Kingdon Ward, but my seed was actually sent back by another collector, George Forrest, under the name of R. *tephropeplum*.

Another charming member of this series, much fancied by Cornish gardeners in R. *leucaspis*, also awarded three stars. This is a smaller and denser shrub with large white flowers with chocolate stamens, but they come much too early to be really useful, in February or March—but in some seasons they are nicely synchronised with those of R. *ciliatum* which also grows easily from seed and flowers within three years of sowing.

Also in this very early-flowering group, in its own series, is the charming R. *moupinense*, a nice little bush with Box-like leaves and coral buds that open to large, speckled, white, scented flowers. There is a very good illustration of it in Captain Kingdon Ward's "Rhododendrons for Everyone" (*The Gardeners' Chronicle*, 1926). It flowers from seed in three years but such early spring flowerers are really better grown in the Alpine House than fully exposed to March weather.

The next series is the Cephalanthum series, now to be known as the Anthopogon series† and it contains some delightful little bushlets, with tiny Daphne-like flowers that, at first glance, few would recognise as members of the Rhododendron family. The one we grow is R. *trichostomum* var. *ledoides* "C" *** which comes from the lovely, but mosquito-ridden, land of Yunnan where it grows in open scrub. The bush is dense and nearly 2 feet high with miniature spherical trusses of tiny pale pink flowers in April or May. It is so free flowering that it makes a real effect and is so dainty and delightful as an individual that

† Dr. MacQueen Cowan and H. H. Davidian, B.Sc., *Rhododendron Year-Book*, 1947, p. 55 *et seq.*

everybody enjoys it. *R. sphæranthum* and *R. cephalanthum* are very similar and equally charming.

The Glaucum series contains the curious *R. pemakoense*, **, "A" class, (which means "hardy anywhere in the British Isles and may be planted in full exposure if desired"). This little shrub is almost a joke, with its tiny framework and relatively huge flowers, which are, regrettably, an unpleasing pale Mallow Purple in colour (H.C.C. 630/3). It is said to make suckers like a Pernettya but my plants do not do this. Although it starts blooming when only a few inches high, usually being at its best in late March or early April, it eventually makes a bush over a foot high.

Now we come to the largest and most important series of these dwarfs—the Laponnicum series, but, as with the other series, we will deal here only with the early-flowering batch that will be in bloom together, as far as possible leaving the later-flowering sorts for our May and June sections. *R. lapponicum* itself, circles the globe around the North Pole and the others are moorland plants, taking the place of heather on their native mountains and tundras. They mostly tend to a mauve, "ponticum", colouring and, therefore, particular care is needed to diversify the effect with pale citron yellow and white which is often best supplied by other genera; otherwise the effect can be dreary.

R. russatum, "A" **** (A.G.M. 1938) with Amethyst Violet (H.C.C. 35/2) or purple-blue, white-throated flowers, forms a rather open, stiff bush said to reach 4 feet although it usually remains more dwarf in an open situation. It is quite an attractive little shrub but requires shelter. *R. cantabile*, a distinct, smaller form with rusty-green leaves, is now, regrettably, merged with it as to name. The general appearance of this plant is very bronzy in tone but its sturdy, compact form and the vividness of the Amethyst Violet flowers (H.C.C. 35/1) make it one of the finest of the mountain dwarfs, though it is sometimes less free-flowering than others. It stands up to exposure much better than *R. russatum*.

R. chryseum "A" **, grows to about 1 foot 6 inches high in the open and has untidy yellow flowers sometimes a little too late in opening to contrast effectively with most of the members of this batch. Forms vary somewhat, but on the whole it is one of the best yellows.

R. fastigiatum "A" ***, has light purple flowers and a rather upright habit. I do not find it so beautiful as many others, but it is, at least, more easily obtainable than most.

R. flavidum "A" **** has pale yellow flowers that sometimes open as early as March, too early for the bulk of the other Lapponicums and often too late for the very early section of the other dwarfs such as *R. leucaspis*, etc.

R. hippophæoides, "A" **** (A.G.M. 1925) is perhaps the easiest to grow of all, making a tallish shrub of up to 3 feet in height. The shapely little flowers are, however, only a pale lilac. It should be grown in an open situation and firmly pegged down at the start or it is a poor gangling thing.

R. impeditum "A" *** is a typically good Lapponicum with a dense mounded habit and, in a good form, has very lovely sparkling Amethyst Violet (H.C.C. 35/1) flowers that completely cover the bush, and beautiful sea-green young foliage. It comes from open moorland at 15,000 feet elevation in western Szechwan but is perfectly happy on my open, peaty slope at 500 feet elevation in Sussex. It is a most delightful plant and in my opinion one of the most beautiful of all miniature evergreens in winter.

R. intricatum "A" *** is rather similar but less fine, with Violet (H.C.C. 36/2) flowers.

Of the hybrids of *R. impeditum* we have already mentioned 'Blue Tit'. 'Blue Diamond' is a lovely dwarf blue-violet-flowered hybrid (*R.* 'Intrifast' × *Augustinii*) for April, with larger and finer flowers, and is available at nurseries. The beautiful 'Blue Bird' (*R.* × *intricatum Augustinii*) with flowers of Veronica Violet (H.C.C. 639/1) is a still newer production but already available. 'Sapphire', raised at the Knap Hill Nursery, is another delightful shrublet of this type.

When buying such Rhododendron crosses it is essential to make sure that the plant is guaranteed to be a clone, that is to say a vegetatively propagated offshoot, of the individual plant that gained the award. Cases have come to my knowledge of mere seedlings of similar hybrid parentage being sold as First-Class Certificate plants. Seedlings vary, of course, enormously in value and the majority are greatly inferior to the outstandingly fine individual plant that was given the award.

Many think that 'Blue Tit' will be eclipsed by some of the above-mentioned, but they will have to show themselves capable of forming the massive, dense, winter-green bushes that make such beautiful winter furniture for the garden which is such an admirable feature of the older hybrid.

R. scintillans "A" ****, has a poor habit but fine flowers in the best form which gained a First-Class Certificate, as these are almost a Royal Blue. It is comparatively easily struck from cuttings and though small, slender and fragile, it is a fairly quick grower so that our nurserymen are able to supply us already with a few plants, and, later on, when they get over the disruptions of the war, the plant will, no doubt, be widely available. *R. scintillans* comes from open pastures on the Lichiang Range at up to 14,000 feet elevation.

R. microleucum "A" *** is a delightful white-flowered Lapponicum species, blooming in late April and growing about a foot high. It thus provides a useful foil to the other colourings and lights up the effect.

In the Maddenii series we have an easily seed-propagated Rhododendron in *R. ciliatum*. But the big pale rose flowers, that seem almost too large for the little bushes, often come in March and, though a large bed of seedlings in fullest exposure makes a great bowl overflowing with a rosy foam of flower, I find it too riskily early in effect and too weak in colour to be worth while in the new small garden, and have therefore discarded it. If grown in the wood, this Rhododendron loses its dwarf form and makes a bush several feet high which is not, in my opinion, particularly attractive.

The series Neriiflorum contains two interesting dwarfs in *R. Forrestii* "B" **** and *R. repens* "A" **** (F.C.C. 1935). They are not really difficult to grow and from their mats of leafy twigs the Turkey Red corollas appear singly and surprisingly large, as though they had fallen from a full-sized bush nearby. In the wild we have great accounts of how these creeping, trailing shrubs carpet and hang down over the rocks blazing with their brilliant crimson-scarlet flowers. In the garden on a shady, peaty bank among rocks they grow well enough, but the flowering is usually hopelessly sparse. In my experience one form only —No. 6832 Kingdon Ward, sent back by that great collector, is really free-flowering, and until this can be propagated sufficiently to become readily available, planters requiring free-flowering plants are well advised to leave these species alone.

Certain hybrids of *R. repens* offer the best compromise as many retain the dwarf habit and scarlet flower quality, and add the blessing of a free-flowering nature. 'Little Bert', whose other parent is *R. euchaites* is one of the best of these, but flowers usually in May. It is unfortunately scarce in commerce, as yet. Others are 'Little Ben', 'Ethel', 'Venapens' and 'Jaipur'. Best of all is 'Elizabeth' (*R. Griersonianum* × *repens*) with an amazing abundance of dark red flowers in late April and a compact and attractive habit. When these delightful little plants become generally and inexpensively available they will undoubtedly adorn almost every lime-free garden.

In the Thomsonii series the only member possibly qualifying for inclusion in this section of April-flowering dwarfs suitable for open positions is *R. Williamsianum*, "C" ****. I am afraid that the "C" is very justly attributed, so I mention it only for a sheltered corner. It is quite a pleasing little Rhododendron with a dense, mounded habit, seldom much more than a foot high. The rounded leaves are pale-coloured below and the young growths chocolate brown. The loose trusses of about five large, pale pink, nodding flowers are beautifully formed and, though owing to its very weak colouring it makes no great effect, it is, perhaps, too charming as an individual to be left out.

In the Triflorum series, only one species comes into this section, devoted to April-flowering dwarf Rhododendrons suitable for growing in the open. This is *R. Keiskei*, "A" **, from Japan, a taller but fairly compact, free-flowering shrub with, regrettably, very pale sulphur-yellow flowers in March or early April. It is possibly one of the best of a rather pale lot of yellows but, unless grown in a shaded, backward place, it is rather too early and is not very vivid in colour and in the small garden it is well to remember to leave plenty of room in the sunnier spots to "embroider in" the plantings of brighter yellow of the dwarf Brooms that will complement and the Helianthemums, late evergreen Azaleas and Heaths, that will succeed the dwarf Rhododendrons in bloom and carry on the decoration through the summer.

In the Virgatum series, *R. racemosum*, "A" **** (A.G.M. 1930) in its various forms is the most useful. The excessively early flowering variety *oleifolium* is, I think, to be avoided, as it opens in March when the weather prevents its being effective more often than not. *R. racemosum* is perfectly hardy in the open and the masses of pale apple-blossom-pink flowers in April are quite pleasing, if sadly weak in colour. It is best in a fully exposed position, as in a shady and sheltered place it grows tall and leggy and does not flower properly. On the whole it is a somewhat over-rated species, but it is useful for bleak places where the more lovely and vivid kinds cannot be grown.

As regards the cultivation of all these delightful little shrubs, a peaty slope with sandstone rocks and a northerly rather than a full south exposure, seems to be the ideal. But in the ordinary garden, on any acid soil, they grow well enough provided that they are pegged down when planted and given water if dry after flowering, and are planted in a fairly moist area made up with black humus and sunken sandstone rocks. Peat or leaf-mould, or just the dark soil from a lime-free Beech wood, all serve equally well. They do not really like woodland conditions and, in my opinion, never look right there, although the shade of distant tall trees is helpful in the dry eastern section of the country to avoid over-roasting when we get one of our hot summers and the frost protection afforded by a canopy of tree branches may be essential in a low-lying garden.

To grow the larger Rhododendrons from seed is a long business, it is true, although the rewards are great. But, with these little fellows that flower within two or three years of sowing, it is obviously well worth everybody's while. The best way of growing them from seed is to collect this carefully when ripe, in November or December, and sow in January in pans of sifted, damp, peat-moss litter, with the bottom half nearly all drainage crocks. Sow the seed on the flattened surface and sift on a scattering of silver sand. This sanding must be repeated when the seedlings appear, to help to anchor them. Air is gradually given, and the pans kept uniformly moist and shaded. Watering is done by partly immersing the pans in a tank of water so that the moisture seeps up from below. When the seedlings are large enough to handle they are very carefully pricked off into boxes and grown on.

With the easier sorts such as 'Blue Tit', I find that sowing in selected spots in the woodland, where a shady bank offers likely conditions, is often quite effective; no reliance can be placed on results, of course, but it is amusing when it succeeds. Cuttings, too, can be rooted without great difficulty and as small plants of good forms now often cost 12s. 6d. apiece it is evidently a rewarding proposition for the amateur. Short firm shoots with a trimmed heel firmly set in sharp sand and peat mixture under a shaded bell-glass in early winter usually respond; but for a masterly exposition of this complex subject in detail, see F. Hanger, *R.H.S. Journal*, Vol. LXX, p. 359.

Those fortunate enough to have a small piece of wooded ground, and an acid soil, may adventure happily with some of the larger woodland Rhododendron species. Some of these flower in April, but as early May is a safer flowering time the greater number of those specially recommended flower then or later still. Consequently a selection of these is grouped under early May (p. 132) together with cultural directions.

Turning now from these acid soil shrubs to a family that is indifferent to soil conditions, we note that several attractive members of the **Viburnum** family flower in spring, usually in April.

Viburnum Carlesii (A.G.M. 1923) comes from Korea and was introduced to Kew in 1902. In the open it forms a bushy, fairly symmetrical, rounded, deciduous shrub, usually about 4 or 5 feet high, with dusty-looking leaves and bun-shaped trusses of very sweet-scented, small, white Daphne-like flowers, fairly freely borne and well displayed, but making little distant effect. Its weak points are that the leaves are rather unattractive until they colour in autumn and that often each of the cymes† of flower has a number of browned florets that spoil their charm. But the young leaves are attractively fresh and green when they expand with the delightful pinkish flower buds in early April.

V. Burkwoodii is a very beautiful hybrid, produced in 1924, between *V. Carlesii* and *V. utile*. Reaching 10 feet in height, it is semi-evergreen and of rather loose and thin habit, with fragrant flowers of very similar character, in slightly smaller cymes than those of *V. Carlesii*. It makes an admirable wall shrub—even against a north wall, and in mild gardens can be delightful as a lawn specimen. It flowers a little later, as a rule, often not opening until early May.

V. B. 'Park Farm Hybrid' is similar in flower but the cymes are slightly larger and this variety makes a more dense and low bush‡ which makes it very valuable for an open site in a favourable garden. On a limy soil near the coast this should be one of the first choices among spring-flowering shrubs.

V. carlcephalum (*V. Carlesii* × *macrocephalum*, wild form) has larger leaves similar to *Carlesii*, and the habit is compact and vigorous. The domed, tightly packed flower cluster is 4 to 5 inches across and very fragrant. Its flowering time is usually slightly later than that of *V. Carlesii*.

V. bitchiuense is a taller shrub of more open habit at first, finally making a large bush, 9 feet high or more, when it may almost equal *V. Carlesii* with the freedom of its brighter, equally fragrant, but smaller flowers. The flowering time is usually early April.

These Viburnums might be described as some of the finest of second-class shrubs; possibly first-class in favoured spots. The flowers being white, they cannot clash with any colour scheme, but assist all, and their fragrance is quite delightful. But one or two plants are enough; one bush is as good to look at as a dozen. They are not particular as to soil, even growing well on chalk, but respond well to a mulch of cow manure; and an open sunny position with shelter from cutting winds is required. Although said to be easily increased by leaf-cuttings, I have not found them to strike very readily or to grow on well. Ordinary cuttings taken at the end of May before the wood gets too hard strike easily but are also very slow-growing. Many make no headway for a whole season. Nurseries usually supply plants grafted on *V. lantana* and these grow well enough, provided that any suckers from the stock are removed at once. The members of this group of the Viburnums do not transplant very well.

† A cyme is a broad, more or less flat-topped, flower cluster, with the central flowers opening first.
‡ "The Genus Viburnum", by A. Burkwood, *R.H.S. Journal*, LXXII, p. 360 (Sept. 1947).

Several beautiful members of the **Clematis** family flower in spring and these are mostly rampant climbers suitable for large house walls or, better still, unimportant trees such as ragged old male Hollies or conifers. Among the finest are the following:—

Clematis montana (A.G.M. 1930) in its finer forms is superb, the great masses of shapely white or pink flowers giving a beautiful effect. A number of poor seedling forms are in circulation, so care should be taken to select the best.

C. m. rubens is a fine pink-flowered form with large, anemone-like, pale purplish-pink flowers.

These Clematis are best planted with their roots shaded but where they can climb up into the sun. They grow well among builders' rubble, and in limy soils generally, and are therefore specially valuable to clothe unsightly new buildings or to decorate an arbor when quick-growing and effective furnishings are required.

Propagation is really best left to the nurserymen as seedlings usually vary in quality for the worse. Layering, however, can sometimes be effected by burying portions of low young branches. No pruning is necessary provided that care has been taken to train out the growths at the start in a well-spaced fan formation covering the required area.

Ulex europæus plenus (A.G.M. 1929), the **Double Gorse,** is one of those innumerable shrubs which nearly achieve great beauty, but just fail. There are always a lot of unattractive dead spines to be seen, the doubled flower is rather a muddle and the habit is very gawky. A poor, hungry soil is needed, or it immediately grows too leggy. Examples of rabbit-topiary of the wild Gorse on the moors are often very attractive, but too much clipping of course prevents free blooming. Though the Gorse makes good windbreaks it is far too inflammable to be safe near valuable shrubs, so perhaps it is best to keep it out of the garden, except for the dwarf species, the 'Petty Whin', whose apricot spires are very welcome in late summer.

In old gardens there is often buried treasure in the form of priceless plants swamped by rubbish. Too often new owners are too hasty in destroying everything in order to make a fresh start. However good the new plan may be, its realisation would probably be both earlier and better if modified so as to include some established features already grown to mellowness and majesty. Among the finds worth keeping at all costs, at any rate until the new work has become furnished, are large evergreens; in particular ancient **Rhododendrons.**

Such an old hardy hybrid Rhododendron is 'Rendall's Scarlet',

formerly known as "*Smithii*," a cross between the early, tender, red
Himalayan *R. arboreum* and *R. ponticum*. It is customary to put this
old variety down as a "has-been" or "no longer worthy of cultivation",
owing to the fact that its flowers are really of rather a purplish pink
colour. But after seeing superb aged specimens in open parkland
gnawed by cattle to the "browsing line", and been greatly impressed
by the picturesque habit of these fine flowering evergreen trees, I am
not at all sure that this is right. A non-gardening friend, whose artistic
taste is widely respected, once told me that, though I had shown him
several hundred different choice varieties of Rhododendrons in the
great Leonardslee gardens during the afternoon, he found that these
gnarled trees were really the most beautiful of all. Forcing myself, with
an effort, to cast aside all horticultural bias for a moment, I had to
agree, but the beauty is possibly that of age, rather than of the variety.
Some Rhododendron hybrids, of course, will never make trees; they
always remain bushes, but this is not invariably such an advantage as
is sometimes thought. Few gardens are so minute that a tree of any
kind is unsuitable, and the most beautiful small trees I have ever seen,
anywhere, are old trees, 30 feet high, of *R. arboreum*, *R. Thomsonii* and
R. Luscombei. The flowers are glorious but the clean, marbled, pink
trunks and weeping branches set with blue-green foliage are a delight
even when the corollas lie in carpets of rose, red and crimson beneath.
So let the old hybrid be spared by all who are lucky enough to find one
on their land, and should a specimen of *R. Thomsonii* or any of its
hybrids *having a smooth bark*, be thought too "leggy" to be worth
keeping, I would plead especially for its life. As this type will not
"break" freely again if cut down, the only alternative is to treat it as
a tree and encourage it to grow in this way. The trunk is as decorative
as that of any of the much boosted trees grown solely for the beauty
of their bark, but too much clearing must not be done, as, unless the
ground is shaded and mulched, the plant soon gets wizened and dried
up, and is no longer an object of beauty. In sheltered spots, immense
plants of the old hybrids, feathered to the ground, are sometimes found
in Rhododendron districts and, rather than destroy them, the wise
course is to plant a complementary flower effect, taking advantage of
the invaluable shelter *without ground-robbing*, that these shrubs provide
so well. Crabs, Plums, Cherries and Narcissi, alone, can build up in a
very short time a group of great splendour around such a main feature,
which would otherwise require a lifetime for its attainment.

Name changes are often irritating but there are times when they are
very welcome. Let us be thankful that the wretched situation of having

Pyrus as the generic name of "Japonicas" (Chænomeles), Pears, Rowans, Apples and Aronias is now brought to an end by general consent. Malus is now the accepted generic name for the **Crab-apples.**

As flowering trees, the Crabs have many handsome species for the garden. They are less beautiful in the individual blossom, as a rule, than the Cherries, and form less shapely trees in the landscape when out of bloom, but their coloured fruits are often brilliant in autumn.

The dull-purple-leaved forms *Malus purpurea Eleyi* (A.G.M. 1925) and *M. p. Lemoinei* (A.G.M. 1937) are very commonly planted, but not everybody finds either the foliage or the somewhat muddy, vinous-pink flowers altogether attractive, and the fruits which are of much the same somewhat uninteresting tint make no great display. *M. purpurea* itself (A.G.M. 1923) has more richly coloured blossom of a bright crimson tint (H.C.C. 22/1) but the dull, reddish-purple foliage, again, makes the tree difficult to place in the summer garden.

M. p. floribunda (A.G.M. 1923), so rightly named, is one of the most beautiful of the Crabs, with its masses of pink buds and white flowers. It should really be allowed to grow as a large bush as it does not make a shapely tree.

M. hupehensis (*M. theifera*) (A.G.M. 1930) is a very handsome Crab with a better, more tree-like habit than the foregoing. It comes from China, whence it was sent back by E. H. Wilson in 1900. The flowers are large, $1\frac{1}{2}$ inches across, and white, or blush-pink in the variety *rosea*, and the globular fruits are yellow and red. It is one of the most attractive members of the family.

M. spectabilis, another tall, upright tree of around 20 feet or more, has red buds opening to blush pink flowers, and yellowish fruits. The variety *Riversii* (or *flore pleno*) is particularly fine. Var. *albi plena* is a superb double white and one of the finest of all Crabs.

M. micromalus makes a smaller, more upright tree, with small pink blossoms in great profusion followed by red fruits.

A singularly fine Crab is *M. baccata mandschurica*, a bigger and more ragged tree with white blossom, violet-scented, very late in the season—towards the end of May. Some forms have abundant vivid red fruits and are especially worth looking out for.

M. prunifolia is one of the best Crabs for fruit as the red and yellow apples remain long on the tree. An interesting variety is *M. p. fastigiata* with an upright habit and fine pink blossom which make it suitable for street planting. 'Cheal's Crimson' has exceptionally vivid fruits.

M. 'Golden Hornet' is a hybrid Crab of erect habit with round, pale yellow, cherry-sized fruits freely borne.

M. 'Cheal's Golden Gem' has attractive, pale blushed flowers followed by small yellow fruits, and 'Gibbs' Golden Gage' is rather similar.

The most delightful bush Crab is *M. Sargenti* (A.G.M. 1927), with shapely white blossom in abundance followed by round red fruits that remain over winter, and a good autumn effect from the colouring of the leaves. The bush is seldom more than 4 or 5 feet high and, anyhow, can be kept to this size quite easily, if desired, by a little pruning.

M. toringoides (A.G.M. 1929) has white blossom followed by very handsome, waxy, red and yellow fruits, but is usually a wretchedly shaped tree.

M. 'John Downie' can make a fine shapely tree with white blossom and bright red and yellow fruits. It is still one of the best of the red-fruited Crabs and unlike many of the others its natural habit leaves little to be desired.

As a matter of fact, the cooking Apple 'Arthur Turner', is as handsome as many of the Crabs, with its abundant, unusually large pink blossoms, and the big green fruits that follow are not without a certain decorative majesty. This variety is worth noting for small gardens where a dual-purpose tree may be essential.

The Crabs are indifferent to soil so long as it is deep and reasonably well drained. For long, Apples were thought to prefer a limy soil, but of late it has been found that the "freezing up" of available iron, caused by the alkalinity, has a bad effect and this is sometimes remedied by injecting iron pills into the trunks. A good mild tonic for a Crab that is not growing well is a light hoeing followed by a top dressing of fresh wood-ash or bonemeal. Like the Cherries, Crabs need regular spraying with both winter-wash and Derris or, sooner or later, they will be made unsightly and checked in growth by a massed assault by caterpillars. In view of spraying dangers to evergreens, the trees are best kept away from the beds of shrubs, being either grown as specimens, complementing groups of flowering Cherries perhaps, or as an irregular line of shade trees for the beds.

Another pink-blossomed lime-tolerating subject in flower at this season is a member of the **Bladder-nut** family.

Staphylæa holocarpa rosea is the best form of this Chinese species which makes a twiggy and rather undistinguished bush about 8 feet high, very pretty when in flower in late April with its innumerable pale purplish-pink flowers. Only introduced from China in 1908 by E. H. Wilson it is still uncommon, but this quality should not lead us to place it in too prominent a position as it is of little ornamental value when out of flower. It is, however, very useful for gardens with a limy soil as it grows perfectly well under such conditions. For gardens with neutral or acid soils there are innumerable shrubs even more brilliantly in flower at this time of year that will, when their flowers are over, still be beautiful parts of the garden composition with pleasing forms and evergreen or autumn-colouring foliage. This Bladder-nut is hardy and can be increased from cuttings of half-ripe shoots treated in the usual manner.

It is in the later part of the early springtime period that the first section of my favourites of all the flowering shrubs come into bloom. They are a very choice family, rich beyond any in plants that have all the qualities for the gardener who seeks the maximum of charm in his garden landscape in miniature. They are the **Evergreen Azaleas** of Japan and their allies, and they give us one of the first displays of densely massed flower colour for the ordinary garden on lime-free soil.

As with the Cherries, the Tree Peonies, the Camellias and the Hydrangeas, these superb garden plants have been so long bred and cultivated by Japanese gardeners that to determine the true original wild prototypes and to trace the crossings that have taken place is an almost impossible task for the botanist. That great plantsman, E. H. Wilson, studied these Azaleas particularly and introduced the lovely 'Kurumes', a cultivated race emanating from the district of that name, to America. But, owing to the fact that intermediate forms between the many extreme types, which appear to gardeners to be quite distinct species, still survived as wild plants among their native hills, he lumped a number of horticulturally distinct kinds together under the name of *Rhododendron obtusum*. We gardeners cannot so generalise, as some are hardy and some are not; some have flowers which fade quickly in the full sun necessary for the health of the plants; others do not fade; some are "mimps" (plants which never really get going); others are first-class garden plants.

When the specific name thus loses horticultural significance the varietal name becomes very important. A good colloquial name is "Evergreen Azalea" and I find the Japanese garden names of the varieties on the whole rather less troublesome than such Latin ones as *Chamæcyparis pisifera plumosa nana aurea Rogersii*, or even French names of the type of 'Souvenir de Claudius Denoyel', 'Petite Sœur Thérèse de l'Enfant Jésus,' etc.

As pet plants for the small garden, charming all the year round and having, each, a distinct personality of its own and delightful to have living close to us, few shrubs can compare with the Evergreen Azaleas.

Furthermore, no evergreens that I know have such neatness and beauty of form in the landscape, and in the great gardens of this country, places that are unmatched anywhere in the world today, they are lavishly used in such a manner that this delightful quality is fully exploited.

According to E. H. Wilson,† the original "type" form of *R. obtusum* was a red-flowered garden form now seldom seen in Britain, named by Jules Emile Planchon, and grown in Japanese gardens for centuries. It is so floriferous that "the whole plant appears blood-red" and its Japanese garden name is "Hiryu", but, to add the usual complications, we learn that around Kurume it is called "Hino tsukasa". Furthermore, it was first introduced from near Shanghai, China, by Robert Fortune who sent it to the Horticultural Society of London in 1844. Wilson states that this Azalea is derived from a wild plant common on Mount Kirishima which has also given birth to the dense, dark, tiered, fully evergreen, purple-flowered var. *amœnum*, to the tall open-habited, partly deciduous, ultra hardy, orange-flowered var. *Kœmpferi*, and the two quite distinct forms which many have grown from wild seed sent from Japan. Now, however, we are glad to discard this theory, which never looked right to those who grew and lived with these plants and to follow Professor Hiroshi Hara who gave species status to *R. Kœmpferi* and *R. kiusianum* also; these species being the chief ancestors of the hybrid garden races generally known as *R. obtusum*.‡

At the same time we should note that two horticulturally distinct types of Azaleas are raised from wild Japanese seed: (1) the type known as *R. obtusum* Planchon, a wild form with bright rose-red flowers with dark purple anthers, flowering too early for safety and incapable either of withstanding full exposure in Britain or of growing healthfully for long in shade and shelter; and (2) the type known as *R. kiusianum* Makino, flowering in late May with purple or deep rose, widely opened corollas with a short tube and revelling in full exposure to sun and wind so that the growths are well ripened and thus hardy and resistant to frost. Although these are not clearly recognisable botanical distinctions, they are vital ones to the gardener who is, after all, the most interested party with regard to these fascinating plants.

The important point is that, being hybrids of multiple parentage like the Hydrangeas also bred for centuries by the Japanese, the varieties differ very widely in hardiness, depending upon which parent they favour in this respect.

The natural habitat of the wild type of *R. kiusianum* is interesting, for it gives us some guidance to its culture in our gardens. Apparently it grows mostly on windswept slopes on the mountains above the

† "A Monograph of Azaleas", by Ernest Henry Wilson and Alfred Rehder, University Press, Cambridge, 1921, p. 30.

‡ "Occurrence of Rhododendrons in Japan", by Hiroshi Hara, *Rhododendron Year-Book*, pp. 112–127 (1948).

7

tree-level in full sun among coarse grasses and other low shrubs.
R. Kæmpferi has a more northern distribution and often inhabits shady
woods.

Two kinds of leaves are produced by these Azaleas: large, deciduous
summer leaves, and smaller, firmer, persisting ones. The commonest
colour of *R. kiusianum* in the wild is a rosy-mauve, but all the other
colours mentioned in dealing with the varieties are said to be also, if
more rarely, found in nature. The fragrance of the flowers is also
variable, though actually I have not found this to be appreciable in the
cultivated forms.

E. H. Wilson sent a selection of fifty of what were considered the
best of the evergreen Japanese Azaleas cultivated at Kurume to the
Arnold Arboretum in 1919. Of these only about five have been commonly obtainable in England up to now, although as many as eighteen
are listed by one well-known Surrey nursery. The R.H.S. have, fortunately, now been presented with a complete set of these†, from the
original American stock, by Mr. Charles Williams, and as their increase
from layers or cuttings is easily practicable we may hope that ere long
they will all be readily obtainable.

Of the fifty Kurumes, the following particularly good varieties appear
to be commonly available in commerce:—

'Kureno Yuki', white "hose-in-hose" (one flower within another)
  flowers, as in a double Canterbury bell; the best white variety.
'Takasago', pale Carmine (H.C.C. 21/2) flowers.
'Azuma Kagami'—large peach-pink flowers, (Neyron Rose H.C.C.
  623/2) hose-in-hose.
'Kirin', flowers bell-shaped, Neyron Rose (H.C.C. 623/2), early.
'Hinodegiri', bright crimson flowers, a very good strong grower with
  beautiful coppery winter foliage, and one of the best.

The flowers of these varieties do not readily fade in full exposure to
sun and wind and thus placed the plants grow healthily and ripen their
wood fully so that they are little damaged by frost.

Among the more distinct of the less common varieties which are
now obtainable at a few nurseries are the following:—

'Shin Sekai', creamy white, flowers soon turning brown.
'Kumo No Uye', flowers pale Vermilion or "salmon", not very
  hardy.
'Benifude', Azalea Pink, fading quickly.
'Tsuta Momiji', flowers deep vermilion red.
'Rasho Mon', flowers scarlet, regrettably early.

In my experience, however, these are of limited value as their more

† See Wilson's "Monograph", footnote p. 202, for the complete list.

tender flower colours require shade and this is bad for the health of the plants.

Outside the selected fifty true 'Kurumes' there are a number of other equally delightful varieties. Perhaps the commonest, and also the hardiest and finest in habit of all the pink-flowered varieties, is one well known as 'Hinomayo'. So well known indeed that it was often sold at the sixpenny stores before the war. Only recently, the January day being mild, I moved about half a dozen brilliant green domes, 3 feet across, from the nursery into my new garden and I remembered that they were the product of a half-crown happily thus spent in an odd moment some seven years before.

'Hinomayo' is a particularly fresh and bright green all winter, enjoying the fullest exposure, and in spring the pure pink of the flowers (Phlox Pink H.C.C. 625) is so clean in tone and these are so densely massed that a complementary planting is advisable. The white-flowered variety 'Kure-no-Yuki', and also a living mulch of simple Forget-me-nots, are perhaps the most satisfying neighbours. 'Hinomayo' was sent direct from the Emperor's garden to Messrs. Van Nes in Holland, whence it was introduced here, prior to 1914. In the admirable *Rhododendron Year-Book* it was accorded two stars of merit, the maximum given to any Evergreen Azalea.

Another good outdoor variety, but unfortunately still earlier in opening its flowers which are of an equally fresh, unfading, hyaline pink colouring but of a deeper hue (H.C.C. Rose Madder 23/1), is 'Myacino'. It was imported by the Yokohama Nursery Company of London from Japan and sold here in quantity before the war.

The variety *amœnum* is very distinct, being notably hardy and of superb form as an evergreen shrub, having a cedar-like habit with dense tiers of branches more persistently evergreen than most. Unfortunately the charming little hose-in-hose flowers are of a Rhodamine Purple very difficult to place. This defect, however, is absent in the gloriously decorative branch-sport sometimes known as Azalea 'Tyrian Rose' (see illustration facing p. 113) and also in the rare crimson-flowered variety *coccineum* which is prominent at Wisley. Sometimes a purple-flowered branch appears, but if this is cut out at the base further trouble seldom occurs. In old gardens splendid specimens of the purple form are sometimes to be found up to 6 feet in height, which leads one to think that this was one of the earliest varieties to be introduced. This Azalea is a particularly good garden plant and grows well in any acid soil with added peat or black mould, rooting "layers" with the least encouragement.

Many other varieties are available but suffer from the grave disadvantage of having flowers whose colourings quickly fade in the sun.

This failing prevents my being able to recommend them for general garden use. This is because, in my experience, unless these Azaleas are grown fully exposed to sun and air they fail to ripen their wood sufficiently to resist autumnal frosts. Thus, instead of being hardy plants they are reduced to the status of rather tender plants. Furthermore, in sheltered shady places these Azaleas are killed-back and disfigured by lichen and fungoid growths.

In the Orient, legend has it, this difficulty was got over by growing the orange-flowered sorts in full sun and air and having small boys on duty with straw-thatched parasols during the time the flowers were open. When the owner appeared to view the flowers these attendants withdrew gracefully to take up their task again later, so long as the sun shone brightly. In our gardens the best course is the compromise of planting these varieties near a Cherry or other specimen flowering tree so that the Azalea receives shade from the midday sun, but is yet in a comparatively airy and open position.

Among these varieties of more fugitive colouring which require shade and are in cultivation in this country, are:—

R. *obtusum* 'Beni Kiren', a bushy variety with medium-sized double flowers of a deep salmon hue flowering a little later than the others.

R. *o.* 'Hino-tsukasa', with flowers of a deep vermilion red freely borne on a spreading and vigorous bush.

R. *o.* 'Ima-Shojo', with small, vivid, crimson flowers, of "hose-in-hose" shape.

R. *o.* 'Koran Yuki', a dense plant with beautiful orange-salmon flowers.

R. *o.* 'Kurai No Himo', with flowers of carmine red, hose-in-hose.

R. *o.* 'Sakata', having larger, Geranium Lake flowers on a strong-growing vigorous bush.

R. *o.* 'Suiyohi', with flesh-coloured flowers.

R. *o.* 'Tama No Utena', with pale salmon flowers.

R. *o* . 'Ukamuse', with orange-vermilion flowers.

Further information covering all the known varieties is to be found in Wilson's monograph already cited (p. 97), in the *Rhododendron Handbooks* published by the Rhododendron Group of the R.H.S., and in an article in *R.H.S. Journal*, Vol. LXXIV, p. 144 (1949) by J. P. C. Russell, "Hardy Evergreen Azaleas for the Garden".

Much suitably prepared, open-ground space and considerable labour, expense and careful recording would be needed to make full tests of the couple of hundred existing varieties. Many are unsuitable for general planting in this country, being less hardy and vigorous in constitution than others, or having flowers which will not stand up to the full exposure to sun and wind necessary to produce winter hardy growth. In my opinion a shaded trial-ground would not provide the essential data. Indeed, the results might well be misleading and tend to cause undeserved setbacks to the popularity of these beautiful plants.

Many seedlings are being bred at the present time and there is very wide variation in the unfading quality of their flower colours and the durability of the material of the corollas. As an example it may be mentioned that the flowers of 'Hinomayo' remain fresh for five weeks or more in full sun while those of 'Shin Sekai' are browned and shrivelled in a few hours. These qualities have little botanical significance but they are of primary horticultural importance. .

R. Kæmpferi. This horticulturally distinct species is only partly evergreen and has certain important characteristics. In the first place it is evidently hardy anywhere in the British Isles as it grows well at the Arnold Arboretum, Boston, Mass., where the climate is too severe for our native Ivy and Holly. Unlike *R. kiusianum* it is abundant on most of the Japanese hills and mountains. The flowers are larger—nearly twice the size of most of those of the varieties of *R. obtusum* and in clusters instead of in pairs, as is usual. This Azalea has also two varieties which are of considerable importance to the gardener owing to the fact that they come into bloom in early July instead of April. These are known as 'Mikado' and 'Daimio' and are available at a number of nurseries. They are not described in any of the works on the genus previously cited, though commonly listed by the trade. I will say more of them under the July headings. Some seedling forms of *Kæmpferi* flower disastrously early and I have seen these destroyed by March frosts. In favourable years such plants are very pretty with the pale violet of R. 'Blue Tit', etc. but on the whole it is better to play safe and select the later-flowering forms. Among other important points, is the wide variation in the durability of the colour and texture of the corollas. Some seedlings of this species are quite useless, as their flowers fade in a few hours—others remain long in beauty. Again, some are unusually evergreen and maintain superbly autumn-tinted leaves for a very long period; others drop nearly all their leaves at once, before they colour in autumn. (See illustration facing p. 256 for my best form.)

R. Kæmpferi has produced, with a hybrid clone called *malvatica*, a number of excellent garden hybrids of nearly equal hardiness to *Kæmpferi*. The latter is given as category "A" in the *Rhododendron Year-Book* while that of the true 'Kurumes' is listed as "C". These hybrids are quite good garden plants, but most require shade to preserve their flower colours and many lack the fully evergreen quality so valuable in the best Japanese varieties and also something of their perfection of refinement of flower form. When flowers are the perfect size in proportion to the bush nothing is gained by making them any bigger. The origin of *malvatica*, a clone with single, mauve flowers, is not known.

The following is a selection of *malvatica* × *Kæmpferi* hybrids:—

'Addy Wery' *, deep mahogany-orange, evergreen, requires shade, superb.
'Anny' **, orange-red, requires shade.
'Betty' **, orange-pink, requires shade.
'Eva', rosy-violet.
'Fidelio' **, deep rosy-pink.
'Frieda', rosy-purple.
'John Cairns' **, Indian red, requires shade.
'Kathleen', rosy-red.
'Mary' *, deep rose.
'Pink Treasure' **, a large-flowered pink.
'Lilly' *, clear pink.
'Zampa' *, orange-red, evergreen, requires shade.

With the exception of those mentioned as evergreen, these hybrids lose nearly all their leaves in winter. They are mostly in the "A" category for hardiness but need to be shaded by a light canopy of branches to preserve their flower colourings.

Crosses have also been made with "Mollis" Azaleas and the name *Vuykiana* is suggested for this new race. One of the best of these is 'Palestrina' a fine white-flowered evergreen variety.

'Hinodegiri' has been crossed with R. *Kæmpferi* producing, among others, the fine variety 'Orange Beauty' ** with rather early, orange-red flowers. A batch of seedlings of this cross will be found to resemble this variety closely, and if care has been taken to select a sun-resistant, long-lasting form of R. *Kæmpferi* as parent, some may be found to improve upon it. These Azaleas are some of the finest of all shrubs for autumn colour, as the richly tinted leaves remain on the bushes right up to Christmas, while those of many species recommended for such effects last only a few days.

Now for the garden arrangement of this early-flowering section. They are such delightful little plants and so singularly decorative all the year round that many of those fortunate enough to have an acid soil will choose them for the first massed colour display of their garden year. There are two colour arrangements that look particularly satisfying.

The first is to give full play to the extraordinarily clean and clear pinks so lavishly provided owing to the hyaline, or translucent, quality of the corollas and add merely white-flowered varieties and blue Forget-me-nots, with a bush or two of, say, *Magnolia stellata* to add its remarkably pure white to this assembly of rich but unmuddied colours. *R. Kæmpferi* and the orange-flowered sorts are kept apart in shady places where the sun will not burn away their delicate salmony tones and the crimson 'Hinodegiri' can be grouped elsewhere with a white-flowered shrub, whilst the purple *amænum* is grown as a specimen in some other part of the garden where its unsociable colour will not clash with other spring bloomers and its noble, darkly bronzed, evergreen habit will adorn the winter scene.

The other method, which I prefer, is to mix all the colours so thoroughly that no large blocks of one tint are able to start a fight. This needs plenty of plants and *all* the colours and a certain boldness in treatment. Thus, if one adds *Kæmpferi* and the salmon and orange 'Kurumes' and the mountain dwarf Rhododendrons with their blue-violets and yellows, and also *Cytisus kewensis* and *C. Beanii*, the palette is practically complete, and it only remains for the artist-gardener to arrange the picture. In this instance he can be absolutely confident of success, because these charming shrublets are so highly portable that trial and error must give the perfect result in the end.

For those who mutter darkly that these Azaleas must be too tender for their gardens it will, I hope, be an encouragement to observe the illustration facing p. 454 in C. G. Bowers' "Rhododendrons and Azaleas" (Macmillan, 1938) showing them in full beauty in the much more exacting climate of New England. More abundant and lovely flowers no shrubs possess and these have the daintiness, the subtle fragrance, the perfection of drawing, the pure and delicate colourings and the hyaline texture that are the very qualities that epitomise the charm that flowers have for us.

No gardeners on lime-free soil in these islands need be condemned to the second-rate; it is purely a question of whether they wish to take the necessary trouble. All are free to grow, in this most favourably situated group of islands, their own choice from amongst the richest garden floras in the temperate world. Some few deliberately seek a certain practical ugliness and no one may blame them, for the pleasure that the growing gives the grower is the criterion, and competition is only for those who wish to compete. As Farrer said once (I cannot remember where) of a fancier of "monstrous Chrysanthemums like mops dipped in lobster-sauce"—"there is not a weed that man treads beneath his feet on his way home from work that is not more beautiful than these." But that is no real point. Gardening for pleasure should have no stern exhortations to growing this or that, I can but indicate certain beauties and hope that the path shown may bring new fields of delight to those who seek that way and would welcome some short-cut which the long and twisted trail I have trodden may enable me to lay bare.

Some eyes are offended at the rich and somewhat "Russian ballet" flavour of orange, magenta, red, white and pink with added blue-violet, but amid the complementary green of spring grass I have found it most enjoyable. The pinks may lose something, perhaps, but the general effect is fascinating, and, all winter, the bright and varied evergreen mounds are a delightful feature of the garden composition

So supreme are these Azaleas as plants to live with, beautiful every moment of the year, that, in the case of a small garden or courtyard with polluted, muddy, unsuitable soil I know no earth-shifting operation so rewarding as its complete removal and the substitution of a mixture of peat or "woodsy" black mould and sharp sand. In a tiny garden to have only the best is more than ever essential. Such a clean, weed-free soil, that is delightful to work and that will grow these superlative garden furnishings and also the newer types of deep blue, violet, crimson and pale blue Hydrangeas, gives better value than many costlier earth-shiftings that only move bad soil from one position in the garden to another, and there prop it up with expensive stone walls.

In low-lying districts the Evergreen Azaleas may lose their leaves in a hard winter and they may be temporarily badly damaged by an unusually hard and late spring frost coming after a long spell of mild weather. But they seldom die, they recover amazingly rapidly and in quite a short time will have regained their old bushiness and vigour provided that they are growing in an open position and in suitable soil.

The cultivation of these Azaleas, garden-bred for centuries, presents few unsurmountable difficulties. A neutral or, better, a definitely acid soil arranged so that it does not dry out in summer (see p. 24), plenty of sun and air, and pegging-down as advised for dwarf Rhododendrons seem to be the chief requirements, In too sheltered and shady places lichen attacks the plants and cripples them so that they make poor growth, with the unnaturally small leaves that betoken ill health in members of the Rhododendron family. Thus it is important to select those varieties whose flowers do not fade in the sun.

These Azaleas can be grown from cuttings, although they often take some time to form roots. On the other hand, any branch trodden into peaty ground frequently surprises me by rooting nicely and layers are at any rate a simple and consistently successful means of propagation.

Seeds sown as prescribed on p. 90 are also an excellent method but the varieties, of course, do not come true. Self-sown seedlings often appear in my garden.

Some hold that true heather peat is not essential for these little plants, but it is an easily obtained and safe material to incorporate with existing soil. Old, black, woods-mould is almost indistinguishable in appearance from peat, though, being richer, it is even better and is so much more quickly colonised by the roots than even a good loam that I always plant these Azaleas in a mixture of this material at the start. Commercial "peat-moss litter" is also effective, and, unless the soil is naturally a suitable black sandy stuff, I would advise adding a half-part of this to the topsoil and well mixing together.

To plant these Azaleas so that the top portion of the ball of roots is covered by ordinary soil is, usually, to ensure their early death. It is wise to keep a few sackfuls of natural forest peat and fine black rotted leaf-mould for the final sprinkling over the root-ball, and never, I would advise, put ordinary soil above the root-ball at any time. These roots require more air than those of most other plants, but sandstone rocks over them do not seem to be objected to, and they certainly help to retain moisture. A mulch of chopped bracken should be supplied every autumn.

In this treatise we have only begun the almost summer-long pageant of these Azaleas; in the sections that follow we shall list those that flower in later May, June and July.

The **evergreen Barberries** are a very valuable group for limy soils giving us both evergreen winter furnishing and vivid yellow and orange flowers very potent in the spring garden landscape.

Berberis Darwinii (A.G.M. 1930), a rather gangling, sparkling, spiny evergreen with orange flowers followed by bluish-purple berries is too well known to need further description. It was introduced from the strange and misty island of Chiloe, off the west coast of Chile, by William Lobb for Messrs. Veitch in 1894. Though ubiquitous, it is only "reasonably hardy" and it is often difficult to make it form a compact and shapely bush. Coming from south of the equator many find its appearance too alien to the northern flora to group really well with them unless special care is taken, and I must confess to being one of these.

A good example of my reasons for using the names of the flower colours, as given and shown in the Horticultural Colour Chart, is provided by this well-known garden shrub. As a rule the colour of the flowers is described as golden. The Chart reveals that they are Orpiment Orange (H.C.C. 10), which is about as pure an orange colour as one can get. I think that anyone holding a piece of orange skin near to a gold wedding ring will probably agree with me that gold and orange are two totally different colours.

This group of Barberries is far the most important of the genus for flower effect and there are a number of very fine varieties among them. Most of these we owe to the skill of that great old plantsman, the late T. Smith of Daisy Hill, Newry, who raised *Irwinii, gracilis*, 'Brilliant', *corallina*, 'Fireflame' and many others.

Mr. W. J. Marchant of Wimborne and Messrs. Cheal of Crawley have also raised fine hybrids.

The ability of the flowers to withstand quite sharp frosts unharmed is a valuable feature of many of the varieties and hybrids, some of the best of which are described below. *B. Darwinii*, like other Berberis, will grow on either acid or limy soils and its chief value will be for use in gardens with the latter type of soil. Its self-sown seedlings appear everywhere and thus propagation is self evident, though I find them bad movers.

There are a great number of improved seedling forms propagated as clones such as vars. 'Flame,' 'Gold,' 'Fireflame,' etc. Another variety —*nana*—is seldom free-flowering.

Early nipping and pegging down improves the habit of *B. Darwinii*, and even its most bushy-habited hybrids such as *B. stenophylla corallina* are benefited by shearing back any shoots that tend to straggle.

B. stenophylla (*B. Darwinii × empetrifolia*) (A.G.M. 1923), a ten-foot mass of spiny twigs with fairly profuse, small yellow flowers in late April greatly admired by many, is perfectly "reasonably hardy", of very tough constitution and very commonly planted. It is excellent as a barrier where a gap has to be completely closed up, but it is too often seen as an ugly, leggy bush with a dense but sprawling and top-heavy head. In my opinion there are better forms for gardeners prepared to give the necessary extra care in cultivation. *B. stenophylla* must be propagated by cuttings, seedlings do not come true. Any necessary pruning is best done immediately after flowering.

B. s. gracilis is a lower-growing and more compact variety with arching branches and soft yellow flowers often not opening until early May.

B. s. 'Brilliant' is a dwarf, drooping form with very richly coloured flowers and rather yellowish-green foliage.

B. Irwinii is a dense and bushy hybrid with curious shield-shaped leaves and arching branches, otherwise resembling *B. Darwinii*, having flowers of a similar hue but slightly lighter in tint. It is one of the best of this type. Dr. Ahrendt considers that this hybrid should not carry the name *stenophylla*, being distinct in certain characters†.

B. stenophylla var. *coccinea*, in the finest form I have, which was received long ago as a tiny sprig as part of an R.H.S. Wisley plant

---

† "Berberis stenophylla Hybrids", by Rev. Leslie W. A. Ahrendt, *R.H.S .Journal*, LXXIV, Pt. 1, p. 36.

distribution, is an even more decorative shrub, being of dense, bushy habit, about four or five feet high, with crimson buds opening to Cadmium Orange flowers that make quite an attractive display of rich soft colour most valuable for limy gardens in the warmer districts. Unfortunately it is not quite hardy enough to be absolutely reliable, fine specimens being very badly damaged by frost alongside Japanese Azaleas, *Rhododendron deleiense, Hydrangea macrophylla* varieties, etc. which, often considered as rather tender, were comparatively unharmed by the low temperatures that destroyed this Berberis. Nothing is more annoying than to have specimen-grown bushes, that after some years have reached perfection, ruined overnight. Some branches in the centre of each dense, twiggy mass remained precariously alive and, by pruning away dead wood and pegging down and shaping up the remains, it has been possible to rehabilitate the specimens. But if more reliable substitutes can be found it is better to use these and avoid such worries.

B. s. 'Crawley Gem', raised by Messrs. Cheal of Crawley and seen by me as small plants, appears to be rather similar in flower but it unfortunately lacks the fine, upright, but bushy, form which makes the last-mentioned variety so pleasing. The branches are wide spreading and loosely arching. 'Crawley Gem' is, however, said to be "reasonably hardy", like *B. Darwinii.*

All these hybrid forms require to be propagated from cuttings, as seeds usually provide plants reverting to one or other of the parents, usually *B. Darwinii.* Cuttings of some of the hybrids are not very easy to strike.

In gardens with limy soils these Berberis may play a fine part with *Kerria japonica, Chænomeles superba, C. japonica, Spiræa arguta,* Forsythias, *Cytisus purgans, C. præcox,* etc., in providing a spring display of vivid yellow and orange flower colour for those who prefer this warm-toned theme to the pink and white theme which is also available.

Berberis linearifolia, introduced by Mr. H. F. Comber in 1927, has larger and brighter-coloured flowers than *B. Darwinii* and ever-green, entire, linear leaves. It is not a very vigorous grower in most gardens and requires a moist woodland soil and situation. In such places the large-flowered Azaleas give a better return but the Berberis is useful to diversify the effect and in gardens just too limy for Azaleas it is very valuable.

B. lologensis is a natural hybrid between the preceding and *B. Darwinii,* also collected by Mr. H. F. Comber, in the Andes. According to the collector's father, Mr. J. Comber (*R.H.S. Journal,* Vol. LXV, Pt. 7, p. 218) it has the rich flower colouring of *B. linearifolia* and the hardiness of *B. Darwinii*. This is borne out by the fact that, though severely injured, it survived frosts at Dawyck, N.B. which killed *Hoheria glabrata*, *Pyracantha atalantioides*, *Escallonia langleyensis*, *Ceanothus dentatus* and almost all kinds of Brooms†. There are various forms of this hybrid, such as 'Orange King', and care should be taken to secure the best.

B. buxifolia nana is a useful species for limy soils where it provides an attractive dense, two-foot, evergreen bush of a dark bluish-green, bearing scattered, solitary, amber-yellow flowers towards the end of April.

Here we will mention an admirable old cottage-garden favourite—**Kerria japonica** (A.G.M. 1928), also long cultivated in Japanese gardens, though actually wild only in China. It has two forms so different that few would recognise them as the same species. The double-flowered form—a gangling, leggy plant with small, pointed, toothed leaves and round balls of confused Saffron Yellow (H.C.C. 7/1) petals for its flowers, was introduced to Kew by William Kerr in 1804. As the deformed flowers had no "works" to them no one knew what the plant was. In 1834 John Russell Reeves introduced the single-flowered form which is a charming twiggy, dense bush bearing rather bramble-like, pure Buttercup Yellow flowers from late April or early May onwards, and that great naturalist A. P. de Candolle accordingly placed it in the Rose Order under the name of Kerria. The single-flowered form is really much the better shrub and perfectly hardy and indifferent as to soil. There are both golden-variegated and silver-variegated varieties, but they are, I think, much inferior to the green-leaved single-flowered type. It is a very pleasing shrub and especially valuable for a soil too chalky for the Azaleas, where, with *Chænomeles superba*, *Ch. japonica*, *Berberis Darwinii*, *B. stenophylla corallina*, *Genista hispanica*, *Spiræa arguta*, *Helianthemum vulgare* vars., *Viburnum tomentosum* and others, it will help to provide a substitute display for the warm and vivid Azalea colourings.

The only really bad feature of the British climate from a flowering shrub's point of view is its habit of making perpetual false promises. The wily Ash of the hedgerows, actually as tender in leaf as most of the exotics of which I write, knows how to discount such deceptions. However balmy the March airs, it keeps its young leaves safely coiled within the black bud-scales. They emerge only when things ought to be pretty safe, and treacherous late frosts are unlikely. Not so the sanguine

† *R.H.S. Journal*, LXVI, Pt. 7, p. 230 et seq.

Moutan, or **Tree Peony,** most splendid of lime-tolerant deciduous shrubs. At any really mild interval, after the turn of the year, it may sprout hopefully forth and usually receives a dreadful snubbing for its pains. The Rose and the Hydrangea are almost as easily deceived and lured into too-early growth.

All we can do, to avoid the consequences, is to study our garden climate, and select as backward a spot as possible or take advantage of a tree canopy or good katabatics†. Katabatics determine the incidence of late, or early, frosts in accordance with the lie of the land. To be very brief, cold air is heavy and slides, if it can do so freely, away downhill. Consequently elevated sites, with free "air drainage", do not suffer very much from spring frosts. Curiously enough this is one of the few fundamentals, comprehensible by mere observation without scientific knowledge, that our grandfathers apparently knew nothing about. This was, I suppose, because folks did not care to live up on a hill if they could avoid it, and, if they had to, they did not wake up early in the morning to have a look at their plants and those of their neighbours below. Nowadays many of us like to live on hills, and, almost any time when we look out of the window in early spring or autumn in the early morning, we see quite clearly that our friends in the valleys below are smothered in white fog and frost while we are up in the clear sunlight. To profit by these recently discovered phenomena we cannot all go and live up in the hills, perhaps, but very many gardeners on sloping lands can improve their garden climates out of all knowledge merely by removing obstructions to free air-flow on the downward side.

Those of us who have to garden in valleys and hollows must either avoid these over-sanguine growers or grow them under a canopy of branches where they are protected, or else in north-facing places where they get no encouragement to start growth until it is late enough to be reasonably safe. Cold, late districts suit the Tree Peony.

The Tree Peony, *Pæonia suffruticosa* (*P. Moutan*) first came to us, like so many oriental shrubs, as a garden plant long cultivated in China and Japan. In the earliest days of the missionaries to China the fame of the beautiful Moutan, that decorates many Chinese paintings and pottery designs, was spread abroad.

It was Sir Joseph Banks, who also introduced the Hortensia and many other valuable plants, who first secured a specimen for Kew from China through a Dr. Duncan in 1787. Robert Fortune, when sent to China by the Horticultural Society in 1843, also sent back many Tree Peonies from nurseries there, and these, according to William Robinson in "The English Flower Garden", were better garden plants than many

† See p. 25 for further data on garden climate.

of the over-elaborate varieties evolved later, in the florist era. They became quite popular and were widely distributed.

Although a rather similar plant had been imported by Sir Abraham Hume in 1802†, the wild ancestor was only discovered in its natural habitat by that fine writer and keen plant enthusiast, Reginald Farrer, in 1913. In "On the Eaves of the World" he wrote—"I was setting eyes on *Pæonia Moutan* as a wild plant. . . . that single enormous blossom waved and crimped into the boldest grace of line, of absolutely pure white, with feathering of deepest maroon radiating at the base of the petals from the boss of golden fluff at the flower's heart." He was not, however, able to introduce the plant or send back botanical material. It was only in 1925 when Dr. J. F. Rock sent back seeds which he collected from a lamasery garden, which afterwards proved to be apparently similar to Farrer's plant, that the wild Peony arrived. Plants of this origin grew and flowered in Colonel F. C. Stern's famous garden at Highdown near Worthing. There is an excellent photograph of this lovely shrub in bloom, p. 552, *R.H.S. Journal*, Vol. LXIV, Pt. 12 (Dec. 1939). From this and flowers exhibited at the Chelsea Show in 1949, we may see that the wild form is as good as, if not better than, many of the garden varieties as a decorative shrub *for appraisal as it grows*, rather than as a cut flower. Of its fragrance, Farrer recorded "the breath of them went out upon the twilight as sweet as any Rose". It is therefore greatly to be hoped that our nurserymen will be able to propagate this fine plant in quantity from seed so that it may be made readily available to all. According to Colonel Stern, in the article accompanying the illustration cited‡, it has been generously distributed by the Arnold Arboretum.

In the meantime we have for long had many fine garden varieties of the Tree Peony generally obtainable. Among these are:—

'Comtesse de Tuder' with blush-pink flowers, over-large and double, raised in France about 1860.

'Athlete', double, lilac.

'Carolina', bright salmon.

'Colonel Malcolm', violet.

'Bijou de Chusan', palest blush pink, a fine double. (See illustration facing p. 112.)

'Reine Elizabeth', cherry-red, a superb variety.

'Mme Stuart Low', cherry-red, shy flowering.

† *R.H.S. Journal*, Vol. LXVI, Pt. 9, p. 310 (1941): " In 24 years this original plant has formed a bush 7 feet high and 14 feet in circumference producing 660 buds".

‡ See also "A study of the Genus Pæonia ", by F. C. Stern, published by R.H.S. (1946), and " The Moutan Tree Peony ", by John C. Wister, *Peonies*, the Manual of the American Peony Soc. [1928], p. 219, published by that Society.

'Prince Troubetskoy', very large double violet.
Van Houttei, large double carmine.
Vandermæli, pale blush.
'Zenobia', purple.
'Mont Vésuve', orange-red.
'Triomphe de Gand', vivid crimson.

At the time of writing, however, there is a temporary shortage of stocks.

Even more effective are the Japanese garden varieties, many of which are still grown and prized in America and also in France. Our nursery-men are importing these at the present time and thus they will shortly be available in this country. Among the finest are:—

'Yomonohomare', early, semi-double, pink.
'Hananosito', deep pink, paler edge, double, large flower.
'Kamada Fuji', Wistaria violet, double flowers 6 to 9½ inches across, dense bush 3 feet by 4 feet only.
'Miyo-Hikari', deep salmon, semi-double flowers, tall and free-flowering.
'Gessetai', pure white, frilled petals, flowers sometimes a foot across and freely borne.
'Ren Kaku', white, double, with golden stamens displayed, fragrant.
'Ukabama', very dark carmine, almost black, incurved petals.
'Adzuma Kagami', rose-red.
'Gioku Senshiu', rose-red.
'Hakugan', white.
'Iro-no-seki', rose pink.
'Kokirin', red, double.
'Kumonano Tsuki', pale violet.
'Konron Koku', deep red.
'Ruriban', violet-purple, very fine single.
'Saishoji', pure white.

A beautiful variety 'Constantia', obtained by Colonel F. C. Stern, V.M.H., from Japan, had carmine, ten-petalled, open flowers with a central cluster of purple stamens and golden anthers forming a delight-ful design.

In cultivation the Moutan requires skill and care. It is perfectly hardy, so far as winter cold is concerned, but as already explained, is a martyr to late spring frosts. Finer specimens are to be seen in the cold north-east than in the alternately mild and frost-ridden Thames valley. Accordingly, it is wise to select as backward a spot as possible, where the sun comes only in the afternoon. It is a gross feeder and appreciates farmyard manure and bonemeal applied after flowering.

It can be propagated by layering or even sometimes by cuttings taken in July and given bottom heat. Plants are often grafted on herbaceous Peonies, and in such cases one can only try everything possible to get these to root above the graft or to layer them all round.

The double varieties seldom set seeds, unfortunately, but single varieties often do so, and these seeds are precious and should never be wasted. After the pod splits, sow as soon as the seeds have lost their first stickiness and become *partly* dry. Dried seeds seldom germinate. A good loam or John Innes Compost is best, and the young plants should not be disturbed for two years.

On the whole, as with Camellias, Roses and Hydrangeas, the garden varieties of the Tree Peony have been grown for the florist rather than for the shrub gardener and I, for my part, would far rather have something nearer the wild form† than some of the varieties with badly presented, over-massive, very double flowers that cannot hold themselves up properly. The florist wants a flower with, say, a hundred petals —we gardeners would prefer, I think, ten flowers instead, with only ten petals each. Most of the petals of these over-double flowers are wasted —we can't see them and the beautiful form of the true, functional flower is lost. This is, I think, why so many experienced gardeners will only grow true species; they are disgusted at the coarseness and enormity of the florists' varieties. But the early crosses and selected seedling forms of the species are, in my opinion, often even more decorative than wild species, and are usually better garden plants.

The Moutan will, under favourable circumstances, make quite a large, picturesque bush having been reported up to 8 feet high and 10 in diameter. Most plants that one sees are only 4 feet high or less. As it will grow well in a limy soil, provided this is well enriched, its chief value will be for limy gardens where, being also a plant of the first quality, it will prove one of the best substitutes for the Rhododendrons and Azaleas that cannot be grown under such conditions. What we really want is a new strain of later flowering varieties and something of this kind has been started in America, see p. 164.

The splendid family of the **Brooms** are now beginning their continuous sequence of flower and the first to open now claim our attention.

Cytisus purgans is a bushy and dense, though almost leafless, Broom up to 4 feet high, giving us a brilliant mass of very intense yellow flowers in late April or early May. To keep it low and shapely, both pegging-down and shearing should be done annually. The colour is almost too

† See *Journal R.H.S.* LXXIV, Pt. 7, Fig. 104 (1949) for a perfect portrait of this exquisite flower.

Pæonia suffruticosa ' Bijou de Chusan '

Rhododendron ' King George '

Rhododendron obtusum 'Tyrian Rose'

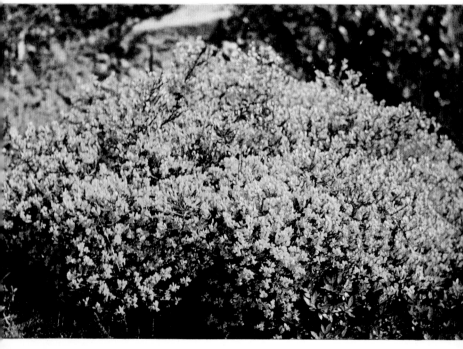

Genista lydia

startling to place easily and needs careful planning so that one may lead up to it with whites, paler yellows and blue-purples. This species comes from southern Europe and is reasonably hardy. Perhaps its best associates are *C. multiflorus* and the presumed offspring of these two, *C. præcox*, whose description follows:—

C. præcox (A.G.M. 1933) (*C. purgans* × *multiflorus*) is a bushy Broom with pale Empire Yellow (H.C.C. 603/1) flowers in April or early May which have rather a heavy and unpleasant smell. The colour, however, is a very valuable one for contrast and for interposing to neutralise possible colour clashes. It originated as a chance seedling in a nursery at Warminster about 1867. With a little trimming, it forms a good, dense, rounded bush about 4 feet high, and is very free-flowering.

Unlike the Brooms of the *C. scoparius* section, *C. purgans* and *C. præcox* will grow well on limy soils.

The cultivation required includes the selection of an open, warm spot, with a soil rather on the poor, dry side for choice, frequent nipping back when young, and, if possible, shearing back and the removal of seed pods the moment flowering is over. Seeds of the hybrid result in variable progeny but *C. purgans* is reliably true as a rule. Cuttings of side-shoots with a carefully trimmed "heel" can be struck in the sand-box in August with a fair proportion of successes.

The **Lilacs** are very commonly planted, and although they are first-class as "cut flowers", with the leaves removed, they are certainly surpassed by very many other flowering shrubs for garden decoration *as they grow*. Their foliage is hardly beautiful, their habit of growth somewhat unattractive and, except for some of the white varieties such as *Syringa* 'Vestale', the colouring of the flowers is so muddy that it does not show up decoratively in comparison with that of many other species. On the other hand, they have their value for gardens on limy soils or in very bleak and cold districts.

Syringa vulgaris, the Common Lilac, is a deciduous bush from S.E. Europe up to 20 feet high with pale Cyclamen Purple flowers in short, blunt spikes in late April or early May.

Of the single-flowered varieties, the following are worth special mention:—

S. v. 'Etna', wine coloured buds, opening pink.
S. v. 'Hugo Koster', attractive slaty-blue flowers.
S. v. 'Massena', tall, large panicles of wine-purple flowers (A.G.M. 1930).

S. v. 'Maréchal Foch', tall vigorous bush, reddish-purple flowers, well presented.

S. v. 'President Lincoln', light bluish-lilac.

S. v. 'Philemon', reddish-purple.

S. v. 'Réaumur', Petunia Purple, moderate height.

S. v. 'Souvenir de Louis Spæth', deep purple (A.G.M. 1930).

S. v. 'Vestale' (A.G.M. 1931), a fine white of good, bushy habit.

The doubles have several good varieties in:—

S. v. 'Edouard André', the best pink for colour.

S. v. 'Emile Gentil', about the best blue for colour.

S. v. 'Kathleen Havemeyer', a fine pyramidal truss, purplish-lavender.

S. v. 'Mme A. Buchner', a tall, later, red-purple with deeper buds.

S. v. 'Mme Lemoine', white (A.G.M. 1937).

S. v. 'Mrs. E. Harding', pinkish wine colour.

S. v. 'Paul Thirion', lilac-pink, late.

S. v. 'Président Loubet', deep reddish-purple.

S. v. 'Primrose', pale Empire yellow flowers.

For a fuller list of varieties of the Common Lilac see Mr. H. G. Hillier's article cited in footnote†.

S. vulgaris varieties can, if on their own roots, be propagated from suckers, otherwise they may be layered.

The Lilacs are not easily placed in the shrub garden owing to their awkward habit of growth. In too sunny a position "few flowers fade more quickly if exposed to light"† and in shady places growth is sometimes rank and shy-flowering. On the whole a north slope, or a position where the rays of the midday sun are tempered by tall distant trees are the best aspects.

With regard to cultivation, the Lilacs really like a rich soil although they will grow well enough on limy soils in a moderately warm position. Faded flowers should always be removed as soon as possible, to prevent seed formation. If, on the Common Lilac, grafted plants are trouble-some owing to suckers, cuttings or layers are an improvement.

Pruning, apart from cutting flowered branchlets back to the first good wood-buds in late May, follows the lines adopted for Apples, aiming at a strong, shapely tree without overcrowded or intercrossing branches. Scraggy specimens may be sawn down to within 2 feet of the ground in November and regrown.

This shrub is at its finest, perhaps, in Scandinavia, where, budded on Privet, it is carefully trained into an arboreal form and much grown as a street tree. The most attractive individual Lilac I have seen was a

† H. G. Hillier in "Flowering Trees and Shrubs", p. 102, R.H.S. (1938).

specimen of the single-blue-flowered form grown as a tree. To achieve this some authorities hold that the best of all root-stocks is the Common Privet, as then there is no trouble with suckers which will emerge even from Lilacs on their own roots. Unless great care is taken, however, the Lilac grows poorly and the union is unsightly.

Many of the other species and hybrids of the Lilac family are interesting. As they flower later, they are dealt with in the later seasonal sections, pages 171 and 202.

The first section to open, of the large-flowered deciduous hybrid Azaleas, are those generally known as the 'Mollis' Azaleas. Before the last war when good seedlings for naturalising in open woodland spots were obtainable at eighteenpence apiece it was a very valuable acquisition, but the flowers come rather too early to be safe in most gardens and it has a weak strain in its composition. This is because the plant is the offspring of the hardy, tough, smooth, orange-red-flowered *R. japonicum* and the soft, downy, rather tender and "miffy", yellow-flowered *R. molle* (*R. sinense*).

In beauty it is one of the elect of all shrubs, and few flowers of any kind have more rich and lovely colourings. Given its requirements of lime-free, open soil, moist and rich in humus, light shade and shelter from cold winds, shallow planting, a leafy mulch and a site where spring frosts are infrequent, it is a good garden plant provided that it is on its own roots. But grafted plants on high, dry beds, planted 2 or 3 inches too deep, with heavy soil piled over the roots, have dwindled and died by the hundred and the plant has accordingly got a bad name as a shrub for general use.

The Dutch, who know a good plant when they see one, were the first mass-producers of these Azaleas and started in 1880, and they are still sending them all over the world today. The firm of Anthony Koster & Sons of Boskoop were the originators and *Rhododendron Kosterianum* is really the correct name for this group of Azaleas; and furthermore, Messrs. Koster are still producing them. The reason why the soft Chinese species was crossed with *R. japonicum* was, I think, because the former is more responsive to forcing. In North America the Chinese strain makes the hybrid too tender to bear their colder winters, although *R. japonicum* itself does well enough in all but the coldest districts. Even in Britain its superiority as an outdoor shrub is very evident.

In English gardens, favourably situated, the hybrid "Mollises" are a very lovely sight when thoughtfully arranged with bulbs, Welsh Poppies and Forget-me-nots among white-flowered Cherries and Birches. One of the best ways, I find, is simply to plant them out 10 feet apart, each plant in a carefully made circular bed 5 feet in diameter, in thin wood-land. One can then practically forget them and they increase in beauty year by year. At least 60 per cent. of yellow-flowered sorts is essential if the effect is to be really pleasing.

For the open garden, their flowers lack the toughness of those of the Evergreen Azaleas, succumbing quickly to spring north-easters, and as the two kinds do not go very well together it is often best, in the small garden, to have the invaluable evergreen types and to leave out the 'Mollises'. Three other sections of large-flowered rather similar Azaleas—the 'Knap Hills', the 'Occidentales' and the 'Ghents' come into bloom later, when most of the Evergreen kinds are over, and, for a main effect, these offer the average garden far better value than the 'Mollises', in view of late frosts, and provide a better succession.

There are innumerable varieties of the 'Mollises' but care should be taken to insist on "layers", or even seedlings, rather than grafted plants which are apt either to dwindle owing to failure to make the essential new wood or to give endless trouble by suckers of the wild yellow stock. A healthy Azalea grows like a Black Currant—it is perpetu-ally in course of renewing itself from the base. When really suited they make, I note, shoots three feet long terminating in a coronet of flower-buds.

Some outstanding varieties are:—

'Adriaan Koster' ***, deep yellow.
'Koster's Brilliant Red' **, "salmon," (Azalea Pink, H.C.C. 618).
'Floradora' **, orange, late.
'Anthony Koster' *, Cadmium Orange (H.C.C. 8/2).
'Colonel F. R. Durham' *, bright yellow.
'Clara Butt' **, deep pink.
'Mrs. L. J. Endtz' **, clear yellow.
'Mrs. Oliver Slocock' **, orange-yellow, a variety of outstanding
    quality.
'Dr. M. Oosthoek' **, vivid unfading orange-red.
'J. C. van Thol' *, Fire Red (H.C.C. 15/2).
'Spek's Orange', large flowers, orange-red with yellow anthers.
'Marmion' ***, pale yellow, deeper flare.
'Mrs. G. A. van Noordt' **, salmon pink.

* Stars of Merit awarded by the Rhododendron Group of The Royal Horti-cultural Society.

These fine varieties may well form the high spots of groups of cheaper and less richly coloured seedlings with, above all, an ample interplanting of the common yellow R. luteum, moving the plants after a season's flowering, so as to get the best colour grouping. So long as the root-ball is kept intact and moist they do not mind being moved at all, at any age.

There are certain essentials that I believe must be faithfully observed to ensure the well-being of these Azaleas, and I would venture to advise accordingly. In the first place, when planting, do not put *soil above* the ball of roots. The plants merely suffocate if you do. If the soil is sandy and well-drained set them so that the upper surface of the root-ball is about an inch below the soil level and then put only half an inch of light leaf-mould or well-soaked ordinary peat-moss litter on the top of the root-ball. If the soil is clayey, efficient and thorough drainage must be provided, as waterlogging quickly kills the roots. It is desirable to add also a generous dosage of rotted leaf-mould or peat to the soil and mix in well. It is essential to keep the beds mulched with forest leaves at all times. Give such light shade as is afforded by Cherries, etc. growing south of the beds or by light shrubs of friendly growth such as *Genista virgata*, *G. æthnensis*, etc. growing in the beds along with the Azaleas. Well grown plants in light shade do not need to have seed pods removed after flowering, but young ones, or those in very dry and sunny positions, are benefited. Limy soil is not suitable for Azaleas of any kind, of course.

No pruning is needed but when really well grown and on their own roots these Azaleas will send up shoots from the base about 3 feet long and as thick as a fountain pen. If these shoots are gently arched over, and pegged down, or the penultimate 6 inches are buried and the end bent up, flower buds are formed all along the shoots in quite a spectacular manner provided that they are in a fairly open position. To feed well to induce strong basal shoots, and then peg them down, rather than prune growth away, is one of the secrets of good cultivation.

The removal of seed pods *before they swell* is always helpful to growth, as the material otherwise put into these is used, instead, to make stronger shoots for next year's flowers. The benefit is only obtained if the deseeding is done the moment the flowers fade. Care has to be taken not to damage the ring of dormant and sprouting buds immediately below. Varieties differ enormously in the ease with which the work can be done. With some, the stalks are sticky and tough, others are easily snapped off at the right place. For the difficult ones, snipping off the cluster of seeds with secateurs is one of the quickest and easiest methods. One snip for each bunch is usually enough, as, if the stalk is even mutilated, the seed capsule does not swell and exhaust the plant.

An excellent dense-growing, ultra hardy, cheap Rhododendron very pretty with the 'Mollis' Azaleas, as it flowers at the same time, is R. 'Cunningham's White' "A". The flowers are white, with a "flare" of orange at the heart. It is a good wind-resister and can be planted practically anywhere in the lime-free garden provided the soil is made right. It can even be grown from cuttings fairly easily.

Few plantings within our power are more lovely in effect than a well diversified group of 'Mollis' Azaleas, where yellow is carefully kept the dominating colour leading up to an occasional burst of soft flame intensified at a few points by vivid orange reds that are cooled by the old 'Cunningham's White'. Few plantings are more crude and unpleasing than a mere row of one lobster-coloured variety affronting the woodland.

A member of the great **Cornel** family, *Cornus Nuttallii*, flowers, as a rule, towards the end of April. It comes from western North America where it makes a tree reported at sometimes 80 feet high, "so beautiful that it is even spared by the settlers". In this country it usually stops short at about 15 feet even if pruned to tree habit, otherwise it forms a large shrub. The clematis-like flowers, at first yellowish and then white, are formed of about six large petal-like bracts surrounding the central, greenish button which is actually the true flower. This button, incidentally, erupts into a bunch of tiny flowers which resemble minute replicas of the inflorescence. The autumn colour of the leaves is a further adornment but, although the flowers are sometimes 5 inches across, it does not, in my experience, make quite the display of flower of *C. Kousa*, which see under June (page 225). Unlike the latter species and *C. florida*, it does not move well when of any size and I have lost some good specimens when transplanting although the other species mentioned all survived without check. Large plants, also, often die suddenly for no apparent reason. *C. Nuttallii* was introduced by David Douglas about 1826 from seeds, gathered in British Columbia, sent back to the old Horticultural Society of London.

This Cornel will grow on a limy soil, if this is well enriched with leaf-mould. The best plan would be to give the young plant a good start with a few barrowloads of turf loam, with which some of the natural soil should be mixed, otherwise it will probably be very slow to get going in the chalk.

A lovely little tree, about 20 feet high, flowering in April is *Amelanchier canadensis*, (A.G.M. 1927). It is sometimes called the "Snowy Mespilus". This English name is also occasionally used for the less attractive *A. vulgaris*. *A. canadensis* is snowy indeed when sheeted with its white blossom which makes a lovely, if short-lived, display among the pinkish, expanding leaves. In autumn the foliage turns to a rich red or yellow and thus the tree gives a double dividend very acceptable in the small garden. It is quite hardy and not particular as to soil though it prefers the acid greensand districts where it seeds itself freely and has even become naturalised. It was introduced about the middle of the eighteenth century. There are a number of other species of Amelanchier but they are, on the whole, of inferior decorative value. The less attractive *A. lævis* is sometimes confused with it, but may be distinguished by the young leaves being quite smooth, not downy on both sides, as in the more decorative species.

Of all the flowering trees of early spring the Cherries, and most particularly the Oriental varieties grouped under **Prunus serrulata** are the most spectacularly beautiful. Though their soft rose or white tones are charming in the vernal landscape, this beauty is one of form rather than of colour—it is the exquisite, delicate design of the massed flowers and the picturesque habit of the trees that appeals to us most strongly.

In dealing with my suggestions for the best associations for the choicer Cherries I am grouping them roughly into sections, as nearly as possible in flowering order. These sections, of course, merge into one another and there are times when one or another variety will flower unusually early or late, but the system forms none the less a useful rough guide for group planting.

I have followed the names used in Major Collingwood Ingram's *Ornamental Cherries* (*Country Life*, 1948).

One of the loveliest in form, of the double-flowered kinds, is *Prunus serrulata* 'Hokusai'. So graceful is the habit of the blossoming sprays contrasted with the dark branches, so exquisite the shape of each individual flower that even very young specimens are highly decorative, but in its maturer years it makes a splendid round-topped tree particularly healthful and long-lived. The colour, however, is such a pale blush-pink that it appears rather washed-out as a landscape effect. 'Hokusai' is therefore best planted where its charm of detail can be enjoyed at close range rather than as a park tree.

P. s. 'Shirotæ' (also known as 'Mt. Fuji' or 'Kojima') has an altogether different habit, being inclined to be low and sprawling, and it is by nature rather soft. If left to its own devices it forms a huge rounded bush rather than a tree. Provided ground space is available this is not a disadvantage and the great mass of its large single or semi-double white flowers turn such a specimen into a mound of snow at blossoming time which will be one of the finest sights in any garden. It is not always long-lived, not having a very strong constitution and I have sometimes lost a specimen from no ascertainable cause.

Another distinct Cherry of high garden value is *P. s.* 'Takasago' (also known as *Sieboldii, pubescens*, etc.). It does not make a tall tree, seldom exceeding 20 feet and is easily distinguished by its downy young leaves. The variety *Watereri* is particularly floriferous and markedly superior to the ordinary form which is slower in growth and rather shy-flowering, though the usual cause of this state of affairs is simply bullfinches destroying the flower buds. The blossoms are pink and mostly semi-double, the young leaves appearing at the same time being of a reddish bronze. E. H. Wilson stated that this variety will root from cuttings and as it flowers when quite small this method of increase should be worth trying.

The true *P. s.* 'Hisakura' is a rare and rather delicate Cherry with small, single, pink flowers opening among reddish-copper young leaves—a delightful combination.

P. s. 'Yedo sakura' (*P. s. nobilis*) is a very slow-growing, but highly decorative, variety with clusters of pale pink, double flowers that often open before the leaves appear. These slow growers are usually worth waiting for and the best way to hustle them is to grow them in top-spit meadow loam and to pinch off their flower buds before they open.

One of the next varieties to flower is *P. s.* 'Mikuruma-gæshi'. It is of notably graceful, upstanding port with the compact, single, pale-pink flowers thickly clustered all along the stems. About the same time *P. s.* 'Ariake', of stiffer, more restricted growth, will open its large single white blooms.

April is now drawing to a close in our calendar of Cherry blossom and the coppery-pink buds of the slow-growing *P. s.* 'Horinji' are so attractive contrasted with the dark calices among the red bracts and rufous-bronze young leaves that one feels that even the semi-double flowers that will follow could not surpass them. When they open we shall not be disappointed and the last section of the Cherries to flower will have begun. They will be described in our next chapter and there, too, will be given cultural directions.

The time when April ends and May begins is so busy with promising buds and opening flowers and so unusually sensitive to the particular complexion of the weather, that ordains an early or a late season, that it is difficult to draw a demarcation line. The other months of the flowering season are much more readily separated.

In most gardens this is the time of greatest danger from frost damage. All too often a promising mild spell followed by a sudden hard frost ruins opening flowers and tender growths. This is so discouraging as to spoil much of our pleasure in the garden. It is therefore very important to study carefully how we may best avoid such disappointments.

Air drainage, tree canopy and nearness to the sea are absolutely decisive advantages but backward sites that discourage too early a start in growth also play a part and backward districts where spring warmth comes late have good points that may be exploited. For every garden it is a different problem and sometimes the factors are so involved that only trial and error can provide the solution.

More often than not, many of the April flowerers escape; it is the May bloomers that suffer most. Hence this chapter is a more bulky one than the following.

CHAPTER IV

MAY

MAY

WHEN the early spring flowerers are over, the plants that bloom in the second flowering period are ready to take over the display, provided that they escape a treacherous late frost.

In this period of the flowering season the largest number of particularly beautiful shrubs are in bloom. Consequently if our gardens are to be equally attractive later on, as they easily may be if we so wish and are ready to take the trouble to plant for that part of the season, we must exercise restraint in the numbers of May flowerers that we plant. Thus we have to be more selective than ever to pick out only the finest possible for our own particular garden conditions.

For acid-soiled or neutral-soiled gardens the claims of the Evergreen Azaleas and the Rhododendrons are again very strong this month, owing to their effective flowering coupled with all-the-year-round decorative value, but we must be vigilant to avoid excessive concentrations of these fine things that, unrelieved by other growth, lose most of their charm and beauty in the landscape.

In limy-soiled gardens we have a choice of dwarf Brooms and Genistas, Daphnes, Choisya, Rouen Lilacs, hybrid Tree Peonies, Ceanothus, Viburnums, Spiræas and the Burnet Roses and allied kinds, assisted by many of the Berberis and the Chænomeles, Periwinkles and Kerria that, although they begin in April, will usually carry on well into the middle of May.

In the last chapter we left April with **Japanese Cherries** in flower and there are more to come this month. Forerunners among these will be the daintily shaped, even, blush-pink rosettes of *Prunus serrulata* 'Ichiyo', each becomingly decorated with one or two tiny green leaves in the centre. Like the earlier-flowering 'Hokusai', this is a Cherry which appeals more for its perfection of drawing when seen near at hand than for its form and colour in the distant landscape. It is free-flowering and elegant to a degree and makes an excellent, healthful, upright-spreading specimen where it can be admired at close range.

P. s. 'Ama-no-gawa' (A.G.M. 1931), being so closely upright in habit as almost to constitute a fastigiate form of the Japanese Cherry, is invaluable in small gardens and confined spaces. The semi-single, blush-pink flowers, borne in clusters, solidly massed, are finely shaped and most agreeably scented. It must, however, be nipped and pinched-back continually in the early stages and annually pruned back in late May at the top, and also regularly sprayed with a fungicide such as "Bouisol" to control the fungus that otherwise destroys the invaluable lower wood-buds. Unless this treatment is religiously carried out it is apt to make a thin, gaunt, awkward-looking, besom-shaped tree instead of the rosy cylinder of outwardly facing blossom which it is our aim to produce. As their achievement requires considerable trouble, such perfect specimens are all too rare.

The original oriental Cherry (*Prunus serrulata*) is a Chinese garden variety which, unfortunately for botanical seemliness, has to stand as the "type" form of the Japanese Cherries owing to being the first to be introduced. It is absolutely the opposite of 'Ama-no-gawa' in appearance, forming a low, wide-spreading tree of the highly picturesque heaviness characteristic of many Chinese garden plants as opposed to the more delicate grace and extreme refinement characteristic of Japanese plants. Obviously this Cherry requires a good deal of space, but the singular architecture of the tree and the profusion of the small, double, white blossoms give it a very high decorative value in the landscape. There are superb specimens at Kew and in many old gardens.

The valuable *double-flowered* form of our native Gean, *P. avium plena* (A.G.M. 1924), flowers at about the same time, considerably later than the wild, single-flowered type, making a stronger, taller tree than any of the Japanese varieties usually do in our climate. It is thus particularly useful as a shade tree, and in some seasons its autumn colour rivals that of Sargent's Cherry. A sub-variety *P. a. grandiflora* exhibited by Messrs. Waterer Sons & Crisp is a particularly fine form.

At this time we may expect the single white blossoms of *P. s.* 'Jo-nioi' and, though the tree is a sturdy and shapely one of very free-flowering habit, it is valued still more for the delicious fragrance of its flowers than for their appearance. A good form of this variety will perfume the air for a considerable distance around, and the scent is always delicate and attractive, never becoming heavy or oppressive.

P. s. 'Ukon' (also known as var. *grandiflora*), the best known of the yellow Cherries, will be out when May is well under way. At first sight it is often rather a disappointing Cherry, for the fact must be faced that it is a very pale, and even rather a greenish yellow. Then, again, it is only when the tree has reached a certain size that it makes any effect at all, and a dark background is particularly essential. Given these requirements the planter's patience is well rewarded in the end. As regards a complementary planting, we can pick up the yellow tone a little more vividly with an early pale yellow Broom, such as *Cytisus præcox*, and then intensify it by contrast with the blue-lavender of one

of the little alpine Rhododendrons or a blue form of the larger-growing
R. campanulatum, if only we can make that shy plant flower freely.

P. s. 'Pink Perfection' is a lovely double pink-flowered Cherry bred
by Messrs. Waterer, Sons & Crisp in 1935. It is very free-flowering and
a valuable addition to the Japanese varieties.

P. s. 'Ojochin' bears white, single flowers with a darker centre and
such outstandingly attractive "drawing" that this makes its portrait
in "Ornamental Cherries" the most pleasing of all in a delightful
selection. The form grown at the R.H.S. gardens at Wisley seems to me
to be a particularly fine one, though the tree in question is not in a
sufficiently open position to show itself to advantage.

We are now nearing the end of the Cherry time but a number of very
choice late varieties are still to come. Of these, P. s. 'Kirin' is a notably
magnificent Cherry of the very front rank. In sunlight the flowers are
apparently of a rich and beautiful pink (though actually of the palest
tint of Magenta) very double but more finely formed, if not quite so
deep in colour *when on the tree*, as those of the better-known P. s.
'Kanzan'. They are borne more evenly along the branches rather than
in dense clusters.

'Kanzan', or 'Sekiyama' (A.G.M. 1930) for so long confused with
'Hisakura', is almost too well known to require description, for it is
the most commonly planted of all the Japanese varieties as a street
tree. It is a fine vigorous Cherry with the richest coloured flowers of
any of these owing to the fact that the delightful coppery young foliage
casts a warm glow on their pale Magenta tint. 'Kanzan' also often
provides a particularly fine autumn leaf colour. If it has a fault it is
that the individual flowers rather lack form and that when top-grafted
standard-high it is not an attractively shaped tree for a good many
years, being of an inverted-pyramid shape, until the crown has filled
out laterally. On the other hand, when grafted or budded low down
it is one of the best for landscape effect and with 'Jo-nioi', 'Shimidsu'
and 'Shirofugen' to provide the white which is so helpful in enhancing
the vividness of the purplish pink colouring, we can contrive a very
rich and harmonious grouping.

As 'Kanzan' fades, one of the last, but certainly one of the loveliest
of all the Japanese varieties, opens. This is the Cherry for long grown in
England as P. s. 'Oku-miyako' or var. *longipes*, and in America as
'Sho-get-su'. Now its name is changed to 'Shimidsu' ("The Gardeners'
Chronicle", 1941, p. 240). It received the Award of Garden Merit in
1933, and has a good constitution, but is not a fast grower unless too
shaded to flower freely, the habit being dwarf and spreading yet rather
dense. It is easily recognised by the long stalks on which hang the daisy-
like, double white flowers. It is an exceedingly floriferous variety, indeed,

so much so as to limit its growth, and is of the highest decorative value, even in early youth. 'Shimidsu' groups well, being white in colour, with almost any of the other shrubs in bloom at the same time, such as the 'Knap Hill' Azaleas with their yellow, orange and pink tones, or the blue of *Ceanothus Veitchii*.

About the same time *P. s.* 'Fugenzo' ("J. H. Veitch") will be in flower; it is one of the oldest varieties and almost as commonly planted as 'Kanzan'. It is a compact, sturdy tree of rounded form, best grown as a lawn specimen in an open situation. The double flowers are of a pale magenta pink that is not very clean in tone; they last well on the tree, however, and are attractively formed with a nice open centre from which project two green leafy carpels. This Cherry is not, in my experience, satisfactory in a rich soil in a sheltered situation as it then runs to leaf and shoot growth.

Last of all comes 'Shirofugen' (sometimes known as *albo-rosea*); it is a strong and rapid grower, and easily outstripped all the other varieties of equal age except 'Tai Haku' and 'Yoshino' which I planted at the same time. Such rapid growth in the early stages usually means that flowering will be somewhat deferred and 'Shirofugen' has to reach a fair size before it flowers really freely. Once well started it is very reliably free with its faintly blushed blossom which turns white when fully expanded, to blush again before it falls. It has the coppery young foliage which is an added attraction to so many of the Japanese Cherries and makes a wide-spreading stately specimen which provides a fitting "finale" to the season. It is one of the varieties which are quite attractive when top-grafted on a strong pole of the wild Gean as its chief beauty is seen when looking up at the pendent blossoms from below.

A late-flowering Cherry whose beauty has much impressed me is the variety 'Morello' of *Prunus Cerasus* whose fruit is so delicious as jam, or in that delicious confection "Kirschkuchen". When it is grown as an open-ground tree the habit is good, the abundant white blossom quite delightful, and the ensuing red fruits are both decorative and valuable. The double-flowered variety *P. c. Rhexii*, on the other hand is, in my experience, not half so decorative and is doubtfully worth growing, as the congested little flowers are more sparsely borne and do not show up well. *P. c. semperflorens* is also inferior, merely producing odd racemes during the summer.

As to soil, the Cherries seem to prefer a good fibrous turf-loam though they also do well both on limy soils and the acid peaty green-sands. They are more exacting as to position, insisting on one that is open and sunny. Strong winds spoil the blossom all too quickly, it is true, and it is here that the Pines, recommended for background and

Lithospermum diffusum 'Grace Ward'

Rhododendron Kæmpferi

Daphne retusa

Cornus Nuttallii

contrast, may perform a third useful function by affording shelter from the north and the south-west.

Cherries may be increased by grafting or budding as described in the chapter dealing with Propagation (p. 35). A complete spraying programme, as for Apples, is really very beneficial to them. In this country aged Cherries often die from fungus attack and are debilitated by lichen. In Japan, small boys whose naked feet do not damage the tender bark, are sent aloft every year to scrub off the lichens and attend to any wounds caused by the wind and thus their Cherries live to a great age and attain a picturesque beauty of the highest order.

Of the later flowering **Crabs,** the American *Malus ioensis plena* with its large double, delightfully scented pale pink flowers, though perfectly hardy, is unfortunately a wretched grower in most parts of this country and a martyr to caterpillar attack and "dieback".

M. baccata mandschurica, on the other hand, is a strong tree and its violet-scented white blossom is very welcome in late May. Its habit is, however, apt to be rather ragged and it requires both winter and summer spraying and also pruning and feeding if it is to look its best. With these attentions its red and yellow fruits, larger than those of the ordinary Siberian Crab, will also make quite a display in late summer.

I have found no way of satisfying the American without endless trouble, but the Manchurian repays an open sunny position and a well drained soil, whether limy, acid, or neutral in an admirable manner.

Rubus deliciosus should really do duty here for the whole Bramble family, for if one of them is worth growing it is certainly this species. Its dry and tasteless fruits could hardly be called delicious, unless so steeped in choice liqueurs as to function merely as a texture. Its wild-rose-like flowers, of purest white, so profusely borne among the black-currant-like leaves as to make quite a splash, are a couple of inches across, five-petalled and glamorously presented. It comes from the Rocky Mountains whence it was introduced in 1870. The difficulty of propagating it has, however, kept it scarce ever since. Furthermore the best-flowered form is even more troublesome to root, even from layers, than the commoner one which has smaller flowers.

A sunny spot with sandy, or at least loamy, soil is needed and the older branches will require removal at ground-level occasionally to keep the plant youthful and vigorous.

R. spectabilis, a thin, erect, 2- or 3-foot shrub with Magenta flowers from late April onwards, will grow anywhere on any soil and

9

may be used to fill odd corners. But the cost of buying a first-class shrub is so little more than that of a second-rater that it does not pay to *buy* any but the best. As it suckers freely this is one of the shrubs that the gardener is particularly likely to be given and it is only mentioned here for that reason.

Let us now examine the **Exochordas,** a genus of tall, deciduous, white-flowered shrubs from northern Asia, distantly related to the Spiræas.

Exochorda racemosa (*E. grandiflora*) grows eventually to 10 feet or more in height, with many stems springing from the ground. The five-petalled pure white flowers, about $1\frac{1}{2}$ inches across, appear in May on short, upright racemes at the ends of the branches of the previous year. It is a beautiful shrub in flower but its habit is not decorative in winter.

E. Giraldi Wilsonii resembles the preceding but the flowers are larger, if slightly less numerous. It seems to require a warmer spot and greater care than *E. racemosa*.

E. Korolkowi (*E. Albertii*) (A.G.M. 1933) is an upright, 12-foot bush with inch-wide, white flowers less freely produced than those of *E. racemosa*. It is, however, a very robust and hardy species. The finest form is *E. K.* var. *Wilsonii*.

E. macrantha (*E. Korolkowi* × *racemosa*) is a fine hybrid raised by Messrs. V. Lemoine of Nancy at the beginning of this century. In freedom of flower this is the finest of the family. The white is a singularly pure one and the racemes of about eight flowers are so numerous that it is very effective in early May.

The Exochordas are hardy and indifferent as to whether the soil is limy or acid. A sunny, open position suits them best. After flowering the flowered twigs may be cut back and, if the stems are very densely set, some thinning may be done by removing old or weak ones.

Cuttings do not root very readily. Seeds are a good method of increase.

Let us turn now from these plants that are suitable for limy soils to a section of great beauty that will only grow on acid soils. Fortunately the greater acreage of the soil of Britain is acid, but unfortunately many gardeners, misled by directions to apply lime as though it were a universal fertiliser, have gravely damaged the soil of their ornamental gardens. Originally the practice arose as a means of correcting the over-manuring of kitchen gardens. Gradually it came to be a stock directive; the ridiculous phrase "lime-deficient" was used for any soils not definitely limy, as though there was something wrong with Nature's acid soil that had to be put right by man to make it fertile. This may be desirable for the purpose of growing coarse fodder-grasses or certain peculiarly constituted lime-loving vegetables, but it is a complete fallacy so far as ornamental plants, trees and shrubs are concerned. By liming acid soil, the essential minerals are rendered unavailable to the plants so that many of the finest genera cannot grow at all. Among these are the Rhododendrons.

Rhododendron yunnanense "B" ****, is one of the few pure **Rhododendron species** of the medium-sized sorts that appears to be admirably adapted for gardens just as it is. It is a shapely, slender-twigged bush with small leaves and delightful masses of Azalea-like white flowers, orange-throated or spotted with red, towards the end of May. It is a treasure that no reasonably favourable lime-free garden will wish to do without. It comes from 9,000-foot elevations in Yunnan. In hard winters it loses many of its leaves and if too much shaded and not pruned back when young is sometimes rather thin in habit. Otherwise it is difficult to find fault with it. The flower colour of seedlings is variable and some are of a purplish-pink which is not pleasing; others, and these should be selected, have white flowers with an orange flare on the upper lobe (A.G.M. 1934).

R. yunnanense, like all its family, insists upon an acid soil rich in humus. It may be propagated by seed, cuttings or layers. I think the most perfect position is when this lovely bush is sited as a lawn specimen in a sheltered but not overshaded spot. In flower it will hold the stage against all competitors and, unlike most wild species, may be considered as an ordinary garden plant for general use.

Specially favoured gardens, that is to say, those that have an acid soil rich in humus, trees to afford light shade and sufficient relative elevation (see Katabatics, p. 25) to avoid the worst spring frosts, may grow certain other Rhododendron species of supreme year-round beauty. Some of these flower in April and some not until June or July, but, as early May is the peak flowering time of this section and also because their culture is rather a thing apart from ordinary gardening, they are grouped here for convenience.

"A" means "Hardy anywhere in the British Isles".

"B" means "Hardy anywhere in the British Isles but requires some shade to attain best results".

"C" means "Hardy along the seaboard and in favourable gardens inland".

The stars indicate relative merit adjudged by the Rhododendron
Group of the R.H.S.

R. apodectum "A" *** is a relative of *R. dichroanthum* with dull
orange or red flowers in June; in an open position it makes a bush of
about 4 feet.

R. Augustinii "C" **** This exquisite species is evaluated by the
degree of blueness of its flowers. The bluest I have seen were of the
lovely, violet-blue known as Aster Violet (H.C.C. 38/2). Most forms
are nearer violet. It is not very attractive as an evergreen when out of
flower and needs a sheltered and favourable spot. In time it may reach
10 feet, each way, and it flowers in early May. A good form is one of the
most spectacularly beautiful of all shrubs, when in bloom (A.G.M. 1924).

R. chasmanthum "C" **** is very similar.

R. campylocarpum "B" ****, in the type form but later makes a
fairly dense bush usually about 4 or 5 feet high in the open. It is generally
considered one of the best yellow-flowered Rhododendrons, but the
colour, which I estimate to be Dresden Yellow (H.C.C. 64/2) is not very
brilliant compared with that of a good yellow Azalea and the flowers
are not very well presented. The variety *elatum* is quite distinct and has
pink buds and a warmer but paler flower colour. The bush is taller
and looser and the flowers are well presented and have a red centre.
Grown near R. 'Blue Diamond' the colour combination is a special
delight. This variety also differs from the type in being quite happy in a
comparatively open, sunny position, and the flowers last well.

R. cinnabarinum "B" **** has blue-green leaves and dull red, clear
rosy red, or yellow, tubular bell-shaped flowers. Its habit is rather thin
and upright at first. Var. *æstivale* is specially valuable as, unlike the
type, which flowers in late May, it flowers in July. Var Blandfordiæ-
florum is a fine form with large Poppy-red (H.C.C. 16/2) flowers.

R. concatenans "C" *** has bell-shaped apricot flowers in early
May and beautiful blue-green foliage but requires care.

R. decorum "C" ** has exquisitely shaped, fragrant seven-lobed
white flowers in May and sea-green foliage. It seeds itself so freely and
stands full exposure so well that I mention it here although it is not so
exciting as others. There are tender forms that are useless.

R. dichroanthum "B" *** has been described elsewhere in this work
(p. 185). A further feature of this curious plant is that it strikes from
cuttings and thus certain specialist nurseries are able to supply the finest
orange-flowered forms on their own roots.

R. didymum "B" ** is a 3-foot bush with black-crimson flowers in
late June. It is a good "doer" but needs side or back lighting to illumine
its dark flowers.

R. discolor "B" ***. This is a big bush with large, fragile, scented, seven-lobed, white flowers with a red centre in July. Some forms are able to stand the severest cold if grown in a sunnier place than one would choose for most other Rhododendrons. My private hardiness-rating would be category "A". See also under July, p. 280.

R. fictolacteum "B" ***. The massive foliage is superb, deep sage green and vividly russet-felted beneath, and the white, dark-eyed flowers in April or early May are very attractive. Care must be taken to get a good, large-flowered, bud-hardy form. There are bud-tender, useless forms. It is a tall shrub or small tree growing up to 30 feet ultimately.

R. Griersonianum "D" **** has been described elsewhere in the work (p. 206). I find that it really grows best in full exposure without any shelter whatever. Under such conditions it is almost category "A" in the south provided that Katabatics are good, (see p. 26). But it is useless except as a tub-plant in low-lying places.

R. hæmatodes "B" **** is a small, wide bush of about 3 feet with brilliant scarlet-crimson flowers in May. Although slow to flower, it is a treasure worth waiting for.

R. lacteum "C" ****. This, the finest yellow Rhododendron, is slow-growing and difficult, very variable in quality and flowers dangerously early, in April, but a good form is a noble and massive plant of fascinating individuality. (See illustration facing p. 49). It is one of the few Rhododendrons that apparently grow better when root-grafted on *R. ponticum* than when on their own roots. Thus grown there is no danger of suckers from the stock and the deadly Honey Fungus which often attacks *R. lacteum* may more easily be avoided.

R. neriiflorum "C" **** is a small neat bush of about 4 feet as a rule, with white-undersurfaced leaves and scarlet-red flowers in April.

R. orbiculare "B" **** is a dense bush with round leaves and large, delightfully shapely but nodding, purplish-pink, campanula-like flowers in April.

R. rubiginosum "A" ***, a small tree completely covering itself with purplish-pink flowers in May, will grow almost anywhere and has a most attractive habit. It would be a most valuable Rhododendron if a form with flowers of more attractive colouring could be obtained.

R. Thomsonii "B" ****. This beautiful bush with rounded blue-green leaves that make it highly decorative at all times, has superb, long-lasting, waxy, blood-red flowers in April and early May. In an open position it forms a dense shrub about 6 feet high but if drawn up by nearby forest trees may make a tree of 15 to 20 feet (A.G.M. 1925).

R. Wardii "C" *** is a shrub up to about 15 feet with exquisite saucer-shaped clear yellow flowers in May, beautifully presented on a shapely bush. It is also the parent of many lovely hybrids.

R. yakusimanum is a superb new species. When it becomes available and if it proves hardy it will be of the highest value. It is a dense, low bush with spoon-shaped leaves felted below and delightful trusses of pink buds opening to shapely white, wide-open, bell flowers in amazing profusion.

The above twenty species are a selection out of over seven hundred grown in this country. They are chosen for their distinction, their effectiveness and their strongly marked individuality and charm. The woodland, rather than the garden, is really their proper home. They can be grown in a suitable piece of woodland with far less labour than that required to grow any plant in the open garden, *provided that they are originally installed with the full specification laid down for this genus.* There is no gardening adventure that I know more pleasurable than to be able to plant these delightful things as specimens in a little woodland corner. Once the planting is faithfully done there is no drudgery and all is enjoyment. Unfortunately few of us have the opportunity, but this treatise, limited as it is, would have been incomplete if I had entirely missed out this fascinating by-way of horticulture. Further suggestions for the late summer effects for such a venture will be found under *Hydrangea serrata* and in that section (pp. 305 and 309).

There are a few large, fairly hardy, hybrid Rhododendrons with yellow flowers, but unfortunately many of these are hardly robust enough for the wind and the sun of the ordinary open garden, being either category "B" or "C". Where, however, there is light shade, good shelter from wind and, of course, a lime-free soil, some of these may be grown. It must be admitted that, compared with the Azaleas, the yellow is often rather a pale, greenish-sulphury tint of no very great decorative value in the landscape. As *R. campylocarpum* ("B" or "C", Thomsonii series, usually flowering in April) figures largely in the parentage of the majority, they are for the most part rather early flowerers, which adds to the difficulty of growing them really well.

A selection of those obtainable follows:—

'Astarte' "B" *, pale apricot; (*R. dichroanthum* × 'Penjerrick').

'Buttercup' "B" **, pale yellow.

'Butterfly' "B" *** ('Mrs. Milner' × *R. campylocarpum*), very pale lemon, brown eye.

'Canary' "C" ('Cunningham's Sulphur × *R. campylocarpum*), bright yellow, a vivid colour but a poor flower often not opening fully, and an ungainly habit.

'Citronella' "B" * (*R. campylocarpum* × *kewense*), quite a bright primrose, red eye.

'Cunningham's Sulphur' "B", very pale yellow, said to be a

form of *R. caucasicum*, but not an easy Rhododendron to grow well.

'Dairymaid' "B" ***, very pale lemon, flushed pink, of very good, sturdy habit and very free flowering.

'Devonshire Cream' "B" *, very pale yellow, red eye, very pretty and of good compact habit.

'Diane', palest sulphur yellow, hardy but addicted to "fly".

'Fabia' "B" *** (*R. dichroanthum* × *Griersonianum*), orange salmon, is very fine indeed, but still scarce and expensive. It is worthy of every care. Var. 'Tangerine' is vermilion.

'Goldfort' "B" ***, pale creamy yellow.

'Goldsworth Orange' "A" ***, Maize Yellow (H.C.C. 607/1), a fine Rhododendron. My private rating is "C".

'Goldsworth Yellow' "B" (*R. caucasicum* × *campylocarpum*), pale Empire Yellow, spotted with green and bronze, rather a straggling habit.

'Hawk' (*R. Wardii* × 'Lady Bessborough') "C", a lovely yellow, requiring a moist, sheltered, shady position and really a wood-garden plant.

'Lady Bessborough' "B" **** (*R. discolor* × *campylocarpum*), very pale yellow.

'Lady Primrose' "B" ***, pale lemon, red spots.

'Letty Edwards' "B" *** (*R. Fortunei* × *campylocarpum*), very pale sulphur yellow, a better grower than most and has more attractive foliage, but needs protection from wind. Very lovely.

'Margaret Bean' "B" **, pale yellow, blushed pink.

'Mrs. Ashley Slocock' "B" **, pale cream, suffused apricot.

'Mrs. W. C. Slocock' "B" ***, pale apricot pink, shaded yellow.

'Penjerrick' "C" **** (*R. campylocarpum* × *Griffithianum*), creamy yellow in best forms, very shapely flowers. One of the loveliest of all Rhododendrons in a wood, and much more beautiful than 'Mrs. Kingsmill' or 'Mrs. R. Davidson' of similar parentage.

'Queen Souriya' "B" * (*R. Fortunei* × *campylocarpum*), pale ochre, mauve edge, shapely flowers.

'Souvenir of W. C. Slocock' "B" ***, Maize Yellow (H.C.C. 607/3), fading to pale yellow, larger truss and slightly later than most.

'Unique' "B" **** (Slocock's form), very pale yellow, orange-pink buds, a very good, compact habit.

'Unique' "B" ** (Wallace's form), pale orange fading to buff, attractive in colour.

'Zuyder Zee' "B" ** (R. 'Mrs. Lindsay Smith' × *campylocarpum*), pale lemon yellow, red spots.

In addition to the positional requirements previously mentioned, the soil should be well enriched with peat or leaf-mould and these Rhododendrons should be kept mulched with fallen leaves over the whole area beneath their branches. They grow so much better in a wood-garden that, on the whole, I would advise growing them in that way, keeping to the "A" class hardy hybrids for the ordinary open garden. Those who do not mind taking a chance on a long-term venture may plant selected, small, low, bushy plants in more exposed places, but shade is desirable in the south-eastern part of the country to prevent scorching of the foliage and bleaching of the delicate flower colours. Both the 'Uniques', 'Dairymaid', 'Goldsworth Orange' and 'Goldsworth Yellow' are particularly suitable for such an experiment.

All these *campylocarpum* hybrids appear to be rather susceptible to attacks by the Rhododendron Fly and, if the pest is seen, need spraying carefully so as to drench the undersides of the leaves several times in early summer wherever the plants are not shaded. Shade generally prevents the "fly" causing much trouble as it seems unable to multiply under these conditions.

Two attractive hybrids that make a charming association with a pale yellow variety such as 'Dairymaid', are 'Mount Everest' "B" **, a sturdy bush with shapely, cupped, white flowers, and 'Susan' "B" *** an Amethyst Violet flowering at the same time. A sheltered but fairly open position shaded by large trees is, I think, the ideal for this type of Rhododendron as they then form shapely and dense bushes well set with flowers, as at Wisley, on Battleston Hill.

I would never advise the making of Rhododendron beds where the larger sorts are herded together by themselves. Culturally it is unnecessary. Æsthetically it is bad because the ultimate result is a dank, gloomy cavern whose outer roof is decorated by largely invisible flowers. The intervening stage is not attractive, either, because Rhododendron foliage demands association with the more vivid leaves and later flowers of deciduous trees and shrubs. Plant Rhododendrons, then, as single specimens grouped among less valuable and less permanent shrubs and all the centuries of their lives they will be rounded, beautiful bushes furnished evenly to the ground. No gloomy groves will make dull the late summer scene. "What is that lovely thing?—Oh, I do believe it's a Rhododendron!" should be the comment evoked, rather than the usual perfunctory response to an overpowering concentration.

To do proper justice to the limy garden and also to mark my insistence that the different sections of the Rhododendron family are as distinct, from the garden angle, as if they were members of different genera, we break off to examine a plant of very different character.

An early-flowering evergreen climber, introduced by E. H. Wilson from China in 1900 is *Clematis Armandi* (A.G.M. 1938). The fragrant white flowers, produced in clusters in the axils of the leaves, are 2½ inches across in the best forms. There are, however, many poor seedling forms about, whose flowers are small and dingy. There is also a very pretty variety, 'Apple Blossom' with pink flowers. In warm gardens this Clematis may be grown on a tree stump or a tripod of poles with delightful effect, but in most places a warm wall is desirable. Plants are reported 30 feet high on suitable walls where the soil, either loamy or acid, is moist and rich, but well drained. No pruning is desirable except for the removal of dead wood. Seeds germinate readily, but there is great variation in the value of the seedlings, so the best forms should be propagated from cuttings. Like many climbers, *C. Armandi* tends to become bare at the base, and it is therefore a good plan to train the young growths out sideways at the start, and to take the opportunity of tying out, similarly, any subsequent young shoot that may appear.

There are several charming **wild Azalea species** that flower, as a rule, towards the end of April and in early May. For convenience I group them here.

Rhododendron Albrechti "B" ****, forms a twiggy bush 3 or 4 feet high with 2-inch-wide exquisitely shaped Fuchsine Pink (H.C.C. 627/1) flowers that open in April or early May before the leaves. It comes from Japan where it grows in woodland on steep slopes and was introduced by Professor Sargent of the Arnold Arboretum and later by E. H. Wilson.

R. Schlippenbachii "C" **** (F.C.C. 1944), is perhaps more attractive than the previous species. It is a taller shrub, said to be up to 15 feet high in its native Korean hills where it is extraordinarily abundant, giving, according to E. H. Wilson, "miles and miles of the purest pink from the millions of flowers of this Azalea". The fragrant flowers (Rhodamine Pink, H.C.C. 527/2) are borne in April in clusters of about five and open before or with the large, heart-shaped leaves. There are good and bad forms, some of the worst being very weak in colour. The plant was first introduced by J. H. Veitch in 1893 from a Japanese garden. It is hardy at the Arnold Arboretum, Boston, Mass., and may therefore be considered quite hardy in Britain so far as cold is concerned, but a moist, lime-free soil, rich in humus, and light shade with shelter from wind, appear to be necessary for the well-being of this lovely plant over here. The autumn leaf colour is very fine and so two pleasing effects are provided.

R. pentaphyllum "C" ****, is a large bush, 6 to 12 feet high in the hanging woods of Nikko where Wilson, who surely saw more flowers than any man before or since, said: "I shall never forget the charm of that splash of lovely colour among the leafless plants of a well-wooded, steep slope". The leaves are in whorls of five at the end of the branchlets, hence the name, and turn to gorgeous tints in autumn. The solitary, or paired, flowers are pure rose pink, unspotted and about 2 inches across, opening April–May. It is rather a difficult plant requiring specially favourable conditions.

R. reticulatum "A" ***, on the other hand, is hardy and easy-going by comparison, and as abundant as the previous species is rare. The flowers are a magenta or purplish-pink colour and appear before the leaves.

R. Vaseyi "B" **** (A.G.M. 1927), is notably beautiful and usually flowers a little later in May. The flowers, of the exquisite finish typical of these Azaleas, are smaller and of a pure pale pink, or nearly white, and open before the leaves. In habit, *R. Vaseyi* is rather upright, growing up eventually to 12 feet or more. Light shade, and well mulched, moist soil with plenty of humus are required to grow it well.

The best place for these Azaleas is really the wood-garden where their individual charm is displayed to the full when in flower, and their bare brown stems melt into the prevailing brushwood in winter. For the open garden the more richly coloured and reliable 'Knap Hill' and 'Ghent' hybrids, flowering later, are much more satisfactory.

China and Australasia have been fairly thoroughly explored by our plant-hunters though more "finds" may possibly yet be made. Japan and North and South America, to our certain knowledge contain considerable numbers of absolutely first-class hardy flowering shrubs, not to mention many herbs, which we lack. Among these several of the most glorious of the known Azaleas are prominent. Unlike the oriental species mentioned, many of the Americans have really good colourings —vivid blood-reds, oranges and yellows instead of purplish-pinks, and, furthermore, several come into bloom at critical periods of the flower sequence of the garden year when such superb colours are particularly desirable. In the hope that the required importations may be made ere long I give below brief particulars of some of these:—

Rhododendron alabamense, a hardy, May-flowering Azalea species with fragrant white flowers, is in commerce here in the "type" form. Some more desirable varieties are, however, described as having apricot-coloured flowers† and these would be a great acquisition to our gardens.

† Mrs. J. Norman Henry, *R.H.S. Journal*, LXII Pt. 10, p. 388.

R. atlanticum var. A hardy dwarf form of this species, a foot high, with rose-scented white flowers in late May, grey-green leaves and carmine stems (*loc. cit. sup.*).

R. speciosum "A" ** is, in its best forms, amazingly free-flowering with orange to blood-red flowers.

R. austrinum is, according to the *Rhododendron Handbook*, an early June bloomer, but Bowers† states that it blooms in early spring with the expanding leaves. According to Mrs. Henry it bears its yellow or orange flowers, in the wild state, before the leaves unfold.

R. cumberlandense, formerly thought to be a form of *R.calendulaceum*, has brilliant blood-red flowers.

R. prunifolium *** has the immensely valuable characteristic of producing its blood-red flowers, which are said to be the largest of all Azaleas, *in July*. That brilliant plant-hunter, Mrs. Norman Henry, (*loc. cit. sup.*) said: "It fairly took my breath away the first time I saw it in bloom . . . twelve feet tall and fifteen feet in diameter".

For my part I would rather have a good specimen of this Azalea in my garden than almost any shrub I can think of. The importation of seed in quantity sufficient to make it readily available would earn the gratitude of all gardeners enjoying an acid or neutral soil.

Turning for a moment from these choice and rare creatures to a commoner and more easily grown shrub of very different character, let us record the excellence of a member of the Spiræa family.

Spiræa prunifolia plena is a Japanese garden form of a Chinese shrub.

It is a graceful, dense, 5-foot bush with arching branches laden in early May with intensely double, white, pompon flowers like "bachelors' buttons". It is specially useful as it will grow on limy soil where it may follow *S. arguta* in bloom and associate with the Kerrias, Berberis and other shrubs of similar size in bloom at this time.

This Spiræa may be increased by detaching rooted suckers from old plants, carefully potting these and growing them on in a fairly warm frame.

Less hardy, but equally easily satisfied as to soil, ***Fremontia californica*** is a soft, partly evergreen shrub of doubtful hardiness and "miffy" nature, like so many Californians in this country. The brilliant golden-yellow Mallow-like flowers, 2½ inches across, are spectacularly free

† "Rhododendrons and Azaleas", by Clement Gray Bowers, Macmillan, N.Y., 1936.

from May onwards but it is only to be recommended for favourable gardens.

A warm, sunny, well-drained spot on a south slope, rather than against a wall, is probably the best place for it and increase is easily attained by seeds. Established plants usually die if moved.

F. mexicana has all the worst traits of this plant accentuated and should be avoided.

More as a warning than a recommendation I mention *Davidia involucrata,* the Dove Tree, a rather Lime-like, 50-foot Chinese tree with large bright green leaves and dark ascending branches. The curious flowers, consisting of a small pompon with a large white bract hanging like a huge petal on either side, just fail, I think, to be really beautiful. They hang down among the leaves and are seldom very well presented and are too roughly formed, so that, in May, from a slight distance, the tree merely looks as though it had a lot of waste paper caught up in it. As a street or park tree it is quite attractive.

The Davidia likes a moist, loamy soil and is apparently hardy. Seeds are the best method of increase.

The finest of the **Pieris** flowers in early May and is a distinguished plant that requires care.

Pieris formosa (a Himalayan species) is too tender for any but the more favoured gardens; it is, in any event, eclipsed by its Yunnanese and Burmese form, *P. f. Forrestii* (A.G.M. 1944) whose flowers appear whiter, having a white instead of a green calyx, and whose young leaves are of a more vivid red.

A more recent arrival, being first introduced in 1910, it was exhibited in flower at the R.H.S. Chelsea Show in 1924. It is a strikingly beautiful shrub growing up to 10 feet high, with fine, dark, evergreen foliage, and large pyramidal panicles of fragrant pure white urn-shaped flowers among the brilliant red young leaves in early May. This latter feature is extremely decorative, and in good forms the plant rivals the Azaleas in brightness of colour. Most unhappily this fine Pieris is by no means really hardy and many good specimens have succumbed entirely to recent cold winters. It is, however, so outstandingly beautiful as to be worth trying in favoured gardens on lime-free soil in a sheltered spot with light shade. Layering or seeds are the best methods of increase.

In those favoured gardens where shade and shelter from wind and a lime-free soil are combined with reasonable freedom from spring frosts owing to good katabatics, the hardier of the **Rhododendron Hybrids** having the "blood" of the great Himalayan Lily-laurel, *R. Griffithianum*, can be effectively grown.

The finest of these is undoubtedly the hybrid with the fragrant, seven-lobed, pale purplish-pink flowered *R. Fortunei*, known as *R. Loderi* "C" ****. The stars are stars of relative merit awarded by the Rhododendron Group of the R.H.S. The "C" means "Hardy along the seaboard and in warm gardens inland", and it is a very salutary precaution always to include the hardiness-category-letter in naming any Rhododendron. The *necessary* conditions to grow a "C" plant are enumerated above.

R. Loderi is one of the loveliest of all flowering shrubs and, where it can be grown, it is worthy of the most important position, such as at the foot of the north wall of the house, rather than tucked away somewhere or lumped up with other Rhododendrons in some dismal concentration. A fine specimen adorned a north wall near the entrance to my old house to the great enjoyment of all. In time it makes a shrub of some 8 feet or more, but a finer occupant of the required space in a lime-free garden could not be found. The immense pearly-white flowers, 6 inches across, are fragrant, though not powerfully so, and expand from pink buds.

There are a number of different clonal forms of the hybrid, as the cross has been made several times. 'King George' is the most generally available at present. It has large and firmly carried flowers in a fine truss. Some seedling forms of the cross are inferior in various ways, some have very lax flower-trusses and others are markedly more tender. Such a tender form, sometimes known as 'Sir Joseph Hooker', with remarkably beautiful, light, bright green foliage, veined with darker green, and having early pink flowers, is often seen. We have very large plants in our favoured wood-garden but it could not be recommended for the open garden. Care must therefore be taken to make sure that one of the hardier forms (many of which have received awards) is secured.

Gardens subject to late spring frosts that destroy the flowers and young growth of *R. Loderi* may well substitute R. 'Angelo' "C" (*R. Griffithianum* × *discolor*). There are many varieties of this later-flowering hybrid, which otherwise much resembles *R. Loderi*. A wide selection in my wood-garden has, through the years, given a better return owing to the flowers escaping frost more frequently as they do not open until the end of May or early in June. At the same time neither the habit of growth nor the form of the flowers of 'Angelo' is quite so decorative as in *R. Loderi*. Both these fine hybrids grow better if root-grafted on *ponticum* rather than as layers.

A degree hardier, but still requiring light shade, regular mulching with leaves, and shelter from wind, are the "B" category hybrids, once removed, so to speak, from *R. Loderi*. This section may be typified by the well-known 'Pink Pearl' "B" **. "B" means "Hardy anywhere in the British Isles but requires some shade to obtain best results", but some amplification and explanation is needed. Briefly the varieties in this section flower early and are consequently at the mercy of spring frosts; they will just tolerate a favourable garden, but grow twice as well in woodland and there become superb plants with huge bold leaves and immense trusses, so different from the usual, shrivelled, garden occupants as to be almost unrecognisable. Any who doubt this statement are referred to the plants themselves which will give a very emphatic confirmation if given the chance. Having given due warning, let us review the different varieties that will flower simultaneously in harmonising colours, assuming that a sheltered spot shaded, say, by tall trees to the south, and having a good, acid, sandy loam enriched with leaf-mould, is available:—

'Pink Pearl' "B" **, rose pink, fading to blush, muddy centre, perhaps the least good of this batch.

'Betty Wormald' "B" *** pale Rose Madder, dark centre, superb when well grown.

'Mrs. A. C. Kenrick' "B" *, Rose Bengal (H.C.C. 23/1), red-purple centre.

'Corona' "C" ***, pale Crimson (H.C.C. 22/2), appears quite as hardy as the others but needs more sun to ripen its wood.

'Mrs. E. C. Stirling' "B" **, blush-pink, hardier than some and able to stand sunlight and exposure.

'Mother of Pearl' "B" *** blush to white, very good.

'Countess of Derby' "B" ** (*R.* 'Pink Pearl' × 'Cynthia'), pale rosy crimson, very large truss.

'Mrs. Charles Pearson' "B" **, pale blush-mauve, spotted, very fine.

'Mrs. Furnival' "B" ***, pale carmine with a red flare, splendid habit in a more open position, rather later-flowering.

'Alice' "B" **, Rose Madder (H.C.C. 23/1), better than 'Pink Pearl', but earlier flowering.

'Raoul Millais' "C" *, Carmine (H.C.C. 21/1), scarlet buds.

'Mrs. Lindsay Smith' "C" **, white, fine, but leggy habit.

'Cynthia' "B" *, Rose Bengal (H.C.C. 25/1), not a very attractive colour.

'King George' "C" **, bright crimson-red, very fine truss. (See illustration p. 112.)

'Marinus Koster' "C" **, warm pink, large flowers, rather later.

The foregoing is only a small selection that I have tested over some years for simultaneous flowering. Many fine varieties are no doubt omitted, in the absence of exact data as to synchronisation of flowering.

A particularly lovely hybrid that flowers before the above group is R. 'Loder's White' "C" **** (A.G.M. 1931). It was raised by Sir Edmund Loder of Leonardslee near Horsham, and is of rather similar parentage to R. *Loderi* but is perhaps more wind-resisting. It is so free-flowering as to give the effect of a cloud of snow, but, as with all the above-mentioned, must be given care and a favourable position as previously described to do well.

Until recently Rhododendrons have been the most pest-free and disease-resistant of all flowering shrubs. Of late, however, a most serious fungus infestation has begun to spread. This is generally called "bud-blast". In late autumn—even if no frost has yet manifested itself —a number of flower buds may be found to be browned and dead. They have been attacked by the fungus—believed to be *Sporocybe azaleæ*† and, unless these infected buds are removed with a small portion of the stem, all subsequent ones nearby are likely to be infected and thus spoiled. Once the fungus gets hold of large plantations the position is grave and I know of superb gardens whose display is sometimes ruined by this pest. On the other hand, with constant vigilance there is no serious danger. We do not yet know much about this new enemy and some form of timed, fungicidal spraying may be found to provide an effective control. In the meantime, the gardener will do well to remove all dead flower buds promptly by early November. Some species such as R. *campylocarpum* and R. *Griersonianum* are reported to be immune (*loc. cit. sup.*). In my view R. *caucasicum* is particularly susceptible.

The first display of **Evergreen Azaleas** is over, the second is under way. One of the members of this later chorus is "Azalea ledifolia", correctly known as *Rhododendron mucronatum* "C" ****, with large, fragrant, white flowers. It has been cultivated in Japan for 300 years. The noble company of fragrant white-flowered shrubs have few more beautiful representatives than this lovely Azalea. The habit is compact and mounded and the evergreen leaves, dark and pointed, show up the massed flowers to perfection. Apparently it was first introduced into England through a collector named Joseph Poole, who sent it from China to his employers, Brookes' Nurseries, at Ball's Pond in 1819. This Azalea is a good garden plant growing to nearly 6 feet high and

† *The Rhododendron Year-Book*, 1949, p. 25 et seq.

15 feet across in favourable gardens, and is reasonably hardy in suitable soil anywhere, but, like all its family, it grows best where the atmosphere is fairly moist. In the ordinary garden it is usually 2 or 3 feet high only, but of much larger spread. Its flowering has apparently been almost everywhere unaffected by recent severe winters. The flowers last longer in the shade of distant trees, but a clear sky overhead is desirable for compact and healthy growth.

The origin of this Azalea is uncertain, being lost in antiquity. No wild species exactly corresponding is known. Professor Hara considers this group to be of hybrid parentage[†].

Varieties:—

> R. m. *Noordtianum* has larger flowers, but, as a growing shrub, is no improvement on the "type".
>
> R. m. *narcissiflorum* is a double-flowered form, and, again, is no improvement.
>
> R. m. 'Sekidera' (*magnificum*) is white, spotted with rose, and is a fine hardy variety.
>
> R. m. *amethystinum* with smaller flowers spotted and flushed with lilac, is evidently a hybrid and flowers much earlier, with 'Hinomayo' and other Kurume types.
>
> R. m. 'Fujimanyo' with double, Orchid Purple (H.C.C. 31/3) flowers, introduced along with the type, is of more open habit and has a slightly later flowering time. It is probably a hybrid.
>
> R. m. *ripense*, purple flowers.

A convenient associate for the charming R. *mucronatum* is 'Azalea Maxwellii' (R. *pulchrum* var. *Maxwellii*) "C" **. The wild form is not known; this variety is a Japanese clone with large, deep Phlox Pink (H.C.C. 625) single flowers that open at about the same time. Though the flower colour is poor it is a sturdy evergreen Azalea and makes quite a pleasing contrast with its white-flowered relative.

R. *pulchrum* var. 'Tebotan' has double flowers with two tiny green leaves peeping from the centre and has petals of the colour, according to E. H. Wilson, of *Bougainvillea glabra*, but I find them, on plants growing here, Orchid Purple (H.C.C. 31/3). It is an old Japanese garden plant and reasonably hardy.

These two Azaleas, *Maxwellii* and 'Tebotan', have passed under various specific names. The above are those cited in the *Rhododendron Handbook*, 1947.

Azalea 'Broadstone Red' (R. o. *Hinodegiri* × *indicum?*) is said to be a sport of 'Hinodegiri' found at Messrs. Maxwell & Beale's nursery. The flowers are orange-red and open late in May, long after those of

† *The Rhododendron Year-Book*, 1948, p. 123

Viburnum tomentosum sterile

Mollis Azalea ' Mrs. Oliver Slocock '

Viburnum macrocephalum sterile

Knap Hill Azalea ' Marion Merriman '

'Hinodegiri'. This is a very attractive variety that helps us to secure continuity in the sequence of flower.

There are also the fascinating , but delicate, little Gumpos. They are a sub-species of *Rhododendron Simsii*, the florist's Azalea from China and Formosa, thus coming under *R. Simsii eriocarpum*.

'Gumpo' has large white flowers; *album giganteum* has larger ones that are not so well presented; 'Gumpo Red' has large pale pink flowers; 'Titugetsuse' has purplish-pink flowers and so has 'Yugiri', but they have darker spots.

Another small but valuable group is tentatively named *Wadai* after the Japanese nurseryman Mr. K. Wada who exported so many beautiful plants to this country before the war. 'Asakanonare' is a beautiful Azalea with large salmon-red flowers opening late in May; 'Bungoni-shiki' has terracotta semi-double flowers and may have *R. indicum* in its parentage, and 'Chichibu' ** is rather like 'Gumpo', with large white flowers.

As a further adornment to this grouping there may be added, although it sometimes flowers earlier, the dwarf-growing form of the yellow-flowered *Rhododendron Hanceanum* "C". One would have expected this form to have been awarded quite a constellation of stars, as that highly experienced judge, Mr. Francis Hanger, the Curator of Wisley gardens, stated that it was his favourite of all the yellow-flowered dwarfs†. But there are many different forms, among them a richer yellow one rarely exceeding a foot in height which is unfortunately very scarce, dwarf forms with whitish flowers, and the "type" form which makes a shrub of 3 feet and is also not particularly attractive, having small, very pale yellow flowers. It is a member of the Triflorum series and comes from the Western Szechwan mountains, China.

Another miniature, blooming in May, is *R. Sargentianum* "C" **, a member of the Anthopogon series. It has pale lemon-yellow flowers and is figured in the *Rhododendron Year-Book* for 1947. Though not so showy as some, it has the dainty individual personality that is such an attractive feature of these little species and is quite a good garden plant, coming from the same habitat as the preceding.

R. 'Yellow Hammer' (*R. flavidum* × *sulphureum*) has small, somewhat tubular, yellow flowers and small neat foliage of a rather dull purplish tone. It is remarkable in the length of its flowering season which begins in early May but it seldom has sufficient flowers out at one time to make a real display. In habit it is thin and upright (attaining seven feet in height) unless grown fully exposed, with all straggling shoots pegged-down.

† Francis Hanger, "Miniature Rhododendron Species", *R.H.S. Journal*, LXIX, Pt. 2, p. 40 (1944).

The May-flowering Alpine Rhododendrons run much to undesirable purplish pinks. Though not recommended they are described below for those who do not object to these colourings.

R. calostrotum "A" ***, is a russet-green-leaved bushlet from the Saluenense series. The flowers, usually in pairs, open out flat and are of an awkward purplish colour (Petunia Purple 52/1) which, lacking the hyaline sparkling intensity of those of the Petunia herself, are not easy to place. *R. calostrotum* comes from 11,000 or 12,000 feet altitudes in the mountains of north-eastern Burma whence it was first introduced by Reginald Farrer. It is very free flowering, but possibly not very long-lived.

Another member of this series is *R. calciphilum* "A". It is a prostrate dwarf with rosy purple flowers towards the end of May or in early June, interesting because it is said to be found only on limestone in Nature. Those stalwarts who struggle to grow Rhododendrons in chalky districts might find it worth trying.

R. radicans "B" ****, Saluenense series, is a very tiny, dwarf and compact grower of attractive habit, but regrettably, magenta-pink flowers, that often delays its flowering until June.

R. imperator "A" ***, of the Lepidotum series, is a creeping shrub that needs some care and in warm gardens grows best in the shade of distant trees. It only rises a few inches from the ground but it will make a little mat, sometimes nearly 2 feet across when it is happy. In early May it is so free flowering that the mat becomes a solidly floral one, composed of the ½-inch wide, often six-lobed, rosy flowers. It comes from 10,000-foot elevations in Burma and was introduced by Captain Kingdon Ward from his 1926 expedition. It was illustrated in the *Gardener's Chronicle*, March 13, 1948, p. 85.

R. aperantum "B" **, is in the Neriiflorum series. So far we have not mentioned a really difficult species, but Reginald Farrer's watercolour of this Rhododendron ("The Plant Introductions of Reginald Farrer", p. 68) is so enchanting that I do not think that anyone who has seen the picture could fail to wish to struggle with the problem of growing the plant. Both the shape of the flower and the colouring vary enormously, but all appear beautiful; either the trumpets or the wide-open bells, and the yellow, orange, red or fresh pink tints of the corollas. Apparently the plant is rather a "miff" in cultivation and this is sad indeed, for it seems to have every good quality otherwise. The Rhododendron Group Year-Book's mention of "mats up to 20 feet across" is certainly exciting and, if only we can go on growing this species from seed, sooner or later a good steady grower should appear.

Before we leave these delightful shrublets of rock garden size, mention must be made of *R. myrtilloides* "A" ***. It is not really effective, but it is very amusing, being only a few inches in height and covered, if a good form, with magenta-rose bell-flowers of a shape that reminds one of *Campanula cæspitosa*. There is a superb illustration of this species in *R. H. S. Journal*, LXIX, Pt. 2, Fig. 6 (1944). It is often not in flower until nearly the middle of June.

For the propagation details of these miniatures see end of April-flowering section of dwarf Rhododendrons, p. 90.

Too often one sees the mountain dwarfs as thin, weedy-looking bushes planted alongside woodland paths, ineffective when in bloom amid the larger-flowered woodlanders and unthrifty and ugly when out of flower. On the other hand, grouped with dwarf shrubs of other genera, such as those described later, among boulders *right out in the open*, on little sloping banks, they are a delight at all times—compact mounds of violet, yellow or purple in spring, dense, blue-green, emerald or bronzy cushions in winter. To attain this, plant them in humus with buried sandstone rocks, with moisture provided as described on pp. 167 and 190. Peg down every possible branch flat on the ground, with bamboo or wire pegs. The centre then grows vigorously and fills up, the whole plant seems suddenly invigorated and in a season or two you have your dense, comely cushion. The simplest pegs are those made by cutting up Bamboo (*Sinarundinaria nitida*) canes with secateurs. When the main stems are cut to size and inverted it will be found that the shortened side growths of the Bamboo hook over the Rhododendron stems most conveniently.

An alternative is to layer the outer branches, but, though good increase is thus secured, the compact dome is not so quickly attained.

Whilst we are still among the little shrubs that are so delightful for the open parts of the garden where a low, cushiony effect is needed, we must not forget the members of another great and valuable family, the **Brooms.** As everyone knows, most of them are yellow-flowered, but it is often a very good yellow. This is a very beautiful and a very showy colour, when embroidered among whites and, either pure and strong colours, or pale colours, depending upon whether the yellow itself is pure and strong or pale. For perfection both associations should be boldly interlaced.

Cytisus Ardoinii, from south-eastern France, usually flowers in early May, growing only from 4 to 8 inches high. It is a free-flowering and pretty little thing with bright yellow flowers.

An outstanding dwarf Broom flowering in May is *C. Beanii* (*C. Ardoini* × *purgans*) with profuse yellow flowers. It grows about one foot or more in height and makes a bright and attractive patch of colour.

C. kewensis is another dwarf hybrid Broom (*C. Ardoini* × *multiflorus*), slightly later in blooming, with flowers of a more creamy yellow (Empire Yellow, H.C.C. 603/1), which is the same as that of *C. præcox*. It is more prostrate, but is a particularly lovely shrub when seen in flower in a well raised position above the cool violet of R. 'Blue Tit'. These dwarf Brooms will grow quite well on limy soils, but of course do so equally well on acid soils. The soft yellow colouring of *C. kewensis* is particularly delightful with the mauves and violets of the mountain Rhododendrons, providing the perfect complement.

C. emeriflorus (*C.* or *Genista, glabrescens*) from Switzerland and north Italy, has an attractive habit, forming a mound about eighteen inches high, completely covered with shining yellow flowers in the latter part of May. It has been rather scarce over here, but I note that it is now listed by several nurserymen specialising in flowering shrubs. One of the loveliest of the dwarf Brooms, it is worth taking some trouble to secure it.

C. procumbens is a less neat tussock, alight with yellow pea-flowers at this season. Rather larger, it will reach 2 feet in height and flowers over quite a long period.

Those who can look after very small plants may add the Hedgehog Broom, *Erinacea pungens* (*E. anthyllis*) from Spain and Morocco. This spiny little hummock, eventually perhaps a foot high and a yard wide, is usually seen no more than mole-heap size, and of a young mole at that. The spines have an attractive silvery sheen and the clear, purplish-blue pea-flowers, two or three together, but not quite as numerous as one might wish as a rule, usually appear in early May. It is quite hardy in a warm dry place where it grows slowly but steadily year by year.

There are a number of other interesting dwarf Brooms, less commonly found, such as *Cytisus versicolor*, a hybrid of *C. purpureus* which has purplish and yellowish tinted flowers; *C. purpureus* itself with rosy-purple flowers in the "type" form and white-flowered and pink-flowered varieties; *C. hirsutus* with yellow flowers stained with brown and also its variety *hirsutissimus* with more downy and vigorous growth.

As regards cultivation, all these Brooms like an acid, sandy soil with good drainage and full sun, but will stand a slight degree of liminess. Many can be struck from cuttings, but it is tricky work and on the whole the amateur is well advised either to buy them in pots or to grow them from seed. As they are tap-rooted and suffer badly if the roots are disturbed it is best to sow three seeds only in each small pot, and, if all come up, either treat the result as one plant or pinch out all but one seedling. The Brooms, apart from *Erinacea pungens*, are quick growers, most desirable for the rapid furnishing of new gardens but they are seldom really permanent, long-lived plants like the Chænomeles,

Azaleas, Rhododendrons, Camellias, Cherries, Hydrangeas, etc.; consequently it is wise to keep a replacement service going. Their lives can be appreciably lengthened by regular pruning-back of the young wood after flowering and by pegging down and layering any suitable branches.

Another dwarf shrub which associates delightfully with the foregoing is **Lithospermum diffusum** 'Heavenly Blue' (A.G.M. 1925), a small, prostrate evergreen with brilliant blue flowers (Gentian Blue, H.C.C. 42) in May and onwards into June and even later. It likes to trail down among sandstone rocks and strikes fairly easily from cuttings placed under a bell-glass in July. Unfortunately, like so many good shrubs, it will not tolerate a limy soil. One of the best of carpeters, it always looks attractive, though to get a mass of blue, as shown in the illustration opposite p. 128, requires some skill. Top-dressing is necessary or the flowers dwindle to half the proper size and growth becomes stunted. Pegging down keeps the plants compact and healthy, but it is a fastidious and difficult plant and very sensitive to drought or untimely frost.

The variety 'Grace Ward' has flowers of a slightly darker blue, perhaps, and the habit is generally more compact, though this feature depends much on feeding and pegging down when a close, bushy habit is desired. An interesting feature is that this variety is reputed to tolerate a less acid soil than the "type", though my own experience is otherwise. It certainly does better in heavy clays and is therefore a plant capable of wider use than the "type".

There is a white variety which I have not seen, var. *album*.

Another pleasing bushlet is **Phyllodoce empetriformis**, a delightful little Heathlike shrub from Western North America. The reddish-purple, pitcher-shaped flowers cover the 9-inch bushes in late April and May and it grows well in any acid, sandy soil suitable for Heaths.

P. nipponica is less easy-going, if even more attractive with its white bell-flowers, with wavy edges, at the tips of the sprigs. Such little treasures as this, exquisite on a near inspection, are among the rewards of the stroller rather than components of the main colour groupings.

The **Genistas,** such close allies of the Brooms that only the botanists can separate them, give us several dwarf growers flowering in May which are conveniently mentioned here.

Genista lydia though seldom mentioned, is a dainty little Balkan species that is absolutely first class, with its densely massed clear yellow flowers covering the gracefully arching branches. It seldom exceeds 2 feet and its hardiness is still somewhat suspect; a warm place, well elevated, seems to suit it best. It flowers towards the end of May, as a rule, often remaining in flower during June. Alas, it does not set seed or strike very readily from cuttings. (See illustration facing p. 113.)

G. hispanica is one of the most useful of all the low-growing members of the Legume family, making dense masses of foot-high, spiny branches completely covered in late May and early June with the rich golden yellow flowers. Not quite reliably hardy in the cold north-eastern and midland parts of our country, it is sound enough anywhere in the south-western half and is a shrub that no chalky garden can well do without. It is a good garden plant provided that it is planted in poor soil, and it is increased easily from rooted fragments, cuttings or seeds.

G. pilosa is a straggling but easily grown dwarf Broom and a native of sandy Heaths in parts of England, it is said, but I have never been lucky enough to find it wild. A more compact form, the best for the garden, is often described as var. *nana* (A.G.M. 1939). It forms a mass of twiggy shoots about 1 foot 6 inches high, sometimes 6 feet across. In May it provides a fine mass of yellow and is very effective on dry banks, carpeting the ground and spreading freely. It may, according to Mr. J. Comber (R.H.S. Shrub Conference, 1938), be propagated from pieces several inches long, put three parts in the ground in February, before growth starts, in the manner used for Sage. It can be grown in a fairly limy soil.

G. Villarsii, a minute shrublet from south-eastern France and the western Balkans is rather slow-growing and less free-flowering than most. Its little hummock is, however, of a pleasing shade of grey-green and as it matures it usually flowers more freely.

G. januensis also from south Europe, has a spreading, procumbent habit and is seldom more than a foot high. It has curious triangular stems and the bright yellow flowers, rather like those of *G. virgata* appear in racemes along the ends of the shoots in May and June. It is not so hardy as the others but is very decorative.

Most of these Genistas can be grown from seed, if and when they produce it. Cuttings are not very easy for the amateur.

Leiophyllum buxifolium, the Sand Myrtle, is a pleasant little North American evergreen shrub of the Heath family. Its white, myrtle-like flowers opening from rosy buds, are very freely borne in May and June and its neat, domed habit, rarely more than a foot in height, makes it very suitable for association with the other dwarf bushes mentioned.

It needs a lime-free soil and may be propagated from layers.

The **Daphnes,** chancy and uncertain plants of poor flower colouring, liable to "miff off" without apparent excuse as they are, have yet a delightful personality of their own and give us a charming May-flowering species in *Daphne Cneorum* (A.G.M. 1927) from South Europe. The abundant trusses of pale Tyrian Rose ultra fragrant flowers almost conceal the low-spreading, lax, evergreen branches that seldom rise more than a foot from the ground. In my experience a sandy turf-loam, on the acid side, and a lightly-shaded position suit this plant well, but good specimens of this, and indeed all the Daphnes, are seen, at least for a time, in almost all kinds of soils. They are pets for odd corners rather than components of the main flower effects.

D. C. grandiflora and *D. C. eximia* are much superior to the "type", being more vigorous in growth and having flowers of larger size and warmer colouring. *D. C. alba* is a weakly dwarf form with small white flowers.

Placing sandstone rocks over the longer branches helps the plants to remain compact and renew their growth and a light scattering of a complete fertiliser should be given each spring, but, sooner or later, they usually die off suddenly. (See illustration facing p. 65.)

D. Burkwoodii, a vigorous hybrid between *D. caucasica*, a deciduous Daphne, and the preceding species, is a well-rounded, semi-evergreen shrub, about 2 or 3 feet high, dappled all over with little trusses of paler, rosy-pink, fragrant flowers in spring. It is fairly robust and easy-going. *D. B.* 'Somerset' appears to be very similar but lower and more spreading in habit.

One of the finest and the most enduring of all Daphnes is *D. retusa*, an evergreen with leathery, oval, leaves (there is said to be a deciduous form), and a dense, stout and picturesque habit, most impressive when seen as a large bush 3 or 4 feet high and equally wide (see illustration facing p. 129). It comes from the mountains of Western China whence it was introduced by E. H. Wilson in 1901. The large flowers, in clusters at the ends of the shoots, are pale mauve, with the interior white, and are deliciously lilac-scented. It is probably the best long-term investment among the Daphnes for a sunny position, but the tragedy of the sudden loss of a fine, permanent-looking shrub, just grown to perfection, always threatens. It is surprisingly easily raised from seeds sown as soon as ripe, though the seedlings grow very slowly, and it can be struck from cuttings placed under a bell-glass in July. This Daphne grows best in a position where its head is in the sun but the roots are shaded, an arrangement easily provided with the help of neighbouring, low shrubs. The Daphne family is one which can mostly be grown in limy soils provided that a little fine leaf-soil is added. On the other hand they grow well in acid soils and the addition of lime mortar to the soil, often recommended, does not, in my experience, do the plants any good at all, but a light dressing of bonemeal is helpful.

D. tangutica (A.G.M. 1949) very much resembles *D. retusa* but it has slightly narrower leaves and the flowers are rather more purple in colour. It was introduced from Kansu by Reginald Farrer in 1914. He described it as "a dense low shrub of very dark glossy foliage about 12 inches high and twice as much through. Dotted in open turf on the slopes, 9,000–10,000 feet, in deep calcareous loam or vegetable mould". According to Mr. E. H. M. Cox†, like *D. retusa*, though hardy, it is both very slow-growing and slow to flower. One of Farrer's plants had 'rose-pink' flowers and the other creamy-white. But the *R. H. S. Journal* (LXXV, Pt. 2, p. 76, 1950) records *D. tangutica* as having flowers rosy-purple outside and white inside, and as free-flowering even when small and the forms available in this country all appear to be of this type. This species flowers rather earlier than *D. retusa*, often opening in early April. Consequently *D. retusa* is probably the better species.

The arrangement of all these dwarf shrubs is most effective on an undulating piece of ground with plenty of mounds, hummocks and little ravines, running downhill if this is possible, so as to let cold air drain freely away. In such a setting a few large, picturesque boulders are invaluable. Æsthetically, such a little landscape is more interesting and attractive than a flat one, and culturally it is of the greatest advantage as it gives many varying aspects suited to the different types of plants. Thus the cooler, northerly slopes suit the mountain dwarf Rhododendrons, the flatter areas the Evergreen Azaleas, the elevated sunny summits the Brooms, and the hot south slopes the essential June-flowering Helianthemums and Halimiums that will be mentioned later, while larger slopes and outskirts may be "lawned" with Heaths, quietly green, until, in August, their turn comes to take over the display. In this way the garden landscape is a miniature, concentrated, expression of the beauties of nature and each "alp", perhaps 2 or 3 feet high, supports a different vegetation on its various faces in accordance with their climate. The more showy plants are so placed as to be visible from garden-house, windows and other viewpoints and those chosen for their interesting individual personalities where they can be closely viewed from the paths that invite a walk.

Occasionally a specimen shrub of dense, bushy habit slightly larger than the others, may emerge from such a low planting—*Kalmia latifolia myrtifolia* (see p. 240) is the type I have in mind—and in such cases we should make sure that the immediately surrounding shrublets are

† "The Plant Introductions of Reginald Farrer."

either plants that will become time-expired by the time the specimen needs more room, or such easily portable little shrubs as Evergreen Azaleas or Alpine Rhododendrons.

The **Wisterias** are beautiful and vigorous climbers all too seldom sufficiently pruned and trained to show their racemes of violet or white flowers to the greatest advantage. The various species provide a succession of flower from May to August.

Wisteria floribunda macrobotrys (*W. multijuga*), the best form of the Japanese Wisteria, has very long racemes of the fragrant, bean-like, violet flowers opening in late May. It is less effective, perhaps, for house walls than its Chinese relative but very attractive grown on strong trellis, pergolas or trees. In Japan it is often trained out over water on poles and screens, when the ropes of flowers hang beautifully silhouetted, perhaps a yard long. The wild type from which this garden form is descended has shorter racemes and is less decorative. By hard annual pruning, this Wisteria can be made to form a picturesque specimen shrub or small tree. The flowers open gradually from the bases of the racemes which makes the display longer lasting but less spectacular than that of the Chinese species. Occasional flowers open throughout the summer in favourable seasons. It is the hardiest of the Wisterias.

W. f. alba is a white variety.

W. f. rosea has pink flowers tipped with purple.

W. f. violaceo-plena has violet, double flowers less freely borne. But, judging from photographs, there appears to be a free-flowering double form in some Japanese gardens.

Wisteria sinensis (A.G.M. 1928), the Chinese Wisteria, has shorter and thicker racemes of a more vivid heliotrope colouring. It is the most decorative of the family on a wall but is less so than others, perhaps, on pergolas, arches or trees. Great care is needed in early training to ensure the form of an immense fan on a wide wall or an espalier to decorate the spaces of a house-wall, between the windows, in an orderly manner. The flowers open somewhat earlier in May and as they all unfold at once the display is very striking. It will grow on limy soils provided that rotted manure or leaf-mould is added.

W. s. alba has white flowers.

W. formosa is a hybrid between the two preceding species, favouring the latter in appearance.

W. venusta is a Japanese garden form of a wild Chinese species not yet introduced. The short racemes of large, fragrant white flowers are substantial and long-lasting, very attractive, and produced in May on very downy stalks. It was introduced in 1912. When pruned and grown as a shrub it is particularly effective.

W. macrostachya. This American species is not often seen but is quite attractive. The flowers are fragrant and lilac-purple, in racemes up to a foot long, and usually do not open until June. It is not so rampant as the others and may therefore be planted where there is not room for the larger-growing sorts.

W. japonica, a July and August flowering species, is mentioned in the section devoted to that month.

The Wisterias all seem to prefer a moist and rich soil and full sun on the upper growth. They may be increased by layering. Seeds are ripened in warm summers in long, bean-like pods but the resulting seedlings are usually disappointing, compared with the selected superior varieties.

Pruning is important and early training even more so. Well spaced shoots should be tied early into their permanent positions and any not required should be cut away. Afterwards all unwanted shoots may be spurred back as with vines. The difference between the unsightly tangle of untrained wall plants and those that have been properly guided is very great. When the Wisteria is used as a tree climber one stout shoot should first be trained spirally up without competition, later it may be allowed to grow as it wills. If required to form an open-ground bush, a strong single stem is first built up and then short strong branches are allowed to develop a certain length each year.

The spring-flowering members of the **Ceanothus** family have their headquarters on the Pacific Coast Range and among the hills of California and, unfortunately, like most shrubs from that part of the world, are rarely hardy enough for these islands. None the less, they are very commonly grown, usually as wall plants, although they are naturally open-ground shrubs, carpeting the baking slopes with their masses of small and rather coarse blue, purplish-lilac or white flowers. Nature's last few sanctuaries are menaced there now, as everywhere else, although good people struggle to protect them.

One of the hardiest species is *Ceanothus thyrsiflorus*, introduced in 1815, which has the habit of a small tree, up to 15 or 20 feet high, with clusters of pale blue, sometimes slaty blue or even whitish, flowers in May. It will grow on a limy soil. Like others of its kind it is liable to be wind-rocked and killed unless either firmly supported and anchored by layering stones, or staked and always pruned back after flowering. It is particularly attractive grown in association with Azaleas as, indeed, often occurs in the wild.

A variety of unusual hardiness and vigour is *C. thyrsiflorus* 'Cascade'; the flowers are Sea Blue. It was introduced by Messrs. George Jackman and Son of Woking, Surrey. 'Treasure Island' (*C. arboreas* × *thyrsiflorus*) is well spoken of in the U.S.A., having abundant masses of lilac flowers. It is not yet available here.

C. t. griseus, the Carmel Ceanothus, is a form with bluish-white or pale-lilac flowers and larger leaves, and is reputed less hardy. It is very fast-growing and can make a fine bush in four years from a cutting†. It is said to be the commonest species on the Monterey peninsular and to have blue-flowered forms "whose blunt-nosed blobs"‡ have cream-coloured anthers.

C. Veitchianus (A.G.M. 1925), was sent back to Messrs. Veitch by their collector, William Lobb, in 1853, and is thought to be a natural hybrid between *C. thyrsiflorus* and *C. rigidus*. It has apparently not been seen since in a wild state. With its comparatively bright blue flowers and free growth it is one of the most effective of this spring-flowering section for general garden use and has the merit of striking fairly easily from cuttings. As an evergreen shrub it is somewhat thin and uglily encumbered with dead twigs unless carefully "manicured". A light soil, quick drainage and a sunny position all help the hardiness and consequently the permanence of the plants, but I have often lost them after hard winters. Most Ceanothus suffer in transplanting and it is better, even, to strike the cuttings in separate small pots, if possible, to avoid a check. Early shaping by the nipping back of open-ground bushes is desirable to secure a bushy habit with low branches that may be anchored to the ground with large stones or pegs as a safer and less troublesome and unsightly method than staking.

C. cyaneus, the San Diego Ceanothus, is more refined in flower than most and an outstanding species for warm coastal gardens with notably bright blue flowers on long spikes and small shining green leaves on green shoots, but a lanky and ragged habit. It is listed by several British nurseries. Cuttings strike freely in small pots plunged under a bell-glass to avoid future root-disturbance, and it blooms when quite small, so it can at least be preserved by replacement.

C. cyaneus × *C. purpureus*, the hybrid 'James Roof', is reported to be a shrub 3 feet high and 5 feet across, with fragrant, rich blue flowers in April. It is not yet available here.

C. papillosus is one of the less tall-growing species with long, strap-like bright green leaves and clustered flowers of quite a pleasing lavender-blue, about the third week in May. Seeds were sent back by

† F. G. Preston, *The Gardeners' Chronicle*, p. 99, 3245, Vol. CXXV, also t. 48, idem.
‡ Lester Rowntree, "The Native Ceanothus of California", *Gardening Illustrated*, 1098, August, 1947.

William Lobb from California. The resulting young plants first flowered "in the open border" at Messrs. Veitch's nursery in Devon in 1854. Although considered one of the hardier species, it died out, except for a plant carefully conserved at Kew and a few specimens in favoured Devon gardens. From these sources it has been redistributed and is now commonly available from nurseries specialising in flowering shrubs. It is notable for its remarkably free-flowering habit. *C. p. Roweanus* is a variety with narrow, creased, sticky leaves growing usually to less than 3 feet high and having deep blue flowers which is increasingly popular in America.

C. rigidus, a somewhat stiff and sparse-branched shrub, with purplish or dark slaty-blue flowers, originally thought to be too tender for the open, is generally grown against sunny walls where it flowers freely. Curiously enough it has survived recent severe winters far better than most other species, so it is worth trying on a warm slope in the open where it makes a fairly dense 3 to 4 foot bush.

C. 'A. T. Johnson' is one of the newer hybrids with flowers of a good blue, often giving a second display in late summer.

C. 'Delight', a hybrid between *C. papillosus* and *C. rigidus*, has flowers of a deep, greyish blue on long-stalked panicles and is a vigorous and hardy variety.

C. dentatus, is of bushy habit and has pale grey-blue flowers in small bottle-brush clusters.

A form generally known as *C. d. Russellianus* is a particularly good variety for mild localities, growing more freely and having clusters of bright blue flowers.

C. impressus (A.M. 1944), is an allied species or a form of *C. dentatus* with profuse, short-stalked flower-clusters of a bright blue in mid May and larger and more orbicular leaves.

Owing to confusion as to the correct names of the species, which merge into one another, being only signposted by an occasional extreme type clearly botanically distinct, it is often difficult to determine whether one has the true plant or not. As with the Evergreen Azaleas, the oriental Cherries and the Hydrangeas, the best solution will probably be to treat the forms available as clones with garden names. Most of the other species, of which there are over fifty, are of lesser garden value, but superlative forms of these have already been collected and propagated by Californian nurserymen. One of these, according to Mr. Lester Rowntree (*loc. sit. sup.*) is a form of *C. impressus* growing 2 feet high and 9 feet across, with abundant, vivid, electric-blue flowers and small wrinkled leaves. Such shrubs may prove valuable acquisitions if suited to this climate, but most are undoubtedly too tender to be reliable in any but warm coastal gardens in the more sunny areas.

The later-flowering, Mexican, hybrid section are dealt with later under seasonal headings.

It is regrettable that the Ceanothus are so tender and unresistant to wind, as there is no doubt that their spring blue is highly desirable in the garden. Though not really pure in their case, it is a lovely and rare colour and very beautiful with pale citron or sulphury yellows, such as the Azaleas and the Brooms supply. In late summer, on acid soils, the purest true blues are easily attained by the Hydrangeas, but early in the season it is much more difficult to provide this colour. A sunny position such as a south slope or the foot of a south wall, good air drainage, a light and well-drained soil, and attention to keeping the plants firmly anchored against wind damage, are all factors affecting the longevity of the Ceanothus, but if the temperature drops below the danger point the plants die. As the danger point for the genus is one often reached and passed in these islands, the mortality is high and, after a time, many turn to more reliably permanent shrubs with relief. Most of the species can be grown on limy soils.

The larger **Brooms** now claim attention and this family contains many beautiful shrubs flowering in May.

Cytisus multiflorus (*C. albus*), the Portugal Broom, (A.G.M. 1926), is a delightful white-flowered species that is a good garden plant and useful for supplying light shade as, like the other Legumes, it has deep roots that are out of the way and in any case do not rob the soil of nitrogen. This food is manufactured for it from the atmosphere by symbiotic (which means "living-friendlily-together") bacteria which form nodules on the roots without which, indeed, the plant cannot grow. The Portugal Broom grows quickly from seed and needs, like all the taller Brooms, much regular nipping-back when young to induce a bushy habit and good framework. On the other hand, if required to shade smaller shrubs, it may be kept to a single, tree-like stem. In height it will reach 8 to 10 feet ultimately, but is usually somewhat battered, gaunt, and leggy by that time. There is a variety, *rosea*, with pale pink flowers that is sometimes seen.

A little later on, the many forms, varieties and hybrids of the common Scots Broom, *C. scoparius*, are in bloom, offering many fine yellows, creams, oranges and coppery reds. The wild type varies greatly in habit, but very little in flower colour. This is, however, a most beautiful clear yellow, being often a combination of Lemon and Buttercup, and in the garden landscape it is really much more effective than many of the garden forms. This is because so many of these are "bicolours" and the colours tend to cancel one another out at a distance. I have even destroyed quite large bushes of named varieties, at times, and replaced them with the common yellow with great advantage to the garden picture as a whole.

The work of producing the multi-coloured garden forms began when a Monsieur André found a wild form in Normandy in 1884 with wing-petals of a brownish-crimson. Then, in 1900, Kew, by artificial cross-fertilisation, produced the first hybrid between this form and *C. multiflorus*, named *C. Dallimorei*. The flowers were of a pinkish-crimson in general effect. The late T. Smith of Daisy Hill, Newry, was one of the first nurseryman breeders and he produced many new forms of attractive mixed colourings. The Donard Nursery and others followed later and a selection of these varieties which come under the heading of *C. scoparius Andreanus* is given below:—

'Daisy Hill splendens', buff standards, lower petals madder crimson.
'Diana', white standard, yellow keel, notably effective at a distance.
'Donard Seedling', pale pink standard, terracotta keel.
'Dragonfly', large yellow standard, bronze, crimson and yellow lower petals.
'Firefly', similar to above but more orange-tinted at a distance, the best of this type.
fulgens, amber standard, russet keel.
'Lord Lambourne', dull red wings, pale cream standards.
'Dorothy Walpole', brownish-crimson wings, rose standard.
Burkwoodii, maroon red, larger flowers than preceding.
'Lady Moore', brownish fiery red and buff.

Most of these, with the exception of 'Firefly' and 'Diana', although amusingly gay on close inspection, make little show at a distance. Much more effective for this purpose is *C. s. sulphureus*, the "Moonlight Broom". This has large pale lemon-yellow flowers which make a mass of fine colour, attractive in association with almost any blue-purple flowers in season. Besides the Ceanothus, *Rhododendron Augustinii* "C" ****, is an example, where it can be given the necessary shelter nearby. *C. s. sulphureus* has a bushier and more naturally compact habit than most.

Another beautiful Broom is *C. s.* 'Cornish Cream', raised in Cornwall. The buds are cream-coloured and open into flowers with white standards and rich yellow wings.

Great as is the value of the Brooms for the delightful flower effects they provide in spring, their quality as all-the-year-round garden furnishings is even more outstanding. Clipped firmly several times in their first growing seasons, and annually trimmed after flowering, they form shapely mounds of beautiful verdure owing to the dense mass of their deep green twigs. In the winter landscape they rival the Evergreen Azaleas in the comeliness of their forms in all weathers. Owing to their wider tolerance of poor soil conditions the Brooms are flowering shrubs of the highest importance to an even greater number of gardeners and their culture, pruning and selection thus merit particular care. Many gardens unable to take advantage of the most beautiful of the flowering evergreens owing to the fact that their soil is just too limy for Rhododendrons, Kalmias, Camellias, Azaleas or Heaths, can grow these Brooms successfully. In such places I know few plants that can equal them as flowering shrubs of year-round beauty in the garden landscape.

Unfortunately the garden varieties are usually grafted on Laburnum seedlings or on the common Broom and this seems to affect their longevity, and cuttings are also often short-lived owing to decay of the pith.

Seedlings do not come true to variety of course, but their flowers are often extremely attractive, if seeds are taken from rich-coloured sorts, and the important point is that they make healthier and more long-lived plants. Two or three seeds may be sown in small pots and the seedlings planted out, and, when they bloom, the inferior ones may be pulled out. Young Brooms, I will repeat, unlike almost any other shrubs, *must* be sheared back all over, again and again, so as to make them form the dense, velvety green mounds so beautiful in the winter landscape and highly effective when in bloom. Old wood cannot be cut without death, or at least serious damage, to the plant, so not only should the young plants be sheared back but it is also advisable to shear back the young twigs of older specimens every year after flowering. The Brooms of this section unfortunately do not grow well on very limy soils. The Genistas, of course, do grow well on such soils.

A most charming evergreen flowering shrub whose praises are seldom sung is **Choisya ternata,** the Mexican Orange, a member of the Rose family. Given proper space it forms a nice, dense, rounded, shapely bush usually about 3 feet high, but it can attain to 9 feet, in time. It has three-lobed evergreen leaves and a succession of clusters of fragrant, white, five-petalled flowers from spring onwards. *C. ternata* was named for a Swiss botanist, Monsieur J. D. Choisy, 1799–1859, and introduced in 1866. Remarkably hardy for a Mexican, being in what I term the "reasonably hardy" class, it has often safely withstood temperatures below zero. Furthermore, it will grow under trees, even, according to the late J. C. Williams, under Beeches, and it flourishes in London. It was killed by forty-two degrees of frost near Selkirk in 1940, but, as all Rambler Roses, and almost everything else, suffered the same fate, this is not surprising. The Choisya is a valuable evergreen for situations too warm for Rhododendrons, enjoying a sunny, well-drained spot. C. *ternata* can be propagated by cuttings of rather ripe wood in the sand-frame and will grow on limy soils.

Another fine shrub from the western hemisphere, **Cornus florida,** the American Dogwood, flowers usually towards the latter part of May. It forms a small tree or large bush, usually about 8 to 10 feet high in this country but sometimes, particularly in the white-flowered "type" form, up to 15 feet or more when pruned to the tree habit. The true flowers are merely small green pompons but they are surrounded by about four large petaloid bracts which make a sizable inflorescence about 4 inches across. Forms vary in the shapeliness, colour, texture and size of these bracts, but most have them of too irregular and ragged a shape for the flower to compare favourably, in individual beauty, with that of a good form of C. *Kousa*. The variety *rubra* is generally considered the finest, but this really depends upon whether one prefers a pure white or a pale crimson-pink flower. In my opinion, a really good white form with symmetrical and shapely bracts is even more beautiful than the pink clone available in commerce here, which has the bracts somewhat irregularly formed. This variety was discovered by Thomas Meehan in 1880, as a branch sport, in what is now Fairmont Park, Philadelphia, and had the Award of Garden Merit in 1937.

In America this Cornel, in the white or pale pink-flowered wild forms, is a small tree of great beauty and there, when making new gardens in the South, darkies are sometimes sent out into the woods to collect young trees. The method is to hack out a lump of root just around the base of the stem and then behead the tree at about 6 feet. Thus an easily portable "set" is secured that can be carried back on the shoulder. I have seen all stages of growth and the final one is a shapely standard tree with a fine bushy head, four years later. I shall not easily forget the sight of such trees near Lake Hall, Tallahassee, covered with the huge white "flowers" shading, with Pines cunningly interplanted, a foaming carpet of the Chinese R. *Simsii* (our florist's potted "Indian Azalea"). But in our climate with its spring frosts and weak spring sun, made still weaker in effect by the prevailing north-easters of May, C. *florida* is usually but a poor shadow of its real self. After a hot summer, however, it is a glorious thing with all the amazing freedom of flower seen in its native land. A neutral or acid soil is required.

In large gardens sufficiently elevated to avoid spring frosts this Cornel is very well worth planting more frequently for its distinct habit

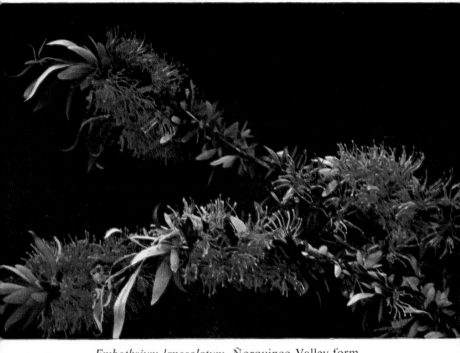

Embothrium lanceolatum, Ñorquinco Valley form

Magnolia Sieboldii

Rhododendron 'Tondelayo'

Ghent Azalea 'Graf Alf von Nipping'

and fine autumn colour. The flowers open on the naked branches, unlike those of its rival, *C. Kousa*, which appear among the full leafage and yet by reason of their greater numbers and superb presentation make an even greater display.

Very different from the gentle Dogwood is *Poncirus trifoliata* (*Ægle sepiaria*) the **Hardy Orange,** which comes from Japan and is a curious and, in warm gardens, quite an attractive shrub. It forms a fairly dense, deciduous bush usually about 5 feet high, sparsely foliaged but profusely armed with the most terrible olive-green spines 2 or 3 inches long. In May the fragrant white orange-blossom flowers appear, often in such numbers as to make a very nice display. Later the fruits, like small inedible oranges, are formed. These contain good seeds from which a person requiring an unusual, but highly effective, hedge might easily raise enough plants for this purpose. It stands clipping well enough, though not hard cutting into the old wood, and is quite reasonably hardy, revelling particularly in the sandy soils of Surrey. It is not, however, over-particular as to soil provided that it has a sunny position and free drainage.

One of the most spectacular of all flowering trees is ***Embothrium coccineum*** and more particularly *E. c. longifolium* and *E. c. lanceolatum* —"Norquinco Valley Form".

The various forms are so distinct in both hardiness and decorative quality that it is best to deal with them separately although botanical distinctions are less clear.

Embothrium coccineum is a native of Chile introduced by William Lobb for Messrs. Veitch of Exeter in 1846 and it first flowered there in May, 1853. It is a sturdy but somewhat thin tree about 15 or 20 feet high with small, leathery, evergreen leaves. In late May small clusters of the brilliant scarlet honeysuckle flowers appear on the ends of the branches. In spite of their vivid colouring the flowers, on typical trees under observation, are not really numerous enough to make much of an effect. On the other hand this form appears to be quite "reasonably hardy", no winter damage having been noticed for at least the last ten years. This plant comes from the most southerly, and thus coldest, part of Chile at a corresponding latitude south to Liverpool north.

In the wild, around the Straits of Magellan, it seldom exceeds the dimensions of a tall shrub and is often not more than 1 or 2 feet in height†. Dr. Wilfrid Fox of Hascombe, Surrey, obtained seeds of an

† R. O. Cunningham, "Natural History of the Straits of Magellan".

absolutely hardy form from Tierra del Fuego, an island lying even further south than the straits†. He kindly gave me a young plant, and its slower and sturdier growth and shorter, blunter leaves are very distinct from the rapid sappy growth and long narrow leaves of *E. c. longifolium* nearby.

E. c. longifolium. According to Messrs. Marchant of Wimborne, who have shown fine specimens at many of the R.H.S. meetings and shows, this form is one long cultivated in Irish gardens. The oldest plant, according to Mr. H. Armytage Moore‡ of Rowallane, is at Rostrevor where it is surrounded by sucker growths at the base. Growth is not slow, hard and twiggy like that of the preceding, but rapid, soft and slender, so that a rather insecure tree is quickly formed. Whether this form is a separate species or not I cannot say, but it is distinct enough from the gardener's point of view to require a distinguishing label. The reason being that *E. c. longifolium* has the valuable quality of producing flowers all along its branches instead of merely at their ends. Furthermore, the flowering season is more prolonged, starting earlier and finishing later, and both fertile seed and numerous basal suckers provide ready means of increase. *E. c. longifolium* is apparently not quite so hardy as *E. coccineum* but it is a faster grower and more vigorous. While I would put the latter in the "reasonably hardy" category I cannot do so in the case of the former. None the less the splendid speed of growth and the astonishing and spectacular brilliance of its flowering make *E. c. longifolium* one of those plants that it is worth taking a chance on. There used to be a saying among the old hands with large gardens: "Do you grow Embothriums? If so, you have a garden—if not, you haven't." I think it is possible to have a real garden without them but I agree that anyone who has a fine flowering specimen of this tree has really got a garden, whatever the rest of it is like. The leaves of *E. c. longifolium* are, as the name suggest, longer and narrower than those of *E. coccineum*.

E. c. lanceolatum. Seed of this sub-species was collected at 5,000 feet elevations in the Argentine by H. F. Comber about 1927. The leaves are still longer and narrower and the flowers, in great fox-brushes of flaming scarlet, even more numerous and effective. The form 'Ñorquinco Valley' is the finest Embothrium I have seen (see illustration facing p. 160). Most authorities are agreed that this form, which Lord Aberconway states to have withstood 34 degrees of frost§, is practically as hardy as *E. coccineum*. When 'Norquinco' becomes generally available it should be tried in every likely garden for it is the most

---

† *R.H.S. Journal*, LXX, p. 289.
‡ *Gardening Illustrated*, Jan. 21, 1939, p. 37.
§ Lord Aberconway, *R.H.S. Journal*, LXX, p. 191.

spectacularly brilliant flowering tree that can be grown in these islands. Like most of the plants from the Southern Hemisphere it has a slightly strange look but, rather than segregate it, as is sometimes suggested, I think the best effect is, probably, to intensify its brilliance by letting it take part in an association with the late-flowering forms of the Scots Laburnum (*L. alpinum*), the white-flowered Manchurian Crab and the Knap Hill Azaleas. Viewed entirely alone its queerness is intensified and the garden as a whole is less assisted.

In years to come, when hardy forms of the best flowering qualities have been bred and selected, the Embothriums will take their proper place as reasonably hardy shrubs or small trees adding to the gaiety of all southern and coastal gardens. In the meantime, like the Eucryphias and Hydrangeas, they are plants that wealthy Local Authorities in tourist areas should plant for the decoration of their resorts. I think that such spectacularly beautiful little trees would pay a very handsome dividend, for by the time they come to flowering size healthful competition in such places might well have been restored.

As regards cultivation *E. coccineum* and its sub-species require a moist acid soil well enriched with leaf-mould. A position where the young tree can get its head up into the sunlight so as to encourage freedom of flower, and where good katabatics are provided to ensure that spring frosts drain away safely to lower levels, seems to be the ideal. Some protection from cutting winds is also desirable as the plant is apt to come into growth rather early in the season.

Propagation may be by means of the rooted suckers which can often be secured from trees growing in cultivated ground, or by seeds. Seed raising is not easy, as many of the young plants, being sensitive to root disturbance, succumb in the pricking off. Possibly, therefore, it would be a good plan to avoid this danger by sowing the seeds singly in small pots.

Another species from the southern hemisphere, **Tricuspidaria lanceolata,** a South American evergreen shrub or small tree introduced by William Lobb for Messrs. Veitch in 1848, is too tender to be effective in any but very favoured gardens or along the south and west coasts, particularly up the west coast of Scotland where the moist atmosphere seems to suit it. None the less, it is commonly attempted. Among the dark green leaves the fleshy, bud-like rich crimson flowers depend on long stalks, reminding one of miniature Chinese lanterns. Every summer it grows vigorously, every winter it is disastrously cut back, almost, but seldom quite, to destruction. Thus its appearance is usually anything but decorative as a growing shrub. In the woodland, provided that the katabatics are good, it survives in better shape, but I must repeat that it is, unlike *Embothrium coccineum*, too tender to be effective in the ordinary garden as a rule. There are exceptional places where, growing perhaps against a whitewashed west wall where the soil is not very rich and air drainage is good, it may provide a spectacular effect; but the vast majority of the many specimens known to me are a sorry sight.

Later flowering **Tree Peonies** would be a valuable acquisition and, indeed, there are already quite a number of such hybrid varieties, derived from *Pæonia lutea* and *P. Delavayi* crossed with the Moutan, such as one with the regrettably long name of 'Souvenir du Professeur Maxime Cornu'. They are attractive in their warm orangy tints but some are afflicted with a shape of flower which reminds one painfully of the grosser and more malodorous members of the Composite family and others have their flowers hidden among the leaves.

On the other hand, Professor Saunders, the Secretary of the American Pæony Society, has made several crosses which have produced a number of beautiful single-flowered forms capable of holding their flowers up properly. Some are only pink or magenta, but many fine yellows and orange-reds have been brought out. 'Argosy', a clear sulphur yellow with a maroon blotch at the base of the petals is already widely available in commerce in America, but propagation is reported to be difficult. A valuable quality of the American hybrids† is their later flowering; they come into bloom in late May when conditions are much more favourable. Thus we may look forward with interest to the arrival of these fine shrubs when imports again become possible. But it would really be best if we ourselves set about breeding a race of hardy, late-flowering Tree Peonies suited to our own conditions. Seeds are freely produced by most species and germinate well if promptly sown, although the seedlings are not very fast growers.

It is a good plan to sow each seed in a small pot and plunge this out-doors as the seedlings require two years without root disturbance. After this, they may be moved into larger pots and again plunged. At five years old from seed they will flower and, according to Japanese growers, the seedlings are almost invariably of high quality though, of course, different from the parent. Indeed, it is very difficult to see how any seedling of *P. fruticosa* could go far wrong because the flower of the original wild plant is quite exquisite in shape and design. One feels that a later flowering date and a better colour are the only improvements possible.

† "Hybrid Yellow Tree Pæonies", by John C. Wister, *R.H.S. Journal*, LXXIII, Pt. 6, p. 190.

The Tree Peony is far the most important shrub, in the grand manner, for the owners of gardens in cold districts with unkindly soils which deny them the charms of the greater Rhododendrons, such as abound in Essex, East Anglia, north east Yorkshire and Midlothian. Indeed, some of the finest specimens in Britain were recorded precisely in these areas. One such is described (*The Garden*, Oct. 18, 1890) as "eight feet high and twelve yards in circumference and during twenty-five years never failed to perfect several hundreds of flowers". The largest and handsomest trees in Midlothian (*The Garden*, Jan. 22, 1887) "grow on sloping banks of light and deep soil well exposed to the sun and protected from fierce winds. During the time they are in bloom their wealth of colour carries all before them". For warmer districts I have recommended more backward positions but the sunny aspect is desirable in such cold districts.

Thus Local Authorities and Parks Departments might well get started on the propagation and culture of such beautiful permanent material instead of spending hundreds of pounds annually on lorry-loads of second-rate temporary plants whose destruction at the end of each season leaves the grounds no better off than before.

The Tibetan form of *P. lutea* recently introduced by Messrs. Ludlow and Sheriff appears to be much superior to the older (1883) Chinese form, being of a more firm and graceful habit, growing up to six feet high and presenting its flowers properly, above the foliage. These flowers are twice as large and of a real butter yellow. Unfortunately, however, it flowers three weeks earlier than the old Chinese form.†
It may perhaps be valuable in hybridising, as it is hardy and vigorous and grows well from seeds.

We now come to the flowering time of one of the most gorgeously coloured sections of all flowering shrubs for lime-free soils and one in which both individual charm of a high order and outstanding garden effectiveness are combined. The '**Knap Hill**' **hybrid Azaleas** are perhaps the finest of all, so far as the individual flowers are concerned, and are the result of a lifetime's work of patient breeding and culling on the part of the late Anthony Waterer. Many species had their part in the production of these Azaleas, and one may recognise in their make-up many of the best qualities of the late-flowering and sun-enduring *R. occidentale*, the flaming, rich-coloured *R. calendulaceum* with its remarkably decorative habit and foliage, the large-flowered, vivid *R. japonicum* and the fragrant, late-flowered *R. arborescens*.

† F. C. Stern, "The Tibetan form of *Pæonia lutea*", *R.H.S.*, *Journal*, LXXII, Pt. 10, p. 394.

On the whole the 'Knap Hills' flower in May after the 'Mollises', already described, and before the 'Ghents', reviewed later, but some varieties are a little ahead and others behind the normal. Where the soil is lime-free and leaf-mould or forest-peat can be added, they, and their cousins the 'Ghents', are pre-eminent for the main display of colour in the month of May. As their hues are mostly pure and unsullied by any muddiness, only equally pure colours and whites go well with them. Some of the cleaner-coloured deep purple hardy hybrid Rhododendrons add a fine note to the scheme, but magenta pinks and purplish-crimsons are to be avoided at all costs and even the very clean pure pinks of some of the 'Knap Hills' themselves are really best kept away from the salmon, orange, yellow and red varieties. Since these Azaleas were first described by the writer in "The Flowering Shrub Garden"† a number of further varieties have been exhibited and named by Messrs. W. C. Slocock of Woking, and the Knap Hill Nursery Company, also of that district. Though multiple hybrids, they should probably be grouped under *Rhododendron albicans*. The following selection is available in commerce:—

'Fireglow', rich orange-vermilion, young foliage reddish.

'Flamingo' (This name is unfortunately already borne by another most valuable Azalea cited later, p. 213), carmine rose, orange flare, frilled.

'Gog', Nasturtium Red, Vermilion and tangerine-orange, of rapid growth, early.

'Goldcrest', Straw Yellow, deeper flare, red outside.

'Golden Oriole', Chinese Yellow, orange flare, early.

'Harvest Moon', pale Chinese Yellow, very beautiful.

'H. H. Hunnewell', deep crimson, late, very fine.

'Knap Hill Pink', Phlox Pink, yellow flare.

'Mrs. Anthony Waterer', pale yellow overcast rose, deeper yellow flare.

'Marion Merriman', Chrome Yellow, orange flare (see illustration facing p. 145).

'Persil', a most lovely white with a yellow flare, rather early.

'Pink Delight', pale Carmine with pale yellow flare, the best pink, being warmer in tone.

'Redstart', similar to 'Satan' but with larger, later flowers.

'Satan', a wonderful Azalea, with flowers of Geranium Lake (H.C.C. 20), which gives an effect of blood-red, and particularly fine autumn-tinted foliage.

† "Country Life", 1st edition 1939, and for further varieties see second edition 1947.

'Seville', orange.
'Tunis', orange and red, late, fine autumn leaf colour.
'Yaffle', Geranium Lake, yellowish blotch, late.
'Unique' **, buff-yellow flushed orange.
*altaclarense**, yellow, flushed orange.
'Nancy Waterer', golden yellow, deeper flare.
The last three mentioned are older varieties sometimes classed with the Ghent Azaleas but they are, I think, of Knap Hill type.

The cultivation required for these Azaleas is similar to that described for the 'Mollis' group (p. 117), but a further word of caution may be added in the treatment of new plants. Restraint in permitting the flowering of newly planted Rhododendrons or Azaleas is well rewarded by much stronger growth, giving a far finer effect the following season. If well flower-budded specimens are received from the nursery I would advise pinching off (or, better, cutting just at the neck with secateurs) all but one or two flower buds at the top centre of the bush. This is best done just before the buds begin to swell in spring. If a dry summer follows, spring-planted specimens will need watering to ensure full growth. The best way to do this is to form a ridge of added peat, like a saucer rim, around the spread of each plant, then the "saucer" may be filled several times so as to soak the soil thoroughly or, best of all, the hosepipe may be allowed to deliver a tiny trickle all night. At all times a mulch of leaves or bracken should be kept over the roots. It is essential that the plants should be very carefully installed and make full growth during that vital first growing season. If this is successfully achieved they can, provided of course, that they are on their own roots, practically take care of themselves, with mere minor attentions, such as mulching, for the rest of their lives.

Besides the Rhododendrons, 'Purple Splendour' (a Doge Purple variety with pale-yellow-tipped anthers), very lovely in association with 'Harvest Moon', and 'Royal Purple' another very hardy variety with rich purple flowers, charming associates for the Azalea groups are provided by the contrasting flower-forms of several outstanding **Viburnums.**

Viburnum tomentosum, a Japanese and Chinese shrub, is best in the superior selected forms mentioned below. The "type" being of somewhat gangling habit and apt to grow too tall and leggy.

V. t. Mariesii (A.G.M., July 1929) is one of the loveliest of all white-flowered deciduous shrubs. The horizontal, arching branches bear, all along their length, pairs of the lace-like flat flower-heads, 4 inches across, composed of a central portion containing the true, functional flowers and showy ray-florets of large size around the margin, like a much finer form of our native Viburnum the 'Guelder Rose', or, for that matter, like the wild Hydrangeas. So numerous are the flowers that the effect is that of a shawl of white lace on a green velvet gown. The bush grows ultimately to 8 feet high or more, though usually seen only about 4 feet high, and has the further merit of turning its leaves to a striking deep wine-colour in autumn. Introduced by Charles Maries from Japan, it first flowered at Messrs. Veitch's Nursery at Coombe Wood, Devon, in June, 1875.

Another fine form was raised from seed at Lanarth, Cornwall, but plants that I have seen growing, though very handsome and larger-flowered, rather lack the beautiful "drawing" and finish of the variety *Mariesii*.

V. t. 'Rowallane Variety' was exhibited by Collingwood Ingram, Esq., Benenden, Kent, in 1942. This variety is quite distinct and very valuable, being later in coming into flower. The inflorescence is more compact and of domed shape and the shrub is of more dwarf habit which is a further advantage for small gardens. Figured in *R. H. S. Journal*, LXVII, Pt. 10 (October 1942).

V. t. sterile, the "Japanese Snowball", is a variety with balls of all-sterile white flowers like the Hortensia types of the Hydrangeas. It is one of the most beautiful of the flowering shrubs of artificial appearance. (See illustration facing p. 144.) As a bush it has not the handsome habit of *V. t. Mariesii*, but is apt to sprawl anyhow, unless pruned and tied to ensure a good framework when young. Robert Fortune introduced the plant over a century ago but its use in the open air only became general of recent years. It usually flowers in the latter part of May.

V. t. var. *rotundifolium* is similar, but earlier flowering by about a fortnight, which just alters the combinations possible with other shrubs. There are said to be two other varieties of the same sort, *parvifolium* and *lanceatum*, but I cannot trace these as being offered for sale in this country at the present time.

V. t. grandiflorum is a form with bolder flowers, but is a slower grower with more rounded leaves, forming a denser bush, It colours its leaves very early in autumn.

V. macrocephalum sterile. The "Chinese Snowball", has very large balls of white flowers, so large, in fact, as to make the appearance of the bush somewhat clumsy (see illustration p. 145). It flowers towards the end of May as a rule and, even in Surrey, seems to require a wall. The scentless sterile form was introduced by Robert Fortune from China in 1844. This shrub grows to about 8 feet high, as a rule, and lasts some weeks in flower but its more tender nature and coarser appearance make the Japanese varieties a still better investment. The wild form, which I have not seen, has only the inch-wide outer ray florets surrounding the small fragrant fertile central flowers, thus forming a flat head 4 to 6 inches across. It is said to be hardier.

V. Opulus, our native Guelder Rose, is attractive in the wild with its translucent red berries and fine autumn leaf colour. In the garden the sterile-flowered or mop-headed form *V. O. sterile* is the more suitable. It is ultra-hardy and grows anywhere, but in view of this it is surprising how seldom it is that one sees a really fine specimen. Messrs. Nottcutt of Woodbridge, Suffolk, introduced a specially fine form of the wild type with improved flowers.

Fortunately the Viburnum family will grow on limy soils and under such conditions other species of this genus may be grown in addition to those described. Many are attractive though they do not quite measure up to the standard of flowering laid down for inclusion in this book. Particulars of these may be found in "Ornamental Flowering Trees and Shrubs", R.H.S. Conference 1938, p. 78 *et seq.* in the section written by the late Lionel de Rothschild.

A curious advantage of the flat-headed types over the globose-headed types with only sterile flowers is that the fertile flowers alone are fragrant. The Hydrangea varieties share this characteristic and thus many growers who have dealt only with the solely sterile-flowered, globose-headed varieties of these genera are probably unaware that the wild, flat-headed forms have a delightful fragrance.

The Viburnums mentioned grow best in ground where plenty of humus is present, and either a mulch or light shade, to retain moisture, seems to help them.

As regards propagation, most will root from cuttings taken in late July or August and placed in a sand-frame, if possible with bottom heat. Layering, especially in the case of *V. tomentosum*, is an easier and more certain method for the amateur.

At this time the Scots or **Burnet Roses,** varieties of *Rosa spinosissima*, open. These compact, dwarf bushes have a delightful habit of growth that is all too rare among the wilder Roses and the yellow-flowered varieties are invaluable, particularly to gardeners on limy soils, as a part substitute for the brilliantly coloured Azaleas. Such is the healthful nature of these Roses that we may grow them in natural ways among other flowering shrubs without censure from anyone for robbing them of the full hideosity of the "Rose-bed". Furthermore, on their own roots, they are good, permanent shrubs that may be relied on to keep their places without endless fuss and replacement. On the other hand, the Burnets only flower once and the best single and semi-double varieties of the H. T. garden Roses are therefore a better investment for the smaller shrub gardens.

The wild species inhabits a vast area that includes Britain and Asia and usually has creamy-white flowers, though pinks and splashed forms are sometimes seen. It is important to get this Rose on its own roots rather than grafted, as its suckering habit is one of its advantages, enabling it to fill out a bed nicely and provide young plants when wanted, as well as renewing its own strength and youth in a natural way.

Like the Camellia and the Hydrangea this Rose was developed during the Victorian era when deformed flowers of large size were in demand and the beautiful, functional design of the normal "single" flower was not esteemed. Most of the innumerable old varieties have become extinct and even the few that survive are not commonly listed by nurserymen.

There are a number of new continental-bred varieties and among these are 'Frühlingsgold', an eight-foot hybrid with fragrant semi-double, 4-inch saucer-shaped blooms of Mimosa Yellow—and 'Frühlingszauber' with pink, creamy-based petals and dark mahogany stamens, flowering later, in June, and sometimes again in September†.

The following is a selection of the older sorts:—

Rosa Harisonii or Harison's 'Yellow' is really a hybrid with the Persian Yellow Rose (*R. fœtida persiana*); it grows taller than *R. spinosissima* and does not sucker so freely. The flowers are a fresh Buttercup Yellow (H.C.C. 5/1) and very decorative though they are apt to "ball" in wet weather.

R. s. lutea, a single Lemon Yellow (H.C.C. 4/1) with rather cup-shaped flowers, is somewhat scarce; the flowers are about $1\frac{1}{2}$ inches across, and the bush about 4 feet high or more ultimately, when well grown. There is also a double form sometimes known as "double yellow Ayrshire" that is otherwise rather similar, but less vigorous in growth.

R. s. maxima lutea has larger, single flowers, but possibly a rather less healthful and vigorous constitution when grafted. On its own roots it is a very fine variety and its flowers open out flat and are very shapely.

R. s. rosea is a pink-flowered form of the "type".

R. s. altaica (A.G.M. 1925), is a Siberian form of much taller growth, up to about 6 feet and has yellowish-white flowers.

R. s. 'William III' has double crimson flowers of a brownish cast and is of rather dwarf growth.

R. s. 'Stanwell Perpetual' is a fragrant pink-flowered, semi-double hybrid flowering all summer. It is a useful Rose, but the shape of the flower is too muddled-up to be really beautiful in my opinion.

R. s. 'Brightness' is a double crimson-purple.

† "Shrub Roses", by G. S. Thomas, *R.H.S. Journal*, LXXV, Pt. 1, p. 10 (1950).

R. hispida is a closely allied species (figured, *R. H. S. Journal*, January 1943) making a 4-foot, spiny bush, suckering freely. The flowers are 3 inches across, ivory white in colour and very lovely.

In the wild the Burnet Rose favours a sandy soil and full exposure to wind, and so makes light of such conditions in the garden and grows well on limy soils. Unlike evergreens, deciduous shrubs cannot be expected to keep down weeds beneath them unless a heavy mulch of leaves, chopped bracken, or mowings, is applied. For these Roses a mulch of lawn-mowings, straight from the box, but carefully spread and patted down so as not to interfere with the stems, is a wise precaution. Otherwise the task of weeding among their fiercely armed stems can be a nightmare that, once suffered, will be avoided at all costs ever afterwards.

All Roses need spraying against aphis and caterpillar attack and must be constantly looked over in their early stages. In places where there are many trees or adjacent woods they are not shrubs that can be left to their own devices. They are too palatable to pests. The pocket dust-gun, at least, has to be applied regularly or reinfestation ruins even bushes that have been carefully kept clean from the start and are perhaps thought to be safe for the season. I find it best, therefore, to restrict even these hardy, half-wild types to places near the house where they can receive the necessary little attentions in odd moments snatched from other work.

In addition to the above, gardeners in warm, limy-soiled gardens, unsuitable for Azaleas, may well adventure with the glorious-flowered but difficult 'Austrian Copper', *R. fœtida bicolor*. The English name is misleading as the species comes from Western Asia. The large single flowers are a glowing Signal Red (H.C.C. 719/1) so far as I can judge, but the petals have a hyaline quality, a translucent orangy fieriness, that no colour on paper can quite equal. A warm, sunny spot, with added humus and bonemeal, free drainage, and timely spraying against each disease or pest the moment it threatens, are the only hints that I can give but I must confess to having always failed to grow this Rose really well.

Rosa Primula, described on p. 198, usually flowers in May. It is a very lovely primrose-yellow-flowered species and worthy of high recommendation. It was superbly illustrated in *Gardening Illustrated*, Vol. LXIV, No. 3318, p. 651 (Sept. 1945).

Syringa persica, the Persian Lilac, a 6-foot Chinese shrub with upright arching branches and pale lilac flowers in broad, loose panicles, opening in May, is not very spectacular. It is, however, hardy and not particular as to soil or position. It was introduced in the seventeenth century.

A better plant is the hybrid known as the 'Rouen Lilac', *S. chinensis* (*S. persica* × *vulgaris*) introduced in 1795, which is justly popular. It is a shrub of more lax habit of growth than the common Lilac, with looser flower panicles usually produced in May with remarkable freedom, making it one of the finest flowering shrubs in this family. It was supposed to have originated at Rouen in the eighteenth century but was apparently also long known in China†. The type has purplish-lilac flowers and there are varieties as follows:—

S. c. alba, white flowers.
S. c. metensis, lilac flowers.
S. c. Saugeana, lilac-red flowers.
S. c. duplex, double, purplish lilac flowers.

Unlike the garden varieties of *S. vulgaris*, the 'Rouen Lilacs' can be propagated like the other Lilac species, from hardwood cuttings inserted in sandy soil outdoors in February.

Coronilla glauca is hard to place in this work, as so long as it thrives it is always in flower. On the other hand it needs a warm south-facing chimney-stack wall or some such favourable spot if it is to last long, as it is scarcely hardy enough to flourish unprotected in the open. The grey-green pinnate leaves and sweet scented yellow pea flowers are very attractive. In very mild districts, or if grown in a tub and taken in in winter, it may reach eight feet in height, but it is easily pruned to a smaller size if required.

C. Emerus (A.G.M. 1930), the Scorpion Senna, is hardy enough for any position but it has not the quality for an important place. It will attain six feet in both directions and the small yellow pea-flowers borne from May to frost are tipped with rusty red.

Cuttings and seeds will increase both species and a sunny position in any soil suits them well.

Actinidia Kolomikta cannot well be left out. It is a very effective climber and it does flower, but this has little to do with its effectiveness. It is the beautifully painted leaves of the male plant, bright rose-pink, white and green that are the great beauty of this species. The shy, sweet-scented little white flowers hide coyly among the leaves while these are

† Mr. F. G. Preston, *The Gardeners' Chronicle*, 3245, Vol. CXXV, p. 99 and fig. 47. See also "Lilacs", by H. G. Hillier, *R.H.S. Journal*, LXI, Pt. 11, p. 449.

still green and have not yet assumed their delightful colourings which usually appear later in the season. Often slow to exceed a modest six feet, this plant has been sometimes reported as attaining twenty feet. It is now rather uncommon although introduced from Japan by Maximowicz, the Tzar's gardener, in 1859. Seeds and cuttings may provide increase and a sunny wall suits it best.

This is one of the many unusual and attractive plants that can do so much to change a dreary town backyard into a pleasure and an ornament to the house. The walls must first be prepared if the best effect is to be attained. Assuming a wall of London Stock bricks in all their grimy "greenery yallery" hideousness, the first step will be the application, with a whitewash brush, of a thick coat of slurry made with one part of Portland cement and three parts of sand thoroughly mixed dry, and then moistened with enough water to provide a creamy consistency that will brush on easily. This is worked in and laid on vertically and then laid off with careful horizontal strokes. When set, the wall may be colour-washed, and then a painted trellis is affixed and the climber may be planted as soon as the foot of the wall has been thoroughly enriched with peat or black rotted leafmould.

It is difficult to place large families with innumerable garden varieties in their proper seasonal flowering order. One must either group them, choosing a time when the majority are in flower, or one must chop and change too distractingly from one genus to another. In my view, however, the significance of flowering time is so important with flowering shrubs that the advantages, for the reader, outweigh the disadvantages.

The **Clematis** family provide one of the most awkward problems in this respect. Their glorious great flowers most generously reward the skilful cultivator and like the Cherries, Azaleas, Camellias, Moutans, Rhododendrons and Hydrangeas they enslave their devotees in a happy bondage which, at least, ensures that never again in all their lives will they know the curse of boredom for an instant.

Clematis patens, an 8-foot Japanese climber introduced by Von Siebold in 1836, is seldom seen but has produced a number of fine garden hybrids. Many of these flower in May and June and are attractive when scrambling up strong-growing shrubs or decorating trellis screens or posts near the garden-house or Loggia. Among the hybrid varieties, commonly available in nurseries are:—

'Daniel Deronda', semi-double blue-purple.

'Edouard Désfosse', violet, "the finest large-flowered Clematis in cultivation". †

† "Clematis", by Ernest Markham, "Country Life", 1935.

'King of the Belgians', light mauve with purple bars.
'La Lorraine', pale purplish-pink flowers and strong growth.
'Lasurstern', very fine deep blue-purple.
'Miss Bateman', white flowers with red-brown anthers.
'Mrs. George Jackman', full pearly white flowers.
'Nellie Moser', large pale mauve-pink flowers, sometimes considered as a C. *lanuginosa* hybrid.
'President', rather later-flowering and continuing into autumn, deep violet flowers very freely borne, sometimes considered a variety of the Jackmanii section.

Many of these beautiful kinds flower at intervals over a long period, being of hybrid origin. Accordingly more detailed mention is made of these in the late summer section where the garden Clematis are dealt with.

These Clematis will all grow well on limy soils and are thus of very special value to those gardening under such conditions. Gardeners with neutral or acid soils, though they can also grow them perfectly will have this flowering season so strongly catered for by the Brooms, Azaleas, and Rhododendrons that they will have less need of these more exacting early-flowering climbers. For them the later-flowering section is probably the more valuable.

In planting a Clematis, care should be taken to set the plant on the shady side of the support and to allow the growth to emerge into the sunlight. A strong piece of wire netting is, I think, essential to protect the highly vulnerable emerging stem. Occasional treatment with "Meta" slugicide is necessary in the growing season or slugs may spoil every emerging shoot. The shoots should be frequently tied out in fan formation, as they grow, or they soon form an unsightly muddle with little chance of bearing the abundant, huge, and beautiful flowers which are the great asset of these rather troublesome and fragile plants. The well-grown and trained specimen does, however, most amply reward the gardener's pains. Further details on the family are to be found in the late-summer section, pp. 215 and 263.

Pruning, for this section, is best confined to the removal of unripened tips and slight thinning if necessary. On very acid soils a light scattering of mortar rubble may be given, but the late Ernest Markham wisely advised restraint in this. The pH value of the soil must not be altered, or mineral deficiencies arise with harmful effects. Bonemeal is better.

Stalwart shrubs that can act as hosts for Clematis have their uses. One of these is a **Staphylea**, S. *colchica Coulombieri grandiflora*, a member of the Bladdernut family. It is a deciduous bush of possibly hybrid origin which appeared in the famous arboretum of Segrez in France about 1870. Usually seen about 8 feet high, it is quite handsome when decked in late May with the drooping panicles of white flowers followed by the large, bladder-like, inflated fruits. While it plays no useful part as an all-the-year-round garden decorator, it is graceful and pretty when in flower and useful for limy gardens as it will grow well on this type of soil. Increase can be effected by cuttings.

Jasminum Mesnyi is an evergreen scrambler which most of us know under the more pleasing name of *J. primulinum*. It is a strange and puzzling plant that has so far not been found wild or bearing seed. E. H. Wilson found it in a garden in Western China in 1900. It resembles the common winter-flowering yellow Jasmine but it is just twice as fine and it flowers in May. The clear yellow flowers, borne singly, are semi-double and an inch and a half or nearly 2 inches across. Unfortunately this Jasmine has not the hardiness of the old favourite and requires a warm and sheltered wall in the south and a cool greenhouse further north. A blue Clematis makes a charming neighbour for it.

Cuttings or layers may be rooted fairly easily in the usual manner.

Were all gardens of the small size I should not mention here many species which do not quite fulfill the requirements for such small spaces, where the maximum of charm attainable must be closely concentrated. There are, however, many extensive gardens in country places whose upkeep, owing to a well-planned naturalistic layout, is no greater than that of many a plot a tenth of the size. Full advantage is taken of mulching and shade as weed deterrents, and groups composed of separate, single specimen trees and shrubs, rather than closely planted beds, are the rule. The motor-scythe, used perhaps only two or three times a year, takes the place of the mowing machine and the swap-hook, or sickle, replaces the border fork. In such places flowering trees are the ideal plant material.

Halesia carolina, the **Snowdrop Tree**, comes from the south-western United States, whence it was introduced in 1756, and is a wide-spreading, irregular, shrubby little tree seldom more than 20 feet high at most. In May, the clusters of short-stalked pendent white bell-shaped flowers decorate almost every naked twig in the most delightful manner. Were it a shapely tree when out of flower we should see it, no doubt, more commonly planted, but unfortunately it is one of those that have not the attractive all-the-year-round appearance so necessary for the small gardens of today. A hybrid form, *H. c. Meehanii*, is a bushy, upright shrub with smaller, more deeply divided flowers.

The Snowdrop Tree requires an acid or neutral soil, preferably sandy. It is hardy, but flowers best in a sunny spot and can be propagated from seed and by layers.

H. monticola. The Mountain Snowdrop Tree is a taller and even hardier American tree species, making a shapely, full-sized tree with longer stalked and larger, white flowers. It is also a more rapid grower and flowers when quite young. It is not readily available yet over here, but is mentioned as it seems to be a tree of great possibilities for the future.

H. m. var. *rosea* is a form described as having pink flowers.

Known here for three centuries yet rarely planted, *Cercis Siliquastrum* (A.G.M. 1927), the '**Judas Tree**' from south Europe, is only seen at its best in the warmer gardens in England. It is, however, remarkably beautiful in Italy and Spain where it is often used as a street tree. The tree, perhaps 15 or 20 feet high, erupts from the naked wood of twig, and even stem, into a cloud of rosy purple pea-flowers in late May. The heart-shaped leaves and bean-like seed pods follow. The Judas Tree is of attractive habit, but, being largely grown from seed, individuals vary and some are of shrubby, rather than tree-like, growth.

A warm position on a south slope is required, but either chalky or acid soils suit it equally well. Seeds are the best method of increase.

The even more beautiful Redbud, *C. canadensis*, though superb in America, unfortunately declines to show its real qualities in our more uncertain climate.

"Ne'er cast a clout till **May** is out" seems to me to refer to the plant rather than the calendar. It is, at all events, in that sense that I have always obeyed the adage.

Cratægus Oxyacantha, the Hawthorn or May, is one of the most beautiful of our native flowering trees, especially when in an open position on chalky soil. Aged specimens have a picturesque habit that can be greatly helped by a little careful "manicuring".

The garden varieties are very commonly planted, yet it is seldom that one sees well-flowered specimens of the finest sorts. Among the best are:—

C. O. rosea, a tree of shapely, twiggy and rounded form, in a properly isolated position, with profuse, pale rose-pink single flowers.

C. O. punicea. This variety appears to me to provide the most

colourful effect of any, with its single crimson flowers, though these
are not always borne as freely as one could wish.

C. O. Pauli (*C. O. plena coccinea*, 'Paul's double scarlet'). The
colour of this fine Thorn bears no resemblance to scarlet, being a
rosy crimson. Curiously enough, owing to rapid fading of the flower
colour, the effect is often less brilliant than that of the preceding.

C. O. plena has double white flowers that become pinkish with age.
In my view a fine selected form of the wild type with large and shapely
single white flowers and bright red anthers is often even more beautiful.
Such a form would be worth propagating as a clone, as the variation in
beauty of flower among wild specimens is very wide.

C. O. candida plena, is a scarce, double, white-flowered form that
does not turn pinkish.

C. O. Maskei is a variety with charming double, pale-pink flowers.

To flower really freely the Hawthorns require more open positions
than they are usually given. When the white, and just a few pink,
varieties are grouped where they have sufficient room, the effect is
delightful and makes them one of the best of flowering trees for chalky
or limy soils. Careful pruning is needed in the early stages to form a
shapely tree with a short trunk and characteristically bushy head.
Bushes rather than standards are really best, for when attempts are
made to keep the tree to a tall clear stem and small head this shape is so
foreign to the nature of the Thorn that results are seldom good, or
permanent.

As lawn or park trees in chalky districts forming 20-foot domes of
fragrant flower in late May, the Hawthorns are superb. On light, very
acid soils, unlike almost all other flowering trees that I know, they are
less vigorous and also less free-fruiting and the fruits are apparently less
vivid in colour.

The garden forms are grafted or budded on the common type and
layers, which may occasionally be got where low branches reach the
ground, are the best means of propagation for the ordinary amateur.
The Hedge Thorn or Quick is of a different species (*C. monogyna*)
and this is quite easily grown from seed if required for hedging
though it is much quicker, of course, to buy young plants.

Two hybrid members of the Hawthorn family provide us with pleasing
small trees for the garden. Judged on flowers alone they would hardly
be called effective, but they add the qualities of decorative fruits and
autumn-tinted leaves and thus qualify for inclusion.

C. Lavallei (A.G.M. 1925) (*C. Carrierei*) is a hybrid Thorn making
a tree about 20 feet high with dull-white flowers about an inch across
in late May or early June. These are followed by large orange-red fruits

12

which last well on the tree in winter. In autumn the leaves turn red before falling. Thus, without ever being spectacularly brilliant, the little tree is a steady worker in the cause of garden decoration.

C. prunifolia is another hybrid of doubtful origin. Unlike the previous variety there are times when this Thorn is one of the most vividly brilliant objects in the garden. Making a rounded tree, furnished to the ground, about 20 feet high, its clusters of white flowers appear, nearly three-quarters of an inch across, in late May or early June among the roundish-oval, brilliant dark green leaves. The round red fruits, about five-eighths of an inch long are often described as falling in October, but having frequent occasion to pass a couple of dozen specimens most admirably planted on the Guildford and Kingston by-pass roads by the Roads Beautifying Association I have been able to note that a large proportion of these often remain decoratively on the trees during the winter. These particular specimens do not colour to any very spectacular extent in autumn. But other specimens under my observation, whose fruits do fall in October, colour their leaves to the most superb brilliant red and orange tones. I have gathered some of the fruits littering the sides of these roads and grown seedlings quite easily. It is as yet too early to say whether they will have the good qualities of the seed parent, but the leaves all appear to be identical.

This fine Thorn, like other members of its family, will grow on limy soils and appears to be perfectly hardy.

The **Laburnums** are among the most spectacular of flowering trees that can be grown in our climate, but their ubiquity and the fact that complementary plantings are hardly ever specially arranged causes them to be held in comparatively little esteem.

Laburnum anagyroides (*L. vulgare*), the common Laburnum from South Europe, opens early in May and the racemes of Canary Yellow flowers are short and do not last very long in beauty. It is, however, very lovely with the white-flowered Cherries, particularly when the colour scheme is kept to white, blue-violet, soft orange and yellow without any pink in sight.

The variety *L. a. aureum* has yellow leaves and is very striking, but not commonly seen.

L. alpinum, the Scotch Laburnum, flowers a fortnight later, as a rule, and some especially desirable seedling forms flower later still. This makes possible a very vivid association with the flaming scarlet flowers of the Embothriums. This is the sort of real "eyeful" that the milder coastal resorts should try out, I feel, instead of the Salvias and other bedding plants which the public are getting tired of. Unlike the common

Laburnum, *L. alpinum* forms a particularly fine, shapely and strong tree and the short racemes are so numerous and well presented that, in my opinion, it is far the most beautiful member of the family. Unfortunately it is now distinctly scarce, but wise nurserymen are again propagating it.

L. Vossii (A.G.M. 1928) is usually in flower a little before the later forms of *L. alpinum*, and is a hybrid between the two species mentioned. The racemes of flowers, of similar Canary Yellow, are very long indeed and provide a fine contrast when the tree is trained over a pergola with Wisterias. It is the finest in the individual flower raceme, but, making only a poor weak tree, is not so valuable in the garden scene, perhaps, as the latest-flowering forms of *L. alpinum*. *L. Watereri* is rather similar but distinct. The buff seed-pods are decorative in winter sunlight.

There has been, until recently, little encouragement for the nurserymen to select and propagate the late-flowering forms of *L. alpinum* so invaluable to the gardener seeking continuity in his garden decoration. Such forms, indeed, transfer a beautiful flower effect from a period when there is too much available to one which is short of good material. To my mind a fine mass of flower is much more acceptable in the dreary "June gap" when most gardens are dull in the extreme, although then at their most climatically enjoyable, than in the bleak days of winter when flowers seem out of place.

The Laburnums are easily raised from seed and are not particular as to soil, even growing well on very chalky land. Careful training and pruning and firm staking in the early stages are needed to secure a fine, shapely tree capable of supporting the great weight of a heavy crop of flowers in later years.

There are shrubs among the Horsechestnuts and of these *Æsculus splendens*, the Scarlet Buckeye, is the most beautiful of all. It flowers in May and is outstanding even among the many lovely plants of the Florida forests. Along the quiet rivers that flow through them its fine scarlet flowers in eight-inch panicles are often to be seen hanging out over the water. It is a shrub of ten or twelve feet and requires a fairly moist and rich soil to do well in this country, but like most other Horsechestnuts moves well and is not over fastidious. Though rare it is available at specialist nurseries and may be increased by layering.

At this point, when June is about to begin, we may lament the passing of a most useful **Broom** which also provided a fine mass of yellow, that most brilliant of all colours at a distance. The late T. Smith of Daisy Hill, Newry, used to grow seedlings from the latest flowering specimens

of *Cytisus scoparius* each year and, after a while, a very reliable June-
and July-flowering strain was evolved. These Brooms are still to be
found occasionally in old gardens in many parts of the country where
they enliven the midsummer scene in the most spectacular manner.
Unfortunately the strain has been lost in commerce, though I have
hopes of inducing some firm to put them on the market again. Even
amid the galaxy of May flowers the common Broom is a very lovely
shrub; in the dogdays of June it is a riot. Furthermore, by constant
shearing back of the young wood the plants form dense velvety green
domes very decorative at all times of year.

Before closing the section devoted to the flowers of May I should
remind readers that in late May some species described along with their
kindred in the June section will often be already in flower. *Styrax
Obassia, Rosa Hugonis, Dipelta yunnanensis, Magnolia sinensis* and *M.
Sieboldii* are examples. Several Potentillas (see page 267) are also in
bloom.

Then, too, the phenomenally long-lasting qualities of the flowers of
some kinds of flowering shrubs enable them to play almost as fine a part
in May as they did in the previous month. Azalea 'Hinomayo', for example, I record as having held its flowers in decorative condition in full
exposure for exactly five weeks from the time the first buds opened.
The evergreen Barberries, Camellias, Moutans, early alpine Rhododendrons and the Periwinkles will also carry on their display well into next
month.

CHAPTER V

JUNE

JUNE

AFTER the late spring-flowering shrubs are over the flowers of early summer open. This time is usually one of the dullest in gardens, though, as the weather is usually then at its best, it should surely be one of the gayest. There are plenty of beautiful shrubs that flower in June—more than enough to fill any ordinary-sized garden completely, but they are too late for the great Chelsea Show, unless unnaturally forced. Thus their names appear comparatively rarely in the nurserymen's order books, and consequently in only small numbers in their propagating lists.

In my view this time of year merits the keenest attention by planters. There is no need for their gardens to drop to a deplorable dullness the moment the rush of spring bloomers is over, Yet the neglect in planning for June is astonishingly widespread. I have ranged the great gardens of England at that time more than at any other, herbaceous borders and all, in search of flowers. There have been many days when the only plants I have found in bloom have been *Campanula glomerata*, *Lilium umbellatum* and a few little oddments. Through the years I have found at last the shrubs to give me flowers in what were flowerless days, and I cherish and enjoy them more than any and judge the garden most critically at this time.

When we have new plantings in mind then, let this be the moment when we visit the nurseries, go flower-hunting in others' gardens where we may, and keep the notebook close at hand. Then, when the results mature, we shall find this lovely time of year in our gardens as flowery as the spring.

Formerly the "herbaceous border" was supposed to take over the decoration of the garden at this stage. But even if one assumed that herbs, unnaturally and densely concentrated in a carefully contrived assortment in one or more rectangular beds, could be an artistic and beautiful feature showing off these handsome plants effectively, the artificiality of the thing is so marked that it upsets the naturalistic atmosphere of the garden at once. The continuity of the whole composition is destroyed by such an unnatural concentration and, indeed, a "shrub border" set down in an otherwise shrubless garden is just as.bad.

Many of the herbs are beautiful plants of fine, individual drawing and attractive flower colour, but they are out of scale with small shrubs.

They are in scale in the composition with trees. In small groups of one fine but varied sort, such as Peony, Campanula, Iris, Lupin, Poppy, Japanese Anemone or Phlox, they can be superb at the foot of a grove or even near large shrubs of a greater height then theirs. But if the garden scene is to be really harmonious, evenly decorated and beautiful all through the year we must really do without that rectangular con- centration of herbs. Consequently we should best look to our shrubs, however many or few we have, to spread their blossoming evenly over the flowering season from the end of March to the beginning of October. This they can do with ease and brilliance; there need be no let-up whatever in the sequence of flower, the whole scene remains beautifully knit and gaily decorated, and there are no cultural complications.

On acid soils, of course, the whole listed selection is available, but the hardy hybrid Rhododendrons, the Evergreen Azaleas of the *R. indicum* section or the Ghent Azaleas make the finest display in the early part of the month and *Cornus Kousa* and Magnolias will be outstanding among the taller subjects, Later on the Roses will take over.

On limy soils Deutzias, Roses, Tree Lupins, Cistus, Halimiums, Helianthemums, Lilac species and Philadelphus offer ample fine plant material to make this month as fine as any. One or other of these genera will be found especially suited to the particular garden conditions of soil and climate and therefore suggest itself for special exploitation.

Intensified beauty, in the language of Nature†, in the garden landscape satisfies our longing for the natural landscape that is now almost everywhere destroyed, for the wild flowers we can no longer gather and the "homes of the wild creatures now far away from us in their own solitude".

Among the indispensables for the lime-free garden are the **Hardy Hybrid Rhododendrons.** There are two fairly clearly marked sections of these which should, I venture to think, be kept entirely separate both in nurserymen's catalogues and in the planter's mind. If this were done much disappointment would be avoided; this is because the earlier flowering section, typified by the well-known *Rhododendron* 'Pink Pearl', "B", or 'Loder's White'', "C", is markedly less suited to withstand the wind-buffetings and sun-scorchings of the ordinary open garden than the "ironclad" later-flowering section typified by *R.* 'Purple Splendour', "A", or 'Mrs. P. D. Williams', "A".

In the wonderful galaxy of colour of the superbly beautiful new hybrid Rhododendrons, the old ultra-hardy types are sometimes put

† As one might say a good building is carried out *in the language of architecture.*

down as quite outclassed; and so they are, *as cut flowers or as denizens of the Wood-garden*, a special type of garden really outside the scope of this work (see p. 134). But, as flowering shrubs to decorate the ordinary little gardens of the majority, many of the new beauties just fail to compete at all. They can only be effectively grown in what approximates, culturally, to a wood. In the opinion of many, a wood-garden is far the nicest kind of garden, but the fact remains that, in these over-populated islands, only a favoured few can have one. Consequently, I hold that no Rhododendron that is not Category "A" ("Hardy anywhere in the British Isles *and may be planted in full exposure*") should be considered as capable of competing with the existing Category "A" Rhododendrons. Having grown all types under varied conditions and made many experiments, these latter are the only ones that I can recommend for the ordinary, but of course lime-free, open garden. Admittedly, the bulk of these varieties have flowers of rather poor and muddy colours compared with the more tender novelties, but there are whites, purples, warm pinks, lavender-blues, crimsons and even an orange-yellow which are reasonably clean in tone. They are all we have got, anyway, and, indeed, if adjudged purely as flowering shrubs for the open garden against other species of flowering shrubs, they are absolutely first-class. Flowering evergreens work all the time and are therefore the most valuable of all shrubs and the hardy hybrid Rhododendrons are some of the finest of these. The late Anthony Waterer, who bred many of the first Rhododendrons and Azaleas that are still unsurpassed, refused to recognise as a *good garden Rhododendron* any which did not possess the following qualifications:—

A strong constitution.

Large, firm foliage.

A compact and conical flower head not easily injured by wind or rain.

Flowering in June or later, thus avoiding frost damage.

In my view, this is as true today as ever.

In a few years' time there will be available a new range of brilliant colours in the truly hardy, "A" category, types. They will be due to an infusion of the "blood" of that remarkable Rhododendron *R. dichroanthum*, "B". In itself this species from "dry, open, rocky meadows" in Yunnan at 11,000–12,000 feet altitudes, does not appear particularly attractive. A low, fairly dense bush with a thin, lax truss of long-stalked, tubular-bell-shaped, small, fleshy flowers of a dull orangy tint, it is not at all striking. Yet this little plant carries the genes that provide the answer to the Rhododendron breeder's prayer. There are hidden fires in that meaty-looking little corolla for, crossed even with the magenta-flushed *R. Fortunei*, the latent orange colour is so dominant that, instead of the purplish-tinged progeny that results from crossing *R. Fortunei* with almost any other mate, a Geranium Lake and Indian Yellow-flowered hybrid can be got. When *R. dichroanthum* is crossed with a red hardy hybrid with a strong, full, upright truss of wide-open flowers, the very first generation, such as 'Berryrose' and 'Limerick', seem to me to be quite remarkably lovely as they are, but no doubt still further perfection will be reached in the second and third generations by skilful breeding and culling. 'Goldsworth Orange', "A", is already available in commerce and I think it is the forerunner of a superb race of hardy hybrids in rich and lovely warm colourings as fine as those of the Ghent Azaleas.

But now let us review the best of those at present available in commerce here, leaving out the more objectionable magenta-pinks, and taking the late May or June-flowering sorts only for this section. All are category "A" unless otherwise stated.

album elegans, palest mauve, a splendid grower and wind resister.

'Blue Ensign' **, pale purplish-mauve, dark centre.

'Blue Peter' ***, pale mauve (H.C.C. 633/2), dark centre, needs shade to avoid "fly".

'Cetewayo' *, dark purple.

'Chionides', creamy white.

fastuosum flore-pleno, double mauve, must have shade or gets "fly" badly.

'Frank Galsworthy', full Solferino Purple (H.C.C. 26), yellow spots, a fine deep colour.

'Garibaldi', salmon-red.

'Goldsworth Orange' **, Maize Yellow (H.C.C. 607/1), flushed orange, very attractive. Not so hardy as others.

'Goldsworth Purple', vivid purple.

'John Walter', crimson.

'Joseph Whitworth' *, deep purple-lake, very dark in tone.

'Lady Annette de Trafford', clear, fresh pink, choclate blotch, very shapely flowers.

'Lady Clementine Mitford' **, a peach-pink effect, actually palest Crimson (H.C.C. 22/3), attractive foliage.

'Lady Eleanour Cathcart' ***, clear rich pink in effect, actually Rose Madder (H.C.C. 23/2), chocolate spots, good, *R. maximum* hybrid.

'Lord Fairhaven' *, shrimp-pink suffused yellow, very lovely.

'Lord Roberts', crimson, blackish centre, very good for an extremely exposed position.

'Mme Ida Rubinstein' **, bright pink.

'Midsummer', rosy pink, yellow eye, late.

'Mrs. Anthony Waterer' *, white, yellow flare.

'Mrs. Davies Evans' *, blue-mauve.

'Mrs. Furnival' *** "B". Pink with a crimson flare, very dense and free flowering, really midway between this section and the 'Pink Pearl' types.

'Mrs. J. C. Williams' **, blush, red flare.

'Mrs. J. G. Millais' **, white with a big flare of gold, fine truss, very lovely with late Azaleas.

'Mrs. John Clutton', white, yellow flare, late.

'Mrs. P. D. Williams' ***, ivory white, greenish-brown eye, very beautiful in an open position.

'Mrs. T. H. Lowinsky' * "B" (Category "A" in my experience), white suffused with the palest flush of cyclamen overlaid on the upper half of the flower with a great orchidaceous flare feathered with saffron, gold and geranium.

multimaculatum, white with orange and black spots, late, a ponticum hybrid and a very beautiful shrub in full sun, deservedly a favourite of the late Miss Jekyll, the inventor of the herbaceous border.

'Old Port', Fuchsia Purple (H.C.C. 28), also good with late Azaleas.

'Orion', clean rose pink, scarlet flare, good.

'Purple Splendour' ***, Doge Purple, black centre, yellow anthers, a very beautiful colour when well associated, as with Azalea 'Harvest Moon'.

'Royal Purple', warm purple, yellow centre, *R. ponticum* hybrid.

'Warrior', rosy purplish-crimson, very late and sturdy, so not altogether to be despised.

It will be seen that, after all, there is quite a fine selection of "iron-clads", bred for the purpose, that may be safely planted in open positions in the ordinary garden with confidence, provided, of course, that the soil is not limy and that peat and leaf-mould are added to improve the humus supply when planting as described on p. 189. In the larger gardens these are the ideal plants for providing the solid back-grounds and mounds of winter green without which the garden landscape would be but bare earth and naked branches for half the year. Unlike some evergreens they may be planted right in the beds with no fear of their robbing the soil for the essential complementary shrubs. The compact root-ball requires only water, tinctured by the leaf-mould of the mulch and the peat, or rotted mould, used at planting time to surround the ball. When, in a limy garden, other kinds of

evergreens have to be used to give solidity to the groups, they compete
actively with the marginal deciduous shrubs and, the effect can, for
this reason, seldom be quite so good.

Beds of garden-bred hybrid Rhododendrons segregated alone are
just bad gardening that will not satisfy the amateur gardener of taste,
today, on any pretext. The worst effects are the result of the greater
carelessness, when varieties of different flowering-times are lumped
together in gloomy, humped beds that can never make any but a spotty
effect, for lack of the care and craftsmanship to sort out these easily
moved plants from the muddle produced by a thoughtless plant order
to the local nurseryman. Had the nurseryman himself carried out the
planting he would have been at pains to achieve a whole-hearted and
harmonious display, and the mere addition of a "surf" of bright-
leaved deciduous shrubs about the margins, and in the bays, would at
once provide something worth looking at, at any time. Almost as bad,
from the artistic standpoint, are the puddings seen in some gardens
where Rhododendrons particularly flourish, where innumerable plants
of the "B" class, almost hardy, but not sufficiently sun-and-wind-
resisting, such as 'Pink Pearl', or 'Cynthia', have been planted in beds
solidly of one variety. Thus exposed, the wizened plants flower freely
enough, but the colours bleach in the hot sun and are soon withered to
brown, and the unrelieved masses, when out of bloom, are a notable
cause of "Rhododendrophobia". As Reginald Farrer so aptly quoted,
"at these repulsive pies, our offended gorges rise!"

The most attractive colour effects can be obtained, whenever there is
space to plant a good breadth of hardy hybrids by making an evergreen
"spine" to a bed, or to fill a corner. These are attained by fairly close
planting of those which bloom at precisely the same time, and so form
an embroidery of interwoven colours.

In the colour scheme, either crimson, pink, white and purple, with
plenty of pale colours to lead up to the richer tints, or, in a sheltered
garden, a warmer scheme of reds, whites, orange-pinks and purples
again assisted by paler tones, may be chosen. Usually, in practice, only
purplish-crimson and scarlet when juxtaposed in large blocks will be
found to make a serious clash.

Where the pure, but brilliant colours of the large-flowered Azaleas
are used, the background Rhododendrons are best limited to the many
superb whites, often with flares of gold which pick up the Azalea
colours again, and to the pale mauves and purples. Scarlet Rhododendrons, of course, blend perfectly with the Azaleas, but I do not know
a true scarlet in the "A" category.

In those favoured gardens where conditions of soil, shade, and
wind-shelter are good enough for the "B" class, that superb

landscape colour, red, can be used with fine effect. Among the truer reds are:—

'Britannia' "B" ***, Turkey Red fading almost to Rose Madder, beautiful emerald foliage.
'Doncaster' "B" **, Turkey Red. The rather dwarf and compact habit is valuable.
'Langley Park' "B" **, red.
'Mars' "B" ****, Turkey Red, a very fine variety.
'Mrs. A. M. Williams' "B" ***, bright Turkey Red.
'Pygmalion' "B" **, crimson-red, black spots, late, of splendid sturdy habit.
'Red Riding Hood' "B" **, red.
'Romany Chai' "B" ***, Turkey Red, scarce in commerce, requires care.
'Scandinavia' "B" **, crimson-red.
'Souvenir of A. Waterer' "B" **, warm carmine, rather leggy habit in shade and fades in sun.
'Vulcan' "B" **, carmine.

And flowering later, well into the latter part of June:—

'Baron de Bruin' "B" **, a fine dark red, but of rather straggling habit unless nipped-back when young.
'Essex Scarlet' "B" *, deep crimson-scarlet, very good.
'G. A. Sims' "B" *, ditto, habit more straggly.

The cultivation of the "A" class ultra-hardy hybrids offers few difficulties if, at planting time, the soil is generously enriched with leaf-mould or peat until its healthy acidity and high humus content is beyond all doubt. Some say that peat is doubtfully desirable but I have always found it highly beneficial and, indeed, necessary, placed round the root-ball. It has the merit of being clean, free of weed seeds, and easily and cheaply bought anywhere, as handy bales of "Peat-Moss Litter". The only proviso is that it should not be used until the bone-dry material that arrives has been completely saturated with lime-free water; if it can be spread out in the rain a considerable time before using, so much the better. Care should be taken that no *soil* is ever placed over the root-ball, a scattering of peat or leaf-mould, only, should be put *over* the roots and then a mulch of dead leaves or bracken. This should be kept a little away from the actual stems or they become soggy and unhealthy.

In light and well-drained soils it is often best to set the plant a little deep in the ground, if grafted, so that it stands in a "saucer" which can be kept well mulched with an extra depth of fallen leaves and chopped bracken which will tempt the variety to form its own roots above the graft.

An excellent plan recommended for very dry and poor, sandy soils† is to bury cow manure several inches below the level of the bottom of the root-ball when planting. Thus moisture rises by capillary attraction from below and the plants withstand dry summers without flagging.

Layers, that is, plants on their own roots, are very much more valuable to the owner-gardener than grafted plants, as with the former there is no trouble with constantly emerging suckers from the *ponticum* root-stock. On the other hand, in unfavourable soils, *root-grafted* plants which are sometimes available are often advantageous as the *ponticum* roots are very tolerant and cannot produce suckers.

The resistance to wind of the hardy "A" class is ample for all requirements but in very exposed places it is best to start with low, bushy plants. In nurseries they are usually grown fully exposed so there is no difficulty in securing these. If grown in too sheltered and shady places the old hybrids make too much soft growth and sprawl about in a very unattractive manner. For such spots the 'Pink Pearl' types and other "B" and "C" class Rhododendrons are much more suitable.

The "fly" mentioned is a dirty, semi-transparent-looking insect that infests the undersides of the leaves of Rhododendrons, particularly those having the "blood" of the ultra-hardy *R. catawbiense* or the yellow *R. campylocarpum*. It seems that it likes the smooth concave undersurface of this type of leaf and can only flourish if the host plant is growing in the sun. The pest is, in general, only difficult to control where there are large numbers of Catawba hybrids grown in full sun, as in nurseries. Certain varieties are martyrs to the "fly" and act as sources of re-infection. Consequently these should either be avoided or grown in the shade. Almost any of the proprietary insecticide sprays or dusts are effective, if applied so as to cover the *undersurfaces* of the leaves in early summer when the juvenile stages of the fly can be seen. Care should be taken, though, to obtain a dust which does not have lime, or ground chalk, incorporated as a "spreader". Specially prepared "Rhodo dust" is obtainable.

Sometimes, particularly near Oaks, the Tortrix Moth caterpillar destroys the young leaves of Rhododendrons. Derris dust, applied with a proper dust-gun is a convenient method of destroying these, but in a "caterpillar year", when the airborne invasion is almost continuous, it is very difficult to preserve the foliage.

"Bud blast", a recently noted plague, has now arrived to spoil the remarkable health record of these sturdy, trouble-free plants. In early

† "Rhododendrons", by O. C. A. Slocock, *R.H.S. Journal*, LXI, Pt. 8, p. 317.

winter, browned flower-buds betray the attack of the fungus responsible.
These should be cut off, with an inch or two of stem, at once, and burnt.
If this is regularly done it is thought, although the pest is not yet fully
studied, that the spread of the infestation is prevented. In large plantations this treatment is hardly practicable and it is to be hoped that, ere
long, we shall have a spraying programme worked out to combat this
new menace. For my part I use green sulphur dust applied in August
with a big rotary dust-gun to protect especially valuable specimens. In
conjunction with the hygiene measures mentioned above the treatment
appears to be effective. At least I have seen no blasted buds for some
years.

The species and varieties of **Deutzia** now claim attention. This is,
incidentally, one of the more perplexing of plant names as to its pro-
nunciation. Those who have learned German usually call it "Doytzia",
others "Dootzia". One should be consistent, without doubt, and
though I am in the first category regarding the name of this shrub I
must admit that I boggle at "Fooh'sia", "Mingizzia", "Mineyolia"
and "Esckaliownia". Presumably, then, the "Dootzias" are right, and,
indeed, a stern anglicising is the rule ordained by custom, though it is
too late for many of us to change our ways.

The Deutzias are a large race of deciduous shrubs belonging to a
section of the Saxifrage family, which some now hold should, with
the Philadelphus and Hydrangea, comprise the Hydrangea family,
with white or pale purplish-pink flowers in early June, and mostly come
from China. If they flowered in early May, amid the huge selection of
beautiful shrubs in bloom at that time, we should not wish to trouble
with them but any effective flowering shrub at its best in June is worthy
of our attention. There are about twenty species of possible garden
value and a larger number of hybrids propagated as clones. A few of
the most decorative have been selected for mention below. Further
particulars may be found in an article by Mr. H. G. Hillier, p 118 *et
seq.*, "Ornamental Flowering Trees and Shrubs", R.H.S. Conference,
1938.

Deutzia albida, a 12-foot, bushy species introduced by Reginald
Farrer from Kansu, China, flowers in early June. The inch-wide, bell-
shaped white flowers, in clusters, whiten the bush in a whole-hearted
manner and it appears to be reasonably hardy so long as it escapes a
late spring frost.

D. longifolia Veitchii is a shrub of about 5 feet with one-inch-wide,
purplish-pink flowers in crowded clusters, during the last half of
June, and narrow, pointed leaves.

D. Monbeigii is a particularly decorative Deutzia flowering in early July, so free with its tiny white flowers as to colour the 6-foot bush. It was found in Yunnan by George Forrest in 1927. It requires a loamy soil.

D. pulchra from Formosa, is taller, reaching 12 feet in height with long arching sprays of Lily-of-the-Valley flowers. It is one of the most beautiful members of the family.

D. scabra (A.G.M. 1928) is a useful old Japanese species introduced in 1822. It will grow anywhere, and the white or pinkish flowers, rather like half-open lawn-daisies, are quite attractive in a quiet way in late June. It does not last well when cut.

D. setchuenensis from China is a very pretty, dwarf, late-flowering species usually seen about 3 or 4 feet high, with starry white flowers in clusters. *D. s.* var. *corymbiflora* is even more attractive and is a plant of great charm and refinement.

D. Sieboldiana is another small species with orange-anthered white flowers with a faint sweet fragrance.

The hybrid Deutzias are of course less distinct and refined in form, if somewhat more vigorous in growth and bolder in flower.

D. elegantissima has purplish-pink flowers.

D. kalmiæflora has cup-shaped, pinkish flowers.

D. magnifica (A.G.M. 1926) is a taller shrub with double white flowers in clusters densely set along the branches.

A very fine sub-variety is *D. magnifica* var. *latifolia* with single flowers 1½ inches across in great profusion.

D. rosea carminea (*D. gracilis* var. *carminea*) has fragrant flowers of a purplish-pink colour in June.

The Deutzias, although they prefer a good loam, will grow on limy soils and, indeed, are not particular as to situation either, though they suffer sometimes from the effects of late spring frosts. They flower on shoots made the previous year, so that pruning, except for the removal of flowered branchlets the moment the flowers are over, is done at the expense of flower. None the less, the oldest branches may also be removed at intervals of a few years with advantage. Cuttings of half-ripened shoots can be struck sometimes in the sand-box, but bottom heat is really required to secure a good percentage of rooted plants.

Buddleia alternifolia (A.G.M. 1924), a hardy, rambling, slender-twigged species with narrow, greyish leaves and abundant clusters of Mauve flowers in late May or early June, is one of the more attractive members of a rather dull family. Introduced by Reginald Farrer in 1914, it was described with his usual remarkable flair as "like a gracious

Magnolia Watsoni

Cytisus Battandieri

Cornus Kousa

Rhododendron indicum macranthum

small-leaved weeping-willow when it is not in flower, and a sheer waterfall of soft purple when it is." Unfortunately the habit of growth has the family weaknesses: it flowers on two-year-old wood which makes pruning unprofitable and soon forms a bush 6 feet high and 16 across. Being an insecure rooter, the weeping-willow-tree form is seldom attainable in the garden and its winter appearance is far from decorative. A dry, sunny spot on either acid or limy soil suits this Buddleia best and cuttings of half-ripe shoots taken in July are an easy means of propagation.

Very similar in its preferences as to aspect and its indifference to soil conditions is *Caragana aurantiaca*, a member of the Pea family. It is a deciduous shrub about 3 or 4 feet high with small, narrow leaves and plentiful orange-yellow, gorse-like flowers in dense rows beneath the arching branches in late May or early June. It is hardy and an easy doer in any well-drained sunny spot in either type of soil. Thus it is a useful shrub for limy gardens where it may take part in the substitute display of Azalea colourings.

Seeds, and July cuttings treated in the usual manner, are the best means of increase.

The **Leptospermums** are a group of beautiful, small-leaved slender-branched evergreens of the Myrtle family, found in Australasia. They are, most unfortunately, too tender for any but unusually warm coastal gardens and these must be further favoured by having the necessary neutral or acid soil.

Leptospermum scoparium, the Manuka or "Tea Tree", is the national flower of New Zealand. The common wild form is a slender-twigged, dense, upright, round-topped bush with small narrow, pointed, evergreen leaves and dull-white flowers, about half an inch or less across, in early June. Specimens over here are usually seen about 5 feet high, but, along the south and west coasts, bushes may be seen up to 18 feet in height.

When wreathed with their masses of white, pink or crimson, May-blossom-like flowers the varieties of this Leptospermum are singularly lovely and the other species described later will provide a succession of bloom almost until summer ends.

The great beauty of the family is a crimson-flowered sport, found about the beginning of this century, named *L. s. Nichollsii*. It was introduced in 1908 and is a beautiful shrub that should be tried in all favoured gardens. It revels in sunny and windy spots rather than in more sheltered situations.

13

L. s. eximium, a Tasmanian variety with rounder leaves found by H. F. Comber, has larger flowers of a purer white than the "type".

L. s. roseum is a seedling form with rose-pink flowers.

L. s. prostratum is a dwarf, prostrate form which is notably hardier than others. It has small white flowers.

L. s. Chapmanni is a variety with singularly large pink flowers.

L. lanigerum, with silky, grey-green foliage and profuse white flowers in late June or early July, follows the previously-mentioned species in flowering time.

L. l. 'Giblin's var.' is a fine Tasmanian form of this species. It was collected by H. F. Comber†.

L. Rodwayanum, of more rigid growth, larger, darker green leaves and large, white, fragrant flowers over an inch across, blooms later still, in late July or in August.

L. Liversidgei is a slender small-leaved species with drooping branches and very small white flowers.

L. pubescens is notable for being hardier than many of the other members of this family. It is of slender, erect habit, being spire-like rather than round-topped like *L. scoparium*. The flowers, about half an inch or more across, are white.

L. flavescens is described as a tall white-flowered species flowering in July.

The Leptospermums require a well-drained, open, sunny position and a neutral or acid soil, on the light side for choice. They do not seem to mind wind at all, a useful quality shared by many New Zealand shrubs. Once planted they cannot be moved with safety which is somewhat surprising in view of the fact that they can be so readily grown from cuttings treated in the usual manner. Seeds sown as advised for dwarf Rhododendrons (p. 90) are also a good means of increase, but the unusually rich-coloured *L. s. Nichollsii* usually gives white or pink-flowered seedlings.

Few trees have more beautiful foliage than *Robinia Pseudoacacia*, the 'Common Acacia'. This American species introduced long ago, in 1640, has had its ups and downs in popularity but it has great qualities as a street or garden tree. The brilliant green, divided leaves come late and hold their fresh colour most attractively when most others are already dull with age and the fatigue of summer.

The racemes of delightfully fragrant white or pink pea-flowers are borne in June when they are particularly welcome and the tree submits to lopping to almost any desired size with perfect good nature. On the

† *Gardeners' Chronicle*, Sept. 5, 1936, Fig. 74.

debit side, it tends to run at the root, though, being a legume, even the most hidebound old tree-hater cannot charge it with "robbing the soil". Normally growing to about 30 or 40 feet high, it is easily kept, as a pollard, to half that height if desired. The branches are unfortunately very brittle, which is a serious drawback in windy places, but by growing the tree on one clean stem and then pollarding, so that a fair-sized head will provide the right height, this trouble is greatly minimized. There are quite a number of different varieties, but only one of floral interest.

R. p. Decaisneana is similar to the type but has pale pink flowers.

R. hispida, the Rose Acacia, is a more tender species. Introduced into this country in 1758, it comes from the Pinewoods of Carolina where it grows to a height of 20 feet. It is even less windproof than the other members of the family, though very lovely when covered with its short, thick racemes of purplish-crimson pea-flowers about 6 inches long and two across. In warm and sheltered places it is very attractive grown as a grafted standard tree carefully trained. In colder and more exposed spots it should be given the protection of a wall where it makes an unusual and attractive decoration. An improved form, *R. h. macrophylla* has larger, brighter flowers and larger leaflets.

In Nature this species runs at the root, covering wide areas in Tennessee by this method. This being so, it might be a good plan to get the plant on its own roots and to let it grow in this way.

R. Kelseyi is another sadly brittle but attractive shrub of the same type from North Carolina, with bright rose-coloured flowers in June. Unlike the last, this species sometimes produces fertile seeds in cultivation. Unfortunately, however, it is usually grafted on *R. Pseudoacacia* and is thus seldom safe from destruction by the wind. Plants on their own roots, on the other hand, could renew themselves in this event in a natural way.

The Robinias are not particular as to soil and indeed the poorer this is the better as otherwise they make soft growth more easily broken by the wind. The Goat Moth sometimes destroys the trees by the tunnellings of its huge caterpillars in the centre of the stems. When the tree is on its own roots increase is possible by rooted suckers.

Another interesting wall plant is *Solanum crispum* (A.G.M. 1939), a climber of the **Nightshade** family. It is barely up to hardiness requirements in the open, but is so quick-growing and floriferous that it is worth trying in any sunny spot against a wall. It was introduced from the island of Chiloe in 1829 and produces its fragrant, pale Heliotrope, inch-wide, potato-like flowers with their projecting yellow-anthered centres from June to the end of summer.

Pruning is not necessary unless it is desired to grow this shrub as an open-ground bush. In this case it requires spurring back each year. It is not particular as to soil and indeed this is probably better if on the poor side as it induces firmer and shorter growth.

An even more beautiful relation, *S. jasminoides*, with pale blue-violet flowers, is slighter in growth and more tender. A form of this with white flowers, var. *album*, is more commonly seen than the "type". They are delightful climbers for unusually favoured places in the south and west but seldom grow well enough to be worth while elsewhere.

The Nightshades may be propagated from cuttings in the usual manner. The Latin name comes from *solari*—to quiet, referring no doubt to the permanently quietening effect caused by eating the poisonous berries.

Among the **Hydrangeas** *H. petiolaris* (A.G.M. 1924) is a hardy climber from Japan with strong rough-barked stems clinging by aerial roots like Ivy. The leaves are bright green and smooth on the upper surface and in June the flattish corymbs of white flowers open. The centre part is composed of the small fertile flowers and on longer stalks around the margin are scattered the larger sterile ray-flowers. The form available here is hardly showy enough for a wall, where so many decorative species compete for our attention, but on a tree stump, or climbing up a tree, this Hydrangea has a picturesque habit that makes it very attractive. There appears to be a superior form of this climber in Japan with much larger flowers and there are many species of climbing evergreen Hydrangeas with red, violet, primrose yellow, pink or white flowers not yet introduced.†

H. anomala comes from the Himalayas and also from Formosa (*H. glabra* Hayata). Resembling the preceding, it suffers from the same drawback, namely that the form we have in this country is not the finest in flower. Herbarium specimens sent back by E. H. Wilson have fine corymbs with many bold and shapely ray-flowers. The form we have has few, and rather small, ray-flowers, but it is a vigorous grower though less hardy than the preceding, requiring a sheltered wall.

These climbing Hydrangeas have the merit of supporting themselves well on walls and thus act as useful hosts for more fragile and larger-flowered climbers such as hybrid Clematis, *Tropæolum speciosum*, Morning Glory, etc. They are not very particular as to soil but, of course, grow better when this is well enriched with humus.

They may be propagated from cuttings in the usual manner although they do not strike quite so readily as the cultivated hybrid races of

† For description, see "The Hydrangeas", by the author, Constable & Co. (1950).

Hydrangea. Seeds, sown as advised for dwarf Rhododendrons (see p. 90) might easily provide better forms than those now available in commerce. Wilson recorded the delightful fragrance of the finer forms of *H. anomala*, and as these climbers can be crossed with the red Hortensias, there are great possibilities for the hybridist.

Another interesting climber, self-clinging and evergreen, is *H. integerrima*. The Cornidia section of the Hydrangeas, to which it belongs, comprises some of the strangest, the loveliest and the least known of all plants, and few Europeans have seen them alive. They are powerful evergreen climbers mostly having large ovate or elliptic leaves. The flower umbel is at first enclosed in bracts so that it looks like the bud of one large flower. When this opens a large umbel of the small fertile flowers with many large and often vividly coloured ray-flowers expands.

There are over twenty different species in Central America and nearly as many in Formosa, the Philippines and the East Indies. Those from both hemispheres have a remarkably close family resemblance yet most species are evidently quite distinct from one another. Some are patently of no garden value, lacking the showy ray-flowers that are the chief beauty of the plant, but others are evidently of the very highest value having gorgeous red, violet, primrose-yellow or white flowers.

These climbers usually resemble Ivy in having two different states; the juvenile climbing state with small, differently shaped leaves and aerial roots on the stems, and the free, bushy, flowering state with large entire leaves.

The other species are described in the monograph on the Hydrangeas already cited. We must return to the one species of the family that we have already got in cultivation in this country.

Hydrangea integerrima (*Cornidia integerrima*) resembles the other members of the Cornidia section, being a powerful liana with elliptic evergreen leaves, ascending to the tops of tall trees, but unfortunately the inflorescence of the form seen and sent back by that capable collector, J. F. Comber, is rather a poor one. The inflorescence opens from a large, bracted bud enclosing the whole thing with numerous small yellowish-white fertile flowers but the ray-flowers are each reduced to one irregular, leaf-like sepal which is white tinged with green.

Judging by herbarium material, forms of this species do, however, exist having the essential valuable feature of four or five well formed four-sepalled ray-flowers to each inflorescence. None the less the important point is that this evergreen climber is reasonably hardy in favourable gardens in this country. Thus, if the more vivid-flowered species were secured, we might expect remarkable results from hybridisation.

Like so many South American plants it dislikes drought or sun heat in this country.

A sheltered wall with moist rich soil, a damp atmosphere and light shade appears to suit this evergreen climbing Hydrangea best and increase may be made from the rooted offsets often found round established plants.

In gardens whose limy soil precludes the growing of the Azaleas with their vivid orange, red and yellow flowers at this season, the various **Rose species** are of particular interest. They flower at different times but it is more convenient to group them in this section as it is about the normal time for their flowering to begin.

Whilst they do not provide the effective mass of bloom over a long season that is such a valuable characteristic of the Hybrid Tea Roses dealt with later, they have often a singularly attractive foliage and habit. Certain of the yellow-flowered kinds provide some of the best substitutes for the later-flowering Azaleas where these cannot be grown.

Among the more outstanding species and hybrids are the following:—

R. Ecæ. This Rose has been confused with *R. xanthina* and *R. Primula*, but the true plant is quite distinct, being a fairly tall shrub with small Buttercup Yellow, five-petalled flowers, red-brown wood and foliage that is not aromatic. It was found in the Kurrum Valley of Afghanistan by Dr. Aitchison in 1880. R. Ecae is quite easily grown but is rare in cultivation, as it is difficult to propagate except by suckers. The puzzling name is based on the initials of the doctor's wife.

A Rose often sent out under this name, which is really *R. Primula* (from Samarkand), is a more easily propagated species forming a 6- to 8-foot bush with spicy, aromatic foliage, red-brown wood, red shoots and thorns, small round leaflets and 1-inch-wide very pale Primrose Yellow flowers in May† At first it is rather shy, but becomes very free-flowering when well established and is a very lovely shrub notable for the beautiful presentation of its flowers and long flowering season (see also p. 171).

R. Hugonis (A.G.M. 1925) is, unfortunately, a disappointing shrub in many gardens. In my own experience it was one of the very few flowering shrubs that died out completely in a favourable garden under the enforced neglect of the "emergency" years. The cause was a form of "dieback" to which this Rose seems liable in places where the atmosphere is moist and favourable for fungal growths. In some districts it grows quite satisfactorily and is then very attractive, making a tall bush of about

---

† For further discussion of these distinctions, see B. O. Mulligan, "Rosa Primula and Rosa xanthina Kokanica", *Gardening Illustrated*, p. 218 (Ap. 27, 1940).

8 feet high with arching branches thickly set with the lovely ferny masses of foliage and 2-inch, pale yellow flowers in May. It takes its name from "Pater Hugo", Father Hugh Scallan, a missionary in China, who first sent its seeds to Kew in 1899.

Much superior as a garden plant is the shapely, palest yellow hybrid *R. cantabrigiensis* (*R. Hugonis* × *sericea*). This Rose is fairly free from "dieback" and is more free-flowering, and the flowers open fully in late May or early June, which those of *R. Hugonis* often do not do.

Another hybrid, *R.* 'Dr. E. M. Mills' (*R. Hugonis* × *rugosa*), is a 4-foot, spreading bush with semi-double cup-shaped flowers of a blushed primrose.

R. 'Canary Bird' is a most attractive, but very early-flowering Rose of *Hugonis* type, with fragrant flowers $2\frac{1}{2}$ inches across of bright Canary Yellow. (See A.M. under *R. xanthina*, p. 202.)

R. Moyesii (A.G.M. 1925), introduced by E. H. Wilson from Western China in 1904, is, in the superlative, red-flowered clonal form, one of the loveliest of all Rose species. It makes a 9- or 10-foot, rather "leggy" bush, with gracefully arching branches, admirable as a shade tree for orange Kurumes or Hydrangeas. The blood-red flowers are superbly formed in one of the most beautiful of all flower shapes, that of the Heraldic Rose, with five petals and an exquisitely formed "old gold" centre. Unfortunately, although sometimes over 3 inches across, the flowers are often sparsely borne for the large framework of the shrub. They do not quite "colour the bush" and thus it usually just fails to be really splendid. The numerous red fruits are very colourful in autumn.

I have not yet fully tested the matter, but I would wager that a good way to grow this Rose so as to induce freer flowering would be to arch-over and peg-down the long growths from the start so as to induce flowers and foliage from every possible bud. Great care in handling the brittle shoots would have to be used but the flowers are so lovely that success would be worth a lot of trouble.

R. M. highdownensis, a variety produced by Colonel Stern of High-down, near Worthing, has even more decorative and numerous heps than the type and the best form is very effective indeed. *R. M.* 'Gera-nium' and *R. M.* 'Underway' are also fine varieties as regards this quality.

R. 'Nevada', a hybrid with 'La Giralda', is an almost perpetual flowering, shapely, strong bush with 4-inch creamy-white flowers (figured *R. H. S. Journal*, LXXV, Pt. 1, 1950).

R. moschata, the Musk Rose, is a delightful climber for a wood, where it may be allowed to scramble up a tree at will. It is too hearty, perhaps, for the small garden where its masses of creamy-white flowers would not quite atone for the amount of room demanded. It will climb 30 feet or more without difficulty and an established specimen is a fine sight.

R. *Rubus*, a less strong-growing semi-climber, introduced from Western China by both E. H. Wilson and Reginald Farrer, is of the Musk type. The fragrant white or faintly blushed flowers, 1½ inches across are borne in large loose clusters from June to August. Hardy and vigorous and flowering very profusely this is a fine but rather neglected Rose. The red heps are decorative in autumn and this species appears to have no particular fads about soil or position so long as it gets full sunlight.

R. *Roxburghii* (R. *microphylla*) forms a large, handsome bush 7 or 8 feet high and is very dense, picturesque and sturdy. The fragrant pale purplish-pink flowers are about 3 inches or more across in a good form, and in spite of the weak colouring are so freely produced and so well presented, in an open position, as to be quite effective at a distance.

R. *Eglanteria* (R. *rubiginosa*), the charming Sweet Briar, is too well known to need description. The improved garden hybrids known as the "Penzance Briars" include a number of quite attractive shrubs, pleasant to have in the wilder parts of the larger gardens. None are, however, in the front rank, in my experience, as they only flower once, and those that are good growers have only pink flowers. 'Meg Merrilees', a sturdy bush with rose Madder flowers, 'Hebe's Lip', white with a pink edge, and 'Lady Penzance', orange-pink but a more weakly and unhealthy grower, are examples. Unlike other Roses the Sweet Briars prefer a limy soil but their growth on acid soils is perfectly adequate.

R. *rubrifolia* has attractive pinkish-grey leaves but the red flowers are few and inconspicuous.

R. *anemonoides* (R. *sinica anemone*) is a distinct Rose of doubtful origin. It is a beautiful climber with very large, single, palest purplish-pink flowers in May. For a south wall it is quite pretty but is, of course, eclipsed by the great climbing H. T. Roses, the Campsis, Clematis, Bignonias, etc. which are a still better investment for such a choice position. Much depends, of course, on the colour of the wall surface, but R. *anemonoides* is a Rose that needs some care and, in my experience, resents pruning and sometimes suffers from "dieback". R. *a.* 'Ramona' (A.M. 1950) is a deeper coloured sport.

R. *rugosa*. The Japanese, or Ramanas Rose is one of the most promising flowering shrubs among the Rose species. The habit is handsome and compact, the leaves have a good autumn colouring, and the tomato-like fruits are highly decorative, but the colour of the flowers is unfortunately very poor indeed. It is a wretched purplish pink that apparently bars any improvement in the direction of true scarlets, oranges, or yellows but yields one or two good dark crimson-red and some white varieties. A number of hybrids are available with large, coarse flowers of a feeble, washy pink or pale fawn colour, such as 'Conrad Meyer', 'Nova Zembla' and 'Dr. Eckener'.

Some beautiful varieties and hybrids of *R. rugosa* now, alas, hard to find, are:—

'Ruskin', a single red.

'Carmen', with 2-inch, single flowers in rich damask red.

'Schneezwerg' (a hybrid with *R. bracteata*), with snow-white flowers in clusters of six to eight, it was raised by P. Lambert, Trier, Germany in 1912.

'Red Grootendorst', with small, fringed, red, double flowers in clusters.

'Pink Grootendorst' is similar, but pink in colour, and makes the charming little bouquets one sees for sale in Swiss flower shops. It sometimes occurs as a branch sport on the red, but may be obtained under its own name.

'Lady Curzon', a single pink, with thin-textured flowers 4 inches across, is thought to be a hybrid with *R. macrantha* and, if well nipped back, makes quite an attractive bush.

'Blanc double de Coubert', this double white variety is particularly lovely and fragrant and, except in a very wet summer when it balls its flowers, is quite effective.

'Mrs. Anthony Waterer', has semi-double, deep crimson flowers.

'Parfum de l'Hay' has double deep rose flowers, and is a fragrant and charming hybrid.

Atropurpurea, deep purplish red.

The *rugosa* family have a good golden yellow autumn leaf colour and their healthy and perpetual flowering nature is most commendable. They grow even in the sea-sand on the beaches, yet they are seldom seen in seaside gardens.

R. pomifera is not remarkable, but a variety of this species, *R. p. duplex*, originally found in the late Mr. Wolley Dod's garden, is very beautiful, with large, soft pink flowers and grey-green foliage followed by hairy fruits.

R. macrantha has single, pink flowers and a bushy habit and flowers for a longer period than most, from May onwards.

R. fœtida, the yellow Persian Rose and its brilliant scarlet variety 'Austrian Copper' are important as the part-ancestors of most of our best garden Roses in these colours. As flowering shrubs they are too difficult to make much of a showing in most gardens, but 'Austrian

Copper' is worth any amount of trouble. It is more fully mentioned in the section comprising the Burnet Roses and their allies, p. 171.

R. Banksiæ. The Banksian Rose is the pride of the gardens of the Riviera, but I have never seen it do well enough in this climate to look really attractive, compared with the other species and hybrids available. The violet-scented wild form recorded by Reginald Farrer does not appear to have been introduced.

R. virginiana has the merit of flowering late and has a lovely pink, double-flowered, possibly hybrid, variety, the 'Rose d'Amour' which is now hard to find. There is also a white-flowered form. This species has notably rich autumn leaf colouring which, with the scarlet heps, give it a second season of beauty.

R. xanthina is a garden form and comes from Korea and North China. This Rose and *R. Primula*, *R. Moyesii* and *R. cantabrigensis* are, I think, the best of this group for the average small garden. The Rose sent out under this name makes a fairly compact and very free-flowering bush about 8 feet high with semi-double yellow flowers about 2 inches across in early June. The wild form, var. *spontanea* Rehder, is of weaker constitution and has smaller, paler, single flowers. Unlike most, this Rose seems to need a sheltered position, and may suffer in hard winters.

An A.M. was awarded to *R.? × xanthina* on May 1, 1945. Unless it was forced, the flowering date seems wrong for this species.

One of the best of all places for these Rose species is probably an open position in a wild garden. There, if the soil is chalky, with Cistuses, Genistas, Halimiums, etc., they may take the place of the Ericaceous families so effective on acid soils. For the Roses, it would be advisable to add turf-loam when planting, or fresh inverted turves, buried below the roots, would serve almost equally well. If it is possible to mulch the bushes with bracken or fallen leaves this is most helpful to healthy growth, as alkaline conditions, and particularly artificially added lime, seems to lower the resistance of the Rose to "Black Spot". Great care should be taken to set the plants in the ground exactly at such a depth that the "burl", or growing point, is only just under the soil. The usual cause of failure is their being planted too shallowly on unmulched ground. Bonemeal is appreciated as a tonic in peaty soils.

Most of the species can be propagated from seed and the varieties may be layered or struck from hard-wood cuttings, formed of flowered shoots about 6 to 8 or more inches long, three parts sunk in sandy soil in the open or, better, in the shade of a north wall.

Some of the wild **Lilacs** are worthy of note as their flowers have the delicate lines and shapely individual formation characteristic of many wild species, avoiding the undistinguished, mongrel look of the typical garden hybrid. For the most part, they also flower much later than the common Lilac which is a further advantage for Lilac lovers, as they prolong the season.

Syringa persica, the Persian Lilac, has attractively formed fragrant flowers of Cyclamen Purple (H.C.C. 30/2). It is a graceful shrub of about 6 feet, flowering in late May or early June.

S. Sweginzowii superba, a long-introduced Chinese species, has small, pale, pinkish-lilac, fragrant flowers which are quite attractive when cut, but the bush is no great ornament to the garden landscape.

S. villosa, another Chinese species, is comparatively free-flowering and compact in habit, with pale rosy-lilac flowers late in the season.

S. amurensis (*S. japonica*) a Japanese and Chinese species, is useful owing to its habit of flowering at the end of June, when good flowering shrubs are scarce. The Japanese form *S. a. japonica*, is particularly fine, attaining, in its native land, it is said, a tree-like habit up to 30 feet in height, with abundant panicles of creamy-white flowers.

S. Julianæ is an attractive and easily grown species introduced by Messrs. Veitch in 1900 and later from Kansu, China, by Reginald Farrer. From lilac buds the fragrant white flowers open in early June in such numbers as to colour the bush, which reaches to 10 feet in height in cultivation. Sometimes it flowers again, less profusely, in August. Farrer described it as growing "in sheer limestone cliff" and it has duly proved to be a good plant for a warm chalky garden.

S. Potanini is another Chinese species from the same district, with very fragrant white flowers with yellow anthers. Farrer also sent back seeds of this previously-known species and the plants over here are mostly from their sowing. It is also a limestone shrub, flowering in June and interesting for warm, chalky gardens, the deep green, lanceolate leaves setting off the white flowers to great advantage.

S. yunnanensis, usually of little decorative value, has superior forms with brighter purplish-pink flowers than the type, but the habit of the shrub has all the family weaknesses.

In a cold and chalky garden some of these Lilacs might well be thought worth growing for their coverage of the "June gap"; for a complete description of all available species, see H. G. Hillier, *R. H. S. Journal*, 61 (1936) p. 450 *et seq.* and also the same author, p. 101 *et seq.* "Ornamental Flowering Trees and Shrubs", R.H.S. 1938.

A number of late-blooming hybrid Lilacs derived from *S. reflexa*, *S. villosa*, *S. Josikæa*, *S. Sweginzowii*, *S. Wolfii*, etc. have been bred at Ottawa by Miss Isabella Preston. The original cross, *S. Prestoniæ* (*S. villosa* × *reflexa*), is commercially propagated in Canada in the varieties 'Oberon' with panicles of very pale pinkish-lilac flowers, and 'Romeo' with phlox-pink flowers on reddish-brown stalks.

S. 'Bellicent' (S. *josiflexa* seedling) is described as a graceful 7- to 8-foot bush with small panicles on the lateral branches and a large central truss of the pink flowers terminating the main branches in late May or early June. In Britain the growth of this variety has usually been less tall, reaching only 5 feet in seven years.

Other varieties, mostly of S. *josiflexa* parentage, are 'Guinevere', "a graceful bush of seven feet"; 'Enid,' "nine feet high" and 'Desdemona,' "seven feet by seven feet."† They are growing in heavy chalky soil at Stansted Park, and were brought back from Canada by Lord Bessborough in 1935.

S. *Prestoniæ* 'Isabella' (S. *villosa* × *reflexa*) has narrowly tubular flowers of Mallow Purple (H.C.C. 630/3) borne in large groups of open panicles nearly a foot in length at the ends of strong shoots set with large dark green leaves. I must state, however, that of the entire range of colours shown in the Horticultural Colour Chart, I think that this hue is the most unattractive that a flower can possibly be.

A number of further crosses have been made with successful results. A seedling of S. *reflexa* × *Sweginzowii* was crossed back to S. *reflexa* producing a very attractive hybrid, S. 'Fountain', illustrated in the article cited, the chief improvement being that the flowers do not split and turn brown soon after opening, like those of S. *reflexa*, although they have not the rich pink colouring of that species, being only a pale purplish-lilac colour‡.

Although these Lilacs display their panicles of flower boldly above the foliage with a good presentation, these are mostly of muddy pink or purplish-pink colours, such as would ensure that any new Rhododendron that dared to flower with such a tint would instantly be labelled "unworthy of cultivation", and consigned to the bonfire, but they have a value for very cold, limy-soiled gardens where the more vivid-flowered shrubs unfortunately cannot be made to grow. Their habit is much superior to that of the common Lilac, as basal growths keep the bushes well furnished to the ground. As regards cultivation, the Lilacs are indifferent to the alkalinity or acidity of the soil so long as it is in good, free, aerated condition, but they need some sun to ripen the growths well and a mulch of dead leaves promotes vigour.

---

† "Notes on New Hybrid Syringas", by T. E. Tomalin, p. 312, *R.H.S. Journal*, Vol. LXVI, Pt. 9 (1941).

‡ "New Hybrid Lilacs", by Isabella Preston. *Gardening Illustrated*, 952 (Dec. 1946).

Wall plants and climbers also provide their sequence of flowers but *Jasminum officinale*, the common **Jasmine,** grown for its delightfully fragrant white flowers from June onwards, makes no great effect on a wall as a rule, and is rather untidy as a climber unless very carefully trained fanwise at the outset. This may be facilitated by driving one large, strong staple into the wall a foot above the spot where it is planted and then driving a number of smaller staples into the rafters, or the roof-plate if this is of wood. When the upper staples are connected to the lower one by wires a ready-made fan is provided to which the young growths may be tied. The first shoots are best secured to the outermost wires as this is more likely to encourage a greater number to spring from the base.

If kept stubbed back to an initial framework of branches, like a Wisteria, this Jasmine may be made to form an open-ground shrub.

J. stephanense is a hybrid with *J. Beesianum* with pale pink flowers.

J. polyanthum is like the common Jasmine but much finer in every way, but unfortunately only hardy enough for very favourable gardens.

J. humile revolutum, a less spectacular species, is hardier. It is not really climbing in habit, having stronger, shorter stems and clusters of numerous yellow flowers from June onwards on the young shoots of the year. It does not, however, make the fine display of that grand old species, *J. nudiflorum*, the most spectacular of winter-flowering shrubs.

The Jasmines are not particular as to soil and can be grown from cuttings of half-ripe shoots placed under a bell-glass in July.

Quite a different type of shrub flowering at this time is *Thymus nitidus.* It is a little gray-green bushlet with pleasing pale pink flowers in June and is the most shrub-like member of the family. It comes easily from seed though it is not very long-lived; thus it is valuable as a "filler" among the many charming dwarf shrubs for undulating open spaces in the garden where the low and rather flat effect of an embroidered mantle for the ground is wanted. The arrangement of such spaces is one of the secrets of good composition that gives the spice of contrast to the taller groupings.

The **Dipeltas** barely attain the requirements of effective flowering shrubs for garden decoration: their tolerance of limy soils and charm as cut sprays for indoors weigh, however, in their favour.

Dipelta floribunda, a member of the Honeysuckle family, is a tantalising shrub from China that was introduced by E. H. Wilson in 1902. The abundant and fragrant flowers, in free and picturesque sprays in late May or early June, are white or pinkish, with a yellow throat and somewhat like small foxgloves in shape. Cut and brought indoors they are a delight, but the bush that grows them is a gaunt, shambling, 10-foot-high brute of a thing, with dirty brown bark peeling off in flakes everywhere so as to defy the "manicurist", and branches sprouting in odd directions all over the place. Thus it is a shrub that the wise planter will keep in the background in some well-jungled corner whence he may emerge at the right moment bearing beautiful sprays of the gay, lacy flowers to the great pleasure of his household. In fact, I have never seen a more pleasing flower arrangement than one I once contrived in a great majolica vase upon a dark and ancient table, with the Dipelta aided by the apricot flavouring of the pink and gold Ghent Azalea 'Aurore de Royghem' and spiced with the fragrant pearly chalices of *Magnolia Sieboldii*.

D. ventricosa, also a Wilson introduction, is an allied species from Western China with larger but narrower downy leaves and sparser flowers of similar colouring. It is hardy and easy going and grows better on limy soils than *D. floribunda*.

D. yunnanensis was found in Yunnan in 1886 by the good Abbé Delavay, to whom we owe the discovery of so many Chinese shrubs. It flowers a little earlier than the other species, often in late May. Less tall than the preceding, about 8 or 9 feet is the usual height. The creamy-white flowers, flushed with pink and with an orange throat, are clustered on the ends of short shoots from the previous year's growths and have the usual foxglove shape of the family. In habit it is more graceful and spreading than *D. floribunda* but does not really produce such masses of flower. On a limy soil it is preferable as it is more vigorous in growth under such conditions.

On the whole, the Dipeltas are hardy and easy-going shrubs that are not fastidious as to soil or aspect. They may be increased by cuttings of half-ripe shoots placed under a bell-glass in July.

Where the soil is acid June offers us a confusingly large number of Rhododendrons but some species are so outstanding and unlike their kindred that they require special mention. **Rhododendron Griersonianum** "D" ****, is I think, much hardier than is generally supposed. Indeed, it stands far better in a warm, open spot in poor soil than when sheltered in the woodland conditions that suit other kinds so well. It forms a dense bush with bright green, lanceolate leaves red-furred and silvered below. In June the brilliant scarlet flowers appear but unfortunately the sun, so necessary to ripen the wood of the late-maturing young growths, soon browns the corollas if the weather is clear at the time. Early autumn frosts are the bane of this species and, as it happens, my katabatic† position preserves me from these. This late growth of the bright young shoots is regrettable, but it is singularly decorative in the September scene. The plant is so easily and quickly raised from seed that it is not at all an expensive Rhododendron for the skilful cultivator and it is my belief that it has great possibilities for tub culture. The plants could be placed in shade as the flowers opened, and, as *R. Griersonianum* is remarkably drought-resisting it could be taken under cover in autumn without the need for much attention. In the open it is worth trying in all gardens where early autumn frosts are not severe, and the effect of a group of seedlings ablaze with their shapely and vivid flowers is one of the finest that June can afford us.

Places too hot and dry even for this Rhododendron will not be objected to by *Sophora viciifolia*, a member of the great Legume, or Pea, family that gives us so many invaluable shrubs among the Brooms, Genistas, Laburnums, Robinias, Lupins, Wisterias, etc. It is a thin but rounded shrub up to 6 feet high ultimately, with little pale blue or purplish pea-flowers in the first half of June. Reginald Farrer collected a particularly good form of this plant in Kansu, China, which he describes as "A thorny delicate-foliaged shrub of four to five feet with countless racemes of blue-white little pea-flowers. From dry, low hillsides of hot and arid districts"‡. I saw this superior form in bloom at Colonel Stern's famous garden on the chalk at Highdown near Worthing many years ago and, noting the fine blue colour of the calices which enriched the paler blue of the petals, was much disappointed when plants of the older introduction (1897, Kew) bloomed in my garden with duller and more purplish flowers.

S. viciifolia can be propagated from cuttings in the usual manner but does not strike very easily without heat. It grows equally well in limy or acid soil but requires a sunny spot.

The genus **Styrax** covers quite a long season with a succession of flowers. As the most valuable members flower in mid June, however, we may well consider them at this moment of our floral calendar.

Styrax Obassia, a Japanese flowering tree of great charm, introduced by Charles Maries for Messrs. Veitch in 1879, bears its racemes of snowdrop-like flowers in amazing abundance in late May or the first

---

† See p. 26 and 109.
‡ "The Plant Introductions of Reginald Farrer", by E. H. M. Cox, *New Flora and Silva*, 1930.

days of June. It forms a shapely little tree up to 20 feet high and is attractive as a lawn specimen, but the flowers are much hidden by the foliage and they only last about three days in beauty, though the snowy carpet of flowers beneath the tree on about the fifth day is very decorative.

S. Hemsleyana, a Chinese species, introduced by E. H. Wilson in 1900, is very similar but longer-lasting, and would, I expect, grow on a limy soil which the Japanese species probably would not. It flowers, as a rule, after the foregoing species is over and the racemes are less pendent and therefore more boldly displayed, making it the better species.

S. japonica is the great beauty of the family and it flowers about a fortnight later—right in the June gap when rivals are few. One of the most beautiful trees that I have ever seen was a specimen of this species grown as a tall standard. One looked up into the faces of thousands of snowdrop-like flowers that hung in rows from every twig. *S. japonica* is usually seen as a dense, bushy, little tree about 8 or 9 feet high but it will grow to 25 feet, in time, in a good soil. It was introduced as long ago as 1862 and it is surprising that it is so seldom seen as it is apparently quite hardy, though sometimes cut by late spring frosts. Like the other Styrax the flowers are white and thus, though *S. japonica* has great individual charm and beautiful "drawing", it is to other genera that we must look for vivid June colour in the shrub garden.

The Styrax, except *S. Hemsleyana*, need an acid or neutral soil rich in humus, to do well, and some shelter from the full blast of the wind. Seeds are the best method of increase. Regular mulching is very necessary to replenish the nourishment expended in the production of heavy crops of flowers. I have seen fine specimens of *S. japonica* dwindling to death from mere starvation.

The most valuable section of the **Magnolia** family flowers in late May or, more often, from early June onwards. They are somewhat vulnerable, alas, to spring frosts, and so are among the delights of elevated or coastal gardens rather than absolutely reliable subjects for general planting in cold districts.

Magnolia obovata (*M. hypoleuca*, *M. officinalis*) is a tree attaining about 30 feet or more in height and undoubtedly one of the most beautiful that can be grown in the British Isles. The large leaves, shaped as the name suggests, are of a brilliant green and most attractive to the eye. The flowers are very large with cream-coloured petals and sepals surrounding a rosette of red stamens from which emerges a club of carpels. The fragrance is very fruity and delightful. Owing to the fact that the flowers open a few at a time, over quite a long period,

Rhododendron indicum ' Satsuki '

Genista sylvestris pungens

Cistus laurifolius

Rhododendron ' Romany Chal '

the tree gives no great distant flower effect but is yet notably good to look at at all times and in particular in autumn when set with fine red fruits. Though it takes time to grow to its full majesty, and does not flower when young, it is quick growing and handsome as a sapling, provided that the situation is open but reasonably sheltered from wind, that the soil is moist and well enriched with leaf-mould and that a fresh leader is grown up after transplanting. In the perfect garden of one's dreams it is the tree to whose shade one brings the tea-things on a warm summer evening. It appears to be reasonably hardy, though in its old age it requires care, and regular feeding, particularly in dry years, is essential. This Magnolia is now placed in a different section from the following species ("A Survey of the Genus Magnolia" by J. E. Dandy, *Camellias and Magnolias*, R.H.S., 1950) but from the horticultural standpoint it has an affinity to them.

M. *Sieboldii* (M. *parviflora*) (A.G.M. 1935) is another superb Magnolia of the highest value for all gardens. Usually a small tree or large shrub about 15 feet high and of wide-spreading habit, it can be kept to a smaller size by occasionally pruning away the oldest stems at ground-level if desired. M. *Sieboldii* usually has quite a crop of flowers at the end of May or in early June and then goes on flowering only slightly more sparsely until August. The flowers have usually nine waxy-white petals and sepals with a red rosette and a green club in the centre. Their fragrance is quite delightful and they are produced by comparatively young trees. The finer forms have the central rosette of a rich red, inferior ones of magenta pink, but even the magenta-centred ones are highly attractive. Spring frosts are the only serious enemy of this Magnolia which is otherwise a good garden plant in enriched soil *on the acid side*. (See illustration facing p. 160.)

M. *Watsoni* is generally considered to be a hybrid between the two previously-mentioned species and in my opinion has the most beautiful flowers of any Magnolia, and the most remarkable perfume. But unfortunately it is a plant of inherently weak constitution, almost invariably dying back badly after it has reached a certain age. I have formed the opinion that this weakness probably results from a deep-seated failing of the stem, caused by moving. Grown up on a new young stem, *in situ*, I think we should get a healthier and more long-lived tree. M. *Watsoni* has otherwise all the good qualities of its parents and flowers when comparatively young. It is to be hoped that it will again become available in commerce ere long, though it is so difficult to propagate that this is doubtful. If the cross could only be made again a seedling of better constitution might appear which would enable this superb hybrid to take its rightful place as the most popular of all Magnolias. (See illustration facing p. 192.)

14

M. sinensis is a Chinese cousin of *M. Sieboldii* and notable in that it can be grown on a limy soil. It forms a fairly tall symmetrical, bushy tree, rather than a rambling shrub like the latter. The otherwise rather similar flowers hang down, facing the ground, instead of being only slightly inclined from the horizontal, and they open out to a flat saucer shape. I have counted as many as fourteen of the pearly-white tepals (midway between sepals and petals) surrounding the rosette of crimson stamens. The central club of carpels is green. So many different seedling forms exist, however, that there is surely some hybridity with the following species to be described. Characteristically the leaves are large and obovate compared with the furry-backed lance-shaped ones of *M. Wilsoni* and the flowers are bolder and broader petalled. *M. sinensis* is reputed, when matured, to flower throughout the summer, like *M. Sieboldii*, but plants under my observation have always flowered very freely in late May or early June and then ceased and set abundant seed. The fruits are very decorative and of a bright crimson, and later the scarlet seeds emerge and remain for some time clinging on gossamer strands to the seed vessels before falling. I have never seen self-sown seedlings even when the conditions appeared ideal for their germination.

M. Wilsonii. This somewhat similar Magnolia has furry young shoots and more lance-shaped, smaller, narrower leaves and narrower petals and sepals and is of less vigorous growth. Extreme forms of the type are markedly inferior to *M. sinensis*, but of recent years specimens under the name of *M. Wilsonii*, equalling *M. sinensis* in size and beauty of flower, but furred and with narrower leaves, have been commonly exhibited by well-known amateur growers of these trees.

This fine hybrid should probably be named *M. highdownensis* (*M. sinensis* × *Wilsonii*). It forms a bushy tree up to 20 feet high with flowers equalling those of *M. sinensis* and is a vigorous grower in the chalk soil at Highdown, near Worthing.

M. globosa is an allied species from the Eastern Himalayas with ovate leaves, red-furred beneath when young, and more globular flowers. It is probably rather less hardy than the other species of this group.

Most of the Magnolias of this group require a good loam, rich in forest humus, to grow fast, as they should to reach a good size quickly, and to bear big crops of flowers. They may be grown from seed, but it is a slow process and not altogether easy. In cultivation the first essential is to get the plant growing strongly, then any necessary pruning to ensure a fresh start with the production of a new shoot from the base that will form a healthy, shapely tree, may be done in March with safety. Many have stated their fears to me of any cutting of Magnolia wood, and to reassure myself I have even pruned mine unnecessarily hard, but I have seen no ill results on trees in good growth. A mulch of forest leaves should at all times be kept over the roots both for their general well-being and to replenish the soil after heavy crops of flower.

M. macrophylla (in spite of its flowers, 16 inches across), *M. Fraseri*, *M. tripetala*, *M. acuminata*, *M. cordata* and *M. Thomsoniana* are really of insufficient garden value relative to their great size for description here. Data regarding these may be found in *Camellias and Magnolias*, Conference Report, R.H.S. 1950. *M. virginiana* and *M. grandiflora* are dealt with later in these pages (p. 294).

From these fragile but exquisite trees, the real aristocrats of the garden, we return, starting with the **Genistas**, to small convenient bushes suitable for restricted spaces and giving the quick results increasingly insisted upon today.

Genista silvestris pungens, generally known as *G. dalmatica*, is a neat, dense bushlet 8 inches or a foot high with thin hairy, spiny branches and a profuse covering of yellow pea-flowers in June and July. It comes from the dry pinewoods of Dalmatia and requires a warm and well-drained spot though it is quite happy in light shade. (See illustration facing p. 208.)

It is one of those delightful low, dwarf shrubs so pleasing when grown in association with other kinds of similar habit to form a close carpet of flower and foliage.

The Dalmatian Genista is not particular as to soil and strikes freely from cuttings placed under a bell-glass or in a propagating box in late July.

Another member of the family, *G. radiata*, also flowers in June. It is not spectacular, but the density of its thin green twigs gives it the winter value of an evergreen bush of the convenient height of 3 feet. Although it comes from south Europe it is reasonably hardy and a good plant for a very hot and dry bank. The small deep yellow flowers are borne in terminal heads only about an inch across and thus its display is hardly up to first-class standards, but in a very dry and warm season when many plants flag, it puts up a superior performance that earns it a position here. This species is easily raised from seeds and is not fastidious.

A large Tree-Broom flowering at this time is *Cytisus Battandieri* (A.G.M. 1938), introduced from the mountains of Morocco in 1921. It has silvery leaves and Aureolin Yellow flowers with an apple-loft fragrance, in corn-cob-shaped spikes. These silvery leaves are rather sparse and the habit is ragged and lanky unless controlled by perpetual early pinching-back. It takes some years to reach flowering size, but a well-grown bush can make quite a good showing though not, I think, up to the very high standard of the July-flowering species mentioned later. (See illustration facing p. 192.)

A sunny position suits this Broom and it is notable in that it does not object to a moderately limy soil, though it is more vigorous in an acid one. It can be increased by seeds. I have not been successful with cuttings.

Another member of the great Legume family that plays its part in June is *Lupinus arboreus*, the familiar **Tree Lupin,** which comes from the Californian coast. It carries a smaller version of the well-known Lupin type of flower-spike in sulphur yellow, palest yellow, pale purple or white, according to variety. The Tree Lupin's remarkably quick growth makes it very useful in new gardens for furnishing the spaces between more permanent and slower-growing species. It is very beautiful at its best, when the delicately formed, divided, evergreen leaves and yellow flower spikes make a pleasing combination on a bushy young specimen that has been well pinched back in the early stages to induce a good framework. All too soon the Tree Lupin gets top-heavy and, inevitably, wind-damaged, dying probably in the following winter from the effect of some frost which it would easily have withstood in its younger days. Fortunately it is easily grown from seed sown in a reserve bed. The seedlings do not move well except when small enough to be moved with a ball of soil adhering to the roots. A rich soil is not desirable as the plants then make excessively soft and rank growth which does not stand the winter so well. They will grow quite well on moderately limy soils.

Perhaps the best position for the Tree Lupin is as a lawn specimen where it can share a little bed with a young specimen tree. Being a Legume, far from robbing the soil of its companion it will advantageously shade the ground and the infant's stem, also helping the young tree materially in later years, when, the top of the now time-expired Lupin being removed, the sapling will profit by the nitrogen stored in the roots of the corpse. Another good association is provided when the white and pale yellow varieties are planted near large existing plantations of *Rhododendron ponticum*. The purple flowers of the latter seem to take on a bluer tone and the combined effect of these two common shrubs is really very enjoyable.

In June the last and the most valuable section of the hardy hybrid deciduous Azaleas, known as the "Ghent" Azaleas, come into flower. Derived from hardy species and flowering so late, they are almost

immune from damage by spring frosts. Thus, with the really hardy
category "A" Rhododendrons, they provide one of the first absolutely
reliable massed flower effects that are safe from damage by spring frosts.
As with other members of the family, grafted plants are weakly and
troublesome and, until layered all round, difficult to make into large
permanent bushes. Bought as layers, on the other hand, they are easily
encouraged to send up strong basal shoots by liberal feeding, and these
are advantageously drawn out, arched over and pegged down, when they
will usually produce young branches all along their length and thus
eventually make fine bushes of dense, mounded habit. By June the cold
north-east winds, so often a feature of May weather, have usually gone
and thus the Ghents have another advantage over the other types of
large-flowered hybrid Azaleas, as they avoid weather conditions which
quickly spoil the delicate Azalea flowers.

Varieties differ a little, but the bushes are usually seen about 4 or 5
feet high, and of equal or greater breadth, when well grown and on their
own roots. In the shadier places they grow much taller, but are thinner
in habit. Under good conditions their ultimate size is about 8 feet high
and perhaps 12 feet across.

Some good varieties are:—

'Aurore de Royghem', orange yellow and pink, in my opinion
   still unsurpassed in beauty *as a growing shrub* by any of the
   novelties I have seen.
'Chieftain', apricot and brown-orange.
'Graf Alf von Nipping', Chinese yellow and vermilion, another
   old variety of unexcelled beauty of form.
coccinea speciosa **, orange-red.
Daviesii *, white, yellow flare.
'Dr. Charles Baumann' *, vermilion.
'Fanny' *, magenta-pink.
'Fritz Quihoui', vermilion.
'Géant des Batailles', deep vermilion.
gloria mundi **, orange-red.
'Mrs. H. White', white, pink and yellow, late.
'Pallas' *, crimson and yellow, very fine.
'Prince Henri des Pays Bas', light crimson, orange flare, late, a
   beautiful variety.
'Sang de Ghentbrugge' *, deep crimson, rather small flower, late.
'Volcano', deep red, orange eye, very late.
'William III' *, orange.
'Flamingo' (Waterer, Sons & Crisp, not Knap Hill), pure orange,
   very late, good autumn colour of a deep beetroot shade.

All these varieties, and dozens that I have not mentioned, are extremely beautiful but a special mention must be made of the last named as unfortunately one of the new Knap Hill Azaleas has since been given the same name. The Ghent 'Flamingo' is the older and, as it happens, the more valuable plant as it flowers long after most others are over. The dreaded "June gap" is apt to be a dull moment even in the better regulated gardens unless special care is taken to plant some of the neglected beauties that flower precisely at that time. 'Flamingo' is one of the most brilliant of these and can provide a most lovely effect grouped with *Cornus Kousa* and the rare and precious Japanese Evergreen Azalea so inappropriately named *Rhododendron indicum*.

The other Ghents, flowering a little earlier, are so lovely as individual flowering shrubs and their colours are so effective that, on an acid soil, they can carry the whole garden during their season. Light shade, such as Silver Birches, Cherries or *Cornus Kousa* afford, is helpful in preventing the hot summer sun bleaching the flowers and it is well worth while taking the measures advised, under the heading of the Mollis Azaleas (see p. 117), for soil improvement and exact planting depth.

Gardens on limy soils have to do without the Ghents and make the best show possible with Roses, *Cornus Kousa*, var. *chinensis*, Helianthemums, Cistus, Halimiums, *Cytisus Battandieri*, etc., but few garden plants produce a greater profusion of more vivid, shapely and fragrant flowers than the Ghents and their absence is painfully marked. For the average lime-free garden these are the most suitable of all the large-flowered Azaleas comprised in the groups Mollis, Knap Hill, occidentale and Ghent. Their hardiness and vigour is outstanding and their flowering-time a most convenient one to follow the Japanese Evergreen early section of the Azaleas. I do not know a deciduous flowering shrub that is a more perfect example of all the good qualities combined. Beauty of form, fragrance and colour are added to sturdiness, freedom from diseases and pests and free-flowering qualities that are all that could be desired.

Owing to lack of demand many lovely old varieties are becoming extinct, particularly the more honeysuckle-like, late-blooming, types with flowers of soft but pure colouring and delighful fragrance.

The true Ghent type has even more perfect "drawing" and finish than either the Mollises or the Knap Hills and owing to its denser flowering, is more effective in the landscape than the latter. As they are so near to that superb species *R. calendulaceum*, the Ghents avoid the coarse and hybrid look, having about nine exquisitely shaped flowers beautifully grouped in a close truss of flattened dome shape, the valuable "top flower" filling the centre superbly, with the lovely foliage and attractive habit of the wild species mentioned. I have seen a great many flowering shrubs but I believe that the most beautiful that I know are two superb old Ghent Azalea specimens, 'Aurore de Rooyghem' and 'Graf Alf von Nipping'. By some, these old varieties are thought to be outclassed today, and no doubt the foot-rule would endorse this, but never, I think, the eye of the lover of beautiful things when comparing them as growing plants.

The varieties 'Unique', *altaclarense* and 'Nancy Waterer' usually classed as "Ghents" are, in my opinion, "Knap Hill" types and are therefore listed in that section.

The hybrid Azalea varieties having a strong strain of **Rhododendron occidentale** in their composition form another distinct section. They are particularly valuable owing to their ability to grow well in full sun and exposure. Thus placed the Occidentales make rounded, dense, 3- and 4-foot bushes so solidly set with flowers that hardly a leaf can be seen. Their colourings are, however, rather pale and weak. Like their relations, the "Knap Hill" Azaleas, they come under the cultigen group of *Rhododendron albicans*. Most commonly seen are the following:—

delicatissima, creamy blush-pink.
exquisita, creamy white and yellow.
graciosa, creamy pink with an orange flare.
magnifica, creamy blush-pink.
superba, pale pink with an orange flare.

The wild type of *R. occidentale* flowers later than most of these hybrid varieties. It makes a taller and looser bush and the more star-shaped white flowers, with a yellow flare, are in a more open truss. Their fragrance is more pronounced than that of the hybrids. It is a variable species and some forms are much more beautiful than others. In a shady position this charming Azalea is not very free-flowering, so a sunny position is best.

The race of **Clematis,** members of the Buttercup family, provide several fine climbers flowering about midsummer in addition to the large-flowered hybrids dealt with later.

Clematis montana Wilsoni is a Chinese variety of that spring-flowering species, that blooms in June and July. The large white flowers, 3 inches across, have gracefully twisted sepals and are borne on downy stalks.

C. chrysocoma is a Chinese species discovered in 1884 by the Abbé Delavay and introduced to Kew from France in 1910. It is not an ultra-hardy species but is most decorative in appearance with its blushed white flowers on long stalks in June and later, and golden downy growths. It grew particularly well at Gravetye Manor, in the late William Robinson's garden near East Grinstead, Sussex, where it was allowed to scramble up trees and bushes, succeeding *C. montana* with an almost equal display over a much longer period. It is easily and quickly raised from seeds.

C. c. Spooneri is Chinese sub-species, introduced by E. H. Wilson in 1909. The 4-inch-wide, white flowers with their four regular sepals are very shapely and appear in late May or early June. It is more vigorous and hardy than *C. chrysocoma* but has not such a long flowering season nor quite such a wealth of flowers.

C. c. S. var. *rosea* is a fine pink-flowered variety.

C. macropetala (A.G.M. 1934) is a graceful Chinese and Siberian species. Though described as long ago as 1829 it was first introduced by Purdom for Messrs. Veitch about 1911, and was again introduced four years later by Reginald Farrer. He wrote of it, "Clematis sp. belongs to the Altragene group and is of incomparable loveliness. I only know it in the Ghyll of Tien-Tang (10,000 feet elevation) where it rambles fraily through light bushes to a height of two or three feet and then cascades downwards in a fall of lovely great flowers of China-blue, so filled with petaloid processes that they seem as double as any production of the garden". There is almost a Dahlia-like look about the form of the flowers and the late Ernest Markham called it the "Downy Clematis" owing to the appearance of the young shoots. *C. macropetala* flowers in June and may well be grown in the manner suggested by Farrer's description. It is quite reasonably hardy.

A fine form raised by Ernest Markham is *C. m.* 'Markham's Pink', with slightly larger, mauve-pink, flowers and stronger growth.

C. lanuginosa, *C. patens* and hybrids such as *C.* 'Miss Bateman' are also in flower in June. (See pages 173 and 265.)

The Clematis mentioned above all grow well on limy or acid soils and, like other members of the family, are best with their roots in the shade and their heads in the sun. Bonemeal is a good fertiliser for them.

They may be propagated from seed, but the resulting seedlings are sometimes inferior to the elect seed parent. Layering is fairly successful but, on the whole, the propagation of these Clematis is best left to the specialist nurserymen who provide the amateur with a sturdy young pot-grown plant ready for planting out. Dogs, and especially puppies, are very liable to destroy Clematis unless the plants are safeguarded by strong wire netting. Care must also be taken to protect the young plants from mice and slugs which have a fondness for the young growths whose safety is essential for the plant's establishment.

Pruning is needed to prevent the growths getting into a thick tangle of stems too crowded to flower properly and to keep them within their allotted space.

When starting a young plant, the roots should be soaked and then gently disentangled if potbound and the shoots may have the first inch or two laid in a little channel formed in the soil to encourage them to form their own roots above the graft. Finally the upper stems are pruned off at a foot from the ground to induce bushiness at the start.

Occasionally a really valuable and lovely species or variety gets lost and goes out of cultivation. As stated previously a surprisingly common cause is simply a muddle over the name. This seems strange, but such are the casualties from various causes other than the weather, that unless a shrub is constantly asked for and planted in new gardens it soon becomes practically extinct. If the name is not known, the essential renewal does not take place and only a few survivors in old gardens may be preserved.

This happened to a certain very beautiful **Late-flowering Evergreen Azalea** usually known nowadays as "Azalea macrantha". According to the rules, the correct name of this plant is *Rhododendron indicum*, but a certain Chinese species, *R. Simsii*, the tender greenhouse Azalea, was known under that name, and, when planters who wanted the hardy Japanese species were sent the tender Chinese species instead, the plants died the first winter and thus demand ceased and the true plant almost died out.

As it happens, it is one of the finest and hardiest of this group of spectacularly beautiful Azaleas. E. H. Wilson reported it as "a prime favourite in Japanese gardens". George Forrest described it as "very beautiful by the sides of mountain streams in June with its large bright red flowers contrasted with *Iris Kæmpferi*". *R. indicum* was first described by Sweet in 1833 when it was introduced to a Chelsea nursery. After about 1850, as it would not "force", a fatal drawback in those days of innumerable hothouses, it was soon superseded by the tender Chinese species *R. Simsii* which is still the basis of the florists' potted Azalea. The true *R. indicum* persisted, however, in its double variety— var. *balsaminæflorum* ("Azalea rosæflora") which has always enjoyed considerable popularity owing to its very unusual, double, rose-like, salmon flowers (pale Vermilion H.C.C. 18/2). The best single-flowered form is, however, much superior for general planting, having large, full flowers $2\frac{1}{4}$ inches across and very freely borne with five broad, rounded lobes of a rich orange-pink (pale Scarlet H.C.C. 19/2) marked with Crimson on the upper lobe. In habit the shrub is low and mounded and a notably vivid evergreen, hence its popularity in Japanese gardens, and it bears clipping well. The lanceolate leaves are of a dark green with a faint reddish cast and the slender shoots are covered with appressed chestnut-brown hairs. In autumn many of the leaves turn crimson.

R. indicum is probably a degree hardier than most of the true "Kurumes", but is rated as about the same hardiness as *R. obtusum* forms "C". Thus we have a beautiful evergreen shrub of convenient size (usually a yard across and half as high ultimately) with notably large flowers of the most highly popular colouring. But this is not all, for in addition to these virtues the plant flowers after most other Azaleas are over—right in the "June gap" when most gardens are particularly ready to welcome a brilliantly coloured and beautiful flowering shrub.

R. indicum is not common in the wild, according to E. H. Wilson, who found it truly so only on Yaku-shima island. It is also, however, reported by others from Hondo and other localities. But in the Japanese gardens it is very commonly planted, nearly two hundred named forms being recognised and it is known there as "the June-flowering Azalea".

A further interesting note to add to the scanty records of this shrub is provided by Reginald Farrer. He imported plants from Japan and though he confused it, as was then customary, with the "Azalea indica" of the trade (*R. Simsii*) and therefore expected the early death of the consignment, he reported with delighted surprise† that over a period of five years these Azaleas never suffered and rarely failed to produce abundance of bloom. "And this", he continues, "though they are planted in merely ordinary garden soil, *permeated with lime*, and though quite unsheltered and unprotected." It will be remembered that his garden lay near Ingleborough in Yorkshire which is generally considered to be a distinctly cold district. The italics are mine.

The clones available here today are as follows:—

R. indicum macranthum ("Azalea macrantha orange"). This appears to be very near the "type" but as the wild plant is reported as variable in colour ("bright red to scarlet, sometimes rose red"‡) and this superlative orange-pink form is propagated as a clone, it is proper to give it varietal rank. This is the finest form I have seen with large orange-pink (H.C.C. 19/2) flowers as previously described. It is very free flowering; in June the tip of every branchlet ends in a flower, making a most lovely display of glorious colour. I would place it in the best

† "Alpines and Bog Plants", by Reginald Farrer, Edward Arnold, 1908, p. 29.
‡ "A Monograph of Azaleas", by Ernest Henry Wilson and Alfred Rehder, University Press, Cambridge, 1921, p. 24.

dozen first-class flowering shrubs for small gardens on lime-free soil with a favourable climate†.

R. i. 'Kokin Shita'. This is, in my opinion, either a variety of *R. indicum* or a hybrid. It is described in the *Rhododendron Handbook*, 1947, as a sub-variety of *R. obtusum*. 'Kokin Shita' is, at all events, distinctly inferior to the var. *macranthum*. The smaller and more thin and starry flowers are the same colour, but they quickly fade in the sun whereas those of the latter hold their colour comparatively well. The habit is weakly and dwarf, with narrower, thinner leaves. The flowering date is the same.

R. i. 'Satsuki'. This variety is sometimes grown under the name of *R. macrostemon*; that Azalea is, however, listed as a variety of *R. obtusum* in the *Rhododendron Handbook* and is obviously no connection, being described by E. H. Wilson as having "small flowers, minute calyx and long exserted stamens three times as long as the corolla"‡. In habit this variety or hybrid much resembles *R. indicum macranthum* and I find it almost impossible to distinguish them when out of flower, but the flowers are not quite so fine, being very slightly smaller, with narrower lobes and they are only a Crimson Pink (H.C.C. 22/2) in colour. I note that this form does not produce fertile seed, which *macranthum* does, so possibly it has some other species in its make-up as well as *R. indicum*. The flowering date is slightly earlier in its commencement than that of *R. i. macranthum* but owing to its peculiar successional habit of flowering it remains in bloom much later, being still effective in July. This quality places it in the noble company of the Camellias, Chænomeles, *Magnolia Sieboldii*, the H. T. Roses, the Spanish Broom, and the Hydrangeas, plants whose continuous succession of flowers over a long period make them invaluable for certain positions where this trait is necessary. When we have this quality coupled with great hardiness, a dense, bushy habit and evergreen foliage of singularly attractive appearance we recognise a great garden shrub (see illustration page 208).

No doubt breeders will one day give us an Azalea incorporating the best characteristics of 'Satsuki' and the fuller and more brilliantly coloured flowers of *macranthum*. In the meantime I raise my hat to *R. i.* 'Satsuki'. It is widely found in commerce and I have had it from half a dozen different nurseries, sometimes under the name of *R. i.* 'Pink'. A less attractive form with petaloid stamens also appears under the latter name which it may well retain. The flowers open all at once and it tends to fade in the sun. 'Satsuki', on the other hand, stands up

† See climatic zones, p. 25.
‡ "A Monograph of Azaleas", by Ernest Henry Wilson and Alfred Rehder, University Press, Cambridge, 1921, p. 24.

very well to full sun exposure. This Azalea is to be seen in most of the great gardens where flowering shrubs are an important feature and, of course, at the R.H.S. gardens at Wisley where, the Curator tells me, it has signally distinguished itself. One of the objects of this book is to bring such little-known but absolutely first-class shrubs to the notice of gardeners. This group has great possibilities for the amateur breeder.

R. i. balsaminæflorum (*Azalea rosæflora*). This is the well known variety with double, salmon flowers shaped like miniature Roses. It is more dwarf in habit than *macranthum* and in the south-east definitely needs shade for free growth, and also to preserve the delicate colour of the flowers. It is a pretty little thing, but of very artificial appearance, suitable for one of those shady little courtyards attached to houses that, if the proper soil is imported, can be made so delightful with Ferns, Camellias, *Hydrangea serrata* and other shade-lovers.

R. i. 'Misomogiri' appears to me to be almost identical.

R. i. var. *crispiflorum* is described as having large pink flowers with undulate petals.

R. i. var. 'Hakatashiro' is described as having large pure white flowers.

R. i. var. 'Tanimanoyouki' ('Coral Ivory') is described as having salmon flowers with a white zone on the petals.

'Vida Brown' (*R. i.* × *obtusum* var. *Caldwellii*), a new hybrid, was shown at R.H.S. Chelsea Show in May 1948 by Messrs. D. Stewart of Ferndown, Dorset, and selected for trial at Wisley. Each inflorescence consists of two large flowers 2 inches across or more, one inside the other. The colour is a crimson-pink and the plants shown were very free-flowering. On small bushes the flowers appear almost too large but on more mature specimens they should be highly effective.

According to E. H. Wilson the Azalea clone sold in America as 'J. T. Lovett', claimed to be of hybrid origin, is simply *R. indicum*. Unfortunately I have not been able to obtain it, so can give no description.

R. i. lasciniatum has, according to the above authority, a deeply lascinate corolla.

R. i. variegatum is described as a variety with white and red striped and spotted flowers, blooming irregularly the year round.

An old Dutch Azalea variety, listed by Messrs. Marchant of Wimborne and others as *illuminata* or *optima*, with large, double, salmon-red flowers and notably shortened anthers, has a strong look of *R. indicum* and may, as I suspect, be found to be a hybrid of this species. It flowers at about the same time as the earliest flowers of the variety *R. i.* 'Satsuki' but blossoms all at once.

I have no information regarding the large number of garden varieties of *R. indicum* cultivated in Japanese gardens. Even without taking into consideration the Japanese garden varieties of *Hydrangea serrata*, *Pæonia suffruticosa* and other species, there is obviously a very rich unexplored field for the plant hunter waiting there, even now.

As regards cultivation "Azalea macrantha" as it is still known in the nursery trade, seems to have no special fads, beyond a cool root-run, rich in humus, and the usual Evergreen Azalea requirements. My plants grow well on a very high and exposed slope with no protection from the wind or sun other than the usual pegging-down when first planted and the provision of a mulch of bracken. These precautions are, how-ever, essential to protect the younger stems from early autumn frosts, where these occur, as this is the one weakness of this species.

Another fine late-flowering Azalea is *R. Kæmpferi* var. 'Mikado'. This Azalea opens its pale salmon (Azalea Pink H.C.C. 618/1), wavy-edged flowers at about the same time as *R. indicum*. Another variety of *R. Kæmpferi*, named var. 'Daimio', has brighter and larger flowers (pale Fire Red H.C.C. 15/3) which open much later, after *R. indicum* 'Pink', and it, also, appears to be scarce in commerce.

These varieties came originally from Messrs. Veitch's nurseries in Exeter and are extremely valuable for their hardiness and beauty of flower late in the season after the others are over. 'Mikado' and 'Daimio' are perhaps best grown in the shade of distant trees as their delicate flower colours bleach somewhat in the hot midsummer sun, though less so than those of most other varieties of *R. Kæmpferi*. This limits their use a little, but *Cornus Kousa*, with its large white-bracted flowers, *Abutilon vitifolium* with pale Cobalt Violet flowers, and *Sophora viciifolia* with its bluish pea-flowers can offer both the necessary shade and timely complementary colourings.

One of the best arrangements that I have had was when these little Azaleas grew in the shade of one of those late-flowering and unusually blue-toned plants of **Rhododendron ponticum** that was my reward for combing a whole hillside in Surrey covered with feral Rhododendrons. The *ponticum* was eventually pruned and trained into tree form, this being an excellent way of dealing with large specimens of this species. Among the beauties of the new gardens in Windsor Great Park not least are the massive evergreen trees, of perfect garden size, obtained by skilful pruning of the old original woodland specimens of this humble Rhododendron. A good coloured *ponticum* "colour-charts" at about Imperial Purple, but exceptional specimens will be found of slightly bluer tone and they are worth looking out for.

Another variety or hybrid of the hardy, free-growing, wind-resisting, sun-enduring, "fly-proof" *R. ponticum* provides us with one of the loveliest and most unsung of Rhododendrons. There are, it appears, several forms of white-flowered *R. ponticum*, collectively named var. *album*, but this variety, propagated as a clone, is of quite outstanding beauty. I can trace no name for this particular hybrid form (believed to be *R. ponticum* × *brachycarpum*) and, as it is highly valuable in my opinion, venture to propose for it the name of 'Tondelayo', the neglected jungle beauty. 'Tondelayo', then, resembles *R. ponticum* closely in habit and general appearance but the leaves are notably longer, slightly downy at first, narrower and more pointed and of a deeper, less shining green. The flowers open from faintly pink-flushed buds, forming a remarkably fine, open truss about 6 inches high and about 7 inches in diameter composed of about eighteen flowers each perfectly poised on a flower-stalk about 2 inches long. The especially valuable distinction of possessing a "top flower" which fills and crowns the centre of the truss is notable. Each flower stands out separately from its neighbour providing a perfect presentation. The individual corollas are deeply divided into five lobes, the lower ones long and narrow and the upper lobe broader and shorter. The colour is an unusually pure and flawless white with, upon the upper lobe, a feathered flare of brilliant Geranium Lake slightly suffused with gold in the centre. The flowering time is appreciably later than that of typical *R. ponticum* which is usually going over as 'Tondelayo' opens.

Thus it will be seen that we have here a shrub with all the well-recognised advantages of *R. ponticum* but without the disadvantage of the purplish-pink flower colour. It is, in fact, a beautiful hardy, evergreen flowering shrub which the nurseryman can sell with confidence for planting in any garden whose soil is not limy, anywhere in the British Isles. Without an effective name this lovely, orchidaceous flower would merely continue to languish unasked for.

The acid-soiled garden has had plenty of lovely plants to choose from in the preceding pages. It is time to consider some lime-tolerant species flowering in June.

Kolkwitzia amabilis, known in America as the "Beauty Bush", is a twiggy Chinese shrub introduced by E. H. Wilson for Messrs. Veitch in 1901. At its best, which is generally after a hot summer followed by a mild winter, it is very attractive when seen near at hand. It forms a cloud of tiny purplish-pink foxgloves on a bush perhaps 7 or 8 feet high. At a distance it is not very effective, as the colour is just that pale, commonplace purplish-pink that one has more than enough of already —so regrettably ubiquitous is this tint in every hedgerow. But the

freedom of flower can be such, and the form of the little corollas is so
dainty, that it must be rated high as a personality in any garden. Its
flowering in early June is a valuable trait; if it came out in the middle of
May we should not give it such a warm welcome. Being Chinese it will
endure a limy soil and, indeed, is not particular in this respect. It is
perfectly hardy and will even flourish in Denmark.

As regards cultivation, as it is found "among rocks at 10,000 feet
elevation", a situation not liable to cause excessive dryness at the root,
yet with full sun, seems to be indicated, and it certainly grows well
under such conditions and appears to be quite hardy. On the other
hand it is a shrub which takes some time to mature sufficiently to flower
really freely. The fruits are not commonly borne except in very hot
summers, so the best means of increase is by means of fairly soft
cuttings in a sand frame with bottom heat in late summer, but firmer
cuttings will sometimes root in the sand-box.

Few of the **Honeysuckles** are very effective in the garden, seldom
surpassing our own wild species in beauty. The wild Honeysuckle is a
sinister plant, deceiving us with its pretty flowers, whose juices no
Honey bee can ever suck. The innocent Ivy is blamed for throttling
trees, though any careful observer can see that it never constricts limb
or branch, merely running lightly up and along. With the Honeysuckle
it is another story; its steely stems, immensely strong and absolutely
unyielding, disdain the well fortified, mature tree but twine round a
sapling's trunk. When the poor thing tries to grow, the Honeysuckle
refuses to relax its grip by even a fraction of an inch. Thus the victim
can only swell unevenly in a spiral bulge, and, with its growth checked,
the Honeysuckle easily overtops and smothers it, often fatally unless it
can support life by some subsidiary stem. So let there be no question
of allowing Honeysuckles to scramble up choice flowering shrubs or
trees.

A short selection follows:—

Lonicera japonica Halliana is a very fragrant, almost evergreen,
Japanese Honeysuckle, often described as hardy; but I lost all my
plants in the severe war winters. The flowers are a pale yellow, opening
almost white, and appear from June onwards over a long season.

L. etrusca, a mediterranean species with almost evergreen foliage,
and a succession of dense spikes of fragrant yellowish-white, purple-
tinted flowers throughout summer, is one of the best of the more
ordinary sorts. *L. e. superba* is a particularly fine form.

L. americana is a fine hybrid of this crossed with *L. Caprifolium*.

L. tragophylla (A.G.M. 1928), is a Chinese Honeysuckle introduced from Hupeh in 1900 by E. H. Wilson. It has large, yellow, scentless flowers in late May and is one of the most effective and reasonably hardy.

L. sempervirens, the Trumpet Honeysuckle, is an American species and more or less evergreen, with unscented orange-scarlet flowers. Although quite hardy in America (Zone III Rehder, includes Newfoundland!), Bean recorded it as not hardy enough for any but specially favoured gardens in the south and west of this country. This is particularly regrettable in the case of *L. s. superba*, a beautiful variety with bright scarlet flowers. Perhaps the form available here is a tender one from the South and a new importation would prove quite hardy.

Certain hybrid forms are hardier.

L. Tellmanniana, a cross between the two previous species, has deep orange-yellow, tubular flowers in clusters in June. It is not fragrant but is quite hardy.

L. Heckrottii is another hybrid, with rich pink flowers, yellow inside, in June. It is quite hardy and a good grower.

L. Brownii fuchsioides has fine scarlet flowers, and this hybrid, (*L. sempervirens* × *hirsuta*) though not as hardy as the last named, is reasonably so in any but a very cold spot. In my view it is the handsomest of all Honeysuckles and is superb on a whitewashed wall or scrambling up some tall shrub of little value.

L. ciliosa, the western Trumpet Honeysuckle, is quite hardy, growing as far north as British Columbia. The "type" has yellow flowers, sometimes tinged with purple, and the var. *occidentalis* is described as having larger and brighter flowers.

These climbers may be grown with Roses and Clematis on the trellis so useful in small gardens to provide ornamental screens, dividing up the various sections of kitchen garden, playground, fowl-run, etc. in an attractive way. The Honeysuckles are not very particular as to soil, but like a fairly moist root-run. Aphis attack often occurs, and unless the plants are well sprayed with a suitable insecticide growth is liable to be spoiled.

Propagation may be effected by seeds, and cuttings of practically ripe young shoots may be rooted in August under a bell-cloche.

Apart from the great families with numerous related species there are genera which offer only one or two species suitable for the garden.

Raphiolepis umbellata (*R. japonica*), is an evergreen shrub of the Rose family from Japan. It has leathery oval leaves and is of good, compact habit and is said to reach 10 feet in height though usually seen about half that size. In June the fragrant white flowers open in dense panicles on the ends of the shoots. They are five-petalled, upright but Cherry-like, and about ¾-inch across. This Raphiolepis is quite reasonably hardy but does best in an acid soil with added leaf-mould or June-cut bracken about the roots. It may be propagated from seeds or by cuttings, if half-ripe shoots are placed under a bell-glass in July.

R. u. var. *ovata* has more rounded leaves.

A hybrid form with rose-pink flowers is *R. Delacourii*.

Penstemon Scouleri is one of the few shrubby members of a large American family, comprised mostly of herbs. Opening in June, the slaty-blue, foxglove-like flowers are about an inch across and 1½ inches long. *P. Scouleri* is a native of Western North America and seldom exceeds 1 foot 6 inches in height. Thus it takes a useful place among the many dwarf shrubs that may be associated so effectively and conveniently in the small garden. It contrasts well with the pale yellow Helianthemums and the similarly coloured Potentillas and the white Cistus that also enjoy the sunny places on freely drained soils, whether limy or acid, that suit the little Penstemon so well.

It is easily increased by July cuttings and, though shortlived, grows and flowers cheerfully enough in all but our coldest and dampest summers. In mild winters the leaves remain but turn purplish.

P. heterophyllus (A.G.M. 1929), with Flax Blue flowers, is also shrub-like and fairly hardy and *P. cordifolius*, a Californian with a looser, more straggling habit, atoned for by scarlet flowers in late summer, is less hardy, but possibly worthy of a position at the foot of a south wall in a mild garden with a limy soil which precludes the planting of the full selection of flowering shrubs available.

P. Menziesii is a prostrate, creeping species with tiny evergreen leaves and blue-violet flowers, 1½ inches long, in June. A white form, var. *albus*, also occurs

All the Penstemons are easy-going as regards soil so long as their position is warm and well-drained and they can be grown from cuttings or seeds in the usual manner.

In freedom of flowering only the Evergreen Azaleas equal **Cornus Kousa,** most spectacular, in our climate, of a large family whose members are mostly somewhat dull shrubs from the gardener's point of view.

C. Kousa, from Japan, forms an unusually picturesque tree about 20 feet high, with tiered branches that bend gracefully down at their

15

ends when loaded with the massed white flowers in June. These flowers are composed of a central green button which is actually a group of true functional flowers, surrounded by four large white petaloid bracts. In good forms they appear to be broad, shapely, waxy, pure white petals, sometimes with a pink tip; in bad ones they are more bract-like, thin, coarse-textured, twisted, narrow and stained. Seedlings vary greatly and, in addition, individual plants even vary the shape of their flowers a little from year to year according to the rainfall and the feeding they receive. In the form of the flower and its spacing on the branches there is a wide range in quality, so that named, clonal forms of shapely flowered individuals are much to be desired. Unfortunately, apart from seed-raising, it is rather a difficult plant to propagate.

It is also a shrub that needs some care, and a well enriched soil, acid and carrying plenty of humus. Furthermore a young plant can be killed by the jobbing, self-styled gardener with a couple of ill-timed snips with his shears. I once heard an old legend to the effect that the Persimmon, *Diospyros Khaki*, was at once killed if cut with the knife. Curious, I therefore secured a healthy specimen and, as soon as it was well established, cut it down with my big Saynor. For some years the plant apparently revelled in this unusual treatment annually and I then let it grow in peace. Years later I absentmindedly snipped a few unwanted side branches off a seedling of *C. Kousa* and was surprised to see it die almost at once from the injury in the most unmistakable way. I had the legend wrong; it probably referred to *Cornus Kousa* and the K was about the only part that I had got right! I would therefore strongly advise anyone growing this lovely Cornel against pruning it in the younger stages. A knock with a motor mower or a wheelbarrow will also, I find, kill young plants more often than not. A wise precaution is to surround the sapling with a ring of wire netting, and an injunction against pruning may well also be attached on a conspicuous label.

C. Kousa flowers when about 6 feet high but needs a few more years of expansion to begin to make its real effect. The best position, I think, is as a lawn specimen, as the habit of the little tree is very attractive and both the red fruits and the rich autumn leaf colour are highly effective additional features. Although the flowers are only white in colour, their delightful design and, literally astounding profusion, make it undoubtedly a first-class shrub and it has a spectacular beauty of form as a flowering tree of a high order. The effect is also one that lasts well, the bracts starting life in a greenish tint and slowly maturing to white as they enlarge. They remain in beauty for a long period and then, as with that other Japanese, bract-flowered beauty, *Hydrangea* 'Grayswood', begin to turn crimson.

C. Kousa var. *chinensis* is a Chinese form that is very similar in appearance. So similar indeed that I, for one, have great difficulty in distinguishing seedling forms. On the whole, according to Colonel F. C. Stern, V.M.H. (*R.H.S. Journal*, LXXII, Pt. 9, p. 371), the Chinese variety has broader leaves and bracts. But I must admit that the specimen with the broadest bracts that I have ever seen was a pure Japanese seedling. The weakness of the Chinese is, perhaps, that a large proportion of seedlings have flowers with coarse, ill-shaped, twisted bracts, though these are sometimes very large. This increase in the size of the individual flowers is very far from being an added beauty as it is their countless numbers, the exquisite finish of their form and their superb presentation that makes the densely packed great flat sprays so enchanting. On the other hand, the Chinese trait of lime tolerance is of the highest value, making it a "first-rate garden plant perfectly hardy and easy to grow in any good soil with or without lime" (*loc. cit. sup.*).

For my part I would advise special care when planting these lovely Cornels. For lawn specimens we prepare, by bastard trenching, a circular bed 6 feet in diameter and add abundant humus which we mix thoroughly with the existing soil. This bed has to support the growth of the sapling to full treehood and, from then on, immense crops of flowers over a long period of years. After the bed is fully made, a part may be turfed over again, perhaps so as to leave only a well mulched 3-foot-diameter bed for the little sapling at first. But the work will have been done before it is too late. I have observed fine trees, 20 feet high, going back badly and in a dry year producing immense crops of wretched, short-lived flowers, each only an inch across instead of nearly 4 inches. Much can be done by regular mulching and top-dressing, it is true, but it is never the equal of a bed really well made at the start which is also kept mulched and thus provides a large "sponge" affording a continuous supply of liquid nourishment, which is, after all, the only kind in which trees are interested.

As summer injury to the wood often causes at least the death of the branch, great care has to be used in staking and only a proper rubber-covered tie as described on page 29 should be used.

Few shrubs provide more beautiful or long-lasting sprays for house decoration, but the risks I have already mentioned should not be forgotten

As regards their value in the garden scene I would go so far as to say that these Cornels are almost indispensable for the June flowering-shrub-garden. They lend themselves well, too, to delightful associations with other shrubs. In lime-free gardens "Azalea macrantha" (*R. indicum macranthum*) Azalea 'Daimio' (*R. Kæmpferi* var. 'Daimio') and the invaluable old Ghent Azalea 'Flamingo', will be found highly effective

as companions, and perhaps, to intrigue the curious, *Hydrangea serrata*
'Grayswood', whose floral bracts undergo the same curious colour
changes, may occupy the shady side. In the warm gardens of coastal
counties, *Leptospermum Nicholii*, with its clouds of little red flowers,
may be risked, and, on chalky lands, *C. K.* var. *chinensis* may be neigh-
boured, on the sunny side, by the pale cobalt-violet flowers of Sophora
or Ceanothus.

The great **Cistus** family is composed of Cistus proper, white, and
occasionally purplish-pink flowered, sun-loving evergreen shrubs from
south Europe, and the yellow and red flowered Halimiums and Helianthemums. So far as my experience goes none of the Cistus are
absolutely hardy, but most will usually survive for some years if planted
in sunny, well-drained spots with the roots protected by a mulch of
bracken in winter, They have the useful quality of growing well on lime.

Cistus laurifolius is probably the hardiest of all, but is also one of
the least decorative in habit. As generally seen it is a gaunt, lanky
evergreen about 6 feet high, with dark, often sooty-looking leaves.†
The wild-rose-like white flowers typical of the family are produced
from June onwards and are 2 or 3 inches across and, like those of most
Cistus, usually drop their petals in the afternoon. It is one of those
shrubs that need constant nipping and pegging down when young to
induce a sturdy and bushy habit. When this is done a vastly improved
appearance is attained. It is a good, hearty garden plant and easily
increased by cuttings or seeds, and is really the only member of the
family that could be called "reasonably hardy". (See illustration p. 209.)

A pretty hybrid is *C*. 'Silver Pink' (A.G.M. 1930), with greyer green
leaves, a more dwarf and compact habit, and large, crimped, pale
Tyrian Rose flowers. It is one of the hardier Cistus but I have often
had it killed out by winter frosts and therefore cannot consider it, or
any Cistus for that matter, a reliably permanent flowering shrub, but it
is so attractive that it is well worth planting even for a temporary effect.

C. cyprius (*C. laurifolius* × *ladaniferus*) (A.G.M. 1926), has silvery
green leaves and clusters of white flowers, with a maroon blotch on a
yellow ground at the heart, that scent the air on warm days. It is a
strong-growing shrub, often reaching 6 feet in height and is among the
hardier Cistus.

C. corbariensis (*C. laurifolius* × *salvifolius*) is fairly free-flowering
and of good, compact and low habit. The flowers are white with a
yellow stain at the base. It is a charming evergreen for a hot, dry bank
and one of the hardiest members of the family.

† The sooty mould is the most serious enemy of the Cistus. Spray at once with
fungicide

C. obtusifolius is very similar but more free-flowering (*C. salvifolius* × *hirsutus*), *and I find it the best of this type.*

C. ladaniferus, the Gum Cistus, with solitary, 4-inch white flowers with a central maroon blotch, is particularly handsome. The variety *C. l. albiflorus* has pure white flowers which are sometimes even larger in size. *C. ladaniferus* particularly needs nipping back when young to induce a bushy habit of growth. It is one of the more tender species.

A superior form of this Cistus with notably broader and less gummy leaves and larger flowers occurs in south-west central Spain. This form was the pollen parent of *Cistus* 'Paladin' (*C. ladaniferus* × *Palinhaii*)†. This is a beautiful hybrid with large white flowers but not, perhaps, one of the hardiest.

C. Verguinii (*C. ladaniferus* × *salvifolius*) is a hybrid with a more dwarf habit of growth and white flowers with a dark centre of maroon and yellow, but is no hardier than *C. ladaniferus*. At least, both kinds quickly succumbed, with me, to winter temperatures which had no ill effect on plants of *Hydrangea macrophylla* and other plants just in the "reasonably hardy" category growing nearby.

C. lusitanicus decumbens (*C. Loretii*), is a much-named Cistus, passing under many aliases, but generally considered to be a hybrid between *C. ladaniferus* and *monspeliensis*. It is a fine, large-flowered, compact, bushy shrub, the white, crimson-blotched flowers lasting notably well on the plant in the afternoon. It is of above average hardiness and quite the finest of its family in my opinion, but it requires a slightly richer soil than the others to grow well.

C. populifolius is, especially in the fine variety *lasiocalyx*, one of the most effective, forming a fine bushy shrub 4 to 5 feet high and having very vivid green leaves and particularly large and well presented white flowers. Although considered one of the hardiest, all plants under my observation were killed by the severe winters of the war years. A large batch of cuttings in the lee of a north wall all succumbed also, although fully rooted at the time of the frost. An illustration of a remarkably fine specimen occurs in "The Flowering Shrub Garden", by the writer (*Country Life*, 2nd Ed., 1947).

C. albidus is a particularly pretty Cistus with white-felted and white-edged leaves and pale purplish-pink flowers. There is also a white-flowered variety.

C. crispus has purplish-pink flowers and is of low habit.

C. pulverulentus is thought to be a hybrid between the foregoing species. It has almost stalkless grey-green leaves and purplish-pink flowers (Fuchsine Pink, H.C.C. 627), possibly rather more attractive than those of *C. crispus*.

† Collingwood Ingram, *The Gardeners' Chronicle*, Jan. 22, 1949, p. 28.

C. monspeliensis is a dense, rounded bush, as hardy as any, with narrow leaves and white flowers in clusters which open over quite a long season.

C. villosus is a variable species, usually with purplish-pink flowers, and one of the least hardy, but the ease with which it grows from seed largely compensates for this weakness. Certain hybrids and varieties are notably fine; among them is var. *creticus* with paler mauve flowers and more crinkled and hairy foliage, the broader leaves being of a greener tint. It inhabits higher elevations than the "type" and is therefore hardier.

C. 'Sunset' is reputed to have the warmest pink flowers of the family (they appear to be the same colour as those of *C. pulverulentus* but I have not checked this), and a dwarf and compact habit of growth. Its parentage is not known for certain, but by some it is thought to be a hybrid of *C. villosus*; others consider it merely a form of *C. crispus* in which they also include *C. pulverulentus*.

C. purpureus (*C. villosus* × *ladaniferus*) (A.G.M. 1927) forms an aromatic-leaved bush 3 or 4 feet high with purplish-pink (Fuchsia Purple, H.C.C. 28/1) flowers with a deeper blotch in the centre. These are borne in clusters and make quite a striking effect when seen close at hand, but the colour is not a very attractive one and the plant is not one of the hardiest. A sub-variety, *C.* 'Betty Taudevin' is particularly vigorous and brilliant.

C. Skanbergii has greyish-green foliage and inch-wide pale rose-pink flowers and is quite attractive in a quiet way though not outstandingly hardy. It is a natural hybrid of *C. monspeliensis* and *C. parviflorus*, introduced in 1929 from Greece.

C. Palinhaii (A.M. 1944) is a newly introduced species from Portugal. It is a dense, low, spreading bush less than 2 feet high with thick, shining, very sticky leaves, and 4-inch-wide, solitary, terminal flowers with pure white crinkled petals and "a conspicuous corona of golden stamens"†. Unfortunately it is not very hardy and is subject to sooty mould.

C. 'Elma' (A.M. 1949) is a beautiful hybrid of the above crossed with the hardy *C. laurifolius*. Raised by Major Collingwood Ingram, this Cistus combines the good points of the parents, being very free with its 3½-inch-wide white flowers.

As regards the cultivation needs of the Cistus, the open, well-drained, sunny position required has already been indicated, but pruning and pegging-down at the start are helpful to induce a bushy habit which helps to protect the stems and prevents wind-rocking. Cuttings and seeds are ready methods of increase and few insects seem to trouble the family. Thus their white flowers, shining from dry banks, may

† *R.H.S. Journal*, LXIX, p. 311.

economically complement the more troublesome and exacting Roses, or temporarily drape a verge which the lower branches of a nearby permanent evergreen will one day cover. The Cistus do not move well and so are best planted out from small pots directly into their garden positions, preferably in spring after the time of frosts is past.

The great asset of the Cistus is their ability to make quick and abundant flowering growth on hot, bare, poor-soiled, dry places which few other shrubs would enjoy. They will even grow under Pines so long as the sun can reach them. The white or purplish-pink flowers are valuable because they appear after the spring beauties are over, but, being so fleeting, they are not to be recommended to those who enjoy their gardens chiefly in the afternoons or evenings.

For the rapid furnishing of new gardens, the temporary filling of spaces between permanent shrubs, and for that fascinating new development—the shrub-rock-garden—they are admirable, but no reliance, of course, should be placed on their permanence. As an example, when our old shrub garden was first installed, on a virgin site, almost all kinds of Cistus were planted. Twelve years later the permanent shrubs had filled their spaces nicely and the specimen flowering trees were grown nearly to perfection, but all Cistus, except the indomitable *C. laurifolius*, had succumbed, and the permanent shrubs had spread their green skirts over the vacant ground, as planned.

Thus in the making of new gardens such transient beauties as Cistus, Brooms of the *C. scoparius* section, and Tree Lupins, have their essential part. They act as temporary tenants or caretakers of the ground, helping to keep it decorated, clothed and fertile until it can be taken over by the permanent ornaments.

Fuller information regarding this family may be found in "A preliminary Study of the Genus Cistus", by Sir Oscar Warburg, M.A., *R.H.S. Journal*, LV, Pt. 1 and "Cistus Hybrids", by the same author, *R.H.S. Journal*, LVI, p. 217.

The **Halimiocistus** are interesting examples of healthy hybrids between two closely related genera. They are only to be recommended for warm sandy or limy gardens but in such places they are so free-flowering and attractive that they are worthy of mention here.

Halimiocistus Revolii (*Cistus salvifolius* × *Halimium alyssoides*) is a rare and very dainty little natural hybrid from the south of France with a continuous succession of exquisite little white flowers stained with yellow at the centre. It holds its flowers until late evening and is the most effective of all these hybrids and quite first-class.

H. Sahucii (*Cistus salvifolius* × *Halimium umbellatum*) is a low, rather sprawling evergreen with relatively large, shapely, white flowers. It is quite effective among the hot colours of the garden Helianthemums but it has not the persistence in flower of the last or its charming bushy habit.

H. wintoniensis (*Cistus salvifolius* × *Halimium lasianthum*) has very striking, tricoloured flowers, 2 inches across, with the white petals blotched with maroon and having a yellow base.

This group consists of delicate and charming little evergreen shrubs for warm perches among rocks. A hard winter often kills them and they are, anyhow, seldom very long-lived, but they are among the most interesting furnishings for suitable parts of a new garden where more permanent and slower-growing shrubs will eventually need their space.

A delightful family of evergreen shrublets flowering in the June gap is that of the **Helianthemums** (A.G.M. 1926) and their close relatives the Halimiums. Although ubiquitous they are seldom given the serious attention that, in my opinion, they deserve. To the plantsman, the garden varieties are too mongrelised to be interesting botanically, perhaps, but for the shrub gardener who believes that the garden as a whole must come first, they are highly important. For we have here a range of dwarf evergreen shrubs of excellent habit, reasonable hardiness, very wide soil tolerance and varied and brilliant flower colouring, making their effect just at the moment when many gardens are duller than in the depths of winter. After all, even in the British climate, fine days when the garden should be enjoyable are more likely to occur in June than in December!

The progenitors of the garden varieties are *Helianthemum glaucum* from Southern Europe and *H. appenninum* and *H. nummularium* (*H. vulgare*) natives of Britain, with white and yellow flowers. The garden varieties differ in habit from small-growing types with brilliant, shining green leaves to larger and more straggling growers with grey, downy leaves. The typical specimen forms an evergreen cushion over a foot across and with care will more than double that size.

There are a large number of varieties† and among the best are the following:—

'Ben Affleck', large orange flowers with a deeper centre.
'Ben Attow', large primrose-yellow flowers with a deeper centre.
'Ben Dearg', orange-pink flowers.
'Ben Lawers', large orange-yellow flowers.
'Ben Ledi', crimson-maroon flowers.
'Ben More', orange flowers with a red centre and good foliage.

† See *R.H.S. Journal*, 1926, pp. 119–123 and 1927, p. 84. Also the standard work, Sweet's *Cistinæ*, 1825–1830.

'Ben Nevis', yellow flowers with a brownish centre, very compact.
'Ben Vane', terracotta-orange flowers.
'Ben Venue', vivid red flowers.
cupreum, flowers of a coppery tone.
'Lemon Queen', large yellow flowers, and rather sprawling growth.
'Loxbeard Gold', orange-yellow flowers.
rhodanthe carneum, flesh pink flowers.
'The Bride', white flowers and grey foliage.
'Watergate Rose', dark red flowers, taller.

The "Ben" varieties, which are outstanding, we owe to many years of patient work by the late Mr. J. Nicoll of Monifieth. Mr. William Christy is another breeder who has produced many fine sorts.

There are also a number with doubled flowers as follows:—
'Rose of Leeswood', rose.
'Snowball', white.
'Jubilee', pale yellow.
'Fireball', red.
'Mrs. C. W. Earle', crimson.
'Golden Ball', rich yellow.
tigrinum plenum, orange.

In addition to the above garden hybrids, there are a number of species of Helianthemum and the closely related Halimium well worth growing in warm dry gardens where their timely flowering may succeed the bulk of the spring flowerers and complement the shade-loving, late-flowering kinds from sunny knolls nearby.

Helianthemum canum (*H. vineale*) is a tiny native shrublet, forming a little mound a few inches high with bright yellow flowers. It is quite hardy but so small that it needs looking after carefully.

H. glaucum is a southern European species with yellow flowers and greyish leaves. From this many of the glaucous-leaved garden varieties are probably derived.

H. lunulatum is a charming, fragile little evergreen, often shaped rather like the glass dome of an old-fashioned clock, with intense Canary Yellow flowers with an orange spot at the base on little stalks in June and sometimes into July. A flower rises and opens daily from each little cluster until all are gone. It comes from the mountains of Italy.

The **Halimiums** are a very valuable but little known family containing many first-class shrubs for the garden.

Halimium ocymoides (*Helianthemum algarvense*) (A.G.M. 1932) is a delightful Portuguese shrub of dense bushy habit usually about 1 foot

6 inches or 2 feet high. The delicately formed flowers, in separate, erect, panicles, are rich yellow with a very dark purplish central blotch and over an inch across, and the leaves are silvered with a white fur, giving a grey-green effect to the bush. It is reasonably hardy and a plant of charming personality, especially valuable for gardens with limy soils where dwarf flowering evergreens are scarce.

H. halimifolium. This species is rather similar but is a taller and more slender grower, with bright canary yellow flowers with a small chocolate blotch at the base of each petal. On the whole, while both species are attractive, *H. ocymoides* is the finer of the two, making a more compact grey bushlet in the winter. It is reasonably hardy but succumbs sometimes, when old, in a hard winter.

H. lasianthum (*Helianthemum formosum*) is an outstandingly fine species from Portugal, forming a low shrub with horizontal branches. The flowers, which open in succession, are $1\frac{1}{2}$ inches across and bright canary yellow with a chocolate blotch at the base of the petals. The leaves are silvery on the under side. It is the hardiest and most long-lived of this group and makes a shrub of good but rather open habit, about 2 or 3 feet high and more in width, maintaining its evergreen foliage well in winter. Its brilliant flowers are effective in June and July.

H. alyssoides has pure yellow, cupped flowers and greyish leaves. The habit is dense and cushiony, but rather coarse, forming a mound about 1 foot 6 inches high and 3 feet across. It flowers over a long period from early June onwards, but presents its flowers less gracefully than the preceding.

H. Libanotis is rather a tender species with a thin rambling habit and small narrow leaves, and short-lived yellow flowers, from the western Mediterranean coast. It is not very effective after midday.

H. umbellatum is an evergreen of erect, rosemary-like habit with white, yellow-centred flowers among reddish young growths. It is not very hardy and requires a warm spot.

The Halimiums, Helianthemums and Halimiocistus are ideal shrubs for planting among dwarf Brooms in the hotter parts of rocky slopes whose moister and more sheltered parts may be planted with evergreen Azaleas, Lithospermum and alpine Rhododendrons. While maintaining the character of the planting they provide a succession of flower of brighter colouring than that of the Heaths, enabling us to cut out those dingy magenta pinks that quarrel with all pure and vivid flower colours.

They will grow on limy soils; indeed, many are found on limestone formations, but they grow perfectly well in fairly acid soil so long as the position is sunny, well drained and elevated. In any event a spoonful of bonemeal is easily given to any plant growing in a very peaty spot, without damage to neighbouring Azaleas. Opinions differ as to the advisability of pruning and shearing back after flowering to aid compactness. Some species seem at times to suffer from this treatment. Pegging-down, on the other hand does, I think, achieve the object even better and can never do any harm. Cuttings of most kinds strike fairly readily, and seeds, even of the garden Helianthemum varieties, are quite a good method. In the latter case the particular variety will not come true, of course, but the plants obtained are often very attractive.

The **Diervillas** are not of very great value as regards their effectiveness for the small garden, but they flower in June and July and as they will grow in alkaline conditions, are therefore of some interest for gardens with limy soils whose owners do not wish to be troubled with more exacting plants. The true species of Diervillas are generally less effective than the garden hybrids and, even with these, the tubular flowers are too sparse and do not last very long, and the colouring is not really brilliant enough for a coarse shrub often 6 to 8 feet high and of equal width.

The following is a selection of garden varieties and hybrids:—

D. 'Abel Carrière' (A.G.M. 1931) has large pink flowers quite freely borne for a member of this family.

D. 'Conquête' has deeper purplish-pink flowers, sometimes 2 inches across.

D. 'Esperance' has pale pink flowers of a warmer tone than most.

D. 'Eva Rathke' is not so vigorous in growth and has dull, deep crimson flowers. Unlike the others, it does not do well on limy soils.

D. 'Le Printemps' has large, pale crimson-pink flowers.

D. 'Newport Red' has deep crimson flowers on a more dwarf-growing plant than most.

D. 'Mont Blanc' has large, creamy-white flowers.

The chief merit of the Diervillas is that they will put up with poor conditions and neglect better than many choicer shrubs and at least provide some colour in June.

They will, mostly, grow on limy or acid soils in sun or shade with equal cheerfulness. Pruning is not necessary, but the oldest branches may be removed after flowering occasionally, so as to keep the shrub on fairly young wood. Cuttings may be struck in the sand-box in late summer.

Very different in character and as rare as the Diervillas are common, *Zenobia pulverulenta*, from the S.E. United States is a curious peat shrub of irregular, thin, arching growth with strange and rather lovely flowers. It was introduced long ago and has been an inhabitant of a few gardens for forty years or more. The leaves and young shoots have a curious blue-white bloom and this contrasts pleasingly with the white flowers, like very large Lilies-of-the-valley, in late June. They make no great display but the plants are very attractive individually.

Z. *p.* var. *nuda* has leaves of ordinary green and smaller flowers.

Z. *pulverulenta* needs a peaty soil and may be increased by July cuttings, or even seeds sown as described for dwarf Rhododendrons.

Another solitary member of a small family flowers in June, *Abutilon vitifolium.* This Chilean shrub, introduced in 1836, is unfortunately rather tender and so only to be recommended for the coastal counties and the south and west. In such places, in a sheltered spot shaded by distant trees, it is often very beautiful, growing, in time, from 6 to 15 feet or more in height. The wood is soft, and among the large, downy, greyish-green vine-like leaves the Mallow-like, pale cobalt-violet flowers appear in groups on the ends of the twigs in late June. There is also a white-flowered variety which contrasts well with the pale violet "type".

It is easily increased from seeds of which a good crop is generally produced. It will grow in either limy or acid soils equally well and though beautiful in flower, has little decorative value at other times. In sunny and draughty situations the Mallow Bush, as it is sometimes called, often drops its flower-buds unopened. It is not a long-lived shrub, even in its native home, and is a miff, being apt to die suddenly when least expected.

The great race of **Philadelphus,** now included with Deutzia in the family of Hydrangeaceæ, with deliciously perfumed, but merely white, flowers hovers on the borderline of the first-class category. The greatest asset of the "Syringa," if I may use for it this charming old name unfortunately belonging, in fact, to the Lilac, is its blossoming time of late June when, so often, it alone provides the flowers of the roadside garden shrubberies. Many of the varieties are somewhat ugly in habit, or have a poor flower presentation that is not decorative, but some are lovely in all respects, except that of winter furniture. The species vary in height from 2 to 15 feet.

According to Mr. H. G. Hillier, a leading authority on the genus (Tree and Shrub Conference 1938), there are about forty species known, but, owing to hybridisation, their exact identification is often a very difficult matter.

Philadelphus coronarius, the common south European species, with small creamy-white, very fragrant flowers, is notable for having a yellow-leaved garden variety—var. *foliis aureis*, which can be highly decorative when grouped among other shrubs with unusually coloured foliage.

P. Delavayi is an "umbrella name" under which shelter a great number of forms, many of which, I know to my cost, are of no value whatever. But there are also some really good forms and among these *P. D.* var. *nymansi* appears to me a particularly fine Philadelphus. Flowering in early June, the inch-wide, cup-shaped flowers, in racemes of about eight, appear among the large, furry leaves that are covered with a glaucous bloom. More desirable still, in my opinion, is another form, 6 feet or more in height, also raised at Nymans, which flowers in late July with a great profusion of fragrant flowers. It was described and figured in *The Flowering Shrub Garden*, 1st edition 1938, by the writer, but is not in commerce. *P. insignis* is probably the best available substitute.

P. pubescens (*P. latifolius*), from the S.E. United States, is the finest of the species in flower in late June and is commonly found as a big shrub often 15 feet high in old gardens. The white flowers are not so powerfully fragrant as those of *P. coronarius*, but carry sufficient perfume to be highly agreeable. It is an admirable shrub for large gardens or wherever there is plenty of room for it to be allowed to grow freely. In the small gardens the choicer hybrid varieties give a much better return.

P. incanus is a useful Chinese species owing to its late flowering, being usually at its best in late July. It has hoary leaves and fragrant cup-shaped flowers in clusters of half-a-dozen or more.

P. microphyllus is of dwarf, dense habit with solitary fragrant flowers, an inch across, in June. It is often very disappointing as to freedom of flower.

P. argyrocalyx, an attractive species from New Mexico, possibly a sub-species of the preceding, was first introduced only in 1922, and has fragrant, usually solitary, white flowers $1\frac{1}{4}$ inches across. It is less tall than many, attaining about 6 feet at most. In habit it is singularly graceful, the arching shoots of the previous year being set with rows of the large and handsome flowers.

P. pekinensis var. *brachybotrys* was the label attached to a fine, but regrettably almost scentless, new Philadelphus with enormous round flowers exhibited in 1948 by Colonel F. C. Stern of Highdown. The wild species is said to be small-flowered and of no great beauty, so this variety is exceptional.

P. grandiflorus (A.G.M. 1923) is the scentless North American species with 2-inch-wide rather narrow-petalled flowers singly or in threes on the ends of the branchlets which has produced many hybrids in which traces of these characteristics appear. It seems to me to lack the most valuable quality of its genus, and, like so many of the Philadelphus species, is hardly good enough as a flowering shrub for the small garden.

There are a number of superior hybrid varieties such as 'Coupe d'Argent', 'Voie Lactée', 'Norma', 'Atlas', 'Conquête' and 'Rosace', with large single flowers, sometimes 3 inches across, usually only slight fragrance, and, often, a somewhat gawky habit. They are all useful shrubs for planting in odd corners to add fragrance to the garden air, but a bed planted up solely with them is a winter eyesore that their summer flowers cannot redeem.

P. insignis (*P. pubescens* × *californicus*) is a fine hybrid of the larger kind, making a graceful bush perhaps 10 feet by 10 feet. The fragrant, single, cup-shaped flowers, with overlapping petals and handsome centre of golden anthers, are borne in panicles in July. Thus the succession of fragrance can be kept going very pleasantly if one has the old *P. coronarius* to start it, P. 'Belle Étoile' to follow and *P. insignis* and *P. incanus* to end up with.

P. Lemoinei erectus is a graceful, small-leaved, and small-flowered variety of twiggy, upright, but bushy habit about 6 feet high. The cloud of little fragrant flowers is very attractive. Curiously enough, if seedlings of almost any Philadelphus are grown they will often be found to be of this type though not quite so fine. The great French firm of Messrs. Lemoine of Nancy who have produced so many splendid varieties of Lilacs, Peonies, Hydrangeas and other plants, was also responsible for the first hybridisations in the Philadelphus family. This produced a whole new race of charming garden shrubs of which the above is an example.

Another group of Philadelphus is that of the purple-centred varieties. Among these *P. Burkwoodii*, with small leaves and large, narrow-petalled flowers with yellow stamens, and 'Sybille', with orange-scented, purple-centred flowers, are outstanding, but the most beautiful of all Philadelphus, in my opinion, is the variety 'Belle Étoile' (A.G.M. 1936). This forms a graceful twiggy bush about 5 feet high of unusually good habit for a member of this genus, with large, rather square, fringed, white flowers with a purplish centre and a delicious fragrance. They are carried with an unusual grace which makes 'Belle Étoile' a first-class flowering shrub for late June and remarkably fine as a lawn specimen.

Among the double-flowered forms the well-known and strong-growing 'Virginale' (A.G.M. 1926) whose buxom appearance suggests a rather fuller life than the French adjective conveys, is outstanding. The habit, with unwise and niggling pruning, can be downright ugly, but when left to its own devices, or when entire branches only are occasionally cut right down, this can be quite passable and the flowers are so large and handsome that it is quite a fine sight in the more highly gardened parts of the grounds. Its appearance, however, does not consort well with more natural plantings, where it looks as jarringly out of place as Hortensias in a wood or Calceolarias on an alpine precipice. Such garden-type, artificial-looking varieties at once make the surroundings look merely unkempt, rather than natural and wild.

'Bouquet Blanc', about 3 feet high, has smaller double flowers in clusters and is very sweetly scented. Having a compact bushy habit it largely avoids the artificial appearance of 'Virginale' and looks well anywhere where double flowers are acceptable.

'Girandole', 'Albâtre', 'Glacier' and 'Enchantment' are other double-flowered varieties, the last-named being one of the latest to bloom, with dense, crowded spikes of small flowers. 'Manteau d'Hermine', with cream-coloured fragrant, double flowers, is notable for a dwarf habit of growth that makes it one of the most suitable for cramped places.

As regards their placing in the garden, the poor winter landscape appearance of the Philadelphus makes their use in quantity in prominent positions inadvisable. Apart from the virtues of 'Belle Etoile' as a specimen, they are best in odd corners where they may scent the air and complement neighbouring plantings of more colourful shrubs.

Their quality of indifference to soil conditions makes them particularly useful in limy gardens and their virtual indestructibility makes them suitable for places where more vulnerable treasures would not be safe.

They may be propagated by seed, which usually gives a small-flowered progeny, or by cuttings of hard wood in the sand-frame in February or, best of all perhaps, by layers.

A June flowerer that is much more exacting as to soil requirements is **Kalmia latifolia,** the Mountain Laurel or Calico Bush, an evergreen from the United States. In its native land it is reported sometimes to reach 30 feet in height but mature specimens are usually only about 8 feet high in this country. In the open the bush is fairly dense and rounded in form and in June appear the clusters of frilled, cup-shaped, crimson-pink, speckled flowers three-quarters of an inch across. In this country, unless the shrub is in full sun, it is seldom as free-flowering as could be desired and the habit is rather loose. On the other hand when fully exposed, it is often very beautiful near at hand, though in most forms the colouring is so weak that it plays no great part in the summer garden landscape.

K. latifolia requires an acid soil with plenty of leaf-mould to grow well and, in my view, full sun to flower well. It is perfectly hardy, making a fine display at the Arnold Arboretum which has a much colder winter climate than any part of Britain. If crowded in among other bushes it is often lacking in symmetry and shy of flower, the best position being as a lawn specimen or among dwarf shrubs. Seed is the easiest method of increase.

K. l. myrtifolia is, I think, a far finer form for the small garden than the "type" and a mature specimen in full sun forms a superb 3-foot dome of pale crimson in late June, when it is most appreciated. It is quite first-class and a notable treasure for the lime-free garden.

Such a choice plant, expensive owing to the difficulties involved in reproducing it, should never be put into a mere shrubbery where all kinds of second-rate, deciduous shrubs are jumbled up together. It is worthy of a prominent position as a specimen, emerging from a carpet of low-growing evergreens.

The propagation of the Kalmias from cuttings is difficult. Even when assisted by hormone treatment they are very slow to form roots, although a fair percentage will do so eventually with this aid. Layers are more certain, for the amateur, but they are also often very slow to root. Seeds, on the other hand, are quite an easy method, following the procedure recommended for dwarf Rhododendrons on page 90, but one cannot be certain of reproducing either an extra rich-coloured form of the common species or the superlative variety *myrtifolia* by this means. The flower colour, being a pale tint of crimson, is what is often called peach pink and this varies in depth though not often in hue. Seeds should be taken from the deepest coloured form available, otherwise most of the seedlings will be found to have flowers of a very pale colouring.

The deepest coloured form is sometimes distinguished as *K. l.* var. *rubra* (see illustration opposite) and the palest, having flowers that are almost white, as *K. l. alba.* Alfred Rehder described another variety, *obtusata*, as being of compact habit and slow growth, but it does not appear to be in cultivation in this country.

Requiring similar soil conditions, **Bruckenthalia spiculifolia,** a small, heathlike evergreen from the mountains of S.E. Europe, 6 inches or a foot high with rosy, open-mouthed, pitcher-shaped flowers in June, joins up the low-toned, pinkish sequence of flower of the Heaths. It is

Potentilla Farreri

Kalmia latifolia rubra

Styrax japonica

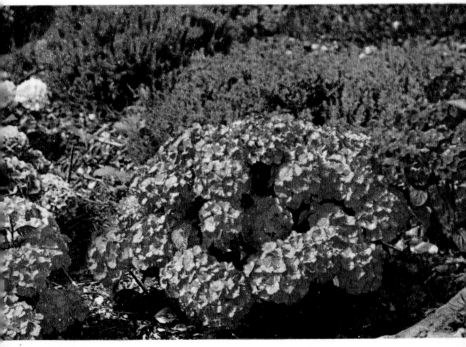

Hydrangea ' Vulcain '

a pleasantly bright and vivid green in winter and may be increased by seeds, carefully sown as advised for dwarf Rhododendrons (page 90). Cuttings, as for Heaths, can also be grown.

From these minor treasures we turn now to one of the greatest, yet one of the most exasperating of garden shrubs; a plant having the very highest qualities but also the most regrettable defects—the **Rose.**

The finest Roses for appraisal as flowering shrubs for the garden include many garden hybrids the details of whose original ancestry are lost in the mists of antiquity. The most important of these ancestors, whose "blood" must be in every good garden Rose, because it alone carried the genes of perpetual flowering, is a certain red Chinese Rose†.

Now the Roses, like the Camellias, the Tree Peonies, the Hydrangeas and now, alas, even the Rhododendrons, have been bred for a different purpose to that for which we shrub-gardeners wish to use the plants. They have been bred primarily for appraisal as cut flowers. Efficiency, of course, demands specialisation and the greater the efficiency for the one purpose the less for another entirely opposed. Consequently it is not among the winners of prizes for cut blooms that we may expect to find flowering shrubs of beauty as such. Quite a different specification is required when we want to see the Rose as a lovely growing bush, densely aglow with flowers at intervals from midsummer to first frost. There are, of course, some Roses ostensibly bred "for garden decoration", but unfortunately the majority of these fail lamentably for one reason or another to measure up to our particular requirements.

It is not everyone that finds altogether beautiful the peculiar shape invented for the very double exhibition Rose, with its high centre and very thick stalk to ensure that the monstrous bloom is seen in profile as it stares up at the sky. In any event, it is too artificial in appearance to consort with more natural-looking shrubs, and the earthy rectangular mess, set with snags and stumps, that so often constitutes the "Rose-bed" is a six months' eyesore that cannot possibly be tolerated, even behind the dense Yew hedge generally used to screen its ugliness from our sight.

Can Roses be grown effectively as flowering shrubs without con-centration-camp treatment in these awful beds? This is the question the artist-gardener asks. The only authoritative answer is that of the plants themselves and it will be found that all those that are really good,

† "Notes on the Origin and Evolution of our Garden Roses", by C. C. Hurst, Sc.D., Ph.D., F.L.S., *Journal R.H.S.*, LXVI, p. 242. See also *Hortus Sempervirens* by J. S. Kerner, t. 114, Vol. X (1804) for a fine coloured illustration of this historic plant.

16

healthful garden plants will, as might be expected, grow to perfection, so long as their pest-control requirements are attended to, in the verges and bays of beds of other flowering shrubs or as lawn specimens.

A plant can only produce so much petal material, so we must decide whether we want this in the form of a reduced number of flowers, each having a lot of petals, or in the form of a greater number of flowers, each having only the minimum effective number of petals. For the decorative *shrub*, I think we want the greater number of "single" or "semi-single" flowers. Fortunately, there is a fine selection of these available in all the usual Rose colours.

Now as to the habit of the shrub, must we suffer the almost herbaceous, snaggy-looking, "leggy" plants which are put up with, as a matter of course, in the "Rose-bed"? The answer is that provided we do not insist upon the individual flowers reaching the maximum size for the variety, and provided that we feed and protect the plants with the assiduity essential to grow any Rose well, many varieties will make large, healthy, shapely bushes with an almost permanent framework that will last for years. Eventually, perhaps, they carry too much old wood and if they are then cut right down to the ground, will reform themselves nicely in a couple of seasons, given a little thoughtful pinching and tying-out to ensure a well-spaced foundation framework.

Good cultivation is admittedly the keynote in forming fine shrubs from garden Roses, and good results cannot be expected unless this matter is carefully attended to. A widespread misconception is that Roses prefer a clayey and even a limy soil. Actually they do not, they become martyrs to "Black Spot"; what they like about the chalklands is the free drainage always given by a subsoil of this nature, not the alkalinity.

According to one of our most successful exhibitors and breeders of Roses† an acid soil, about pH 6 and very rich in humus, is the ideal. I find that Roses that are kept heavily mulched with fallen leaves grow quite well enough in a very sandy soil as acid as pH 5·50 a figure which I like to aim at, as it pleases the Rhododendrons that precede the Roses and ensures blue flowers on the Hydrangeas whose duty it is to complement them and to succeed them when their first flush of bloom is over. A turf-loam, made simply by rotting down turves until the grass and weeds in them are dead, is, I think, a particularly favourable medium for Roses and the practice of burying turves well below the roots when planting is very effective. Our shrub-rose has to decorate the garden for many years with the minimum of fuss and bother and

† Bertram Park, "Some Modern Roses", *R.H.S. Journal*, LXXIII, Pt. 1, p. 18 *et seq.*

this precaution, and the addition of plenty of humus to the topsoil, will make certain that it can do so effectively.

Next we must consider the requirements of the Rose as to aspect. The plant is very definite in its preference here; the aspect must be fully exposed to sun and air, but very violent winds are, of course, harmful, as indeed they are to all shrubs that are expected to grow 4 or 5 feet high.

Thus the optimum conditions we have arrived at for our Roses have, we find with some surprise perhaps, a remarkable resemblance to those suitable for our hardy hybrid Rhododendrons and Azaleas and for our Hydrangeas. But the aspect requirement is slightly different; the Rhododendron likes the lightly dappled shade better than the full day's sun and is grateful for some tempering of the full blast of the wind. The Hydrangea does not mind the wind but its delicately tinted flowers are sometimes faded by the sun. Our beds, however, have usually a sunny and a more shaded side and this difference is just enough to please all three of these splendid garden shrubs, if they are given their preferred aspects.

What the Rhododendron family is in spring and the Hydrangea in late summer, so is the Rose in midsummer, the king. Difficult as it is to select the best from the hundreds that just fail to provide the perfect shrub for one reason or another, the immense variety makes them adequate collectively.

Already, I am sure, breeders seeking the mammoth prize bloom have put many a perfect shrub-rose on the bonfire. I would venture to give a tentative specification for such a variety in the hope that some breeder may give us shrub-gardeners a treat. Let them give us, then, a Rose capable of making a shapely, strong and healthy permanent bush 10 feet across like 'Felicia', an almost indestructible, single flower like that of 'Betty Prior', and a glorious vivid colour combined with an enchanting fragrance like that of 'Catalonia'. We need not worry about the defect of the over-thick flower stalk, as this will be corrected by the "large bush" method of growing. Needless to say we do not want the flowers to face the sky—so that we only see their thin edges; we want them to look at *us*, so that we see them full-face. The outsides of the petals of Roses are naturally duller in colour and partly obscured by the calyx in the earlier stages.

Another point that will determine our choice of varieties for growing as flowering shrubs and to be viewed as such, is the system of flower production. Some varieties bloom mildly but continuously, others make a tremendous display and then take a short rest, and then repeat. I think the latter type is much the most effective for our particular purpose. This is quite another matter to the "Rose-bed" requirements, let us remember; we are giving first consideration, as always, to the garden scene as a whole. The spring effects are over—our Rose orchestra is tuning up and then, suddenly, it starts. To be as good as what has gone before, and what will follow later, it has got to be very good indeed and no "Ca' canny" policy can be good enough. The rest period will coincide with the full glory of the Hydrangea and Genista effect in July so we shall not grudge the Roses their quiet time. They will then come again with greater vigour to take a full part in the grand finale in August.

There is an amazing difference in the beauty of flower of the different varieties in distant effect. Some appear as mere lumps of formless colour, and surprisingly weak colour at that, compared with many other flowering shrubs. Indeed, in general the Rose is not so very vivid in colour; it is really rather on the weak side. Some varieties, however, and 'Donald Prior' is notable for this, have such a presentation as to give a lovely *flowery* effect at a distance. Much can be learnt by study of this important feature at nurseries and trial-grounds. I used to go to the National Rose Society's grounds and, standing on the highest and most distant spot, direct an assistant to selected patches of effective mass display. Curiously enough it was for the shapely masses of its bloom on small plants, rather than for its superb deportment as a large shrub and wonderful sprays for cutting, that I first selected 'Felicia'.

As I have said, I do not know a perfect Shrub-Rose, but many varieties have one or other of the necessary qualities.

The following selection includes some of the best of the **Hybrid Teas.**

'Picture' has remarkably attractive sea-green foliage and Carmine Rose flowers of a rather upright and artificial, but very charming, shape. It is a strong, reliable Rose, and quite outstanding among the modern H.T. types for growing as a large bush.

'Mrs. Sam McGredy' is a fine orange-pink, opening warmer in colour but quickly fading colder than 'Picture'. It is a fine Rose but regrettably from our point of view, very double, so that at a distance it looks like a blob instead of a flower.

'McGredy's Sunset', 'Lady Forteviot', 'Heinrich Gaede', 'Katherine Pechtold' and 'Angèle Pernet' are all rather similar. Their glorious soft orange flowers have a brilliance no garden can well do without. All require care to grow well, and success is especially well rewarded when a few plants are grown, rather surreptitiously, among the blue Hortensias. 'McGredy's Sunset' is particularly beautiful in both flower and foliage.

'Mrs. Wemyss-Quin' is an old Rose, with pale yellow, double flowers, that has remarkable strength of constitution and longevity. It is often seen as a huge bush in abandoned gardens, as the last survivor of a mixed "Rose-bed". It is one of the most reliable and healthy of the yellow varieties when grown as a large bush, but not outstandingly beautiful.

'Catalonia' is a Spanish Rose. Though the flower is a huge, formless cabbage, it is so free and intensely vivid in its colour, that I mention it here. The petals, Indian Yellow at the root shading through Nasturtium Red to Geranium Lake, give an effect of Orange Scarlet. In the north of England it grows poorly, but in the warm gardens of the South it is like some great June-flowering Tree Peony, the huge vivid flowers making a gorgeous display. I counted sixty-two open flowers on one bush of this Rose on May 31, 1949.

'Golden Dawn' is a rather washed out, pale yellow but it is strong-growing and free for a yellow Rose, if somewhat coarse and ragged in the flower.

'Easelea's Golden Rambler' is a climber that can be grown successfully as a large bush and with its fine foliage and shapely, double, clear yellow flowers is very beautiful among the early Cambridge-blue Hortensias, such as 'Mousseline".

The following are Singles and Semi-singles:—

'Réveil Dijonnais' (Clg. H.T. 1931) is a climber that is so outstanding, grown as a bush, as to be worthy of special mention. The wood carries very large thorns, and the semi-single flowers are, I estimate, Geranium Lake, with Indian Yellow centres, opening out flat and fading paler, but the petals do not fade in an ugly way, so that the bush is always decorative. The flowers are produced in great numbers over quite a long season so as to make a fine picture. With some nipping, pegging-down and encouragement, it can be made to form a bush that is reasonably compact and sturdy and about 3 or 4 feet high. It is one of the nearest to the perfect Shrub Rose that I have seen but needs a fairly warm spot and some care.

'Isobel' (Pernetiana, McGredy 1916), Cherry orange, single, perpetual blooming, is very beautiful but now, unfortunately, rather scarce.

'Cuba'. Lincoln red and orange, semi-double. This was a wonderful shrub Rose but, alas, almost if not quite extinct.

'Mrs. Oakley Fisher' (B. Cant, 1921), is an apricot yellow, fragrant, single, of compact growth, now regrettably rare.

'Irish Fireflame' has small, rather thin flame-flushed apricot single flowers with red buds.

'Innocence' has white, semi-double flowers of delightful shape.

The following are a selection of **Hybrid Polyanthas**:—

'Donald Prior' is a deep Turkey Red, semi-double; it is disease-free, has good foliage, is of rather dwarf, compact growth, and is freely available. It is one of the finest of all red Roses when grown as a shrub about 3 ft. high in an open position, but it sets seed so readily that it requires frequent dead-heading or it will stop flowering.

There are a number of new varieties of this type which are being tried out at present as shrub Roses. 'Frensham' is a very promising variety but I doubt that it will surpass 'Donald Prior' as a flowering shrub. 'Our Princess' is notably sound in colour but the habit is not suitable for a shrub, admirable though it may be for cutting purposes. 'Commonwealth' has very large crimson, single flowers but its habit of growth is not yet fully tested. 'Fashion' is promising.

'Fortschritt' is a bushy and charming variety with large, very pale, salmon-blushed, shapely flowers very well presented. It is rather like a miniature 'Felicia'.

'Betty Prior', single, Rose Madder, long-lasting and floriferous, makes a strong bush for a specimen, but is rather upright in habit and a poor colour for the garden landscape.

'Kirsten Poulsen' (A.G.M. 1933), cherry red, single, makes a good, strong bush as a specimen, but is also too upright in habit and poor in colour, as it fades badly. 'Kirsten Poulsen Improved' has the colour of 'Karen Poulsen' and is certainly an improvement.

'Karen Poulsen', Turkey Red, single, and very shapely, is rather dwarf in habit and unfortunately the colour quickly fades.

The following are a selection of **Hybrid Musks**:—

'Felicia' has pale pink (Rose Madder, H.C.C. 23/2) and yellow double flowers in clusters on long thorn-free stalks, making a huge, firm bush. It is fragrant, and very good in autumn, but regrettably weak in colour.

'Prosperity', similar in habit to 'Felicia', has semi-double salmon (H.C.C. Azalea Pink) buds opening paler and ageing to white, and is a superb shrub Rose making a tremendous display of beautifully presented flowers.

'Vanity' is also similar in habit to the preceding, but the flowers are crimson pink.

'Moonlight' has small white, semi-double flowers in sprays. It is a strong bush that can take care of itself anywhere. On its own roots it quickly colonises a large area.

'Danaë' has soft, yellow, semi-double flowers in clusters and rather loose growth. 'Callisto' is rather similar.

In addition to the British-bred Hybrid Musk Roses there is a further

valuable section that was bred in Germany. Two fine reds of this kind
are 'Wilhelm', crimson, and 'Hamburg', a fine bright red, and they
are now available at nurseries in this country.

It should be mentioned that I have, over a period of many years,
tried out a very large number of Roses. For instance, I had great hopes
of a lovely, single, orange Rose, 'Collette Clément', that I imported
from France many years ago among a number of other kinds. Like so
many others that I have had to discard, this variety had not sufficient
natural vigour and resistance to disease to prove serviceable for the
shrub garden.

The above selection are perfectly suitable for growing interspersed
with Hortensias in the verges and bays of beds whose evergreen centre
planting is formed by Japanese Azaleas or hardy hybrid Rhododendrons or, in limy soils, other flowering evergreens of garden type. The
more natural-looking single-flowered varieties consort best with the
Lacecap Hydrangeas similarly backed by Evergreen Azaleas or by
Rhododendrons of less pronounced garden type. Among the almond-
green young leaves of the Hydrangeas in spring the ruddy young growths
of the Roses are highly decorative against the background of the bright
Rhododendron flowers and their dark foliage. The stronger-growing
Roses may also be grown as large lawn specimen bushes with delightful
effect.

As regards colour schemes, the most effective that I know is when
the yellow, white and orange scheme is interlaced with the Cambridge
and the Royal blues of the Hydrangeas and the stronger yellows of
Genistas. When this comes off, the July effect is as vivid and lovely as
that of the Azaleas in May. In the first few years, in important places
near the house, the display may be reinforced with annual plants,
always the best temporary trimmings among shrubs. In sunny spots
deep purple small-flowered Petunias are also particularly effective and
the delightful combination remains gay and colourful until the first
hard frosts. Following the unusually mild winter of 1948, the Petunias
revealed their true character as tender flowering shrubs, by flowering
profusely from hard woody branches in 1949.

On limy soils we cannot have blue Hydrangeas, and then we may
intersperse the red and white varieties of these among the Roses and let
the late Ceanothus hybrids and Clematis 'Perle d'Azur' provide the
blue among Genistas backed by Choisyas, evergreen Barberries and
Escallonias.

As to the vexed question of pruning, before I dare to speak I must
repeat that the shrub gardener's target is quite opposed to that of the

ordinary rose grower and my method would doubtless not suit his requirements at all.

What makes the rosebush, when pruned in the usual manner, unsightly to our eyes is the snaggy, bare base and, above all, the unnatural-looking angles of the pruned branches, with their new shoot duly sprouted from the outward bud below the cut. My method, which was suggested by the plants themselves and not by any human being, is never to cut a shoot anywhere but at the base and to do so only when that shoot appears to be too old to be useful. Flowering young shoots from the base are religiously *not cut at all* after flowering, only the seed heads are removed. The idea is *not to stimulate* a new shoot from a flowered stem. Good feeding and cultivation stimulate the Rose to grow and if it is not incited to make secondary new growth from a shortened stem it will often make it right from the base, and this is what we want it to do.

Much depends on the vigour of the basal "burl" and this is always treated with great respect, and surgical care is taken to keep it healthy and clean of all dead snags and exactly positioned just below ground-level.

Those little spindly shoots from the base, which occur as well as the big strong ones, are not cut away but carefully preserved, as they shade and screen the base and thus help the health and comeliness of the bushes.

Not all Roses respond to this method, I admit, but quite a number do very well indeed and the principle at least secures the most comely and well furnished shrub possible. Some kinds tend to make long growths, and these are gently arched over and tied down in a natural-looking curve to suit the furnishing of the bed.

Occasionally an old Rose may die when moved, but usually if the plant to be moved is then and there cut down to within a few inches of the stump or base and this is pared clean of all dead wood with surgical care and the patient is then at once very firmly replanted with the burl just below ground-level, more often than not that Rose will make a fine new top and provide as good a display as any hard-pruned young plant in the garden. It is useless to move a Rose without cutting away the top. Few shrubs respond more spectacularly to a mulch of fallen leaves than Roses. Plants growing in almost pure white sand, kept mulched, are far more vigorous than unmulched plants growing in heavy loam.

Many of my buxom Roses, smiling in their beds among other shrubs, were old stumps that have been moved several times. The age of a Rose is simply the age of its oldest wood. If it gets worn out it means, I think, that either the variety or its cultivation is at fault.

In the critical first growing season of a Rose daily vigilance is needed to protect the vital new shoots from pests. One or two concealed caterpillars or a few bunches of aphis can be fatal, and with a delicate patient I prefer the finger and thumb to any chemical insecticide.

For the house walls the great **Climbing H.T. Roses** are unbeatable. The reason for the wretched performance of the usual wall Rose is almost invariably that the unfortunate plant has been merely half buried, with its roots still twisted up in a bunch, in the appalling rubbish filled in around the foundations by the builders, when the house was built. It is remarkable that such plants survive at all. It would be much better to install one climber properly, by excavating and carting away the rubbish and replacing it with a couple of barrowloads of turf loam, than six, merely stuck into the existing, impossible, growing medium. Properly planted†, fed and tied-in, almost any of the climbing H.T.'s will cover the front of a post-war-sized house in a reasonably short time and produce the effect of a vertical bed of Roses that will be a sight really worth seeing.

Ramblers, that is to say varieties of *R. wichuraiana* parentage, are not suitable for walls. They need the air blowing through them.

I do not find there is so very much difference, of effect on the Rose, in the various aspects of walls. The main point is to choose a flower colour which will best suit the tone of the building material. At the worst, it is not difficult nor, moreover very expensive, to alter the colour of—say—a repulsively red wall, to a reasonably quiet grey by the mere application of a single coat of tinted cement-and-sand slurry put on with a whitewash brush.

As for the method of tying and training, there is nothing better than inch-square oak trellis or wiring the wall completely with vine-eyes (iron driving pegs with a hole for the wire) strung with strong wire in such a manner as to form 2-foot squares. With this support the Roses can almost be left to their own devices, once the initial tying-out in fan formation is achieved. Another good method is to fix a big staple firmly in the wall a foot above the plant and then fix a row of them into the wall-plate below the guttering. When all are connected to the bottom staple a ready made fan is formed.

Among a wide selection of climbing Roses available today may be mentioned the following:—

Climbing 'Etoile de Hollande', dark crimson red, a fine climbing sport of the well-known old bedding Rose.

Climbing 'Mme E. Herriot', orange shaded red, rather drooping flowers, a Pernetiana, so needs care.

† See Installation, p. 27.

'Paul Lède', apricot, double, good on a warm wall.

'Allen Chandler', semi-single, deep carmine fading to deep Rose Madder with a beautiful golden centre.

Climbing 'Shot Silk', cerise, shaded orange-salmon, with very bright green foliage.

Climbing 'Mrs. Sam McGredy', orange pink, large flowers.

Climbing 'Mme Butterfly', pale pink, shaded apricot, fragrant. Good on a north wall if reasonably sheltered.

Climbing 'Lady Hillingdon', deep golden yellow, dark foliage.

'Fortune's Yellow', orange-yellow, shaded red, very thorny, suitable for a south wall, one flowering only, but very good in a hot summer.

'Lady Waterlow', carmine-pink, semi-double and of lovely shape and fragrance, giving two or three big crops of bloom every year when established and well cared for.

Some of the **Rambler** section are so attractive that an opportunity to grow them on fences, or the trellis screens so useful as divisions in the small garden, should not be missed. Such a screen can produce a wall of flowers that can hardly be equalled by any other kind of shrub. The "Barbier" types have all the charm, and none of the disadvantages, of the "old Roses", in my opinion. They should therefore be especially sought for by those to whom such Roses appeal. On the other hand, they are less effective for brilliant colour at a distance and where such an effect is required the stronger coloured modern varieties should be chosen although they may lack the dainty form and fragrance of the "Barbiers" and, unlike them, must be pruned and retied every year.

The following is a short selection of the choicer Rambler Roses suitable for trellis screens:—

'Felicité et Perpétue' (not "happiness perpetuated" as one might have hoped, but two girls); a notably evergreen, old-fashioned climber with attractively shaped rosettes of an off-white tone.

'Mermaid'. This much boomed variety is, I think, somewhat disappointing. The flowers are seldom really shapely or produced in sufficient numbers at a time to make a display, although individually sometimes 5 inches across. Possibly it is just an example of what a charming simple and well chosen name can do for a plant (A.G.M. 1933).

'Easlea's Golden Rambler' has fine large yellow flowers and an attractive habit.

'Climbing Crimson Conquest' has semi-double, glowing, deep carmine-crimson flowers in clusters. It is very effective.

'Léontine Gervais' has salmon-rose tinted yellow, double flowers with an exquisite fragrance and a lovely, delicate form. It is one of the most delightful of the "Barbier" ('Gloire de Dijon' × *Rosa wichuraiana*) section.

'Francois Juranville', with orange-pink flowers, very fragrant and charming, is another of the "Barbier" type, though actually raised by Bizot in 1873.

'Sander's White' is pure white and fragrant and has the typical hybrid *wichuraiana* habit.

'Rêve d'Or,' a buff yellow Noisette, flowers again in autumn, but requires more time.

'René André' has deep saffron-yellow shaded orange-red flowers. It is a lovely, fragrant little "Barbier" type Rose.

'Albertine' is carmine pink and fragrant; another "Barbier" type, and a wonderful Rose.

'Miss Helyett' has pale carmine-pink flowers, shaded salmon.

'Emily Gray' (B. Cant, 1918) is golden yellow, and has glossy foliage, almost evergreen. It is best in a warm position being apparently a hybrid of mixed parentage.

These Ramblers repay careful pruning, training, spraying and feeding when they show signs of needing it. The difference between well-cared-for plants and those that are neglected is immense. In the small garden the essential screens are ideally provided by inch-square oak trellis, or easily formed of interlaced bamboos, or bought ready-made and at once treated with one of the green-colouring preservatives. The usual tiresome erection of larch poles does not really suit these Roses at all as it does not provide a sufficiently spacious support on which to train the growths out fanwise; even tall chestnut fencing or wire netting is better. It is surprising what these Roses can do, even with a fowl run, if they are well looked after, but the true *wichuraiana* ramblers such as 'Dorothy Perkins', 'Crimson Rambler', 'Bonfire', 'Veilchenblau', etc., are not shrubs for places where there is not time to prune, train, clean and feed them properly.

Another delightful way of growing the "Barbiers" is over the trees of a derelict orchard. Once well established and trained to the top of the trees, they will cascade down in flowery waterfalls, making a most delightful picture. There is also the system of budding Roses of this type on the top of strong Briar poles so as to form the well-known "Weeping Standards". These are seldom effective unless a vast iron stake is used to support the arrangement and then the whole thing is apt to look too artificial. Compared with those seen in sunnier climates, even the properly built, classic-columned pergola often looks forlorn

and out of place in England. One feels that the vast expense incurred
would have given a better return even if only half of it had been used
to purchase really choice shrubs and flowering trees.

The "**Old Roses**" have many admirers but I must confess to never
having succeeded in getting them to grow with the healthful vigour
and freedom of flower characteristic of the more modern hybrids,
although the Hybrid Teas in the same beds may have made shoots a
yard high crowned with a veritable umbrella of flower buds.

An exception has been the thornless 'Zephyrine Drouhin', an old
"Bourbon" hybrid with reddish leaves and very fragrant double
flowers of a rather regrettable Rose Madder, that too commonplace
"cake pink", so hard to place, which unfortunately colours many
otherwise charming flowers. Zephyrine makes fine specimen bushes
and strikes easily from cuttings which are just stuck into the bed,
wherever a plant is required, and left there. Actually the tone of pink
of 'Zephyrine' harmonises quite happily with pale blue Hydrangeas.
An extraordinarily cheap bed that I once planted simply by sticking in
shoots of both these easily "struck" shrubs made a very fine effect a
few years later.

There are, however, a number of outstanding old Roses that are
particularly worthy of note. As one usually sees them, diseased, gaunt,
pest-ridden, almost flowerless, and herded into depressing collections,
they are not very decorative. Some hold, however, that with care and
pruning at the right time, which is, with most, immediately the flowers
are over and not in spring, they can, with the frequent sprayings necessary to keep any Rose clean and thriving, be grown so as to be quite
attractive as flowering shrubs.†

For the red and white-splashed *Rosa gallica versicolor* I can raise
little enthusiasm, but the habit is good and there are, fortunately,
self-coloured varieties.

The Damask Rose, 'Madame Hardy', is a beautiful old white-
flowered variety with very shapely flowers, symmetrical, double, and
opening flat to show the golden stamens, and is generally acclaimed as
one of the most beautiful of all the old-fashioned sorts.

'Queen of Denmark', a fine pink Rose with grey foliage and delicious
fragrance, is another notable old variety.

'Tour de Malakoff', with large, typically "cabbagey" flowers of
cerise, carmine and purple, is probably the finest of the survivors of the
Rosa centifolia race, making a strong but "leggy" bush that should

† "Shrub Roses for the Modern Garden", by G. S. Thomas, *R.H.S. Journal*,
LXXII, Pt. 6, p. 170 and illustrations.

surely be pegged-down rather than tied up to a stake like a Delphinium, as shown in an illustration accompanying the article cited above.

The "Mosses", cousins of *R. centifolia*, have their followers, and nine or ten varieties are still listed by nurserymen, but they are too vulnerable to mildew for the shrub garden.

In the notes mentioned above it is pleasing to find a word of praise for the curious old Rose 'de la Grifferaie', often found in ancient gardens as the surviving rootstock of a long defunct 'Maréchal Niel'. Its masses of ultra-fragrant cerise flowers, that quickly fade to pale purple, are often very decorative. But, in my opinion, the charm of the old sorts is very perfectly exemplified in the lovely, trouble-free, healthful climbers of the "Barbier" strain such as 'Léontine Gervais' and 'François Juranville' which are described in the section devoted to climbers.

Mention of these climbers reminds us that several members of the **Clematis** family are in bloom in June. Owing to the fact that the most effective Clematis are hybrids of mixed parentage whose peak flowering time generally comes in July, they are grouped together, in a section dealing with their parent species also, in the chapter devoted to that month. (See pages 263–267.)

Another gorgeous climber having a variety that flowers earlier than the normal, in June, is *Campsis radicans*. This variety, *præcox*, and its parent species will be found described on page 320.

But now we must leave the environs of the house where the more sophisticated garden varieties, needing frequent care and attention, are planted. The wilder parts of the garden, where less domesticated species provide less spectacular and lasting effects with but a tenth part of the work must not be forgotten. Here June flowers should be as plentiful as they were in spring and, for that matter, as they will be in late summer also.

Fabiana imbricata, an erect, rather Heath-like, evergreen shrub from Chile, which really belongs to the Nightshade family (Solanaceæ), is seldom seen. About 6 feet or more across and high, the bush has long, downy, tapering branches evenly set in June with short, slender twigs each terminating in a narrow white trumpet-flower about ¾ inch long. Unfortunately *F. imbricata* is rather tender and can only be recommended for a sunny position in an elevated garden with a well-drained soil, either acid or limy, in the southern and western counties. It has been well illustrated (Fig. 20, Jan. 31, 1948) in the *Gardeners' Chronicle*.

F. i. prostrata is a dwarf form with smaller leaves and pale mauve flowers, rather hardier than the "type".

F. i. violacea recently introduced (1925–27) from the Andes by H. F. Comber, is hardier than *F. imbricata* and has pale mauvish flowers and shorter leaves. The habit is more lax and spreading and it makes a wider bush.

Late summer cuttings of side-shoots may be struck under a bell-glass. It is best, however, to lift these when rooted and winter them under glass for planting out in spring.

Chionanthus retusus, the Chinese Fringe Tree, is a deciduous member of the Olive family like the Ash, the Lilac, the Privet and the evergreen *Siphonosmanthus Delavayi*. This species forms a shrub or small tree usually about 10 feet high in this country. In late June the feathery masses of snow-white, very narrow-petalled flowers, in upright panicles on shoots of the current year, cover the tree in quite a spectacular manner in a warm season, much less so if it has been cold and wet. It was introduced from China by Robert Fortune in the middle of the last century, but few plants were seen until about 1880 when it was reintroduced by Charles Maries. It is beautiful as a lawn specimen, in flower at a time when there are not many flowering trees in bloom.

C. virginica, the American Fringe Tree, is very similar, but the slightly fragrant white flowers are borne on hanging panicles densely packed like a fringe beneath the branches.

Both species are better when propagated from layers, as budded or grafted trees are weakly and of poor habit. A good rich loamy soil is required, but no objection is made if this is slightly limy. The Chionanthus move well, like Cherries, and, on their own roots, grow quickly in any sunny spot and are quite hardy.

The midsummer garden has few more spectacularly beautiful decorations than **Genista virgata** and particularly, its near relative *G. cinerea*.

G. virgata (A.G.M. 1923) comes from Madeira whence it was introduced to Kew by Francis Masson in 1777. It is a tall shrub, branching low and rising to 9 or 10 feet as a rule, though, by frequent shearing of the young wood when young and after flowering, it can be made to form a dense low bush. Though resembling *G. cinerea* in general appearance, the softer, more numerous, larger, broader, silkier leaves, with a silver edge, the more evenly distributed racemes of flowers, and the abundant seed that is set, usually serve to distinguish it. Young plants of this species are noticeably much more lush and leafy.

In late June or early July the Madeira Genista covers itself with fragrant little yellow pea-flowers, delightful in effect from near or far. Indifferent to soil and asking only for a reasonably sunny spot, it is one of the indispensables of the shrub garden. When out of flower, though deciduous, the mass of green twigs makes young specimens appear as mounds of vivid pale verdure most attractive in the garden landscape. Few young shrubs achieve a more rapid rate of growth and *G. virgata* is thus particularly valuable in new gardens.

Easily raised from seeds sown as soon as ripe in small pots in the greenhouse, or in spring in the cold-frame, the amateur can soon raise a good stock. The seedlings must be planted out before they become potbound or they will fail to anchor themselves properly. In cold districts plants that are kept sheared back so as to shelter the stems by their own twigginess are safest, and this is also helpful to avoid wind damage which often kills top-heavy young plants. But anywhere in the south *G. virgata* is hardy enough for any position and Mr. Bean recorded that it had almost naturalised itself in the Kew woods.

Genista cinerea (A.G.M. 1933) comes from South Europe, particularly Southern Spain, and is a lean, tall shrub usually rising on several stems from near ground-level to 8 feet or more. The fine specimen, however, in Cambridge Botanic Garden is, after thirty-seven years, 18 feet high and 25 feet through according to Mr. F. G. Preston of Cambridge. The leaves are small, very narrow, firm and pointed and the racemes of highly fragrant little Aureolin Yellow pea-flowers hang grouped in bunches in amazing profusion in late June or early July. The flowering-time is usually a little later than that of the preceding and the bunched racemes, the small stalkless, narrow, pointed leaves, the thinner habit and the fact that this species rarely or never produces seed in this country, serve to distinguish it from *G. virgata*, which, though probably only a geographical form of *G. cinerea*, is distinct from the garden viewpoint.

G. cinerea is one of the most spectacularly beautiful of all summer flowering shrubs and as it will grow equally well on limy or acid soils, should be in every garden. Unfortunately it is still extremely rare owing to difficulties in propagation.

As this leguminous shrub, like others of its kind, does not draw its nitrogen from the soil, it is particularly valuable for giving light shade to Rhododendrons, Azaleas and blue Hydrangeas, where it is desirable

to have the shade-providers growing in the same beds as the bene-
ficiaries. This Genista can sometimes be propagated from cuttings taken
with a "heel" and put under a cloche in July, but I have not been very
successful, nor have many of my nurserymen friends. Seed, which
provides the strongest plants, is rarely formed or ripened here, so supplies of fresh seed from Spain would be exceedingly welcome. By this
means this absolutely first-class flowering shrub could be propagated
in such quantity as to make it an effective feature in every good garden.

G. *cinerea* is usually just too early in flowering to complement the
blue Hortensias for long, but flaunts its glorious mantle of flower
among the Roses, the reddening, but slowly shrivelling bracts of
Cornus Kousa, the lively masses of crimson-pink of *Rhododendron
indicum* 'Satsuki' and the white avalanches of Philadelphus.

A light, warm, well-drained soil is the most favourable for both these
Genistas, but either acid or limy conditions suit them almost equally
well. Their one weakness is their failure to withstand strong winds unless
planted out from pots before the tap root has become bent. Even then
the young plants should be repeatedly pinched back or a sudden gust
may twist and destroy the tap root. I have lost many fine specimens
from this cause.

On the whole, G. *cinerea* is the more decorative and fragrant of the
two species as it displays its flowers to greater advantage with a better
presentation. In the young stages G. *virgata* looks more attractive, but
as the plants reach maturity the European species indubitably proclaims
its superiority. At the same time, G. *virgata* is so much more easily
propagated that it can be used much more freely as a Wild Garden
plant wherever it can be protected from rabbits.

Much better known, but of more questionable value is **Carpenteria
californica** (A.G.M. 1935), an evergreen shrub of the Saxifrage family
from California, of doubtful constitution and hardiness in this country.
Most specimens have a shabby look owing to winter damage. Miss
Jekyll first flowered this species in 1885 at her famous garden at Mun-
stead Wood near Godalming in Surrey. The fragrant flowers are white,
about 3 inches across, and appear in clusters in late June and the
yellow anthers make an attractive centre. On the whole it is too tender
to be a really reliable investment for the small garden, but good specimens are sometimes to be seen even in the midlands.

A warm sunny spot at the foot of a south wall, with well drained,
but moist soil, which may be limy, neutral or acid, is the best place for
this species. The plant suffers particularly from the effects of fog which
prevents its being a success near London and other large towns. It may

Genista cinerea

Rhododendron Kæmpferi 'Daimio'

Hydrangea serrata 'Grayswood'

Hoheria glabrata

be raised from seeds but forms vary widely in the substance and beauty of their flowers, so that plants raised from cuttings of the best form are more desirable.

Another shrub that can only be recommended for warm gardens is **Convolvulus Cneorum.** It is a beautiful silvery, blue-green, leafy evergreen a foot high and 3 feet across, with fragile, blushed flowers of the typical shape of its genus, opening successively over a very long period. Unfortunately it is only hardy enough for the South and West and needs a warm sunny bank, but it is so decorative in the garden land-scape and grows so easily from cuttings struck in the greenhouse, that I include it here. In warm gardens, whether limy or acid, it is indis-pensable for foliage effect alone but proper contrast with darker and warmer coloured bushes, such as *Erica vagans*, Azalea 'Tyrian Rose', Cistus, clipped common Brooms, *Berberis Thunbergii*, etc., is necessary to get the full value of the effect.

In association we may plant another silvery-leaved shrub having rather similar requirements. **Phlomis fruticosa** (A.G.M. 1929), the Jerusalem Sage, belongs to the Mint family and was introduced from the Mediterranean in the sixteenth century. In June the small, dense clusters of yellow flowers appear in the axils of the leaves but they are not particularly effective. Like *Senecio laxifolius*, this Sage is grown more for its silvery-grey foliage effects, so attractive in the composition of the all-the-year-round garden. Unfortunately it is scarcely hardier than the Senecio or *Convolvulus Cneorum*.

The Jerusalem Sage will grow on limy or acid soils equally well but requires a warm, sunny position. Cuttings can be struck under a bell-glass in July.

The **Escallonias** are a race of South American evergreen shrubs of rather doubtful hardiness. They are, however, invaluable for seaside or warm gardens on chalky soils, as, except for *E. virgata*, they will support almost any kind of soil conditions quite well. The flowers are small, and somewhat coarsely formed and seldom colour the bush solidly, and the hue is, unfortunately, often of a weak purplish-pink. Thus the Escallonias hardly measure up to the specification laid down for in-clusion in the first-class category for the small inland garden. The hardiness of the species is also, with the exception of *E. virgata*, barely up to the "reasonably hardy" standard according to my tests, many

17

plants having been killed-back severely by the cold war winters whilst those I list in the "reasonably hardy" category, growing nearby, were practically undamaged. Furthermore, inland, instead of growing more beautiful with age like other flowering evergreens, the Escallonias gradually become shabby and ugly so that they stand out as eyesores in old gardens among shrubs of other species that have reached the full glories of maturity.

None the less, for the benefit of seaside gardens, I list the more effective below, due warning having been given.

Escallonia macrantha, a denser evergreen than most, is useful for seaside hedges. It has rather sparse, crimson-pink flowers throughout the whole late summer period.

E. montevidensis is a tall species that requires the protection of a south wall in most places. The white flowers, $\frac{3}{4}$ inch across, in panicles about 6 inches or more in length have a faint, unpleasant smell, when closely sniffed. It is often at its best in late August and good even in September.

E. punctata is probably the best of the crimson-pink-flowered species and grows fairly rapidly to a height of nearly 15 feet. The habit is loose and the panicles of flowers appear from June onwards.

E. rubra pygmœa (*E. r. uniflora*) forms a compact bush about 3 feet high, as a rule, with small, dull crimson flowers in late summer; it is a "witches broom" form of *E. rubra*.

E. virgata (*E. Philippiana*) is a "reasonably hardy" member of the family, but not evergreen like the others. It is a rather open-habited shrub about 7 or 8 feet high, with arching branches well covered with the small white flowers in short racemes on the ends of the branchlets in late June.

The hybrid varieties are more effective, on the whole, and somewhat hardier than the species; the following is a selection:—

E. 'Donard Seedling' has pinkish buds, opening white, in June and often again in autumn.

E. 'Donard Beauty' is more free-flowering than the others with purplish-pink flowers and notably small, but abundant, leaves; it is usually seen about 4 feet high.

E 'Donard Brilliance' is a taller variety with larger (up to an inch across), but sparser, crimson flowers with golden stamens. The foliage is bright green and abundant and the habit is elegant. According to Mr. H. G. Hillier it is a good shrub for planting against a whitewashed wall, in a chalky district.

E. edinensis (*E. virgata* × *punctata*) is one of the hardiest sorts, with pale crimson-pink flowers opening from crimson buds. 'Slieve Donard' is very similar.

E. 'C. F. Ball', raised by the late C. F. Ball at Glasnevin in 1911, is a taller variety with fairly large crimson flowers.

E. exoniensis (*E. pterocladon* × *rubra*), was bred by Messrs. Veitch of Exeter and is a tall shrub sometimes 15 or 20 feet high, worth consideration as an informal windbreak or hedge. It bears blush-white flowers.

E. newryensis (*E. pterocladon* × *langleyensis*) is somewhat similar.

E. Iveyi chance-bred at Caerhays, Cornwall, is thought to be a hybrid of *E. montevidensis* and *exoniensis*. It is a tall evergreen with large white flowers and very handsome, but a really hard winter usually kills it.

E. langleyensis (A.G.M. 1926), (*E. virgata* × *punctata*?) is another variety bred by Messrs. Veitch of Exeter in 1897. The crimson-pink flowers, on short sprigs all along the arching branches, appear from June onwards. It is one of the finest varieties and hardier than many. If cut back by frost in winter, it often breaks from the base in spring again, and against a wall it is fairly safe. According to certain good judges 'Donard Brilliance' may eventually supersede this old variety.

These hybrid Escallonias will put up with careless planting in unimproved, poor, rough soils, polluted with builders' rubbish, in the most creditable manner. They survive where most shrubs would perish. As the average person who is not much interested in gardening will rarely take the trouble to install a flowering shrub properly at the start, this is a very valuable quality. The nurseryman can sell the plant with less than the usual, all too well-founded, misgivings as to its fate at the hands of the purchaser. The little bush struggles along and usually manages to establish itself in time. For the rougher parts of limy-soiled gardens in coastal districts the Escallonias are in their element; wind does not worry them much, and, though rather thin, they are at least evergreen and so give some shelter to other plants.

Most kinds can be easily struck from cuttings of half ripe shoots in the sand-frame, or even against a north wall.

Pruning-back in spring is helpful to encourage the production of young flowering wood, and as an aid to compactness. Old plants in neglected gardens are usually a sorry sight in contrast to the healthful maturity of other flowering evergreens. Thus, in gardens able to grow better things, their use will be chiefly as temporary fillers whose space will be required by more permanent plants later on.

Caesalpinia japonica is an 8-foot deciduous shrub of great qualities and grave defects. The doubly pinnate (twice divided) ferny foliage and foot-long racemes of canary yellow, red-marked flowers, each nearly

$1\frac{1}{2}$ inches across in June and July, are certainly very beautiful. But it is not hardy, it bears the most ferocious thorns and its habit of growth is very straggling. Thus it can only be recommended for a warm corner, preferably against a wall, in a fairly extensive garden. It has no objection to limy soil.

C. Gilliesii, a South American counterpart, is more tender, though it will grow quite well against a wall in the south. The racemes are upright and more compact and the flowers have conspicuous protruding scarlet stamens.

So we have shown, I think, that this month offers us abundant material for the decoration of our gardens with fine flowering shrubs. Yet when June ends the wise gardener can feel that he may look forward to an equally fine display of flower later. All this time the July and August flowerers have been perfecting their young shoots of the year that will bear the succeeding flowers. It is just this happy circumstance of growth that provides us with such a full and satisfying succession. There need be no repine for past glories, an equally fine display is yet to come.

It should be pointed out that many of the hybrid varieties of Clematis described in the succeeding chapter are in flower in June. *Potentilla fruticosa* will also have commenced flowering though usually its best display comes later. The unusually early-flowering variety of the American Trumpet Vine, *Campsis radicans* var. *præcox*, described in the next chapter, will also be in flower this month.

CHAPTER VI

JULY AND AUGUST

JULY AND AUGUST

THIS period covers the later summer from July right up to the first frosts. Fortunately there is a wide selection of good shrubs available though, possibly, the effectiveness of the flowering during this period is more dependent than any other on a favourable garden climate and a neutral, or, preferably, acid soil. Gardens with such fortunate conditions show at this time massed flower displays every bit as spectacular as those of May. Hydrangeas, Eucryphias, Spanish Brooms, Genistas and Fuchsias carry the garden and on warm walls the splendour of the scarlet Trumpet Vines eclipses all that has gone before.

The elimination of blue Hydrangeas, Heaths and Eucryphias is rather a severe handicap for limy gardens, and of Spartium, Senecio, Ceanothus, Hoherias and Fuchsias for very cold ones. Roses, Hibiscus, Genistas, Clematis, Potentillas, Hypericums, Buddleias and Hydrangea species and those hybrids of crimson and other colourings must therefore receive the more attention and, fortunately, they can provide superb flower effects. A greater difficulty is the dearth of good flowering evergreens for such places. As a result, if the winter scene is to be really good, it may be necessary to use some non-flowering evergreens and this inevitably robs the flower effects of some of their whole-heartedness.

Among shrubs with really large and gorgeous flowers the **Clematis** takes a high place. It is so beautiful as to be desirable for all gardens, but its value is even higher for those having a limy soil which are consequently denied the beautiful blues of Lithospermum and the hardy Hydrangeas. On such soils it is a shrub of the very first importance.

The wild species are, on the whole, less spectacular than the garden hybrids. Among the more important parents are the following:—

Clematis lanuginosa, was originally introduced from China by Robert Fortune about 1850. It has very woolly leaves, and large white, or pale lilac flowers nearly 6 inches across in early June and has a somewhat dwarf habit of growth, reaching only to about 6 to 8 feet.

C. florida is a rather fragile Japanese and Chinese species with longer and more wiry stems, smaller, creamy-white or violet flowers in June and July, and glossy, dark green leaves.

A Japanese garden variety of this species, *C. florida bicolor*, flowers earlier, in June, but is mentioned at this stage for convenience. The stamens are transformed into petal-like organs forming a central rosette of a purple colour which contrasts well with the white petal-like sepals surrounding it. The flowers are about 3 inches across and borne with great profusion. It was a favourite of the late Miss Wilmott of Warley. Var. *flore pleno* is similar, but all white in colour.

C. patens is a Japanese species, introduced by von Siebold in 1836, with pale violet flowers 6 inches across, in May and June. With its hybrids, it is dealt with earlier in the work.

C. Viticella is a free-flowering, 20-foot, south European species with 2- to 3-inch violet or blue flowers and divided leaves, dying back in winter nearly to the ground. The late Ernest Markham, an authority on this genus, estimated that a plant of his that had scaled a holly hedge, bore five thousand fully open flowers at one time. *C. V. alba luxurians* (A.G.M. 1930) is a fine white-flowered variety.

These were the wild species from which among others the following garden hybrids were evolved:—

C. Jackmani (A.G.M. 1930) is one of the commonest and most hardy and handsome of the hybrid Clematis. It was raised in 1860 by Messrs. Jackman of Woking and is said to be a hybrid of *C. lanuginosa* and *C. Viticella*. Identical plants have, however, been long grown in Japanese gardens. The well-known, deep violet flowers are highly decorative, but the foliage turns black and remains on the stems in a very unsightly way in winter. Consequently some study has to be given to the placing of the varieties of this type, so that their unattractive appearance in the dead season will not be too prominently displayed. If grown for the decoration of house walls, the provision of a host-shrub, such as the charming and ultra-hardy *Euonymus Fortunei gracilis* (*E. radicans foliis variegatis*) with its brilliant winter foliage, helps to preserve the Clematis growth and hides many of the blackened leaves. On the whole, in the open garden, the Clematis is best grown and trained up some unimportant tree or bush or so as to decorate a trellis screen in company with climbing Roses of almost any type but the Wichuraiana Ramblers, whose pruning would be dangerously untimely for the Clematis. I once had the most delightful summer effects with this Clematis simply grown on tripods of Bamboo canes in the beds, but the winter effect was unsightly unless the plants were cut down in late autumn instead of spring, and the tripods were removed. Though it is said to be better to prune them in spring the plants usually survived this treatment. Like the others of this section, this Clematis has curious flowers in that they have no petals, the petal-like sections being really sepals, but the design of the flower is none the less exquisite and traditional. As pruning depends upon the group to which the hybrid belongs (see p. 266) the name of the group is mentioned with each variety.

C. J. alba is a white-flowered form, otherwise similar.

C. J. rubra has brownish-crimson flowers.

'Beauty of Richmond' is a fine mauve-flowered variety of the *C. lanuginosa* group.

'Comtesse de Bouchaud' is not a strong grower and has 6-inch, pale purplish-pink flowers over a long season in summer. Jackmani group.

'Ernest Markham' has crimson-purple flowers and is probably the finest of its colour. It is a hybrid of *C. Viticella* parentage.

'Lady Betty Balfour' has flowers, often 8½ inches across, of a deep violet-purple with yellowish-white stamens and is one of the finest varieties for the later part of the season. Viticella group.

'Lady Northcliffe' has deep violet-blue flowers with pale yellow centres in May and June and is one of the finest of all of the *C. lanuginosa* group.

'Huldine' is a very strong grower of *C. Viticella* parentage, blooming rather late in the season, with white, translucent flowers barred and flushed with lavender-pink on the outside, produced in charming sprays with great freedom. Ernest Markham, who bred this Clematis and was in charge of William Robinson's superb garden at Gravetye Manor, East Grinstead, Sussex, always reckoned this the finest as a cut flower for table decoration.

'King George V' is a newer variety with flesh-coloured flowers barred with pink. Lanuginosa group.

'Marie Boisselot' is a very lovely white-flowered variety of the Lanuginosa group with a broad-sepalled, full flower of beautiful form.

'Mme E. Desfosse' has very large violet flowers, sometimes 10 inches across, and is of moderate growth, blooming fairly early in the season.

'Mme Van Houtte' has beautifully formed, white flowers equally large and is also a moderate grower of the Lanuginosa group.

'Miss Bateman' is an early flowerer with white flowers with brown anthers, it is a member of the Patens group.

'Perle d'Azur', of the Lanuginosa section, is an excellent August-flowering pale blue, especially recommended for its informal growth and freedom of bloom among shrubs.

'Pourpre Mat' is valuable for being the last to open, deferring its flowering usually until late August. The flowers are a glowing crimson purple and very freely borne. The growth is very vigorous indeed. It is a member of the Viticella group.

'Royal Velours' has deep purple flowers freely produced on a vigorous plant. Viticella group.

'Ville de Lyon' flowers early and also late and is a very free flowering and vigorous variety. The flowers are crimson and particularly effective against light coloured walls. It is rather prone to mildew attack which requires spraying with one of the copper fungicidal sprays or dusting with green sulphur dust when the foliage is moist. Viticella group.

C. 'W. E. Gladstone' has extra fine, large flowers of a blue-lavender shade, with deckle-edged sepals, and belongs to the Lanuginosa group.

The above selection will cover the long flowering season of these glorious-flowered climbers from June or July to frost and the spring-flowering kinds, such as C. montana, C. patens, etc. combine to cover the greater part of the garden year when flowers are enjoyable.

The Clematis of the groups dealt with here grow best, like most climbers, when their roots are in the shade and the upper part of the plant can emerge into the sun. They do quite well in neutral or acid soils provided that the situation is well drained, and grow excellently in limy soils. Most authorities hold that the Clematis is one of the few shrubs benefited by added lime and they are certainly among the most beautifully flowered shrubs that can be grown in the limy garden. In an article in the R.H.S. Journal† Mr. Jackman recommends that the soil should be rich, open, stony and well drained and kept moist by a mulch and that, under very acid conditions, some old mortar rubble may be added with advantage. Ernest Markham, however, counselled caution in this. If too much is given the soil develops mineral deficiencies which are quickly resented by the Clematis.‡ Bonemeal is really better.

Few climbers are more beautiful and effective for the decoration of the trellis, so useful for screening and background purposes. The chief drawback is the constant attention required to train the young growths out in spring, fanwise, for if this is not regularly attended to the plant often gets into a hopeless tangle and wastes its energy in unprofitable growth. When some unimportant shrub or tree is used as a host for the Clematis and there is no question of covering a definite area with decorative growth they can be left largely to themselves once they have been guided up the host's trunk or branches. At Gravetye, previously mentioned, they were very lovely grown in this way. At Kew a fine collection is grown up untrimmed oak branches formed into rough tripods by fastening them together at the top.

As regards pruning, all types are best shortened back when they are first planted. The Jackmanii type are best looked over in spring and any dead stems removed, then one or two of the shoots may be cut off about a foot from the ground so that new growth may clothe the base, as

† "The Clematis as a Garden Plant", by Rowland Jackman, R.H.S. Journal, LXXI, Pt. 12, p. 349 et seq.
‡ "The Clematis", by Ernest Markham, Country Life, 1935.

otherwise this gets somewhat bare in time. Young plants of all varieties are best cut back to one foot from the ground in their first spring. Varieties which flower on the old wood such as the Patens group (for most of these see under late May, p. 173) and the Lanuginosa group, obviously need little pruning, otherwise the flowering wood is removed. On the other hand, those that flower on the young shoots of the year, like the Viticella group, can do with quite severe cutting-back to encourage new growth. Ernest Markham recommended shortening all growths by half in February.

Mice and slugs are two pests which are so troublesome as almost to debar the large-flowered Clematis from the more outlying and wooded parts of the garden. Breakback traps, set under large inverted flower pots to save the birds, and Meta slugicides are the best remedies.

Propagation, for the amateur, may readily be effected by layering low shoots into plunged pots. The "serpentine" method by which the selected branch is alternately buried and brought out into the air all along its length, is not always successful by any means, but very rewarding when it comes off. The practised seed grower may also sow the seeds and raise interesting young plants, but these cannot be expected quite to equal the glories of the seed parent, which was probably the finest seedling out of many hundreds raised. On the other hand, their health and vigour is better than that of grafted plants.

When installing a young Clematis the precaution of firmly fixing a strong piece of protective wire netting round the lower part of the stems should always be taken. Otherwise the first puppy, or indeed, any dog short of tooth exercise, will inevitably chew them up and destroy the plant.

Provided that the plants are in the fully dormant state the roots may be gently uncurled and spread out when planting. When installing a Clematis against a wall the best plan is to set the young plant carefully and firmly in the ground at the correct depth and about 2 feet away from the wall. Then the lower part of the stems may be gently bent over into a shallow trench formed in the direction of the wall and lightly covered with loose soil. The true variety will then probably form its own roots on the buried portion. Where slugs are to be feared a final spadeful of weathered and sifted coke ashes may be spread round the stems. The mortality among newly planted Clematis is very high but if these measures are taken there is little risk of loss.

The **Potentillas** or Cinquefoils are admirable garden shrubs for any type of soil, except perhaps a badly drained clay.

Potentilla fruticosa is a small, untidy, deciduous bush widely found

in nature in the northern hemisphere, even in England near the High
Force of Teesdale. The leaves are divided into about five leaflets and
the yellow or white, strawberry-like flowers are an inch or more across.
Potentillas start flowering in May, in June, or early July, and they
often continue to open a few flowers until summer ends. They seldom
have sufficient flowers out at one time to make a really whole-hearted
display but are nearly always able to show a fair number. In height
they are usually about 2 or 3 feet but the varieties differ greatly in
size and flower colour and there are over twenty of them. All are greatly
superior to our wild form as garden plants.

Among the more distinct and valuable are the following:—

P. f. arbuscula is a bold 3 foot bush with the stems and shoots covered
with bronzy hairs and clear yellow flowers 1½ inches across. A fine,
continuously flowering variety.

P. f. Beesiana is similar to *nana argentea* described later, but bolder
and slightly larger.

P. f. dahurica is a compact dwarf suitable for rock garden use with
inch-wide, pure white flowers.

P. f. Farreri is one of the most brilliant and effective varieties, with
vivid Buttercup-yellow flowers, but it does not make such a large and
shapely bush as *Friedrichsenii* or 'Katherine Dykes', being rather
dwarf in habit.

P. f. Forrestii is of stout habit and has pale yellow flowers.

P. f. Friedrichsenii is a cross between the "type" and var. *dahurica*,
and is an unusually tall vigorous bush up to 6 feet high with dark green
leaves and large pale yellow flowers.

P. f. grandiflora. The leaves and flowers are larger than the "type",
the latter being yellow and 1¼ inches across.

P. f. 'Katherine Dykes'. This is thought to be a cross between
P. fruticosa and *P. f.* var. *Friedrichsenii*. The flowers are about an inch
across and of a soft Canary yellow and open rather earlier than those
of most varieties. 'Katherine Dykes' makes a fine large, shapely bush
and is one of the finest of all as a garden shrub.

P. f. mandschurica has creamy-white flowers and leaves silvered
with dense, whitish silky hairs. It is a dwarf shrub seldom exceeding
1 foot in height.

P. f. nana argentea is a dwarf variety with silvery leaves and small
yellow flowers.

P. f. obtusifolia is a free-flowering 2-foot bush with small clear yellow
flowers.

P. f. ochroleuca has large pale sulphur-yellow flowers on a sturdy,
upright 3-foot bush.

P. f. Purdomii is a dwarf variety about 1 foot 6 inches high with large deep yellow flowers. It was found in Tibet.

P. f. pyrenaica. A dwarf form, usually only a foot high; flowers yellow.

P. f. Veitchii. The leaves are a silvery grey-green, and silky haired; the large flowers are pure white; a fine 3-foot Chinese form, particularly notable and opening very early—in May.

P. f. Vilmoriniana (A.G.M. 1926). A fine Potentilla growing up to 4 feet in height with intensely silvered velvety leaves and large creamy-white flowers. A very beautiful variety.

The Cinquefoil is perfectly hardy and, given proper drainage, will grow on any, even on limy, soil; thus it is surprising that it is not more commonly seen. It is a very attractive shrub provided that it receives occasional "manicuring" to remove old seed pods and dead leaves, which is essential if it is not to look very shabby in winter. Whilst not really spectacular, it is valuable as a constant bloomer late in the season and always gay and charming except in winter, when its appearance is deplorable. Propagation can be done by seeds or, in the case of special varieties required true to type, by cuttings of fairly ripe side shoots in late summer. If taken with a "heel" of older wood these root very readily. The Potentillas are not particular either as to soil or position but do best in a fairly sunny and well drained spot.

It is most regrettable that such a beautiful foliage shrub as *Senecio laxifolius* (A.G.M. 1936), is barely hardy enough for any but southern or coastal gardens. A shrubby member of the composite, or Daisy, family from New Zealand, it makes a spreading four-foot bush of silver grey with the shapely leaves very gracefully presented so that it is always most attractive to the eye while it is in good health. In early July heads of bright yellow daisy-flowers appear but they are of no great ornamental value. Indeed, I soon cut them off so as to get more of the beautiful young leafy shoots. It is when contrasted with dark-foliaged shrubs or rusty-coloured shrubs such as *Erica vagans*, or when complementing the orange-red of autumnal leaves that this beautifully drawn, silvery shrub makes its best effect. To do this really well, an odd plant or two is quite insufficient—a dozen are needed in the picture, planted singly or in groups of three, so that the whole foliage effect of the garden landscape is lighted up by the contrasting silveriness boldly interlaced among the deeper tones. It will grow equally well in limy or acid soils and, apart from frost damage, is a good, rapid-growing, healthy garden plant. Fortunately it strikes easily from July cuttings placed under a bell-glass or in pots of sandy soil in the greenhouse and thus, even if a hard

winter kills it, its retention is a practical proposition. Certainly few
shrubs are more worthy of this trouble, for this Senecio is of the highest
year-round effectiveness in the garden landscape. It requires a sunny,
well-drained, open position; in shady places it grows soft and sprawling.
Rabbits destroy it in winter if they get the chance, so it is not to be
recommended for the Wild Garden, or unprotected places.

Other members of this family, *S. Greyii*, similar but bolder, and *S.
rotundifolius*, a noble, rounded bush of 7 or 8 feet, though both too
tender for most inland gardens, are superb in the sea-wind along the
warmer parts of the coastline.

Santolina Chamæcyparissus, the "Lavender Cotton" is another silvery
bush. It is a shrub of the Daisy family with curious qualities and
curious drawbacks. A well-grown and regularly trimmed plant provides
a plumy mound of silvery-white persistent foliage that is very effective
in the composition when well contrasted with shrubs of suitably varied
foliage tints. The yellow flowers, in July, themselves also contrast
attractively and there is a form with flowers of a much paler yellow
which I have seen in Cornwall which adds greatly to this effect when
associated with the "type". Hardier than *Senecio laxifolius*, *Convolvulus Cneorum* and *Phlomis fruticosa*, it provides gardeners in colder
districts with a more reliable grey-leaved shrub.

The Lavender Cotton can be divided or struck from cuttings placed
under a bell-glass in July, provided the weather is warm, otherwise
heat is necessary. It is not particular as to soil, growing quite well in
limy soils, but is best in a sunny, open position. After a time the plants
get untidy in habit unless regularly pinched, pegged down, trimmed
and layered. Indeed, it is one of the few shrubs that I would recommend
cutting hard back to the stump every spring if one has not the time to
attend to it constantly.

The common **Lavender**, *Lavandula officinalis* (*L. Spica*) though dear
to us for its pleasant associations and the scent of its flowers and, to a
less degree, of its leaves is, by nature, of rather an ungainly habit.
Clipping every spring keeps it to a reasonably compact form but, all
too soon, it gets shabby and must be started all over again from cuttings.
It is therefore a matter for rejoicing that a compact and naturally
shapely variety of this plant should recently have come to light. This is
L. o. nana atropurpurea or 'Hidcote variety'. It forms a shapely, dense
mound covered with the flowers on their long stalks in July and August.
In colour these are a notably deeper and of a more vivid purple than

those of the old favourite. In other respects it resembles the common
Lavender and similarly responds best to a warm light soil.

Among late flowering plants for a wall or bank we may consider
Berberidopsis corallina, an uncommon, rather tender, evergreen
sprawler, or climber. It was introduced from the forests of Valdivia in
1862. The racemes of red, globose flowers hanging from stalks that are
also red are produced from the axils of the uppermost leaves and form
a fine picture, where conditions are sufficiently mild, from July to frost.
A shaded wall, protected from the bite of the north wind by fairly
distant trees appears to be the best site. Leaf-mould should be added
when planting and an acid or at least neutral soil is necessary. Propagation may be effected by layering or by cuttings of half-ripe short shoots
placed under a bell-glass in July.

Feijoa Sellowiana is a difficult, curious, and spectacular member of
the Myrtle family from South America. An evergreen with glossy green
silvery-backed leaves growing up to 18 feet high, it does not get enough
sun heat to flower freely in mild south-western gardens, and in places
where winters are colder it seldom lives long enough to give a good
account of itself. The solid, waxy, solitary flowers in July are, however,
highly attractive. They are $1\frac{1}{2}$ inches across and white with crimson
centres and showy red protruding stamens. The Feijoa needs a really
warm south wall and a moist, light acid soil, and even then it is a chancy
proposition, but when it succeeds it is a magnificent sight.

Seeds from the edible fruits which are only produced in very hot
summers may be sown in a greenhouse or cuttings of half-ripe shoots
may be struck there in a propagating box in July.

Among the indispensables is *Spartium junceum* (A.G.M. 1923), the
Spanish Broom, an absolutely first-class garden plant rewarding the
industrious gardener with a dense bushy shrub continuously and
spectacularly in flower from June to frost. On the other hand it reacts
immediately to ill-considered positioning and neglect by making a
gaunt, twisted leg from which straggle many dead, and a few live,
rush-like stems only spasmodically bedecked with the large, honey-
scented Aureolin Yellow (H.C.C. 3/1) pea-flowers whose standards
are a full inch across. The Spanish Broom has been with us for several
centuries, but well-grown specimens are not common, as its natural
habit in the wild is to creep up among spiny "maquis" shrubs and

then burst into a cloud of stems safely out of reach of the goats that usually infest its native regions along the shores and among the islands of the Mediterranean. Hence the clippers or, better, the razor blade must be constantly at work to induce branching and keep down the height, and the position must be sunny, fully exposed and, preferably, isolated. On hot, dry banks, in either limy or acid soils, this great Broom is particularly at home and its extraordinarily long season of bloom makes it a most valuable garden decorator as, if it is prevented from seeding, it outlasts the glorious but fleeting Genistas with an almost continuous late summer display. It is very easily grown from seeds sown in small pots, from which the young plants should immediately be planted out into their permanent positions. Once the tap-root has become frustrated and curled around the inside of the pot the plant cannot hold itself firmly in the ground and will blow over just when it appears to be reaching perfection.

Two varieties are recorded, but not seen by me—an old double form —var. *plenum*, still grown at Kew, and a whitish-yellow-flowered one— var. *ochroleucum*, which sounds much more attractive.

On the whole the Hydrangeas are the best associates as their long season of flower parallels that of the Broom. On a slightly limy soil the many white-flowered Hydrangeas complemented by the rich red varieties that show their best colour only under these circumstances, will make an interesting combination. On an acid soil the blues and whites will group superbly with the Aureolin Yellow of *S. junceum* and the Lemon Yellow of *Hypericum patulum*. All that is lacking is a really good orange-flowered shrub to complete the picture, although Hybrid Tea Roses such as 'McGredy's Sunset' will be found to provide that telling spice to the composition in a reasonably satisfactory way.

The **Stewartias,** which rather remind one of deciduous Camellias, qualify very doubtfully for inclusion here as really effective shrubs. Making quite large trees, up to 30 feet high they bear their fine white flowers in June and July, when they are welcome enough. Their presentation, however, is so singularly bad that they make no distant effect, and every plant photographer knows how difficult it is to find even one small branch bearing flowers well enough displayed to make a passable picture.

None the less, flowering trees are such an essential part of the shrub garden at all times that we must take a lenient view of the short-comings of any species kind enough to flower in late summer. We have to provide the shade which reduces the labour of weeding and improves the growth and beauty of the majority of the finer shrubs, and the trees also give us additional flower effects at a greater height than the shrubs can attain.

Stewartia koreana, a tree up to 50 feet high in its native Korea, flowers in late June or early July and is one of the more decorative species. The wild-rose-like white flowers, 2 or 3 inches across, appear singly or in pairs in the leaf axils, facing in all directions. Introduced to America by E. H. Wilson in 1918, it is a more beautiful tree than the more commonly seen *S. Pseudo-camellia*, and the foliage colours attractively in autumn. In habit it is stiffer and more upright than the others and when fully established flowers more freely. As a partly fastigiate (like a Lombardy Poplar) hardy tree of decorative flowering and autumn foliage effect this species might be considered suitable for seed propagation in quantity for street and park planting in the future.

S. Malacodendron is a shrubby American species introduced as long ago as the early part of the eighteenth century. It is not often seen, however, owing probably to its miffy temperament and awkwardly placed flowers. These are on the verge of being very beautiful, being about 3 inches across with somewhat thin white petals and a bold and arresting centre of black-purple stamens and anthers. Unfortunately the texture of the petals is so papery that they do not hold their form but flop about almost at once, and furthermore the flowers face all ways and so do not complement one another so as to achieve a pleasing group effect.

It is not an easy shrub to grow well, but I think the best position is actually one where, in spite of a moist soil, it gets a good roasting in summer and is really sent off to sleep by the cold in winter.

S. serrata is an uncommon Japanese species with small, cup-shaped white flowers, stained with red outside, about $2\frac{1}{2}$ inches across, with an attractive centre of yellow anthers. They are very freely borne but in the usual awkward manner of the genus. It appears to be reasonably hardy, but is not commonly obtainable in nurseries. The autumn colouring of the leaves is often particularly vivid.

S. sinensis is a Chinese species with brightly coloured bark introduced by E. H. Wilson in 1900, making a small tree up to 38 feet high. The small white flowers are about 2 inches across and fragrant. The autumn colouring of the leaves is very good and this species is listed by several nurseries.

S. ovata (*S. pentagyna*) is a smaller species, up to 15 feet high, native of the southern United States and introduced over a hundred years ago. The flowers borne, in late June or early July, singly in the leaf-axils as usual, have creamy-white petals attractively waved, and conspicuous yellow anthers. Unfortunately the symmetry of the flowers is often spoiled by deformed petals and other irregularities.

S. ovata grandiflora is a finer form with purple stamens and larger

18

flowers, 4 inches across. It is now somewhat rare in commerce, which is to be regretted as this is about the finest of all the Stewartias.

S. Pseudo-camellia. This common Japanese species introduced towards the end of the nineteenth century by Messrs. Veitch of Exeter is rather disappointing. It grows easily enough, but makes but little show, so hidden are the flowers among the foliage and branches. They are white and slightly cupped, with a central boss of golden stamens. The autumn foliage sometimes colours quite attractively.

As regards the placing of the Stewartias they may be planted to provide, ultimately, the shade trees for beds of flowering shrubs such as Azaleas and Hydrangeas. It is, however, doubtful if they are sufficiently effective to take the place of the Cherries, Crabs, Peaches, Magnolias, Robinias, Laburnums, Cornus, Koelreuterias and others that so admirably carry out the double function of providing both valuable shade and spectacularly decorative flower effects.

The cultivation required is the provision of a fertile acid soil enriched with leaf-mould and kept mulched with fallen leaves to prevent both drying out in summer and excessive frost penetration in winter.

Seeds are the best means of propagation, mature trees, especially those of *S. Pseudo-camellia*, ripening large crops of seed in favourable seasons. Cuttings can sometimes be struck of fairly well ripened wood taken in August and placed under a bell-glass.

Cotinus Coggygria is the new name of our old friend *Rhus Cotinus*, the **Venetian Sumac,** a member of the Cashew family from south Europe. In the "type" form, the handsome, spreading, 12-foot bush has roundish green leaves and plumy masses of feathery purplish-crimson inflorescence that almost cover the plant in early July. In autumn the leaves turn a fine yellow.

The variety *C. C.* var. *purpureus* (A.G.M. 1930) has beautiful foliage, opening a rich crimson and turning purple, and similar curious flowering to the "type".

C. C. var. *purpureus* "Nottcutts variety" is even deeper and more vivid in its colouring.

The "Smoke Plant", as it is also called, is one of those shrubs that flower better in a poor soil, either limy or acid. It may be increased by cuttings of half-ripe shoots placed beneath a bell-glass in July. The red-leaved varieties are among the most brilliant of foliage shrubs, but like all those with such colouring, some care has to be taken in their placing so that the unusual tone does not make too sudden a contrast with normal coloured leaves. Among other shrubs of unusual foliage colour, or in autumn, these Sumacs are superb.

Cotinus americanus (*Rhus cotinoides*) is a rare shrub of no floral beauty but of such flaming vividness of autumn leaf colour as to be almost unsurpassed in this respect. Like *Berberis Thunbergii* and *Acer* 'Osaka Suki' its solo display is so spectacular that all the surrounding leaf tints of autumn are shown up to advantage, reflecting its intensity in quieter tones.

An acid turf-loam and an open position seem to be necessary to get the best effect and a year or two must pass before a specimen will show its true quality. The leaf-colouring is varied as well as vivid: orange, scarlet, purple, yellow and green being often shown on one plant. Layers are probably the best method of increase but it is not a very rapid one.

One of the most lovely of white-flowered deciduous shrubs, *Hoheria glabrata Plagianthus Lyalli* var. *glabrata*) (A.G.M. 1926) flowers in July. The name has been much argued over but a seldom mentioned but important point for the gardener is that there are two horticulturally distinct **Hoherias** in cultivation in this country. *H. glabrata* (the word means "nearly not hairy") forms a shapely shrub with bright, pale green, faintly lime-like leaves, and the white, honey-scented, Cherry-like flowers, 1½ inches across, are waxy yet translucent and cover the bush in a spectacularly beautiful manner provided that the soil is not very rich, in which case overleafiness may hide many of the flowers. The largest specimen that I know is at Grayswood Hill, Haslemere, and I estimate its spread as being nearly 20 feet with a height of about 8 feet. I have seldom observed this species to set good seed and it flowers towards the end of July.

Hoheria Lyalli is more treelike in habit, with duller, greyer green, more markedly serrated leaves and more numerous but slightly smaller and thinner-textured flowers. It is, I think, equally beautiful and flowers regularly about a fortnight before *H. glabrata* and usually sets good seed if the season is propitious. Seedlings grow very rapidly indeed and provide most effective shade trees growing among Rhododendrons who protect the trunks of the Hoherias from excessive winter frost and are in their turn benefited by the overhead canopy provided. Seedlings of *H. Lyalli*, although planted many years after a large group of *H. glabrata* grown from layers, have easily outstripped them in height, being over 10 feet tall. The fragrance appears to be similar, but, when young, the seedlings have a curious juvenile foliage much waved and serrated at the margins. It seems to be desirable to have both species, as the presence of the two kinds provides a succession of bloom. The finest form of *H. Lyalli* that I have seen (at Nymans, Handcross,

Sussex) is *H. L.* var. *grandiflora*, which has superbly presented medium-sized flowers with dark anthers. Mr. James Comber informed me that this lovely variety was sent out by Messrs. Le Chenault of Orleans.

These Hoherias are among the few shrubs from the Southern Hemisphere which avoid the queer and incongruous appearance which so many of these have for eyes accustomed to the northern flora.

In very hard winters Hoherias are sometimes reported to be killed to ground-level, though all my plants passed through the severe temperatures of the war winters quite unharmed. The trunks of many specimens are partly protected by other shrubs and possibly this is a desirable precaution. Where this is not possible it is probably a good plan to prune young plants so as to induce the formation of several stems from the ground-level so that, should the trunks be killed, shoots will the more readily spring from the base again.

These Hoherias come from New Zealand where they are known as "Mountain Ribbonwood". They are first-class shrubs that should be grown in all gardens in the southern counties. They will grow in a limy soil and, under such circumstances, should be one of the first choices for a warm spot. Curiously enough they are quite rare in gardens, although many equally tender species such as Ceanothus and Escallonia are very commonly grown.

As regards cultivation, the usual precautions to prepare the site with humus and a good and well-worked but not over-rich soil are advisable in view of the fact that the shrub can be expected to produce huge crops of blossom for many years. Both species can easily be grown from seed and they soon make bushes of flowering size. Seed is more often set by *H. Lyalli* but a warm summer will usually enable *H. glabrata* to ripen a few pods. So strong and numerous are the seedlings that these fine shrubs will undoubtedly become available at very reasonable prices. Thus one may hope to see them ere long decorating hundreds of gardens in coastal and southern districts. To these, such beautiful July-flowering trees will be a great acquisition and be yet another reminder of the debt we owe to the good people of New Zealand.

Another species of Hoheria, *H. populnea lanceolata* (*H. sexstylosa*) is a small, willowy, white-flowered evergreen tree that, unfortunately, is insufficiently hardy for any but specially favoured south-west or coastal gardens. It was discovered in New Zealand in 1825 by a Mr. C. Fraser and inhabits both the north and south islands. Flowering in August, the thinner and more starry white flowers show up well against the rather dark green, lance-shaped shining leaves. Thus, where conditions allow, the gardener should take advantage of his good fortune and plant this lovely species.

The late-summer-flowering section of the **Ceanothus** family provides us with several attractive blue-flowered shrubs. They are, if anything, slightly less hardy than the Hydrangeas which easily provide superb blues in acid soils, so their chief value will be for warm gardens whose soil is too alkaline (limy) for these to give blue flowers. The best garden shrubs of the family are of very mixed hybrid origin containing the "blood" of the tender *C. cæruleus* (*C. mexicanus*) and of the hardier *C. americanus*. The late Alfred Rehder, whose "Manual of Cultivated Trees and Shrubs" is followed in the nomenclature used in this book named this section × *C. Delilianus*. Few Ceanothus are really quite up to the "reasonably hardy" standard, almost all having succumbed during severe winters which failed to kill plants which I have considered fully entitled to be placed in this category.

One of the toughest and best known is *Ceanothus Delilianus* 'Gloire de Versailles' (A.G.M. 1925). It is a somewhat rambling, 10-foot shrub, making strong soft shoots in all directions, with panicles of pale Lobelia Blue flowers from July onwards. Though partly evergreen in mild climates, it usually loses its foliage and looks very battered in winter. It is one of the hardiest of the section. 'Topaze' is similar but less vigorous, though brighter in colour.

C. D. 'Indigo' has flowers of a fine deep blue colour but is markedly less hardy, barely surviving in any but favoured gardens.

C. D. 'Henri Desfosse' is one of the brightest blues; 'Marie Simon' has pink flowers; 'Ceres', a strong grower, has pinkish-mauve flowers; 'Georges Simon' is one of the hardier sorts with pink flowers; 'Gloire de Plantières' is rather dwarf and has deep blue flowers.

There is also *C. D.* 'Charles de Trichet' (*C. Albertii*). This variety, introduced in 1878, is described as having flowers "of a clear, soft blue, most admirable planted near water in shade'. † This recommendation no doubt applies to the mild Irish climate. In England autumn and spring frosts might be too severe in such a situation. At any rate this variety is proving hardier than most and is being again taken up by nurserymen.

C. Burkwoodii (*C. D.* 'Indigo' × *floribundus*) (Cory Cup 1930) is a hybrid between the summer-flowering and the spring-flowering sections and is one of the hardier sorts. It is a fast-growing shrub of good bushy habit with shining, oval, evergreen leaves about an inch long and ½ inch wide. The flowers are a good bright blue for a Ceanothus, with cheerful yellow anthers, and are borne in panicles 1 or 2 inches long from July onwards. 'Autumnal Blue' is similar, with larger flower trusses of a slightly softer blue and is one of the hardiest of the race. Parryi is another of this type.

† Sir Frederick Moore, R.H.S. Shrub Conference, 1938.

Although they will grow under limy conditions, these Ceanothus are best on a deep, warm, well-drained soil and in a hot, sunny position. Pruning, for this section, is done in late March to encourage the production of flowering shoots; it is really best restricted to the removal of weak or damaged branches. Cuttings can be rooted fairly easily, though often rather slowly, in the sand-frame.

The splendid family of the **Brooms** continue their summer-long service of providing us with a sequence of fine yellow-flowered shrubs highly decorative in the garden.

Genista æthnensis (A.G.M. 1923) is a 10- or 15-foot, thin-habited, almost leafless shrub ablaze with sprigs of little yellow pea-flowers, individually very similar to those of *G. cinerea*, in July. It comes from Sardinia, Sicily and the slopes of Mount Etna whence it takes its name. It is perfectly "reasonably hardy" in these islands in any sunny spot with free drainage, and is a shrub that should decorate every garden, as it will grow on almost all types of soils. The thin shade it provides is very helpful to many other shrubs and never too dense, while its roots do not rob the soil. It is long-lived, for the family, and very aged specimens nearly 20 feet high are sometimes seen in old gardens, precariously propped up, and, perhaps, sporting but one little tuffet of flowering growth on the topmost twigs. Sometimes it is grown by skilful cultivators as a naturally weeping standard tree when it is spectacularly beautiful, particularly as a lawn specimen. The decision as to whether it is to be allowed to grow naturally, as it wills, or to assume the standard-tree shape must be taken immediately it is planted. If the latter is required it must be kept to one stem and carefully tied up to a stake, all other growth being pinched off when young, until the required height is reached.

G. tinctoria. The "Dyers' Greenweed" is too coarse to be a first-class shrub, but it flowers late into autumn and is a useful temporary caretaker for odd corners. It is a native weed in many parts of this country. The most effective form is probably the variety *flore pleno* which forms a dense bushlet often only 8 inches or so in height, densely covered with bright yellow but shapeless little flowers in July and August. Unless a watchful eye is kept, it easily becomes a martyr to a purplish aphis which is such a persistent infestor that frequent sprayings are necessary.

Cytisus nigricans, a bushy shrub about 3 feet high, comes from Central and S.E. Europe and was introduced long ago, in 1730. The yellow flowers are borne in spire-like racemes in July and August. Like

some other members of this family it is one of the few flowering shrubs
that actually *require* pruning. This takes the form of removing the flower
spikes, when over, to save the plant's energies in seed production, and
also, to induce a compact and bushy habit, cutting back any straggling
shoots before growth commences in spring. *C. nigricans* is an attractive
and effective Broom very decorative in the late summer garden and
really more valuable that most of the various-coloured, spring-flowering
garden hybrids which flower at a time when there are so many other
colourful shrubs in bloom.

A sunny, well-drained position suits it and seeds are the best means of
increase. Like most other Brooms it requires to be protected from
rabbits.

Indigofera Gerardiana is a very late-leafing shrub, allied to the
Brooms, with arching slender shoots, attractive, lush, pinnate leaves
and racemes of small, purplish-pink pea-flowers in July. It is not really
very effective but has a possible use for screening some plant which
becomes dull and unattractive in late summer when its flowering is over.
A white variety, var. *alba*, is now seldom seen.

I. decora is a pretty dwarf species from China with pink and white
flowers freely borne in late summer. There is also a white form.

I. hebepetala, a Himalayan like *I. Gerardiana*, has crimson and rose-
coloured pea-flowers, much more pleasing in colour than those of that
species.

I. Potaninii is a somewhat hardier Western Chinese species with
racemes of pink flowers over a long period from June onwards. It is
rather loose in habit unless attended to.

Most of the Indigoferas require a sunny position. They can be
increased readily from seed and are not particular about soil.

An attractive complementary display to the charms of the Genistas,
and other pea-flowers, is provided by some of the latest flowering
Philadelphus. As a family they interbreed so readily that seedlings of
many varied types and flowering dates appear. The late-flowering ones
are worthy of care as they add fragrance to the garden in late summer
when scented flowers are scarce.

One of the finest late-flowering sorts is a form of *Philadelphus
Delavayi*, raised at Nymans, Handcross, Sussex.

P. incanus is a Chinese species flowering in later July. Both these are
more fully described with the other members of the family in the June
section on page 236.

A family whose flowering time centres about July is that of the **Abelias.**

Abelia floribunda is an evergreen shrub from the high mountains of Mexico, with small ovate leaves and rosy-purple jasmine-like flowers in June. It is slender in habit and usually about 4 feet high. It is rather tender and is most likely to succeed against a wall facing south.

A. uniflora, an evergreen Chinese species introduced by Robert Fortune, is the finest member of the family, being "reasonably hardy" and having blush-white flowers, orange tinted at the throat, an inch long and as wide at the mouth, It is free-flowering and from June onwards makes quite a fine display. Unfortunately it is very scarce.

A. grandiflora, an evergreen hybrid of the above, is much more commonly seen. The flowers, of similar colouring, are actually smaller, but is a more vigorous plant. Its great quality is the persistence of its flowering from July right into autumn. Although attractive on close inspection, it makes no display for distant effect.

A. Schumannii is a deciduous species introduced from China by E. H. Wilson, with purplish-pink flowers abundantly produced singly from the leaf axils of the shoots over a long period. It is not very hardy but even if cut back in a hard winter, usually shoots up again in spring. But for the singularly poor colour of the flowers it would be a most attractive little thing.

Though not first class, the Abelias are useful for their late flowering and their ability to grow in limy soils. With the exception, perhaps, of *A. uniflora,* they make no great display. All like warm, well-drained positions and most can be increased by cuttings of half-ripened branchlets in the sand-frame.

In gardens favoured with neutral or acid soils a number of **Rhododendron hybrids,** having in their ancestry the August-flowering *R. auriculatum* "B" ***, the blazing scarlet-flowered but tender *R. Elliottii* and *R. eriogynum* "D" ****, the dwarf, deep plum-coloured *R. didymum* "B" ** or the large-leaved, hardy, fragrant lily-flowered *R. discolor* "B" ***, may play a fine part in late summer decoration.

Though hardy, *R. auriculatum* is too difficult a plant for the average garden. Even in our favoured wood the large and fragrant white flowers are often spoiled by adjacent scorched leaves, and plants in Cornish gardens seem little better. The hybrids are an improvement, it is true, but seldom sufficiently so to qualify them as really good garden plants according to our definition, but the hybridists are ever at work and no doubt ere long such plants will be available. A forerunner is 'Polar Bear' (*R. diaprepes* × *auriculatum*) with very large fragrant white flowers in August.

R. eriogynum "D" ****, a splendid species from open thickets in Yunnan, is unfortunately only hardy enough for very favourable gardens in the southern and western counties. It has superb, vivid red flowers in late June and has produced a number of fine hybrids which are better garden plants.

R. 'Redcap' "D" *** is, I think, one of the most attractive hybrids ever produced, the parentage being *R. eriogynum* × *didymum*. It is a sturdy little evergreen bush alight with blood-red flowers in July when it may complement *Hoheria glabrata* and *Genista cinerea* most delightfully. Unfortunately its use is limited, as the "D" means that it can only be grown in favourable gardens where care is taken to give plants of this genus the best possible conditions.

R. 'Romany Chal' "C" *** (*R.* 'Moser's Maroon' × *eriogynum*) delights me every July with a superb display of its fine Geranium-lake flowers, but its position is a perfect one with the dappled shade of Rowans and naturally peaty, moist soil. In dry, earthy beds hybrids of this delicate type do not thrive. I estimate our plant to be 8 feet high and as much through and, being layered all round, it is still increasing rapidly. It is a plant for the keen amateur with a favourable garden.

R. discolor "B" *** is a fine, ultra hardy, late-flowering Chinese species. The huge pale-coloured flowers are fragrant and beautiful but unfortunately of such a thin and papery texture that they are all too vulnerable to battering by wind. It is also slow to flower; seed that I sowed twelve years before only showed me flowers in 1948. When there is more demand for late-flowering Rhododendrons such plants will certainly be produced—at present the hybrids of this kind generally available in commerce are very limited.

R. 'Azor' has large rose-pink flowers and is a hybrid with *R. Griersonianum* to which that brilliant creature, as usual, has not, unfortunately, bequeathed its rich colouring.

R. 'Goldsworth Orange', a cross with *R. dichroanthum*, has already been mentioned under the hardy hybrids on page 186.

R. Ungernii "A" **, is a hardy species from the Caucasus, but its little pinkish-white trusses, borne in July, are not very showy, being somewhat buried among the leaves.

Whilst we are considering this family we may mention two attractive Azaleas that also flower late.

R. viscosum "A" *** (A.G.M. 1937), is an American Azalea species growing up to about 6 feet high with sticky white, or pale purplish-pink, fragrant flowers in July. It was introduced here early in the eighteenth century. The clove-like fragrance is very agreeable but the flowers are too small and concealed to make it a first-class shrub.

R. arborescens "A" **, is greatly superior to the preceding, with larger white flowers, with purplish filaments, better presented and with a more pleasing and powerful scent. It comes from the Appalachian Mountains, where it grows up to 20 feet high by the banks of streams. It is rather scarce in commerce although *R. viscosum* is quite a common shrub. *R. arborescens* was introduced in 1818 but has never "taken on" for some reason. While it is not very showy it has a refinement of drawing that the previous species lacks and should adorn every lime-free garden because of its delicious heliotrope fragrance which perfumes the summer evenings in the most delightful manner. It flowers a fortnight or so earlier than *R. viscosum*.

Some interesting varieties have been described in America. They sound highly attractive and desirable and are as follows:—

R. a. flavescens having pale yellow flowers with a deeper blotch on the upper lobe.

R. a. rubescens which has rose or purple flowers with some yellow on the upper lobe.

Both the above Azalea species are perfectly hardy and grow well in any lime-free soil which is reasonably moist. They may be propagated by seed or layers.

Undoubtedly the hybrid Azalea known as 'Flamingo' (Waterer, Sons & Crisp's variety) has *R. arborescens* in its parentage. Flowering very freely, with rather small, soft orange flowers in late June or early July and having a fine autumn leaf colour of a deep beetroot hue, it is a very useful variety described on page 214.

R. amagianum is an interesting and rare Azalea from Mt. Amagi, Japan. It was first exhibited by Lord Aberconway on July 6, 1948 at the R.H.S. meeting. The flowers, in trusses of two or three only, though larger and more solid and fleshy, rather resemble those of a good form of *R. Kaempferi*, but the foliage and habit are totally different. The leathery, round, but pointed leaves, in threes at the ends of the branchlets, have a remarkable resemblance to those of *Gaultheria Shallon* in their texture and surface veining, but they are not evergreen. Early July is the natural flowering time, I am told, and therefore this species is at once one of great interest. A flower of a soft and lovely orange pink at such a moment of the garden year, borne on a shrub of natural appearance would fill a gap that many would like filled.

There are other lovely late-flowering Azaleas, but unfortunately they are scarce and difficult to get.

R. cumberlandense from Kentucky, flowering after *R. calendulaceum*

(p. 214), has exquisite orange, scarlet or blood-red flowers and grows about 7 feet in height. It should be perfectly hardy in the British climate.

R. prunifolium, from Georgia, U.S., is, even in its wild form, probably the finest of all the deciduous Azaleas. Flowering in the latter part of July with scarlet or orange-red flowers of unusually large size it is a strong and vigorous grower making a bush about 8 feet high. It is quite hardy, withstanding sub-zero temperatures without harm and is "easily and fairly quickly raised from seed".†

We should remember that *R. cinnabarinum* var. *æstivale* (see p. 132) also flowers at this time.

In addition, *Viburnum tomentosum* 'Rowallane' and *Leptospermum Rodwayanum*, mentioned in our June section, will also be in flower in July and the latter will last into August.

Twelve years ago I installed a young plant of *Rhododendron Thomsonii* with some care as a specimen in a favourable position. I had in mind an experiment to determine the results of completely eliminating *all* maintenance attention. That plant has never been touched by anyone since, and it is in perfect condition today. So, indeed, are many others installed with similar care, but they may have had an occasional dead branch removed that has fallen onto them from the canopy above, or a few dead leaves swept over their roots off the path. The point I wish to make is that the Rhododendron, *once properly installed,* needs remarkably little attention and in view of the fine display of flowers produced annually can be considered as a labour-saving decorative plant of unusually high value. Brooms and Roses, and, to a less extent, Hydrangeas, need attention to look their best and we are therefore grateful to plants that by their limited demands on our time enable us to grow greater numbers of their more exacting brethren. Thus I, for one, deplore the limited numbers of effective, late-flowering Rhododendrons available and look forward eagerly to new hardy hybrids of rich colouring to decorate the August garden.

In late summer the sequence of flowering trees continues, though the choice becomes rather more limited. Particularly welcome are the charms of **Koelreuteria paniculata**, the China Tree. This interesting Chinese and Japanese tree has never become common, although it was introduced in the eighteenth century, is reasonably hardy and produces deep yellow flowers well massed in July, when such rich colour

† "Deciduous Rhododendrons at Gladwyne, Pennsylvania", by Mrs. Norman Henry, *The Rhododendron Year Book*, 1946, R.H.S.

is particularly welcome. Perhaps the reason for its neglect is that it needs warm sunny weather to appear at its best. The habit, when young, is rather gaunt and the pinnate (or ash-like) leaves are at first reddish-green. The pyramidal panicles of small yellow flowers are produced on the ends of the branches and are followed by bladder-like fruits, and the leaves colour early in autumn to a fine yellow. *K. paniculata* was named for Professor Koelreuter of Karlsrühe.

The China-Tree is very well worth planting for its excellent contribution to late summer decoration and is of help in balancing the garden effects, so that spring does not have an excessive preponderance of colour. It might well be tried out as a street tree as it is quite hardy and though not very long-lived, grows well in towns, eventually making a compact tree about 30 feet high.

K. p. fastigiata is a narrow-columnar form.

K. p. apiculata was introduced in 1900 by E. H. Wilson from Szechwan and is a good hardy form with smaller and more numerous leaflets and flowers and fruits particularly freely when young. It is one of the most desirable trees for the garden and quite undeservedly neglected.

In hot summers *K. paniculata* sometimes sets seed which may be sown in pans in the frame and the resultant seedlings grown on. It may also be propagated by root cuttings but this is rather a complicated matter for the amateur. It is not particular as to soil but needs a warm sunny position.

The genus **Veronica** is a large one containing an enormous number of rather tender species of which only a few members of the more woody section, now placed under **Hebe,** are of value as outdoor flowering shrubs for favourable gardens.

Hebe Traversii (*Veronica Traversii*). In my opinion, this is one of the finest of the family as an outdoor shrub, even in Cornwall where many of the more tender species flourish. There are a number of flowering shrubs that demand single specimen positions and *H. Traversii* is certainly one of these. In a bed, mixed up with other bushes, its curious extending method of growth makes it a shabby and lopsided mess just when it should be at its best. Isolated plants, on the other hand, often form noble rounded specimens 6 feet high and 8 feet across. The small evergreen leaves are almost hidden by the 2-inch long racemes, packed with the little white flowers with their purplish anthers, from July onwards. 'White Gem' is a hybrid of smaller and more compact growth.

H. cupressoides is another species hardy enough to be worth planting in warm seaside gardens. It has a curious cypress-like appearance.

forming a slender bush about 4 feet high, with pale bluish-green, needle-like leaves and pale blue flowers in clusters from late June onwards. To preserve the attractively bushy, rounded habit, which is its chief charm, it should be given an open position on a sunny slope.

H. Hectori is a smaller, rather Juniper-like species of similar type with white or pink flowers in small heads rather sparsely produced.

H. anomala is another of the hardier species. Its habit is too besom-like to be attractive as a growing shrub, unless sternly pruned back each year to keep it bushy. It is evergreen and the white or pinkish flowers are quite pleasing but seldom very freely borne.

H. pimeloides is a dwarf species making a nice dense little bush with spikes of purplish-blue flowers in late June, July and into August, and rounded, glaucous leaves. A variety, *glauco-cœrulea*, is more vigorous and pronouncedly bluish, with darker purple flowers.

H. vernicosa is a particularly attractive little "Veronica" with small deep green glossy leaves, making it a pretty little bush, usually about 1 foot 6 inches high and 2 feet or more across. Its white flowers are freely borne in June and July.

Other similar small species and hybrids are *H. Pageana, H. pingui-folia, H. canterburiensis* and *H.* 'Bowles hybrid'. In coastal limy-soiled gardens the smaller kinds can take the place of the alpine Rhododendrons and late summer Heaths. They associate well with Helianthe-mums, dwarf-growing Genistas, *Cotoneaster Dammeri* and other small flowering or berrying evergreens, to form those attractive low, evergreen carpet plantings from which larger specimens may emerge into telling effect. *H.* 'Autumn Glory' is a bushy, hardy hybrid with purple flowers.

There are almost innumerable other kinds of Hebes but the destruction of thousands of bushes of 'Blue Gem' and other hybrids by recent unusually severe weather in the West has given them a severe setback in popularity. On the whole it is only as shrubs for seaside gardens that most members of this family are to be recommended as likely to have any permanence. *H. Hulkeana* is an untidy sprawling species with oval, serrated, evergreen leaves and 18-inch panicles of small lilac flowers from midsummer onwards. It is somewhat tender but succeeds against a warm wall.

The larger Hebes, as one should now call these shrubby Veronicas, will also grow on chalky soils and are thus particularly valuable for such districts along the coastline where, with Fuchsias, *Senecio laxifolius, Hydrangea maritima, Spartium junceum*, Rosemary, Escallonias, *Phlomis fruticosa, Abutilon vitifolium, coronilla glauca*, Olearias Hoherias, Tamarisks and other maritime shrubs they revel in the moist and salty winds.

Half-ripe shoots will strike fairly readily if placed under a bell-glass or in the warm sand-frame in July.

With some plants it is not easy to decide whether they should be considered as herbs or shrubs.

Romneya Coulteri the **Californian Bush Poppy** (A.G.M. 1929), is, in this country, almost herbaceous in habit, making soft shoots from the ground with divided green leaves, and the well-known huge, golden-centred, fragrant, papery, white poppy-flowers are aglow from July onwards. It is a charming plant for the foot of a south wall with a deep rich soil in which the roots will wander and send up shoots as often as not on the far side of the wall.

R. trichocalyx is a closely related sort with blue-green leaves, a less finely formed but firmer flower and a slightly hardier constitution.

In place of the circlet of rich golden-yellow fluff from which a dark-based, slender cone emerges, *R. trichocalyx* has merely a pompon or button of stamens in the centre of the flower and the more separated petals are stiffer, lacking the crinkled perfection of *R. Coulteri*. Yet at a distance it is the more decorative shrub, for the firmer "drawing" of the flowers shows up most attractively, while those of *R. Coulteri* appear merely as a series of formless blobs. But, alas, instead of the delightful fruity scent, likened to the bouquet of a fine old Hock†, which charms us in *R. Coulteri*, *R. trichocalyx* can only offer us a rather nasty daisy-like smell.

For perfection we need both kinds perhaps, and, in the warmer gardens, a group planted against a dark evergreen background will present a particularly lovely sight when well established. At Grayswood Hill, Haslemere, a large clump of *R. trichocalyx* at the foot of a retaining wall has sent its roots under this and produced a straight row of flowering offshoots in the gravel of the terrace 4 feet above. In warm gardens, particularly on limy soils, the Romneyas are most valuable for late summer display and they are not expensive to buy. Their habit is dashing, but untidy, and a position sheltered from strong winds and a little training, and even light staking of the young growths, is helpful to good deportment.

In the colder districts the plants should be cut to the ground in late autumn and have a thick mulch of bracken placed over the roots.

The Romneyas do not object to a limy soil so long as it is well enriched and reasonably deep. Root cuttings with an "eye", taken from short pieces of surface roots, just buried in sandy soil and put in gentle heat will usually send up shoots and thus form new plants. It

† "Romneyas", by C. T. Musgrave, V.M.H., *R.H.S. Journal*, LXIV, Pt. 12, p. 353.

is not, however, an easy method for the amateur. Young plants must be carefully potted-on until set out in their permanent positions, as these Romneyas do not move safely, being very sensitive to any interference with their root-system.

It is possible, in a good warm summer, to get fertile seed if *R. Coulteri* is hand-pollinated with pollen from *R. trichocalyx* (*loc. cit.*). When ripe, the seeds should be sown, preferably in thumb pots, as otherwise many plants die in pricking off.

A Holly-like evergreen South American shrub is **Desfontainia spinosa**, introduced by William Lobb for Messrs. Veitch of Exeter, where it first flowered in 1853. Its hardiness is really only sufficient for gardens in the coastal counties along the English Channel and the Irish Sea. The leaves are opposite instead of alternate, otherwise most would take the plant for a small Holly, but the $1\frac{1}{2}$ inch long, tubular, red and yellow flowers are highly unusual. Unfortunately they are too narrow, being usually less than $\frac{1}{2}$ inch across at the mouth, and they droop among the leaves so as to be rather poorly presented. Their best point is that they are borne in July when such rich colouring is not common. If grown in the shade the plant grows well enough but is rather shy-flowering; in full sun it is apt to be damaged by the sun shining on the frozen leaves in the mornings. On the west coast of Scotland very large and healthy plants are to be found and I am always surprised not to see well-grown specimens more commonly in Cornish gardens where one would expect this plant to make a fine display. In the average garden it is a disappointing shrub and I would only recommend it for the west coast.

D. spinosa requires an acid soil well enriched with leaf-mould, and above all, a moist atmosphere, and can be struck from cuttings in the sand-frame fairly easily. In warm years it sets seed and can then be propagated in this way also.

The shrubby St. John's Wort, or **Hypericum** genus provides several good species for the garden; the Lemon or Buttercup-yellow flowers are both gay and superbly shapely, and, furthermore, borne with remarkable freedom late in the season.

Among the most important is *Hypericum patulum*, yet the original Japanese form of this shrub is of no great account, being somewhat tender and short-lived. The following forms, however, are superb garden shrubs:—

H. p. var. *Forrestii* (A.G.M. 1924) is a more or less evergreen shrub of good bushy habit about 4 or 5 feet high and as broad. From July or early August onwards, the Buttercup-yellow, saucer-shaped, five-petalled flowers, 2 inches across, appear, making a charming picture among the red-barked branchlets and bright green, tongue-shaped leaves. No shrub in my garden seeds itself as freely as this, old plants being soon surrounded by innumerable true seedlings. This useful quality enables us to use the plant freely as a "filler" but care should be taken to cut off the seed pods before their contents ripen or the good work may even be overdone. Some of the leaves colour superbly in autumn if the weather is favourable. *H. p. Forrestii* was collected by G. Forrest in the Lichiang Range in Yunnan.

H. p. var. *Henryi* is another superior form from China, introduced by Professor Augustine Henry at the close of the last century. The flowers are slightly smaller than those of the var. *Forrestii*.

H. p. 'Hidcote variety' is the finest of all the Hypericums that I have seen. Its habit is very bushy and compact; the unusually large flowers do not fade so quickly in the sun and are freely borne over a very long season. When this plant becomes generally available it will undoubtedly gain high popularity. At present it is rather scarce.

H. Hookerianum. This species was originally introduced from Assam by Thomas Lobb. On the whole it is a better garden shrub than the original type form of *H. patulum* but less effective than its variety *Forrestii*. It is said to be distinguishable by the fact that its branchlets are round in section while those of the latter are two-edged. *H. Hookerianum* is, however, thinner and more lanky in habit and the leaves are rounder, rather than tongue-shaped like those of *H. patulum* var. *Forrestii*.

H. Moserianum is a hybrid between *H. patulum* and *H. calcynum*. It only grows about 1 foot 6 inches tall and is unfortunately rather tender. The top growth is often killed back in winter but it usually shoots again in late spring. The flowers are large for the size of the plant and open one at a time from the usual cluster formation. It does not creep at the root like the following species.

H. calcynum, the "Rose of Sharon", is a low shrub about a foot or 1 foot 6 inches high, very useful as a carpeter in rough places. It is hardly up to garden standards although the Lemon Yellow flowers are very large, being about 3 inches or more across with a conspicuous brush of stamens in the centre. It is quite hardy and grows well on chalky banks. It is easily increased from pieces of the creeping root-stock.

H. Leschenaultii is a Malayan and Javanese species less effective than *H. patulum* var. *Forrestii*. It gets badly cut back in winters that leave the latter species unhurt, and in the wet and sunless summers all too common in England, it often does not flower until September is well advanced. Even grown to perfection, as in 1949, it is a disappointing species except, perhaps, in a few very favourable localities.

H. 'Rowallane Hybrid', raised by Mr. Armytage Moore by crossing *H. Leschenaultii* and *H. Rogersii*, is a shrub reaching 5 or 6 feet with bowl-shaped Buttercup-yellow flowers (H.C.C. 5) 3 inches across. In my experience it suffers from all the defects of the preceding species, often flowering too late and lacking the splendid vigour and fine deportment of *H. patulum* var. *Forrestii* or 'Hidcote Variety'.

The shrubby Hypericums are very valuable in the late summer shrub garden in association with the blue Hydrangeas, thus providing a delightful blue and yellow effect. On limy soils they grow well in the more moist positions, with added leaf-mould.

Light shade and a well-drained position with a moist subsoil is preferred. They are often attacked by small grey insects which eat away the surface of the leaves, making the plants dirty-looking and unthrifty. When this occurs the pocket dust-gun provides a convenient remedy. Some authorities recommend cutting back *H. p. Forrestii* nearly to the old wood in April but all such cutting interferes with the natural symmetry of the growth to suit its position. With me this species is of fine, dense, twiggy habit when old, and has gracefully arching sprays when young. I have not seen the need for the secateurs on any of the considerable number of plants grown, except to remove over-abundant seed pods.

These Hypericums are an easily propagated group, seeds and July cuttings placed under a bell-glass offering ready means of increase.

Ceratostigma Willmottianum (A.G.M. 1928) is a slender little shrub found in China by E. H. Wilson in 1908 and the great Miss Willmott was the only person who raised plants from seeds he sent back. She thus, most deservedly, gave the plant its name. *C. Willmottianum* grows about 2 feet high with many thin stems from the base, terminating in a cluster of bright blue flowers in July in which only one or two are open at one time. The succession is therefore good but the distant effect rather weak. Its hardiness is just up to the "reasonably hardy" category. The summer growth usually dies down in winter and in early spring the plant often looks as though dead. A light scattering of bracken over the roots, however, preserves it and the little shrub has time to grow enough new wood to make its contribution in late summer.

Of no great account, it is a pretty little thing for a sunny place, included for its timely flowering and easy increase by either seed or cuttings. Its Chinese habitat ensures its growing in limy soils and it is therefore especially valuable under such circumstances to complement,

19

with Caryopteris and the larger-flowered, bluer Clematises, the many
yellow-flowered shrubs available at this season.

Perowskia atriplicifolia, the Afghan Sage, qualifies doubtfully for
inclusion here, but as it flowers in August, is given the benefit of the
doubt. The long upright silvery-white shoots are set with slender
branchlets bearing little whorls of the tiny, labiate, brilliant violet-blue
flowers. In certain lights and certain positions these can be very decorative but for most positions the habit of the shrub is almost too gawky
to be bearable. It is a sun-loving plant from the hot and arid parts of the
Himalayas, forming a large part of the almost invisible vegetation which
shimmers in the heat haze among the blazing rocks of the N.W. frontier
of India. Pruning to the base every spring is recommended but new
spindly shoots, 3 feet or more long, merely emerge and on these the
flowers appear in due course. Possibly incessant nipping might make a
more compact and comely shrub of it but the best course is probably
to plant it in a small group so that the evening sun illumines the slender
silvery spikes against a shadowed background.

It is not particular as to soil, growing even in limy soils, so long as it
gets the sun. Cuttings are reported to root under a bell-glass in July,
but I have had few successes by this method.

Easier to grow than most but less decorative in flower, **Polygonum
baldschuanicum** is a rampant climber really too obstreperous for the
small garden. Given an eyesore to cover as quickly as possible at all
costs, it has its uses. The feathery sprays of tiny white flowers backed by
bright green foliage are quite pleasing in August. It is not self-support-
ing, so requires wires, or a length of wire netting fixed to the wall, to
twine into or the whole thing may come adrift in a high wind. It is not
particular as to soil and may be propagated from cuttings taken with a
heel, the end being just trimmed smooth with a sharp blade before
insertion in sandy soil under a shaded bell-cloche in a warm spot.

In August, flowering trees continue to offer their sequence of flowers
and the **Catalpas** are particularly valuable at this time when much tree
foliage has begun to assume a dull tone.

Catalpa bignonoides is a beautiful late-flowering tree introduced in
1726 from the eastern United States. It has large leaves of a fresh
yellowish-green and Horse Chestnut-like panicles of white flowers,
striped inside with yellow and spotted with brownish-purple, in early

August. It is a very bushy-headed tree and withstands wind surprisingly well. There are also a number of oriental species and hybrids some of which are equally effective. The Catalpas will, no doubt, be grown more widely now that planters are beginning to take more interest in the later summer flowers.

C. b. aurea is a variety with rich yellow-green leaves making quite a striking mass of colour. It is notable for park plantings where copper Beeches, blue Cedars, Negundas, Silver Poplars and other trees of unusual leaf colourings are used for massive effects.

C. b. Koehnei has yellowish centres and yellow margins to the leaves.

C. b. nana is a dwarf, bushy form which very seldom flowers. Grafted standard-high it provides the mop shape which is thought desirable for certain formal situations.

C. b. pulverulenta, with white-spotted leaves and *C. b. variegata* with leaves blotched with yellowish-white are not particularly ornamental.

C. ovata, a Chinese species cultivated in Japan, forming a tree about 30 feet high with white, yellow-stained and pink-spotted smaller flowers, is not commonly seen or offered by nurseries.

C. o. flavescens is described as having flowers suffused with yellow but even smaller than those of the "type".

C. hybrida (*C. Teasiana*) is an American-raised hybrid flowering in July and of great vigour in the hotter summers of the United States. In Britain it is reported to be less effective than *C. bignonoides*.

C. h. japonica, also thought to be a hybrid between the preceding species was introduced from Japan about 1886. The flower-head is more pyramidal in shape and the flowers are of a purer white than those of *C. ovata*, and dotted with violet. They are notable for being fragrant. This is a strong and quick-growing form, but unfortunately now scarce.

C. h. erubescens, another hybrid, has small but very numerous fragrant flowers of a more purplish cast, as is also the foliage. As described by Mr. F. G. Preston†, a tree 30 feet high in the University Botanic Gardens, Cambridge, is a conspicuous sight when in bloom in August.

C. speciosa, a southern United States species, is a fine timber tree in its native forests, sometimes 100 feet in height and the wood has extraordinary durability. The flowers are sparser but individually larger. It is not so well suited to our climate as *C. bignonoides*.

C. Fargesii is a western Chinese species with pale purplish-pink flowers spotted with brownish-red and stained with yellow.

† "The Gardeners' Chronicle", Jan. 15, 1949, p. 22.

C. F. Duclouxii is a particularly fine form described by Mr. J. S. L. Gilmour† as "up to 65 feet in height with pink-dotted, pale pink or white flowers with yellow-banded throats". The best clonal variety of this fine Catalpa is generally considered to be 'Borde Hill', with lilac-pink flowers in dense clusters.

C. Bungei is a bushy-habited small tree of 30 feet reported to be shy-flowering in this country.

The Catalpas are attractive trees for gardens where a tropical-looking atmosphere is sought. A garden, I think, should always look more fertile than the surrounding land; there should be something of the oasis about it. Such large-leaved species as these and the Bamboos, Mahonias, Fatsia, Yuccas, large-leaved Rhododendrons, etc. have a great effect in achieving this object.

The Catalpa is best as a lawn specimen tree; cramped up with other growth its natural symmetry is lost.

The species are not very particular as to soil but do best, like all trees, when this is enriched by the addition of a mulch of leaves or bracken.

With *C. bignonoides*, if the tree form is desired, young specimens require care in encouraging a definite leader by cutting back competitive shoots, otherwise this Catalpa grows as a large bush.

Seeds produce the best trees, but cuttings of the hybrids and special forms may be struck, if bottom-heat is available.

Though a member of a family mostly known as flowering trees, *Æsculus parviflora*, the "**Dwarf Buckeye**" is a deciduous, bushy shrub about 8 feet high, like a miniature white Horse Chestnut, flowering in July or August. It is hardy and vigorous and it is a pity that the beautiful red or yellow flower colour worn by some of the other Buckeyes is not present in this sturdy species.

It forms quite an attractive lawn specimen and like all the members of this family submits well to moving, responds quickly to good cultivation and has no rigid soil requirements.

Seeds, sown as soon as they fall, are the best means of increase but unfortunately they are only ripened in quite exceptional seasons. Rooted pieces may sometimes be detached and grown-on to form new plants.

Mere rarity is seldom a virtue but there are times when we seek a plant that is new and strange to our eyes. There are, curiously enough,

† *R.H.S. Journal*, LXII, Pt. 3, p. 139.

many old established occupants of our gardens that have, for one reason or another, never become widely known.

Wisteria japonica is an uncommon member of its family flowering in July and August, introduced in 1878 by Charles Maries for Messrs. Veitch of Exeter, that great nursery of the past to whom we owe so many fine trees and shrubs.

The flowers, a pale yellowish-white and in racemes up to a foot long, are individually rather small but so numerous as to make a charming effect when this climber is grown up some unimportant tree or suchlike support. Forming an attractive feature of a distinct type in the August garden landscape this Wisteria is worthy of more attention than it has received. It takes time to reach effective size but grows steadily and will finally envelop a small tree in a most remarkably picturesque manner.

Like the other members of the family a moist rich soil is preferred and it may be increased by layers.

The greater convenience and clarity gained by splitting up unwieldy genera containing species of widely differing types has already been acclaimed in the Apple, Pear, Whitebeam and other families. The **Spiræas** also benefit. The fluffy-spired herbs are now Astilbes, only the typical Bridal Wreaths now remaining as Spiræas. Most flower earlier but some species retard their flowering until late summer.

Spiræa bullata is a pretty little dwarf shrub from Japan, compact and rounded and about 1 foot 6 inches high with rosy-pink flowers in dense corymbs in July. At that time it forms a dome of colour that is quite acceptable unless the gardener has achieved the triumph of eliminating this colour from his composition; failing this, it will play a useful part in providing a succession of flower with the evergreen Azaleas, Helianthemums, dwarf Brooms and Heaths that are so attractive for those low effects of flowery carpeting which it is one of the objects of this book to recommend.

S. japonica, in its typical form is almost a weed, with its magenta-pink flowers and rank growth, coming up from self-sown seedlings in every likely spot. It is quite useful for rough places where its flower colour is not objected to.

S. Bumalda 'Anthony Waterer', a hybrid of the above, has brighter and deeper coloured flowers in July and a more dwarf and compact habit of growth, making a shrub of 3 or 4 feet each way. This is quite a useful thing for rough, unimproved soils.

These Spiræas will grow quite well on moderately lime soils, though more vigorously in acid soils. Where it is desired to keep the plants to a small space the shoots of the previous year may be cut back to the older wood in spring, but such pruning is to be avoided if possible. Bushes thus treated have an ugly, snaggy appearance that is markedly less attractive to the eye in winter than a bush of natural branching. With some kinds flowering is slightly improved, it is true, but it is at the expense of attractive and natural-looking form in the winter landscape. Cuttings root freely in the sand-box or under bell-cloches in late summer.

Sorbaria Aitchisonii and *Holodiscus discolor,* formerly considered as Spiræas, may be taken together. They are tall, 10-foot, rather tropical-looking shrubs with feathery plumes of white flowers that make a short but impressive display in late July or early August. They are at their best on the flanks of some noble, semi-woodland glade, perhaps in the background of Hydrangea groups where their graceful arching habit may be well displayed. *H. discolor* is, I think, the more decorative of the two and may well be used in a corner of quite a small garden with advantage. The name change from the familiar Spiræa is to be welcomed as, from the gardener's viewpoint, these shrubs seemed to have little in common with the other members of that family.

Both shrubs are hardy and not particular as to soil. They may be increased by seeds, though hybrid offspring may result, or by detaching rooted pieces. Some thinning out of the growths is desirable when these get too crowded to flower well.

Two valuable members of the great **Magnolia** family flower in the later summer.

Magnolia virginiana (*M. glauca*) the "Swamp Bay" of the south-eastern United States, is a charming little tree usually about 12 to 15 feet high. The waxy-white flowers, about $2\frac{1}{2}$ inches across, are endowed with one of the most delicious of flower scents but last for only a few hours in perfection. The leaves are glaucous beneath, that is to say, covered with bluish-white bloom, and the whole appearance of the little tree is delicate and charming. It does best in a moist, rich soil, such as regular mulching soon provides, with its head in the sun to encourage freedom of flowering.

M. grandiflora, the "Bull Bay", is the most beautiful of full-sized evergreen flowering trees in its native home in the southern United States, where, alas, it is all too often destroyed wholesale by the Negroes without a thought. I have seen specimens 100 feet in height in some of the Florida backwoods and, especially where the scarlet Bignonias decorate the trunks, the sight is one of the most splendid I have known. For garden purposes there are two forms that are so greatly superior to the others that care should be taken to secure them. One of these is the variety 'Exmouth' which has large, rather pale green, shiny leaves, foxy-red beneath, and grows very quickly, flowering when quite young and, indeed, at all times with remarkable freedom. In my old garden a plant of 'Exmouth' had grown to 20 feet and produced hundreds of flowers before a seedling form of the common type planted near had grown above 6 feet or ever produced a flower. 'Exmouth' also appears to be hardier. The other variety, *gloriosa* (or 'Goliath'), is also preferable to the common type; it has larger flowers and broader leaves rounded at the ends and green beneath and is a less upright grower. The south walls of all sizeable mansions should, I think be decorated by these superb and lovely evergreens. In the open, when grown as a tree, gales and snow often break down the branches and these may be braced with steel cables and eyebolts bolted through the trunk with advantage. As is now generally recognised, a small bolt passing completely through a limb, or the trunk, does much less damage to the tree than any form of band around the bark. The bark, and more particularly the cambium layer just beneath, are the actively living portions of the stems; the centre wood is more structural than vital.

As regards cultivation, a good turf-loam enriched with a leaf mulch grows these Magnolias as well as any soil that I know. Propagation is difficult for the amateur, and even layering *M. grandiflora* is by no means always quickly accomplished. Well damped, half-rotted Pine sawdust is said to tempt rootage better than anything else. Increase is always worth trying with such an expensive subject and particular care should be taken to bend the young branch up *abruptly* and to fix the base of the bend very firmly in position.

The **Tamarisk** family are mostly thin-habited maritime or sand loving shrubs very valuable for exposed, sandy, seaside gardens.

Tamarix pentandra (*T. hispida æstivalis*) is one of the most beautiful. It is a deciduous species with racemes of pink flowers covering the ends of the current year's shoots in plumy masses. Sternly cut back each year it produces these the more freely and is a fine sight in August and September and the spicy scent, which has been compared to gingerbread, is not unattractive.

T. tetrandra the spring-flowering Tamarisk, *T. juniperina* with very decorative summer foliage, and *T. anglica* the evergreen English Tamarisk that flowers in late summer are all worth growing, close to the sea.

They are easily propagated from cuttings put in the ground in early winter, as for Roses. By the sea the natural sandy, salty soil suits them perfectly but inland they will be found to require a good moist loam.

Like the Camellias, the **Hydrangeas** have for long borne a largely undeserved reputation for tenderness owing to misunderstandings as to their positioning, pruning and cultivation. In general it may be said that in the British Isles it is only cold gardens that are situated in frost-holes or low-lying situations subject to frequent severe spring and autumn frosts, that cannot grow the more suitable varieties quite successfully out of doors.

Like the Rose and the Tree Peony, the Hydrangea is over-sanguine and starts making growth too early and continues too late in the season for safety in low-lying places. When travelling through the countryside of Britain the observer will note superb plants in the cottage gardens on all the hills and few or none in the closed valley bottoms where the cold airs collect in late spring or early autumn. Even in such places as these, however, certain varieties and species of the Hydrangeas can often be grown quite successfully provided that they are planted in full sun and exposure with a thick mulch of bracken kept over the roots in winter and that they are carefully pruned in spring and have controlled liquid feeding in early summer.

A bar to their planting by gardeners has been the misconception that there is only one variety, called "the common Hydrangea" which is of service only as an indoor pot-plant. There is, of course, no such thing; one might as well call any ubiquitous garden Rose variety "the common Rose" when, of course, all these varieties are selected seedlings propagated as clones just as the garden Hydrangea varieties are. Many of these are "reasonably hardy" in the British Isles. The important point is to select those hybrid varieties which flower freely from side shoots if the terminal bud is winter-killed. The names of these are singularly important as they also vary widely in effectiveness and in hardiness as outdoor plants.

Hydrangea macrophylla (*H. hortensis*, *H. opuloides*, etc.) is a hybrid race containing the "blood" of both the maritime and the woodland species and may be divided into two separate sections—the Lacecaps, or flat-headed forms with an inflorescence similar to that of the wild prototypes, composed of a central area filled with small fertile flowers surrounded by an outer ring of large and showy sterile ray-flowers, and the Hortensias, which were mostly bred on the Continent and in which the flower-head is globose in form and composed almost entirely of the large sterile flowers.

Taking the **Hortensias** first, a Chinese garden form of *Hydrangea maritima* first reached this country when imported from China through the agency of the great Sir Joseph Banks in 1739. This original variety, of Hortensia type, is still to be found in old gardens. It is a large, coarse-growing plant for which the varietal name 'Joseph Banks' has been proposed†. Usually bearing very large, lumpish heads of pale purplish-pink flowers, it is actually one of the least attractive as a garden shrub, although very fine almost anywhere *close to the sea*. Inland it is much less effective than others as it does not flower from side shoots if the terminal bud is killed by frost.

Following on the importation of the Japanese hybrid Hortensia clones 'Otaksa' and *rosea*, from about 1907 onwards extensive breeding of the Hortensias took place in France and, to a slightly lesser extent, in Germany and Holland. In the course of time hundreds of varieties have been produced for use as pot plants. By chance some of these inherit hardiness, freedom of flower, resistance to sun and wind and vigour of constitution. Others, though perhaps good for pot work, are not suitable for outdoor growing.

For growing as open-air shrubs in the garden, certain varieties are pre-eminent; others fade or burn and are insufficiently hardy and free-flowering for outdoor life. But which to choose out of these depends largely upon whether the soil of the garden is alkaline or acid. In the first instance the flowers will be pink or red, in the latter, blue or purple. The reason for this is that limy conditions make the aluminum and other mineral elements in the soil unavailable to the plant. It is the aluminum, not iron, as formerly believed‡ that causes the crimson pigment in the sepals to turn blue. Consequently the gardener whose soil is limy will be well advised to grow the warm pinks, carmine-crimsons and whites rather than spend endless labour on feeding aluminum to obtain, with difficulty, a few blue flowers. On a neutral soil it is worth growing a few good blues carefully fed with extra aluminum.

If the soil is very limy, so as to make the plants chlorotic (yellow-leaved and unthrifty), feeding with a quarter-ounce of sulphate of iron dissolved in a gallon of water will usually cure the trouble. The alkalinity of the soil also locks up the available natural iron so essential to the Hydrangea and indeed, though to a lesser degree, to other plants, so that even fruit trees have to be dosed with iron pills inserted in their trunks when grown on very limy soils. Sunlight usually enhances rather than fades the red flower-colouring.

† *The Hydrangeas*, by Michael Haworth-Booth, Constable & Co. (1950).
‡ R. C. Allen, *Contributions to the Boyce Thompson Institute*, Vol. XIII, pp. 221–242.

The following is a selection of Hortensias for limy soils:—

'Princess Beatrix' is a fine early rosy-red that is unusually free-flowering.

'Carmen' is a mid-season flowerer with rich crimson-carmine flowers. It is very fine, but in some soils will not grow well.

'Vulcain' is a charming little dwarf no more than a foot high with large heads of glowing Carmine flowers. It is a good outdoor plant in full sun. Under glass it is very subject to "damping off". (See illustration facing p. 241.)

'Parsifal', in colour Rose Madder, early, with serrated sepals, has medium growth. It fades badly in the sun but is mentioned here as it is very commonly seen.

'Ami Pasquier' is early-flowering, with crimson flowers and moderate growth, and is one of the most vigorous of red-flowered Hortensias. It is remarkably free-flowering.

'Mme Mouillère' has white, serrated sepals and is early flowering. It is a very beautiful variety, particularly against a north wall.

'Gloire de Vendôme', also known as 'Brightness', is a deep crimson. It is a late-flowering variety of dwarf growth, lasting long in beauty.

'Mein Liebling' is flesh pink, a dwarf grower and does not go bluish in slightly acid soils.

'President Doumer' is a vivid velvety red and of dwarf growth.

'Heinrich Seidel' is a fine deep cherry red with serrated sepals and a moderate to tall grower. It is remarkably fine when well established but requires a favourable climate.

'Westfalen' is vivid Crimson, similar to 'Vulcain' but stronger in growth, with very shapely flowers. It sends up flowering shoots from the base like a herbaceous plant if well fed. It has the most intense colouring of all the Hydrangeas. (See illustration facing p. 304.)

The blue varieties that give a Cambridge blue in acid soils are best avoided in limy districts as their pale pinks are colder in tone, and less attractive than those mentioned.

On the other hand, on an acid soil of pH 5·50 or lower, the best Hortensias for the purpose will become blue- or violet-flowered naturally, in time. In any event they are easily assisted in such soils, to attain a beautiful pure colour by feeding with aluminum sulphate, a quarter ounce to a gallon of water or, though this is rather risky, by adding from one to seven pounds of the same to the surrounding soil in Autumn, depending upon the size of the plant from 5-inch pot size to that of a 3-foot established bush. As with those recommended for a limy soil, iron should be given in the same way if a plant shows yellowish foliage at any time. When they are grown blue-flowered light shade helps to preserve the flowers.

The following are specially desirable Hortensia varieties for an acid soil.

'Vibraye' ('Générale Vicomtesse de Vibraye'). This hardy old variety is still valuable owing to its ability to flower from side-shoots, should the terminal bud be killed, and its very marked readiness to give a pure Spectrum Blue flower. It is a tall grower with rather slender shoots and mid-season flowering.

'Mousseline'. This early variety has better formed, less crowded flowers and more shapely heads than the preceding but does not "blue" so intensely. Once settled, it is very good indeed. It is a strong grower, with almost unspotted green stems and flowers both very early and very late. The autumn colouring is particularly good and it is notably hardy.

'Holstein' is a sky blue with serrated sepals and is rather a weak grower, flowering early and very freely.

'Hamburg' is a good deep blue in acid soil and of strong growth; in neutral soil it comes a bright rosy-pink and the flowers always last well, turning a beautiful deep red in autumn. It requires shade and a favourable climate but the huge fringed flowers are superb.

'Maréchal Foch' is one of the best dark blues for distant effect and quite remarkably free-flowering.

'Goliath' is a tall grower with fairly small heads of large mauve-blue flowers at midseason. It is remarkably fine near the sea.

'Domotoi' is an old Japanese variety with picturesque pink or blue-lilac, strangely doubled flowers. It is a vigorous but medium-sized plant making a good display late in the season. It is not a very ready bluer but has a quaint charm of its own.

'Mme J. de Smet' is a late-flowering pale blue; very useful to prolong the flowering season.

'Mme F. Travouillon' has peacock-blue flowers that do not fade in the sun but are often spoiled by rain, and is hardy and vigorous.

'Merveille' is a fine deep violet with bold heads and handsome foliage.

'Kluis Superba' is a splendid dark blue of compact free-flowering habit.

'La Marne' is violet-blue, late, a tall grower, and rather soft, but very fine when well fed, particularly by the sea.

'Altona' is a magnificent blue for those who like very large flower heads. It is a stout grower and one of the finest as a specimen plant in a tub or for exhibition, but not very hardy. The flowers last for months.

'Ami Pasquier' is, in acid soil, one of the best rich purple-flowered
varieties, the colouring being exceptionally vivid. It is a moderate
grower, up to 3 feet high, and has the shapely individual flowers
characteristic of the best varieties. The leaves turn a fine red in
autumn.

'Amethyst'. This is the latest of all to flower, being at its best in
September; thus it is only suitable for the more frost-free gardens.
The colour is violet-blue and the doubled sepals are attractively
serrated. Growth is very stout and the leaves are of an unusually deep green.

'Westfalen' and 'Vulcain' have intense violet or deep blue flowers
in acid soils, depending on the degree of acidity. In three or
four years they build up into dense low bushes, only a foot or
so in height, ideal for the small garden. (See illustrations facing
pp. 241 and 304.)

As to the garden use of the Hortensias, I think that the rather artificial
appearance of the flower-heads makes them unsuitable for naturalistic
or woodland planting. They demand the more formal beds near the house
where they associate most delightfully with the H.T. Roses, the hardy
hybrid Rhododendrons and other "garden variety" types of flowers.
There are no more delightful furnishings, if Camellia japonica varieties
are also added for spring effect, for the entrance courtyard, front
garden, or porch. I give these descriptions because the principle of
decorating this important part of the garden effectively, right at the
start, is, in my view, equally essential for Castle, Manor or Cottage.

For woodland and naturalistic plantings, rather than the Hortensias,
we should plant the informal Lacecaps, described later, which resemble
the wild species in the form of their flowers and are perfect for this
purpose.

Few plants are more effective when grown in tubs than the Hortensias,
as the soil can be controlled exactly to suit the flower colouring required
of each variety. In a very acid-soiled district the gardener may grow
the red varieties in neutralised soil with the extra iron so easily fed to
the plants in such containers and in a limy district he may rejoice in the
purest blues and richest purples grown in specially prepared acid soil
watered only with soft rain water.

The hardiness of certain varieties of the Hortensias is much greater
than is generally supposed. In gardens where spring and autumn frosts
are rife they are sometimes killed nearly to the ground and though
the roots of established plants always survive and send up fresh shoots,
the flowering is spoiled for the earlier part of the season. Some varieties
of this hybrid race have tender species in their ancestry and are thus

unsatisfactory outdoors. The planting of tender varieties grown "soft" for use as pot plants has given the Hortensias a largely undeserved reputation for tenderness; established old plants of the hardier sorts have withstood the severest cold probable in these islands with impunity.

There are fine bushes over a hundred years old in gardens in good positions in some parts of this country. An interesting example is that of Bingham's Melcombe, Dorset, where an old picture by Joseph Nash drawn over a century ago showed a number of strong Hydrangea bushes in front of the house. A *Country Life* photograph taken recently showed them to be still there and in superb health, and the late owner, Lady Grogan, wrote to me and confirmed that they were the original plants.

As regards cultivation, the Hortensia enjoys most an acid turf-loam —about pH 5·50—fairly rich in humus and having plenty of moisture such as a stony clay subsoil often provides. In short, any soil that suits Rhododendrons should suit blue Hydrangeas. Excessive manuring with farmyard manure, or excessively limy soil, may produce Chlorosis, signified by yellow leaves, and this is curable by feeding with bonemeal in the first case and sulphate of iron in the second as previously described (p. 298).

In soils of an acidity of pH 5·50 and more, the flowers of suitable kinds are naturally blue and the leaves a healthy deep green, as such conditions make the natural aluminum and iron freely available to plants. Lime locks up plant foods of this kind making them insoluble and unavailable to the plant and itself burns up the humus so that its valuable water-retaining qualities no longer come into play. By mulching and adding humus and feeding the Hortensia with available iron, in the form of sulphate of iron, the plant is able to grow quite happily in fairly alkaline soil. The aluminum, on the other hand, has only slight beneficial effect, other than making the flowers blue by chemical action on the crimson pigment in the sepals, but such feeding is only readily feasible on neutral or acid soils. On limy soils it is best to go in for the red or white varieties.

As regards pruning, the object for outdoor shrubs is to obtain a large number of small heads well distributed rather than a few, top-heavy, monstrous blooms that will look out of proportion and possibly flop at the first heavy shower. To encourage this, some growers pinch out the top bud of strong shoots, in early spring. The two buds immediately below then plump up, and both flower in the same or the following year.

This type of pruning may be done but it is not essential. What is absolutely essential is the thinning out of over-numerous shoots when the old top growth has been destroyed by an unusually severe winter.

The young shoots which emerge in a dense sheaf must be thinned out until each has plenty of light and air all along its length. Otherwise the overcrowded growths do not ripen fully or flower and are sure to be killed the following winter. Dead wood must be removed promptly.

It is a mistake ever to cut down a Hydrangea bush. If the plant is too large for its position, move it, complete with a ball of soil like a Rhododendron. Then replant a variety of the correct size on the old site. The varieties range from 1 foot in height, like 'Vulcain,' to 5 feet, like 'La Marne' and there are all sizes in between.

When starting young plants it is best to let them grow for a couple of seasons before giving aluminum, as it tends to check growth if they are forced to produce blue flowers before they are well established.

The next section of the varieties of *H. macrophylla* is that of the **Lacecaps.** These are, in my opinion, even more beautiful as flowering shrubs whose natural grace makes them ideal subjects for informal planting and, owing to the form of the head, even as cut flowers for appraisal in the hand or the vase, but they do not give quite such solid masses of rich colour as are attainable with the Hortensias.

The flower-head follows the pattern of the wild species†, being a flat corymb composed of a central mass of the true fertile flowers, whose shape somewhat recalls those of the common yellow Stonecrop. They are surrounded by a ring of the large, sterile ray-flowers which are similar to those of which the Hortensia flower-head is composed but much larger in size. The shape of these ray-flowers is often enchanting, the sepals being exquisitely formed with wavy and serrated edges of delightful pattern.

The artist, who often turns sadly away from the somewhat shapeless corymbs of too carefully fattened exhibition Hortensias, finds in the Lacecaps a new flower-shape of classic perfection that before long, I venture to prophesy, will take its place in floral designs.

The difference in the flowering times and hardiness of the various Lacecaps is so marked that careful attention has to be given to this point or planned effects will fail from lack of synchronisation. As this section, which comprises the finest of all the Hydrangeas for growing outdoors in the naturalistic shrub-garden, has been but little studied and recorded, I give fuller particulars below than are given for the better-known Hortensia types.

Most of the Hortensias are scentless, but the Lacecaps have the added charm of fragrance. The scent is not of the very highest quality, it is true—rather reminding one of that of the wild Meadow Sweet—

† All varieties and species of Hydrangea are described in a recent monograph by the writer, *The Hydrangeas* (Constable & Co. Ltd., 1950).

but it makes a pleasant contribution to the atmosphere of the late-summer garden, adding "body" to the tang of the Roses and the sweetness of the Spanish Brooms and late Azaleas.

What we lack are Lacecap varieties of the really vivid colours of such Hortensias as 'Westfalen', 'Ami Pasquier' and 'President Doumer'. Since the richest-coloured Lacecap, 'Bluewave', was the result of a chance shot in 1904, it should not be beyond the powers of future breeders to give us this alliance of lovely flower form and really rich colouring. All the following varieties may be grown in moderately limy soils with the special feeding necessary which is described in the Hortensia section.

H. m. 'Lanarth White'. This Hydrangea was first observed in the famous garden of Mr. Michael Williams of Lanarth, and there, to this day, are to be seen the most glorious great ancient bushes of this beautiful shrub. The numerous ray-flowers are a singularly pure white and have four or five somewhat irregular-sized, sharply pointed sepals, and a few sterile flowers are also sometimes produced among the bright blue central fertile flowers. The pointed leaves are usually rather a yellowish-green unless the plant is iron-fed. 'Lanarth White' is one of the earliest of the Lacecaps to flower, being often in bloom when July begins. Its unusually irregular flower shape does not lend itself to cultivation for increased size and it is therefore best in an exposed sunny position in fairly poor soil where it will produce a larger number of smaller and shapelier flowers on a very dense and decorative bush about 2 feet high. It is one of the most free-flowering of all Hydrangeas.

H. m. Veitchii is the next to flower and is one of the finest of the white-flowered Lacecaps for a shady position. This hybrid forms a tall, rather slender-branched bush with broad, bullate and notably acuminate leaves. The large ray-flowers have usually three entire, or slightly notched, sepals of large size fairly regularly formed, but, like all Hydrangeas, it reacts so readily to rainfall and position that there is much variation.

H. m. Mariesii (A.G.M. 1938) is a fine Japanese variety and one of the oldest in cultivation, having been introduced from Japan by Charles Maries in 1880. The inflorescence is bunshaped and, in form, midway between that of the Hortensias and the Lacecaps. Sterile ray-flowers of various shapes and sizes appear mixed with the central fertile flowers and the larger ray-flowers of the outer ring have usually four entire, rounded sepals pale pink in colour—only bluish under very highly aluminous conditions. This variety responds well to good cultivation, such as a moist soil and generous feeding afford. In a neutral turf-loam the pink colouring, though pale, is warm and attractive and the shapely flowers are large and beautiful. In time it forms a graceful bush 6 feet high. The true variety is rather scarce.

H. m. 'Bluewave' is probably the commonest and most spectacular of the Lacecaps and, owing to its great hardiness, one of the most valuable of all Hydrangeas as an outdoor flowering shrub for gardens enjoying an acid soil.

This Hydrangea was bred by Messrs. V. Lemoine of Nancy and introduced in 1904. It is not described by E. H. Wilson or other authors so far as I can discover, but fortunately the plant can speak for itself being greatly appreciated in the many gardens all over the country that it decorates so well.

'Bluewave' forms a large, strong, dense, permanent bush usually 5 or 6 feet high and even wider across, though by pruning it can be kept to 4 feet if absolutely necessary. Its hardiness is exceptional and, once well away, it rarely suffers winter damage but strong direct sunlight sometimes scorches the foliage. The flower-heads are flat and strongly supported on the stout branches. The ray-flowers, typically, are large and beautifully shaped with a delightful waved pattern of symmetrical serrations. The centre part is paler but the four sepals are a tint of Gentian Blue (H.C.C. 42/3) in acid conditions and some shade of pink or lilac depending exactly on the degree of alkalinity, in a neutral or limy soil. It does not "blue" as readily as many Hydrangeas, but once well fed and settled does not often throw odd pinkish flowers and better repays the trouble of aluminum feeding to give a pure blue than almost any other variety. It is a common shrub in old gardens, surviving neglect and the bitter winters of nearly half a century with ease. In full sun, in an unusually hot summer, the leaves scorch and the flowers bleach to a purplish tinge and thus the shade of a wall or distant trees and a little seasonal feeding with aluminum are needed for this glorious flowering shrub to show at its best. (See illustration facing p. 305.)

A curious feature is the very late flowering-time of this Hydrangea; it is rarely fully out until August is well on, when it associates superbly with the Ecuryphias, the Hypericums and also many of its own kindred whose phenomenally long flowering season keeps them still in bloom. It is common in Cornwall and the West and, indeed, all the southern counties of England.

H. m. 'Whitewave', is a superb variety found in a number of old gardens. It is a sister seedling to 'Bluewave' and was brought out by Messrs. V. Lemoine in 1904. We received plants in an importation from Messrs. Smith of Guernsey before the war. It is a strong grower rather resembling 'Bluewave' but easily distinguished by the concave, spoon-shaped leaves and the huge, white or faintly flushed, ray-flowers which have the same delightfully waved edges.

Hydrangea ' Westfalen '

Hydrangea macrophylla Veitchii

Hydrangea ' Bluewave '

Campsis Tagliabuana ' Mme. Galen '

It flowers about mid-season, with *Mariesii*, and is best in full sun in an open position in rich, well-mulched soil. It is one of the finest of all Hydrangeas, the inflorescence being about 8½ inches across with numerous beautifully shaped ray-flowers each often 3 inches across. It lasts in beauty for many weeks and is one of the most striking of white-flowered shrubs.

H. m. lilacina is an attractive hybrid variety. Messrs. V. Lemoine of Nancy also raised this interesting Hydrangea from naturally pollinated seed of *H. m. Mariesii*. This variety has a strong look of *H. serrata* in the matt, acuminate leaves and reddish shoots. A chocolate-brown line around the edge of the young leaves is characteristically very distinct. The ray-flowers are markedly serrated and rather thin in texture and small in proportion to the size of the plant. In a limy soil they are pink, ranging to quite a clear blue in highly acid soil.

H. m. tricolor is an old variety with brilliantly variegated foliage of three colours, sea-green, pale yellow, and deep olive green; the flower-head rather resembles that of *H. m. Mariesii*. Although somewhat prejudiced against such leaf-colourings I must admit that the fine qualities of this variety have made it one of my favourites, as the corymbs are very attractive and very freely borne over a remarkably long period and the healthful-looking and vigorous foliage is very decorative indeed. With aluminum feeding the flowers are a pale blue and the plant is then one of the handsomest of this artificial type, and looks particularly fine in a tub or large pot.

The Lacecaps have an advantage over most of the Hortensias in that wind and rain do not bow the flowers to the ground, but they remain erect and comely upon the bushes, indifferent to the blast. Both kinds associate particularly charmingly with yellow Roses, the Hortensias among the double garden sorts in the more formal parts, and the Lacecaps among the "singles" in more naturalistic plantings. The kitchen-garden appearance of the Rose-bed is thus, at a stroke, happily abolished and the flowery display of late summer rivals, and often indeed eclipses, thanks to safer weather, the glories of spring.

My earlier attempts to grow the Lacecap varieties of *H. macrophylla* in the wood-garden failed at first owing to the fact that insufficiently large individual beds for the specimens were made, too dry positions were selected and mineral feeding was not given to plants on steep slopes where such nutrients had been for centuries leached away from the leaf-mould and peat by heavy rains; also no slug poison was applied to check these destructive pests. When care is taken to avoid these mistakes the Lacecaps will be found to be amazingly effective in bringing late summer beauty to woodland glades glorified by Azaleas and Rhododendrons in spring and early summer.

20

Few shrubs are more easily propagated than these Hydrangeas. Short July cuttings of side-shoots with four leaves left, root almost invariably in the simplest glass-covered sand-box or even in sandy soil against a north wall. Damping-off is the one danger in frames, and fungicidal sulphur dusts have enabled even this trouble to be obviated.

¶ *H. serrata* is a Japanese hybrid race containing a preponderance of the "blood" of **H. acuminata, H. Thunbergii** and **H. japonica** which are woodland rather than maritime species. Unlike the varieties of *H. macrophylla*, the *serrata* varieties were mostly bred in Japan. The first crossings between the various woodland species were made centuries ago and I know of no new varieties that have been produced of recent years.

H. serrata varieties really require shade and a moist rich soil to look their best. They are, however, somewhat hardier than the varieties of *H. macrophylla*, and flower particularly freely from side-shoots. Slugs seldom eat their young shoots.

The parental species of the woodland hybrid race are attractive garden plants in themselves. Among these are the following:—

H. Thunbergii is a charming miniature Hydrangea usually 1 or 2 feet high, but attaining 3 feet under good conditions, with a ring of rounded, almost orbicular, three-sepalled ray-flowers, of quite a rich crimson-pink surrounding the central fertile flowers. The shoots are slender and crimson in colour when young, later turning brown, and the puckered, acuminate leaves are also reddish with a greyish bloom. It is commonly available in commerce.

H. acuminata is a very beautiful and distinct Hydrangea for a moist, shady situation on an acid soil, as the ray-flowers which have four large entire even-sized, ovate sepals, are very numerous and take on a brilliant blue colour under such conditions. The shrub is remarkably floriferous and of dense and bushy habit. It is rare in commerce, though stocks are now being built up. This species was first described by Von Siebold and is well figured in Siebold and Zuccarini's "Flora Japonica". According to several authorities it is common in Japanese gardens. The leaves are dull surfaced, slightly puckered, and often reddish or purplish when exposed to the sun. They end suddenly in a sharp point, being what is termed acuminate, though no more markedly than those of many of its kindred. Its wild habitat is Japan and Korea.

H. acuminata var. 'Bluebird'. This is a fine selected form with flowers of a slightly more vivid blue and larger size. Unlike *H. macrophylla*, all these woodland species require light shade except in the west, and the blue colouring of the flowers of this variety is particularly readily faded by the sun.

H. japonica var. *macrosepala*. This is an old Japanese variety of von Siebold's species *H. japonica*. This lovely Hydrangea was beautifully figured by Regel in his "Gartenflora" (1866, 15 t. 520) and I think we may assume that he got the plant from his friend Maximowicz, gardener to the Czar of Russia, who brought back a large consignment of Hydrangeas from Japan in 1864. Forming a 5-foot, densely twiggy bush with long slender deep green leaves, *macrosepala* flowers with amazing freedom in July. The corymbs have usually only four or five unusually large white ray-flowers with boldly serrated sepals and the fertile flowers are a blushed white. Thus the lacelike effect of the plant in full bloom is singularly beautiful; indeed even finer, in my opinion, than that of *Viburnum tomentosum Mariesii*.

I shall not forget my first sight of this plant in the romantically lovely gardens of Lanarth. We had passed through a grove of red-trunked Myrtle trees when, rounding a corner, we came upon a great bush of this exquisite Hydrangea. The waved and fretted flowers enveloped the plant in a mantle of white lace through which peeped the velvety green leaves. Only Nature in her most decorative mood, or selective breeding during more than two centuries of eclectic gardening, could produce such a beauty. From this unique survivor are descended those that we have today.

The garden varieties of the **H. serrata** group are becoming increasingly popular, as they grow well in shady places where Rhododendrons provide the spring and early summer flowers. Succeeding them in bloom they give the wood-garden an all-summer display which adds greatly to its interest and beauty.

H. serrata var. *intermedia*. This clonal variety is of such an indestructible and easily propagated nature that it is very commonly seen. It is a coarse, strong-growing shrub over 6 feet high in acid soil and shade. The foliage is intermediate between that of *H. Thunbergii* and *H. japonica* and so are the flowers. The ray-flowers are three-sepalled and deeply and regularly serrated, usually hollowed in the centre. In neutral or alkaline soils the fertile central flowers are pink, in acid soils blue, but the ray-flowers open white and gradually turn crimson whatever the soil. Owing to its objectionable habit of twisting its few ray-flowers over to face the ground, its decorative value is not great.

H. s. var. *rosalba*. This clone bears some resemblance to the preceding, but is much superior as a garden shrub. The ray-flowers are usually four-sepalled and turn a brighter crimson and do not twist

so soon; furthermore the inflorescence has usually from five to seven
of the showy ray-flowers instead of the meagre three or four of *H. s.
intermedia*. The foliage has a characteristically pale, bloomy look
which makes it easily distinguishable even out of flower. It is common in
commerce, but the preceding variety is often mistakenly sent out instead.

H. s. var. 'Grayswood' is one of the finest of all the clonal varieties
of *H. serrata* that I have seen. It forms a tall, slender-branched shrub
5 feet high or more. The leaves are at first markedly concave and
matt, yellowish-green and reddish-brown and acuminate. The flowers
are as beautiful as those of the Lacecap varieties of *H. macrophylla*
and almost as large. I would place it absolutely in the front rank
of first-class late-flowering shrubs for a shady position. The large
ray-flowers are particularly numerous, there being usually seven
or nine surrounding the inflorescence; they have four beautifully
serrated sepals, the lower one being characteristically elongated which
gives the flower a distinctive and singularly attractive shape. In colour
they are at first white, then they gradually turn to an even brighter and
more intense crimson than those of the variety *rosalba*. They last long
in this condition and though they finally twist to face the ground the
effect of the shrub is often highly decorative until hard frost comes,
owing to the fact that the under-surface of the sterile flowers becomes
brightly coloured by exposure to light. Thus, unlike most Hydrangea
flowers, those of 'Grayswood', instead of fading, get more brilliant
in colour as they age. (See illustration facing p. 257.)

H. serrata var. *stellata* (*H. s. prolifera*) is an extraordinary variety
with attractive doubled flowers. It may turn up in some old garden but
I am afraid that it is apparently extinct in this country. Indeed, all the
plants in cultivation in Europe were propagated from one surviving
plant brought home by Maximowicz. The foliage is rather similar to
that of the variety *intermedia* though this form has not the remarkable
vigour of that plant.

The garden value of the Japanese woodland species and hybrids
is high. The finest forms, such as *H. s.* var. 'Grayswood', *H. japonica
macrosepala*, and *H. acuminata* 'Bluebird', are ideal late summer shrubs.
A degree hardier than *H. macrophylla*, they grow with equal ease from
cuttings and, preferably in rich acid soil and light shade, can be grown
anywhere in these islands. If the terminal bud is killed by an unusually
severe winter they will flower cheerfully enough from side shoots
formed along the surviving stems.

Although, in favourable soils these Hydrangeas can make a plant
almost as large as the average run of *H. macrophylla* varieties they are
usually smaller and more slender-branched and can be kept to a height
of 2 feet or so with pruning, if necessary.

A rich, deep, acid soil containing plenty of humus seems to suit this type of Hydrangea best and, though it will survive in full sun, the finest plants are always to be found enjoying the shade of distant tall trees. In Cornwall, on the other hand, I have seen superb plants growing in full exposure in cottage gardens, but the grey skies and frequent showers, together with the moist maritime atmosphere, make a different climate from the plant's point of view.

Unlike the Hortensias, with their typical "garden variety" look, the Hydrangeas of this section have the delicate refinement of wild species and are thus ideal to enliven, in late summer, the wilder woodland sections too often entirely monopolised by Rhododendrons. There is no reason why such spots should be flowerless from July onwards, except perhaps for the somewhat fugacious blossoming of *Rhododendron auriculatum*. Azalea 'Daimio', *Rosa Moyesii*, *Rhododendron amagianum*, *R. indicum macranthum*, *Genista virgata*, *G. cinerea*, *G. æthnensis*, *G. tinctoria*, *Hoheria glabrata* and *Cytisus nigricans* all help the continuity of flower; but the woodland Hydrangeas in their various forms are outstanding for this purpose and can "take over" the decoration of the wood-garden in late summer with surprising effectiveness.

There are a great number of other species of Hydrangea, but not many that are really sufficiently decorative to require mention in this work devoted only to outstandingly effective garden plants, are available in this country.

Hydrangea Sargentiana, a tall grower with massive foliage, perhaps over-large and bold for the flowers, can hardly be considered as quite up to the decorative standard demanded by the small garden. Though quite pleasing in the shady woodland, it is outclassed in flower effect by the finer forms already mentioned, even in Cornwall. Shade is essential for it.

H. arborescens, an American species, has the merit of great hardiness to recommend it. In the variety *grandiflora* the flower-head is globose and almost entirely composed of sterile flowers, like that of the Hortensias, but the colour is only a yellowish-white and the habit is often so weak that the flowers flop over on to the ground. At Grayswood Hill colonies have practically died out whereas *H. macrophylla* and *H. serrata*, alongside, have made huge permanent bushes. With regular feeding and no pruning, however, the plant can be built up to form a stronger and more decorative shrub than those usually seen. Thus grown it is useful for cold gardens where *H. macrophylla* will not thrive.

H. quercifolia, the Oak-leaved Hydrangea, comes from the S.E. United States and is a handsomer shrub, but owing to frost damage the white-flowered panicles are seldom sufficiently numerous for the framework, and thus it requires a favourable garden climate to show its true beauty. The autumn leaf tints are notable.

H. paniculata, from Japan, is a popular shrub owing to its great hardiness. The flower-head is, in the form *H. p. grandiflora* which is most commonly seen, a large blunt panicle of sterile flowers of a creamy-white tint. When well fed and hard pruned these are often of enormous size, but somewhat shapeless and gross. In my view the beautiful Japanese garden variety *floribunda* is really far more decorative, and the more shapely bush with better presented flowers consorts more harmoniously with other flowering shrubs. *H. paniculata* is a late bloomer, seldom at its best until August is well on, except in the case of the curious, narrow-sepalled variety *præcox* which opens in July.

H. Bretschneideri, a Chinese species, is hardy and vigorous, making quite a large and sturdy bush about 8 feet high. The flat corymbs, 6 inches across, are composed of creamy white flowers. It is quite an attractive shrub for an odd corner, but not effective for so long a time as the garden sorts. In woodland it makes a pleasing small tree.

H. involucrata, a dwarf Japanese species with decorative white ray-flowers and blue fertile flowers, is one of the most attractive. It has a curious whorl of bracts at the base of the flower-head and is almost sub-shrubby in habit. It is just "reasonably hardy" but dies back some-what in winter. It flowers very late, often not opening fully until August or even September. There is a valuable Japanese garden form with pink doubled flowers *H. i.* var. *hortensis*. This is hardier and has a stronger constitution besides being more effective.

H. strigosa, a Chinese species, has a superior form usually known as *H. aspera macrophylla*, but, according to Alfred Rehder, correctly named *H. strigosa macrophylla*. This has large leaves sometimes nearly a foot long and flat flower-heads 8 inches across of a pale purple. It forms a vigorous, upright shrub up to 8 feet high and the flowers remain decorative far into autumn. It is, I think, more decorative than *H. Sargentiana*, and somewhat hardier, though often killed back to the ground in hard winters in all but the southern and coastal counties. E. H. Wilson found this plant in Western Hupeh in 1901. Unfortunately it is now rare.

H. aspera is a closely allied species, not very hardy in its common Himalayan form, it has downy leaves and purplish ray-flowers. The upright habit of the flowering shoots distinguishes it from *H. villosa*.

H. villosa. This fine species, introduced by E. H. Wilson from Western Szechwan, China, in 1908 has superlative forms of special merit. The finest I have seen is a superb specimen about 8 feet high and across growing in Colonel J. C. Stern's famous garden on the chalk at Highdown, near Worthing. It grows admirably in this soil and, in spite of the limy conditions, its flowers are a beautiful pale violet-blue, and these are qualities of the very highest value. In mid-August the flat corymbs about 6 inches across and of charming form and excellent presentation covered the great bush with a lacy mantle of colour.

Another form in commerce here and also ascribed to this species, has serrated edges to the sepals of the sterile flowers and a less compact inflorescence with small ancillary heads alongside the main corymbs. This is similar to that described by Mr. W. J. Bean as having first flowered at Kew in 1915†.

H. villosa is readily grown from seed, and slightly different colour forms are found, mostly with pale violet flowers. It is one of the finest of the species for general garden use, forming a fairly large shrub about 8 feet high, with deep sage-green leaves, golden and furry on the underside.

The Hydrangeas of these hairy-leaved Asiatic types occur in scattered habitats over a vast range of country across China to the Himalayas and the sorting out of allied species and forms is a complicated business. Many species of great beauty and, probably, hardiness remain to be imported‡. There is no doubt that when the best and hardiest forms are generally available, clonally propagated from cuttings, we shall have a very valuable addition to late-flowering shrubs capable of being grown in either limy or acid-soiled gardens.

Most of the species like a moist soil and light shade, and can be propagated from half-ripe side shoots in the sand-box or under a cloche in July. As with most Hydrangeas the critical time is the young plant's first winter and therefore it is best either to plant them from pots in early autumn so that they have time to get established before severe frosts come or to set them out in spring after frosts are over. Those who have a greenhouse may grow most of the species from seed. This is ripe about December and may be at once sown thinly in *well firmed* sifted sand and leaf-mould, much in the manner described for Alpine Rhododendrons, p. 90.

But, in our sequence of flowering bushes, we have lingered too long in cool and bosky places. It is time to consider what may be afoot on sunbaked hillsides where the garden climate is the very opposite. In such spots the Yuccas are at home. They are an extraordinary genus of tropical-looking plants from the southern United States and central America. Why the Yuccas should be hardy it is not easy to understand,

† "Trees and Shrubs Hardy in the British Isles", Vol. III, p. 188.

‡ For a description of all the known species see *The Hydrangeas*, by Michael Haworth-Booth, Constable & Co. (1950).

but they are. To my eye they always appear out of place grouped near
more typical plants, shrubs and trees of the northern hemisphere. On
the other hand in courtyards near modern garden-houses or loggias
where a rather tropical atmosphere is often highly pleasing or, again,
on hot sandy slopes, where other southern plants affect the landscape,
they are superb. They need, I think, as careful placing as the hardy
Palm, the Canna, Phormium tenax or the Mahonias and Fatsia that,
in association, so readily provide the sub-tropical décor fitting and
enjoyable in certain places.

Yucca filamentosa, with low tufts of the pointed blade-like evergreen
leaves and profuse panicles of loose yellowish-white flowers; *Y. glauca*
of more formal outline, with narrow glaucous green leaves and erect
spires of greenish-white flowers; *Y. gloriosa*, the most striking of all
with huge erect panicles of superb, drooping, creamy-white flowers
above the clusters of stiff, straight, spine-tipped leaves, are all effective
for the purposes described, and, when matured, flower in July and
August.

When the plants get too leggy, the tops can be cut off and rooted in a
pot of sandy soil in the greenhouse. They can also be propagated from
rhizomes detached from the plants and potted off in heat. A warm light
soil suits the Yuccas best but they are not very particular.

The **Buddleias** are a popular family owing largely to their vigorous
and indestructible nature and the fact that their flowers attract butter-
flies. Their habit of growth and general appearance when out of flower,
and too often actually when in flower as well, is, however, hardly that
required for year-round beauty in the garden landscape.

Buddleia Davidii (*B. variabilis*) (A.G.M. 1941), the common Buddleia,
is too well known to need description. The purple flowers turn brown so
readily that it is almost impossible to find a perfect spike unspoiled by
such decay. The habit is coarse and the growth so naturally successive
that the pruning-away of the older wood is desirable to ensure the
larger spikes produced on the young stems. Thus age, instead of bringing
picturesqueness of form, leads only to a more unnaturally disjointed
framework, possessing neither the advantage of the permanent shrub
nor the winter-disappearing herb.

In its favour it may be said that the common form of this Buddleia
is virtually indestructible and propagates itself freely both by seed and
trodden-in shoot. The hearts even of those who do not care for it in the
garden are warmed by its cheerful colonisation of blitzed ruins and suchlike waste places.

The variety 'Isle de France' is unusually vivid in colour and massive in spike and, of late, breeders have produced a number of other varieties which also excel in this respect. 'Royal Red' with foot-long Imperial Purple spikes, 'Fascinating' with even longer pink ones, Royal Purple, violet, and 'Peace', a pure white, are notable.

Other forms are *B. D. Veitchiana* raised by Messrs. Vilmorin Andrieux in 1893; *B. D. magnifica,* the variety most commonly seen, with brighter purple flowers produced a little later in the season; *B. D. Wilsoni,* with a more pronounced orange centre to the individual flowers; *B. D. alba,* with narrower leaves and white flowers and *B. D. nanhoensis,* a more dwarf and compact grower introduced by Reginald Farrer from Kansu, China, in 1914.

B. globosa has, if anything, a more gaunt, coarse and ungainly habit than the previous species described. The flower-head is a panicle of eight or more ¾-inch, ball-shaped clusters of Tangerine Orange fragrant flowers. Unfortunately the shrub is so large that they are too small to be proportionately effective.

B. Weyeriana (*B. Davidii* var. *magnifica* × *globosa*) is an interesting hybrid with the ball-like flower clusters of *B. globosa.* In colour these are a combination, being yellowish-orange suffused with mauve. The brightest variety commonly obtainable is var. 'Golden Glow', 'Moonlight', with pale, creamy flowers with an orange eye, is another. Breeding continues and no doubt varieties with brighter coloured flowers will appear.

B. Fallowiana, from Yunnan, China is a vigorous shrub of 6 feet or more with the leaves and young shoots partly covered with whitish fur and dense spikes of fragrant mauve flowers† in late summer. It is only hardy enough for favourably situated gardens. For a warm and elevated position where the soil is too limy for more year-round decorative subjects it would be a good choice.

There is a white-flowered form—var. *alba*—with orange centres to the flowers, which is more attractive than the mauve-flowered "type" and one of the finest of all the Buddleias.

Like the other members of its family *B. Fallowiana* is readily increased from July cuttings placed under a bell-glass or in the sand-box.

Nandina domestica is a curious Bamboo-like Chinese evergreen shrub of the Berberis family. It is much prized in Japanese gardens but is barely able to show its full beauties in any but the warmer parts of this country. The stems are erect and unbranched, reaching 6 feet or more in height. The much divided leaves are very decorative, being a foot or so in length and usually bright red when young and again, though often

† *R.H.S. Journal,* Vol. LXIV, Pt. 11, p. 544.

more purplish, in autumn and early winter. The flowers, in foot-long white plumes at the top of the bush in late summer, are not particularly decorative but the large panicles of red berries that follow them are vivid and well presented. Furthermore the "Heavenly Bamboo", as Reginald Farrer called it, is one of the precious band of shrubs giving us a really lasting leaf colour whose display carries on sometimes right up to Christmas, instead of leaving us with bare stems after only a few days of autumn colouring.

N. d. var. *atropurpurea* is a variety with bright purple leaves.

As regards soil, a moist and acid one is preferred and a sheltered position in full sun suits the Nandina, as I may call it, being the only species of its genus. In Japan it is usually grown in some courtyard near the house and indeed it looks best as a specimen in such a position rather than closely associated with other plants.

Propagation is easiest from seeds, cuttings being slow to root, or grow.

Fragrant evergreen flowering climbers are rare and we therefore especially value the **Trachelospermum** genus. They are allied to the Periwinkles and come from Japan and China.

Trachelospermum asiaticum (*T. divaricatum*) is a "reasonably hardy" species from Korea and Japan with leathery, oval leaves, an inch or so in length, and abundant yellowish-white, fragrant, inch-wide, periwinkle-like flowers in slender, terminal cymes during July and August. A vigorous twiner, it will reach 15 feet or more and cover quite a large area. A fine specimen at Kew showed, according to W. J. Bean, no signs of injury from frost over a period of thirty years. This is a charming climber in a quiet way.

T. jasminoides, a Chinese species introduced by Robert Fortune in 1844, is less vigorous and tall-growing and has larger and more pointed leaves and larger and more fragrant, pure white flowers. It has generally been found to be much less hardy than *T. asiaticum*.

A variegated form, *T. j.* var. *variegatum*, has the leaves blotched and bordered with creamy white in quite an attractive manner but it is very shy-flowering. Var. *Wilsonii* has narrower leaves which often turn crimson in autumn.

A form common in southern Europe, sometimes distinguished as var. *japonicum*, is hardier and more vigorous, with broader leaves which often turn to attractive crimson and bronze tints in winter.

T. jasminoides likes a warm wall and a light sandy and peaty soil. *T. asiaticum* is less particular and grew and flowered beautifully for many years in ordinary soil on an east wall in William Robinson's garden at Gravetye Manor, East Grinstead, Sussex. Increase may be made by July cuttings placed under a bell-glass.

Passiflora cærulea the "**Passion Flower**" of Brazil really needs a warm wall in a mild district. The strange design of the large and handsome bluish, five-petalled and five-sepalled flowers is thought to have a religious significance—there is no question of the fruits having any amatory consequences. Orange-coloured and egg-shaped, they are rarely ripened here and, anyway, unless grown in a warmer climate, are too full of troublesome seeds. From these, however, young plants are very easily raised, but cuttings are equally effective. Perhaps more curious than really beautiful, the flowers open, as a rule, in small batches from June to September without ever making a real display. To get real freedom of flower a restricted root-run or a really poor soil is necessary and the growths require shortening back to half their length in early spring. With this treatment this old climber, which has been with us for well over two hundred years, will give a fairly good account of itself and may be expected to make quite a good showing in July. In mild winters the hand-like leaves are often evergreen and the strong tendrils readily attach themselves to any convenient support but, without a sunny wall behind, the flowers are seldom abundant, even when the other precautions mentioned are taken.

P. c. 'Constance Elliott' is a variety with white flowers.

The **Clethras** are a family of, mostly, rather dull shrubs with small white flowers in dense spikes late in summer. Far the most beautiful species, *Clethra arborea*, the Lily-of-the-Valley Tree, is an exquisite flowering evergreen but is, unfortunately, too tender for Britain proper, though it grows well enough in the Channel Islands, on the south coast of Ireland and even in a few favoured Cornish gardens.

Clethra Delavayi, a deciduous species from Yunnan, has dense racemes of downward-pointing white cups in July. It is the most attractive of the Chinese species, but needs a moist, acid soil with shelter from wind and a mild climate. It is said to reach 40 feet in height.

C. monostachya, also a deciduous Chinese species, was introduced by E. H. Wilson and has solitary spikes of fragrant white flowers. This is a hardier plant, but grows to only about half the height of the preceding.

C. Fargesii, another Chinese species introduced by E. H. Wilson, has densely-flowered, slender, 6-inch racemes in terminal clusters. It requires a mild climate and moist peaty soil.

The common hardy American species *C. alnifolia* has, in the best form sometimes distinguished as var. *paniculata*, terminal panicles of small fragrant white flowers in August. It is an easily grown shrub in moist soil, reaching to about 8 feet high.

Clethra barbinervis is a Chinese and Japanese species with small white flowers in compact, downy panicles five inches or so in length. It is not quite as hardy as *C. alnifolia*, being caught sometimes by late spring frosts, but it is rather better looking.

The Clethras may be propagated by seeds, cuttings and layers. Their late flowering qualities are their best recommendation and they may play a useful part in woodland gardens in association with other shrubs that succeed the Rhododendrons in bloom. A soil free from excess lime, what is known as acid, is required. An acid soil may often be recognised by *Rhododendron ponticum* growing almost wild where it occurs. The presence of Heather or Heath is another certain guide.

Kadsura japonica is an uncommon evergreen twiner from Japan allied to the Magnolia family. The small, fleshy, solitary, cream-coloured flowers, in July, make no great display, but the leaves turn to rich red and purple tints in autumn and in favourable seasons this effect, which lasts well in favourable weather, is intensified by the addition of round clusters of scarlet fruits. In a courtyard, against a grey or whitewashed wall facing south, it can be quite attractive. The Kadsura prefers an acid soil enriched with leaf-mould and can be struck from cuttings placed under a bell-glass in July. There is a variety, var. *variegata*, with leaves broadly margined with white.

The **Mutisias,** a race of South American Gazania-flowered, climbing Daisies, are, like so many plants from that region, very exacting in their requirements and thus have a name for being tender and difficult. Even when cultural success is attained I am not at all sure that the result is really beautiful, even without taking into consideration the naturally untidy habit of the plants. Possibly this is just another example of a personal opinion that the flora from south of the equator very seldom looks right mingled with the northern flora. When one has ranged across the northern hemisphere, with eyes constantly alert for plants, the northern flora comes to form a harmonious picture in one's mind. The southerners seem to introduce a bizarre and jarring note that is slightly irritating. Possibly this is mere whimsy and on that assumption the Mutisias shall receive their due.

Mutisia decurrens is a scrambling, tendrilled evergreen with many slender stems, narrow oblong leaves and the usual Gazania-shaped flowers 4 inches or more across, of an orange vermilion colour with yellow disk-florets. Messrs. Veitch introduced it from Chile about 1860 but it has never become common, being difficult to propagate and rather a "miff". Like so many South American plants it succumbs quickly to sun-heat and drought and, in addition, is easily destroyed by slugs which may prevent the growth of the suckers necessary to its well-being. South walls are usually too dry at the foot to suit it, and north walls too cold. Thus, while a west wall offers quite a favourable site†, it is really best when planted in the shade of a host-shrub through whose branches it may scramble into the sunlight while its roots remain cool, yet well drained.

M. Clematis is a vigorous species and more responsive to culti-vation, but too tender for any but the most favourably situated gardens. In a cool greenhouse it is a rampant climber, flowering all summer and needing regular pruning to keep it in bounds. The leaves are pinnate (divided) and the drooping, 2-inch-wide, orange-scarlet flowers are solitary and borne on the ends of the shoots.

M. ilicifolia, another Chilean species, with leathery, holly-like, ever-green leaves, has pink or pale mauve flowers with a yellow centre framed by the numerous disk-florets, in all about 3 inches across. It is really a cool greenhouse plant, but has survived outdoors for many years in favourable gardens where it has received careful attention.

M. oligodon, a pink-flowered species also from Chile was introduced by H. F. Comber in 1927. It is a low-growing plant as a rule and best grown scrambling over rocks. It supports a drier soil than most. Unfortunately it holds its leaves after they are dead in an ugly way which makes it unsuitable for a prominent position.

M. retusa resembles *M. ilicifolia* but is thought to be a better garden plant. A fine specimen scrambling over a large thorn bush at Nymans, Handcross, in Sussex, produced many self-sown seedlings. *M. r.* var. *alba* is a variety with white ray-florets.

There are about fifty other species known but there is no evidence that they surpass the preceding in hardiness or beauty.

To sum up the cultivation required, it appears that the Mutisias insist upon a continuously moist but sharply drained soil, lightly shaded against the sun. Protection of the young shoots from slugs is also necessary and facilities for the top growth to emerge into the sun-light must be afforded. It is considered probable that the plants exhaust some constituent of the soil and consequently regular top-dressings are advisable.

† "*Mutisia decurrens*", by C. T. Musgrave, V.M.H., *R. H. S. Journal*, Vol. LXIII, Pt. 4 (April 1938).

Seeds, when available, seem to be the best method of increase, as the removal of rooted suckers is thought to imperil the life of the parent plant, and cuttings are rather uncertain with many species.

Lapageria rosea is another beautiful late-flowering South American climber that is really just too tender and too vulnerable to slugs to be reliable outdoors. I flowered it well for some years, outside, on a north wall, in black woodsy soil; but unavoidable neglect regarding protection from slugs and the cold winters of the war period proved fatal. The heavy, solid, waxy, pink bell-flowers are very beautiful but usually open rather too late in such a position. In a cool greenhouse, or even an unheated greenhouse, it is much more satisfactory.

Some love **Ivies** and others dislike them. For my part, I like Ivy on a strong tree such as an Oak. Everyone who has used his eyes carefully, and pondered the matter in an open-minded way, knows perfectly well that this climber does no harm whatsoever to such a host. Unlike the deadly Honeysuckle, it exerts no pressure whatsoever upon trunk or limbs neither does it work its way outside the leafage of the Oak and so cut off its light, nor, even, does it compete with the deep roots of its host. Benign and wholesome in death, as in life, I have in years past regaled my farm beasts, sharp-set in a hard winter, with its palatable foliage. I deplore the foolish who cut it down, preening themselves on a noble act, and I condemn utterly the false wiseacres who instruct the young to do the same, acting on a false premise. It is only in those very rare cases where an Ivy has found and run up a very young sapling that any harm is done. Of the innumerable fancy sorts I commend *Hedera Helix* var. *aureo-variegata* (*H. H.* var. *chrysophylla aurea variegata*) with large handsome leaves boldly blotched with gold.

In smoky towns where bare walls abound and few plants flourish, the Ivies provide pleasant greenery, so long as the dirt is frequently hosed off their leaves and they are occasionally rejuvenated by the addition of clean fresh soil. Almonds, Robinias, Catalpas, Cherries, Pyracanthas, Hydrangeas, Figs and *Magnolia Soulangeana* are also notable for surviving a smoky atmosphere with great fortitude. H.T. Roses of the varieties having shiny leaves are, by the way, notably more soot-resistant than the matt-leaved sorts and should therefore be chosen in preference to others by the town gardener.

The **Eucryphias,** a southern hemisphere family with exquisite, fragrant, four-petalled white flowers, bloom in August. They have, unfortunately, a grave defect from the garden point of view for, although few flowering trees are more beautiful when in flower, their display is regrettably short-lived. In addition, many of the hybrid seedling forms take many years to grow to flowering size. On the other hand many are beautiful, merely as evergreens, for favoured gardens.

Eucryphia glutinosa (A.G.M. 1935) is a beautiful little flowering tree, introduced from Chile by Messrs. Veitch in 1859. The largest specimen I know is about 15 feet high and much wider, as it has layered itself in many places where low branches have touched the ground. The branches are upright but pliant, bending over to the ground beneath the weight of the massed, 3-inch-wide, white, four-petalled flowers with their ample tassel of stamens whose form recalls those of *Hypericum calcynum*, the "Rose of Sharon". The divided rose-like leaves have almost an evergreen look and turn to vivid orange-red colourings in autumn and they hang on so long that this Eucryphia is one of the finest of all shrubs for early winter colours. The flowering time is early August, and for a day or two this Eucryphia is one of the most beautiful of white-flowered shrubs. All too soon the petals fall, or brown, and all is disarray. Grown from seed, a large proportion of the young plants will be found to have ugly little double flowers. They may often, but not always, be detected before flowering by their bushier habit. To grow *E. glutinosa* well, a rich acid soil is needed and, duly fed, mulched and attended to, the young trees grow fast and flower when about chest-high. In poor soils, unmulched and with meagre care, they are slow and loath to flower. Were it not for the extra boon of fine autumn and winter leaf tints I would almost hesitate to include this charming species among effective flowering trees and shrubs, so short-lived is the flower effect. During its spendour, however, it is of the first class and that moment is as fortunately timed as the autumn leaf display which outlasts all but that of the Evergreen Azaleas.

· *E. lucida* is a Tasmanian tree up to 60 feet high in its native island. The exquisite almond-scented, white flowers, though much smaller, being but an inch across, are even more beautifully formed, and the red-tipped stamens filling the centre are beautifully drawn. It has a delicate charm of a high order and the small, divided, evergreen leaves and slender, strong, ascending branches make it decorative at all times. Layers sometimes flower at 6 feet high, but seedlings are often very slow to flower, in my experience.

E. cordifolia, a stouter, even later-flowering Chilean evergreen tree of great beauty is, alas, too tender for any but warm coastal gardens or those sufficiently elevated to avoid untimely frost.

E. nymansensis, a hybrid (*E. glutinosa* × *cordifolia*) is probably the most effective, reasonably hardy member of the family. It forms, eventually, a sturdy tower perhaps 20 feet high covered in August with a profusion of lovely waxy, white, four-petalled flowers, honey-scented and always abuzz with bees. An awkward winter will destroy the ever-green leaves and spoil the flowering for the season but it makes up for these defects when all goes well. It is definitely a long-term investment, being very slow to flower, but a good one for a reasonably favourable place. (See illustration facing p. 321.)

Thanks to its parentage including the lime-tolerating *E. cordifolia*, it can even be grown on a chalky soil, but regular feeding is needed to keep it growing strongly under such conditions.

E. intermedia is a hybrid between *E. glutinosa* and *E. lucida*. In its best forms it is a delightful little tree, but seedlings are often a long time growing before they flower freely and the variety 'Rostrevor' is of this type. Particularly fine forms, flowering freely when young, have been bred at Grayswood Hill, Haslemere; they have not yet been named.

The Eucryphias practically require a garden free from excessive frosts owing to relative elevation, and they prefer an acid soil well enriched with humus. Seeds and layers are the easiest means of propaga-tion. I have even obtained fine young plants by breaking low branches half through and then burying that point carefully in good turf-loam. Cuttings can also be struck beneath a bell-glass but are often rather slow to root.

In late summer bloom some of the most gorgeous of known climbers that will grow in our climate. They provide a soft rich scarlet flower-colouring of the utmost brilliance complementary to the splendid flowers of the later-opening pale blue-violet Clematis. Yet how seldom does one see the great Trumpet Vine of China, *Campsis grandiflora*, in even the most celebrated gardens. More often the ultra-hardy American species *C. radicans* may be found rioting on cottage walls, but the invaluable hybrid *C. Tagliabuana* is so rare that I know of but one mature specimen in this country.

The banal Ceanothus and the ubiquitous Firethorn or Escallonia are really no more hardy than these more naturally scandent wall adornments, the **Campsis, Tecomas,** or **Bignonias** (as they have been variously named) true climbers that will hold their places with but small attention once the early training and tying is accomplished.

Campsis grandiflora is a Chinese climber long cultivated in Japan. The twining stems are set with divided leaves and on the ends of the season's shoots in August the long open panicles of large orange-scarlet trumpets, 3 inches across at the mouth, are borne (see illustration opposite). On a sunny wall this most gorgeous of all climbers is

Campsis grandiflora

Eucryphia nymansensis

Hibiscus syriacus ' Rubis '

"reasonably hardy". Layers and hard-wood cuttings are successful methods of propagation but few nurseries have parent plants. Now, however, this species can again be obtained and wise planters will secure it while the supply lasts. Once grown and trained so as to fill the available space, the young growths may be spurred back to the old wood as is done with vines. *C. grandiflora* flowers when quite young so is an excellent investment for a south wall. It is never over-rampant and always free-flowering by nature, although in a very cold, short and wet summer it may fail to open its flower buds in time.

C. radicans is an American species and, surviving the destruction of the forests, has even become a weed in that country "taking to fence-rails like a song-sparrow". It is hardier, but more rampant and with smaller, more tubular and much less vividly coloured trumpet-flowers. This climber was brought back to this country early in the seventeenth century and is absolutely hardy. Unlike *C. grandiflora*, *C. radicans* attaches itself by aerial roots quite efficiently when the support is a tree stump or cliff. On a house-wall wires or nails are desirable as well, or it may be wrecked by a storm, but it is really not good enough for such a position. On a tree in the wood-garden it is highly decorative.

C. r. præcox is an early-flowering variety blooming in June.

C. r. flava has dull orange-yellow flowers.

C. r. speciosa is a shrubby form making annual shoots 2 feet long from the framework of old wood. The flowers are less vivid in colour than those of a good form of the "type".

C. Tagliabuana var. 'Mme Galen' is a superb hybrid combining all the virtues of the two preceding species. The foliage is intermediate and the flowers, in shorter and more crowded panicles, are deeper-coloured but as vivid as those of *C. grandiflora* and almost as large. (See illustration facing p. 305). This superb, perfectly hardy climber should be, I think our first choice for a south wall, being capable of the most gorgeous effects. Unless spurred back like a Vine, it is not quite so free flowering as *C. grandiflora* when young. At the same time the flowers open earlier than those of *C. grandiflora* so that it is certain to be effective, even in a bad summer when the still unopened buds of that species are finally destroyed by September frosts. This most desirable hybrid is at last obtainable in this country so we may look forward to seeing it decorating south walls in many parts of Britain in future.

C. T. Thunbergii is another hybrid variety with flowers having a shorter tube and the lobes turned back.

The origin of these hybrids is not known. There is a fascinating account† of how, Mr. W. T. Smith the curator of the Washington Botanic Gardens noticed that both the American and the Chinese

† Bulletin, Arnold Arboretum, Series 4, Vol. I, p. 1.

21

species of Trumpet Vine were in flower at the same time on the walls of
the buildings. Now the natural pollinators of these long-tubed flowers
are the humming birds. Indeed, these flowers, like most berries too, owe
their scarlet colouring to the fact that that hue is the one that most
attracts birds; it is not attractive to bees. The humming birds were
flying from one species of Campsis to the other, busily sipping the
nectar provided and incidentally interchanging the pollen adhering to
their burnished feathers. Mr. Smith, observing this, carefully saved the
seeds, which produced evident hybrids of the two species. The origin
of the hybrid race is not known, and it is to his sowings of these that we
owe our knowledge of the hybridity of this race. They were named
many years previously, in 1859, when Roberto de Visiani applied the
term *Tagliabuana* in honour of two famous Italian gardeners—the
brothers Tagliabue. The variety 'Mme Galen' is far the finest of these
Campsis and provides a good example of the indubitable value of
successful hybridisation. 'Mme Galen' combines the beauty of flower
of *C. grandiflora* with the vigorous constitution and great hardiness of
C. radicans.

Bignonia capreolata is another most beautiful species of Trumpet
Vine. Like many of the finest of the American Azaleas, this glorious
climber is, in its best *red-flowered* form, almost non-existent in this
country.

There is a plant at Shrewsbury and a layer from it at Reading, but
so far as I know the other plants in this country are all of an inferior
form with ragged, dull yellow and brownish-red flowers. This Bignonia
is one of the most lovely of all climbers, even out of flower, the lanceolate evergreen leaves, one above another, covering the ascending
stems that form aerial roots like Ivy. In the best forms the gentian-
shaped flowers are a rich, pure red, making quite a cloud of brilliant
colour amid the tree tops of its native Florida forests. On a house-wall
its deportment is admirable and two large plants on the south wall in
my old garden were quite unharmed by the severe winters of the war
period, though *Ceanothus Veitchii* and other plants of uncertain hardiness succumbed, alongside.

The Campsis and the Bignonia require a warm wall where they can
get well roasted in summer and also a well-dug loamy soil to secure
good, but not excessively soft, growth. The Campsis are best secured
to light wooden trellis fixed to the wall, but the Bignonia can attach
itself to rough stone or brick, although it is safer to nail the wall and tie
it in occasionally. For an attractive contrast one may grow nearby the
huge blue Convolvulus flowers of the 'Morning Glory' (*Ipomœa*

cærulea) or the wide violet stars of the great garden Clematis. All these are plants of the first class, repaying the care of the keen amateur in no uncertain manner. For propagation, layers are an easy method for the Bignonia. Cuttings of the Campsis of ripe short dormant shoots, taken in winter and carefully trimmed at the "heel" will root under a bell-glass, but even more readily with bottom heat in the propagating-house.

Tropæolum speciosum, the Flame Flower, is another vivid late-flowering climber. It is less woody, often disappearing almost to ground-level in winter, and, unlike the others mentioned above, is really best either on a shaded wall where it may scramble up another wall shrub, or in a bed of tall flowering shrubs among which it can climb at will. The rich green, hand-shaped leaves are always attractive and the delightful flower buds, poised and shaped like a flight of minnows, even more so, but the pure carmine flowers, of an exquisite crimped and tailed shape that is all their own, are unique. I have seen the Flame Flower doing wonders on a Yew hedge in the bleakest part of the Midlands, so no qualms need be felt at trying it anywhere.

A cool, leafy, shaded soil is advisable with good drainage and above all no hoeing, "digging over", or other destructive interference. To complete the intriguing personality of this fascinating plant it produces azure-blue peppercorns as seeds and from these, or pieces of the white root thongs, it may be propagated in well shaded, woodsy soil. An unproved theory of mine is that the morale and vigour of a small emerging shoot of this plant is greatly helped by the immediate pro-vision of a tempting, twiggy support. The top of a cane of *Arundinaria nitida*, with its many slender branchlets, is just the thing for the purpose.

While the Campsis and Bignonia set aflame the hotter walls the Flame Flower may perform this service for the shadier ones. This charming little plant is also an essential late summer adornment for the Rhododendron groups and has often delighted me among the white-flowered Lacecap Hydrangeas.

Few members of the **Fuchsia** family qualify for our "reasonably hardy" category, although many of the large-flowered garden forms can be grown in warm gardens near the sea-coast or indeed any garden enjoying good katabatics. (See p. 25.)

There is a wide choice of such varieties suitable for outdoor culture and it is best to select those with the more boldly presented and vivid flowers. Many kinds recommended as hardy are more quaint than effective. On the other hand 'Achievement', a splendid vigorous, erect variety with large red sepals and purple petals, 'Mme Cornelisen', an unusually hardy vivid red with a pure white skirt, 'Rose of Castile', violet and cream, and 'Mrs. Rundle' and 'Aurora Superba', with carmine and orange flowers, are good examples of the showier kinds. In a well-drained sandy soil, kept well mulched with a thick layer of dead leaves to protect the roots in winter, such plants have flourished outdoors for over a decade in many gardens, to my knowledge. Less striking, but unusually vigorous sorts are 'Dorothy', 'Margaret', 'Phyllis' and 'The Doctor'.

Fuchsia magellanica var. *riccartonii* is an unusually hardy and free-growing, but less spectacular member of the family, effective as an out-door shrub in districts having too cold a soil for the large-flowered varieties. Making free, sturdy growth it is notably more decorative than the equally hardy *F. gracilis* which has more slender stems and less vivid and boldly presented flowers.

The intense Turkey Red of the buds and calyx lobes of the Fuchsias is a most welcome colour in the late summer shrub-garden. The Fuchsia is so readily struck from cuttings that it is one of the most convenient shrubs to use to fill up any vacant spaces in the beds, and we can seldom go wrong by using such late-flowerers for this purpose. In hard winters the upper growth of even *riccartonii* is killed back, but the root system of most varieties almost always survives if given a forkful of litter or suchlike protection, and sends up a strong sheaf of flowering shoots that provide one of the brightest patches of colour in the following August. In favourably situated gardens *riccartonii* and *gracilis* often retain their permanent framework over winter but are then seldom so free-flowering as plants that have been cut back.

A warm position where the soil does not get too dry suits the Fuchsias best but they are not particular so long as the soil is not cold and ill-drained. Being easily propagated and inexpensive plants it is worth risking them outdoors in all gardens in the south and west. When planting, it is a good plan to place a shovelful of rotted bracken deep down below the roots. Such is the avidity of Fuchsia roots for this material that they will seek it out and colonise it intensively at such a depth as to make their safety from winter frosts a certainty. For the same reason bracken is not a good surface mulch for Fuchsias as they then make yard-long surface roots which will be too much exposed to winter frost.

The later-flowering **Heaths** are the most valuable members of their genus for the garden, to my mind, but the family weakness in colour unfortunately persists. Muddy and dull purplish-pinks are to be avoided at all costs, for not only are they unattractive in themselves but they spoil all the beautiful pure colours by their presence. But if one wishes to convert the untidiness born of unavoidable neglect into a picturesque and attractive natural wildness, the Heaths, particularly *E. cinerea*, will be found to achieve this in an almost magical manner if planted as informal edgings.

Erica cinerea, the **Scots Heath**, or "Bell Heather", is the most vividly coloured of the hardy species. The wild "type" has flowers of an intense Orchid Purple (H.C.C. 31/1) and in poor acid soil in an open position grows very quickly to an effective flowering size. The wiry stems, clothed with the short evergreen needle-like leaves, end in a raceme from 4 to 6 inches long clustered with the urn-shaped flowers, in groups of seven or eight on small branchlets. In my experience an acid soil is particularly necessary for this Heath and the poorer the better, as in a good loam it grows so rank and soft as to be much less decorative than when kept somewhat starved, when the shorter and firmer racemes remain upright and unharmed by any frost.

The best garden varieties have flowers of more attractive colourings than the "type" but are more expensive and often less vigorous in growth. The following is a selection:—

E. c. var. *coccinea* is a dwarf variety, only about 6 inches high, with vivid deep crimson flowers borne rather earlier in the season. It is probably the finest of the crimsons.

E. c. atrorubens is another good crimson-flowered variety.

E. c. atropurpurea has brighter purple flowers than the wild form, with large, showy flower spikes.

E. c. atrosanguinea ("Reuthe's variety") is similar to *E. c. coccinea* but stronger and later-flowering. "Smith's variety" is rather brighter in colour in the mass.

E. c. 'Frances' is more of a cerise red and an attractive variety of good habit.

E. c. 'Golden Hue' is valuable for its golden foliage, which, turning red in winter, enlivens the deeper tones of the other Heaths.

E. c. 'Golden Drop' has coppery foliage also turning red in winter and 'John Eason' has similar foliage to 'Golden Hue' and deep pink flowers.

E. c. 'Domino' is a fine white with black sepals and flower-stalks and is of dwarf habit.

E. c. alba has white flowers.

E. c. 'P. S. Patrick' is a strong grower with long spikes of vivid purple flowers over a long period. One of the finest varieties for garden decoration when interspersed with the "type" and other sorts.

E. c. lilacina has paler green leaves and spikes of lilac flowers.

E. c. 'C. D. Eason', one of the most attractive of the many pink-flowered varieties, has deep green foliage and a good habit. Others are *carnea*, 'C. G. Best', 'Eden Valley', 'Knap Hill', 'Rose Queen', 'Apple Blossom' and *rosea* (A.G.M. 1928).

E. c. pygmæa is a dwarf form with pink flowers; others, similar, are 'Startler' and 'Mrs. Dill'.

The Scots Heaths are among the most effective of all carpeters for lime-free soils, covering the ground with an attractive and labour-saving green and russet mat and enlivening the later summer garden with their massed flowers whose purplish tones harmonise quite well with the pure deep blues of certain Hydrangeas.

In their cultivation the labour of weeding is minimised and the decorative value of the Heaths is improved if the soil conditions are made rather extreme. The poorest and most acid and firm soil suits them well and does not give weeds much chance to become troublesome. Full exposure is desirable also to keep the plants compact and free-flowering. Pruning, which takes the form of shearing off flowered shoots in early spring, is very helpful and the product will be found a useful addition to the mulch around larger flowering shrubs.

These Heaths may be propagated by layers, scooping out a little hole in peaty, sandy soil and bending a shoot into it and out again so that an elbow-bend is formed, made as acute as possible without breaking the shoot. The abrupt bend checks the sap-flow, and roots are usually made quite quickly. For cuttings, bottom heat and a propagating house are really necessary for a good "take", but success is often achieved under bell-glasses when conditions happen to come right. The little side shoots, about an inch long, are pulled off with a "heel" and this is trimmed with a razor blade, then the lower leaves are carefully cut off so as not to tear the stem. Then the little cuttings are half buried in pots of peat and sand, particular care being taken to make the base of each quite firm with the dibber. Finally, the pots are stood in a trough of water until the earth is well saturated and then sunk to the brim in the soil and the bell-glass is firmly put over all with a piece of light hessian tied to the knob to keep off direct sunlight. These Heaths transplant quite easily providing that care is taken to preserve the fine roots within a ball of soil.

Erica vagans, the **Cornish Heath,** is another valuable species for the shrub gardener. It is a dense, bushy Heath of excellent habit and fine winter appearance and a good variety will have flowers of a pale Crimson tint (H.C.C. 22/3). Unfortunately, adjacent browned corollas infuse a muddy tone into the bush, so that we do not get the value of this beautiful clean "peach pink" for very long. The short blunt spikes carry whorls of rich green leaves below and the bush may attain a height of about 2½ feet and a spread of 4 feet.

E. v. 'Mrs. D. F. Maxwell' is one of the finest of all the Heaths, with flowers of a Crimson pink (H.C.C. 22/2).

E. v. 'Lyonesse' is a splendid white-flowered variety with glossy, rich green foliage and fine large spikes.

E. v. 'St. Keverne' (A.G.M. 1937) has rose-pink flowers.

E. v. nana is a dwarf with creamy-white flowers and chocolate anthers.

E. v. rubra has flowers of a crimson pink.

The Cornish Heath is, I find, assisted both in compactness and vigour by a little spreading out of the branches with a trowelful of tempting peaty soil added to hold them in position. A poor, but moist peaty, sandy soil and free drainage in an open position suits this species best and shearing back of straggling shoots and old flower heads helps the appearance of the bushes. Propagation may be effected as described for *E. cinerea*, but more moisture is needed for this species which cannot resist dry conditions so well as many others.

E. ciliaris, the **Dorset Heath,** has a more rambling habit with small greyish, oval leaves set closely in threes on the stems. The flowers, narrowly pitcher-shaped and also in threes, form short upright racemes on the ends of the shoots. The wild type has unpleasantly coloured purplish-pink (H.C.C. Cyclamen Purple 30/2) flowers but several of the varieties improve on this.

E. c. Maweana is a stronger grower with larger flowers, from Portugal.

E. c. 'Mrs. C. H. Gill' has purplish-crimson flowers and dark green foliage.

E. c. 'Stoborough' has large white globular flowers superior to the old white form *alba*.

The Dorset Heath will thrive in richer ground than most of the other species and can be similarly propagated.

The **Irish Heath** is a notably beautiful and easy-going species of dense and compact habit and having a remarkably long flowering season. It needs little attention beyond an occasional top-dressing with peat and cutting back the flower shoots in winter. Often opening in June, this Heath continues in flower almost until winter begins. *Daboecia cantabrica*, (*D. polifolia*) (A.G.M. 1930, is a bold and handsome species about 2 feet high, with large, egg-shaped, Cyclamen Purple flowers borne in upright racemes over a long period.

D. c. alba is a white-flowered variety of great charm and vigour.

D. c. atropurpurea has more vividly coloured flowers than the "type".

D. c. Prægeræ is a remarkable form with clear pink flowers that was found on Connemara Heath, hardy and vigorous.

D. c. bicolor has mixed white and purple flowers.

D. azorica is a closely allied species from the Azores. It has an attractive, low, dense habit, forming a mound about 6 inches high with erect racemes and Fuchsia Purple flowers of similar shape to those of *D. cantabrica*.

Erica Tetralix, the common Heath, is, in comparison, hardly sufficiently decorative in habit to be effective in the garden, and browned corollas spoil the small clusters of very pale purplish-pink flowers.

E. terminalis, the Corsican Heath, is not a very showy species and the flowers, of the all too common vinous pink, are not remarkable.

There are also a number of hybrids such as the much-boosted *E. darleyensis*, with dull purplish-pink flowers from November onwards, and *E. 'Dawn'* (*E. ciliaris × Tetralix*) with abundant pink flowers which are valuable for gardens where Heaths are an important feature. Care should, however, be taken to interplant with species having more vividly coloured flowers as too much purplish-pink is extremely depressing.

Calluna vulgaris, the **Heather,** is less vivid in colour than most of the Heaths, being only the palest tint of Petunia Purple (H.C.C. 32/3) and its little flowers are so much more widely spaced on the stems that its effect is less vivid at a distance than that of many Heaths of the same flower-colouring. On the other hand, it grows more vigorously than the Scots Heath and self-sown seedlings appear more freely. In sandy soils free from lime it is a useful "filler" between growing shrubs eventually needing the space, as single plants are so easily pulled up when no longer required. Some improved varieties are listed below.

C. v. 'H. E. Beale' (A.G.M. 1942) is a pale purplish-pink double-flowered form found in the New Forest. The variety 'County Wicklow' is similar, but prostrate. *C. v. flore pleno* has slightly deeper-coloured flowers and blooms a little earlier.

C. v. 'J. H. Hamilton' is a pretty little Heather of dwarf growth, with pink, double flowers forming attractive little rosettes.

C. v. 'Camla' has double pink flowers on short, upright stems.

C. v. Serlei is a fine white-flowered form with a handsome habit and bright green foliage.

C. v. S. aurea has bright golden foliage all the year round and white flowers.

C. v. S. grandiflora is a late-flowering purple variety.

C. v. 'Carlton' has white flowers produced on the laterals as well as the main spike.

C. v. Hammondii is a strong-growing white-flowered variety.

C. v. H. auræfolia has similar flowers but the young growths are golden-coloured.

C. v. H. rubrafolia has the new growth bright red and the flowers purple.

C. v. alba plena is a fine double-flowered white variety that originated in Germany; it is one of the finest of all the varieties of Heather.

C. v. 'August Beauty' has white flowers on drooping spikes.

C. v. Alportii has deep green foliage and dark, dull purplish-crimson flowers on a somewhat stiff and upright plant.

C. v. 'C. W. Nix' is similar but brighter in colour and later in flowering.

C. v. 'E. Hoare' is deeper still in colour than *Alportii*.

C. v. coccinea has flowers of a brighter crimson and pale greyish, downy foliage.

C. v. 'David Eason' is another crimson and has a more dwarf and spreading habit and blooms later.

C. v. 'Goldsworth Crimson' is a late-flowering variety with long spikes of deep crimson flowers.

C. v. 'Tib' is a variety with double, purplish-crimson flowers that was found in the Pentland hills.

C. v. alba aurea has golden foliage and white flowers.

C. v. aurea has golden foliage turning red in winter and pale purple flowers, like the wild type.

C. v. cuprea has coppery foliage turning red in winter.

C. v. alba pumila is a dwarf variety with white flowers.

C. v. Foxii nana is a minute dwarf form with purple flowers.

C. v. Foxii floribunda is a dwarf form with a more free-flowering habit.

C. v. 'Sister Anne' is a minute dwarf with greyish foliage and pink flowers.

C. v. 'Tom Thumb' is compact and fairly dwarf, with pink flowers.

C. v. 'Mrs. Ronald Gray' is a prostrate variety with reddish-purple flowers.

C. v. minima ('Smith's variety') is very minute, forming tiny cushions that turn red in winter.

C. v. 'Silver Queen' has silvery hairs on the foliage giving a grey effect.

These Heathers are of reasonably compact growth and, as late-flowering evergreens, have their value as labour-saving carpeters for peaty, sloping gardens. Although the flower-colouring is weak, it comes, at least, at a time when most shrubs are going over and turning their leaves to their autumnal tints rather than competing with more vivid flowers. Plenty of white is needed to relieve the sombre purplish-pinks and to lead up to the occasional splashes of yellow provided by some of the Legumes.

A poor, sandy soil, which must be free from lime, suits the Callunas best; on strong loams the plants soon become too rank and leggy.

Propagation of the named varieties may be effected by layering and the wild type may be grown from seed. Clipping off the old, flowered stems in early spring, before growth begins, improves compactness.

Some of the larger shrubs including the **Clerodendrons** defer their flowering until late in the season. *Clerodendron trichotomum* is a tall, rather coarse, Chinese shrub of the Verbena family, usually about 10 feet high with 6-inch-long, oval leaves and starry white, fragrant flowers about an inch across, with a red calyx. These are very freely borne and are followed by blue fruits. It is no more than just "reasonably hardy", the downy young shoots being often cut back by frost in late autumn. Blooming in August, this is a handsome shrub for large, warm gardens, especially if it can be viewed from higher ground, in colder places it is less effective. It will grow in a limy soil. Seeds and suckers enable it to be readily propagated.

C. t. Fargesii is rather similar, but the calyx is green instead of red and the fruits are a brighter blue. It is slightly hardier, but seldom quite so effective in bloom. It was introduced from China by Père Farges in 1898.

Both these Clerodendrons require an open, sunny but sheltered spot and free drainage. Mixed up in a "shrubbery" with other large shrubs they are not attractive but a specimen rising from a carpet of dwarf-growing, low shrubs makes quite a fine late summer picture.

Among the medium-sized shrubs flowering at this time is a beautiful **Caryopteris**, *C. clandonensis* (A.G.M. 1942). This hybrid, raised by Mr. A. Simmonds in his garden at Clandon near Guildford about 1931, is superior to its parents (*C. incana* and *C. mongholica*) as a garden shrub. The Aster Violet flowers, in trusses in the leaf axils of the outer ends of the shoots of the year, appear in late summer when it can provide a pleasing mass of soft colour. To attain this it should be pruned annually in spring, each shoot of the previous year's growth being cut back to two pairs of eyes. With this treatment the bush assumes a reasonably compact form, about 4 feet high. The parent species come from China and Japan and are less reliable in the garden. *C. clandonensis* should be struck from cuttings of the best form, which is quite an easy matter. Seedlings vary greatly and, though possibly an even finer form might turn up, they usually vary for the worse. A sunny position is desirable, but the plant seems to have no particular preference as to type of soil and is therefore of special value for alkaline districts.

Whilst the hybrid surpasses *C. incana* (*C. Mastacanthus*) and *C. mongholica*, there is another species that is very well worth growing, particularly on limy soils where the Hydrangeas cannot provide late-summer blue. This is *C. tangutica*, discovered long before, but only introduced from Khansu, China, by Reginald Farrer in 1915†. It is of denser and more bushy habit than *C. mongholica* and is also hardier. The flowers open at the end of July covering the bush in a haze of violet-blue. The leaves are a more attractive, deeper green than other kinds and in cultivation *C. tangutica* will reach a height of 5 feet by 8 feet in diameter. Unfortunately it is now rather rare in nurseries.

An attractive foil to the Caryopteris is **Ulex nanus,** the dwarf Gorse or Petty Whin. It is a native species entirely distinct from the Common Gorse. In nature it rarely exceeds a foot in height and flowers in September. The short, upright, densely spined stems are thickly furnished with the Buttercup-yellow (H.C.C. 5/1) flowers. The distant effect is more apricot, owing to russet-brown withered flowers. The Petty Whin is useful for a late summer effect, as by the time it is at its best even the long flowering season of the Spanish Broom is practically ended, and the complete sequence of yellow thus secured is of great help to the all-summer-flowering garden. In rich garden soil the plant loses character and grows tall and gangling and flowers poorly. In a thin, dry soil, however, it forms compact mounds of timely and attractive colour.

Propagation may be achieved by seeds sown in small pots and even so, the young plants should be put early into their permanent positions as they do not transplant well and the long roots soon either get through the bottom holes of the pots or make the plants unthrifty by getting twisted into a ball.

There are shrubs that are all-the-year-round decorative pieces of garden furniture. Others are frankly ugly in their winter dress of bare

† "The Plant Introductions of Reginald Farrer", by E. H. M. Cox, p. 33.

branches. When this characteristic is coupled with an unusually late-leafing habit we must insist on quite an outstanding flower display to compensate for these defects. Even then, we must plan the position of such a plant with extra care so that the long period of ugliness is not too obtrusive, yet the moment of glory is well displayed. William Robinson and other good judges have condemned the **Hibiscus** as making an insufficient return in flower for its seven months of drabness. Yet a big bush of a good variety in full bloom will demand recognition as one of the great flowering shrubs.

Hibiscus syriacus, the Bush Mallow, is a very old inhabitant of our gardens yet, although perfectly hardy, it is very rarely seen. The bush grows slowly to about 10 feet in height, with upright, twiggy branches and somewhat oak-like leaves. The flowers, Magenta in the wild form and shaped like those of the Mallow to whose family it belongs, are about 3 or 4 inches across, usually with a darker eye and an attractive column of yellow stamens in the centre. (See illustration facing p. 321.)

There are many varieties and the following is a short selection of the best:—

- *H. s. cœlestis* has flowers of a violet blue with a darker eye and opens earlier than most. Unfortunately the habit is rather thin and upright.
- *H. s.* 'Hamabo' has bluish-pink flowers with a large crimson blotch at the base and flowers rather late. It is one of the loveliest varieties and came from Japan.
- *H. s.* 'Woodbridge' has vinous-red (H.C.C. Magenta 27/2) flowers very boldly displayed. The true variety has very large, wide-open flowers.
- *H. s.* 'Rev. W. Smith' has pure paper-white flowers of good open shape.
- *H. s. monstrosus* has white flowers with a dark eye.
- *H. s. totus albus* has creamy-white flowers.
- *H. s. Leopoldii plenus* has fine pink-blushed and dark-centred double flowers, beautifully presented, and a good habit.

There are many other double-flowered forms but they are mostly less effective. In a cold, wet autumn the Hibiscus drops many of its flower-buds unopened but in a warm September it can be highly decorative. At other times it is rather a bare and ugly bush so care should be taken not to give it too prominent a position.

This shrub seems to have no special preference as to soil but needs a warm, sunny spot to flower freely. Cuttings will often root under a bell-glass but the resulting plants are unusually slow to get going and though the usual grafted plants are by no means quick growers they are so much better than cuttings in this respect that they are preferable. The Hibiscus does not always transplant successfully, so care should be taken to get the bushes into their permanent positions at an early age.

Quite the opposite of the Hibiscus in its qualities is *Fatsia japonica* (*Aralia Sieboldii*). This noble evergreen shrub is best known as an indoor pot-plant but is really quite "reasonably hardy" outdoors in the southern counties. The huge, nine-lobed leaves are very handsome and in late autumn the panicles of ball-shaped heads of white flowers appear. It is a common inhabitant of Japanese gardens and is very decorative near formal masonry or wherever a somewhat bold and tropical evergreen effect is required. A plant bought from the sixpenny stores reached 9 feet in height and became one of the most effective features of the terrace in my old garden. In spring the unfolding, hand-like, young leaves assume a charming attitude and are covered with a soft red fur on a silver ground. In courtyards, near loggias and arising from paved areas there are few better shrubs of architectural form and it has been undeservedly neglected for this purpose. The designer seeking plants of tropical character to give the desired atmosphere to the surroundings of a modern outdoor garden-room will find in this plant one of the answers to his quest.

Any good soil that is not excessively limy seems to suit the Fatsia, and, though it can be propagated from cuttings of half-ripe shoots under a cloche in a warm summer, this is somewhat chancy, and it is probably best to buy young plants in pots and put them out in spring after frosts are over. Pruning is not necessary but a stem may be cut out at ground-level before growth starts in spring if the plant gets too leggy. New shoots will then spring from the base and clothe it effectively. On the other hand it is singularly effective when grown in tree form with a single clean stem.

Another fine evergreen is *Mahonia lomariifolia*, a handsome new Mahonia from Yunnan, China, with huge spiny leaves divided into about thirty leaflets rather similar in character to *M. japonica* (see p. 46). The cluster of numerous short, upright, yellow flower-spikes opens in late October or November and thus one or other member of this family covers the season from early winter to spring. With its whorls of fierce tropical-looking leaves it is an impressive plant for a snug courtyard position where its appearance is more telling than when it is secluded in a woodland dell.

M. lomariifolia is not very hardy and a sheltered position and an elevated garden free from early autumn frosts are really necessary to ensure its growing well. Any good deep soil, whether slightly limy or not, suits this Mahonia. Propagation is not easy for the amateur. In a favourable season seed may be ripened and this should be carefully sown, if possible in thumb pots plunged in a box of sand and peat mixture so that the risky business of transplanting these difficult movers may be made safer.

Another late flowerer that is almost too late is *M. Fortunei*. Even when a propitious warm autumn gives it every encouragement its October flowers have rather a thin unhappy look and its architecture lacks the bold design of that of *M. lomariifolia*.

The **Lespedezas**, leguminous, clover-like, Japanese and Chinese sub-shrubs with rosy-purple pea-flowers at the end of summer are hardly effective enough for general planting.

Lespedeza Thunbergii is much the best of them. Its growth is luxuriant and attractive or it would not be so highly valued in Japanese gardens; but it starts its growth so late that it is unsightly among the spring-flowering shrubs and a cool spell in early September will often spoil its display just as it begins. In a favourable season its pendulous branchlets terminate in large panicles of flower in impressive profusion.

Viburnum Tinus, the common **Laurustinus,** is an admirable winter flowerer beginning often in November and, wisely dodging the worst weather, it is often still in bloom in April. Its good qualities have, however, been its downfall for it has become so common that few bother to plant it when planning new groupings. It requires a sunny position to flower really freely, and, above all, to enable it to assume the pleasingly dense and rounded form proper to the bush.

V. T. var. *hirtum* is hairy and has larger leaves but is less hardy in the open.

V. T. var. *lucidum* is less compact in habit, if larger flowered, and, again, less hardy.

Cuttings may be rooted beneath a bell-glass from July shoots in the usual manner and this Viburnum is not particular as to soil.

Now, at the end of this period comes the unexpectedly beautiful moment when, though flowers are over, the colouring of the leaves gives the well-planned naturalistic shrub garden a new pattern in soft and rich tones, even more closely in harmony with the surrounding landscape than that which has gone before. The beauty of subtly contrasting forms and foliages, without the distracting flowers, shows up the more clearly and often surprises us with its loveliness. The dark blue-greens, pale yellowish-greens, sea-greens and black-greens of Rhododendron, Evergreen Azalea, Alpine Rhododendron, Camellia and Holly show up the bright almond-greens of Hydrangea foliage, contrasted with their autumn-reddened flowers, the red-greens of Roses and the silver-greens of Senecio and Santolina. The Brooms, solid cushions of velvet (thanks to the ever-busy shears!) complement the silvery yellow-green, plumy mounds of the Genistas or the stern, spiky architecture of the Mahonias.

Already the Japanese Maples are aflame to add that vivid red that every picture craves—like Turner's floating carrots in the storm. *Viburnum Mariesii*, Sargent's Cherry, *Berberis Thunbergii*, *Koelreuteria paniculata* and certain Hydrangeas give other early leaf colour effects that hint of more to follow. Their show is brief but bright and in the end it will be the turn of the evergreens to carry the garden all winter till the new leaves come again. If there are not enough of such plants to do so effectively, the remedy is simple; there are plenty awaiting our call, for these Islands have that essential characteristic of a great gardening country, they suit the beautiful broad-leaved flowering evergreens that are the backbone of all enduring beauty in the garden landscape and are denied to so many other places.